AN ARCHAEOLOGICAL SURVEY OF THE CHOLLA-SAGUARO TRANSMISSION LINE CORRIDOR

VOLUME 1

Prepared for Arizona Public Service

Assembled by

Lynn S. Teague
Linda L. Mayro

Contributions by

Neal W. Ackerly
Richard S. Ciolek-Torrello
Gary T. Cummins
David A. Gregory
Richard C. Lange
Susan D. Morton
Alan H. Simmons
Lynn S. Teague

Edited by

John F. Robertson

Submitted by

Cultural Resource Management Section
Arizona State Museum
The University of Arizona

Report submitted to Arizona Public Service
in final fulfillment of
Contract No. 74-00586

July 1979

Archaeological Series No. 135

ABSTRACT

The Arizona Public Service Cholla-Saguaro Transmission Line corridor extends from Red Rock to Joseph City, Arizona, a distance of about 386 kilometers (240 miles). The corridor, a transect 100.5 meters (330 feet) wide, is associated with numerous access roads. The Arizona State Museum began archaeological survey of the corridor in 1974; field work was completed in 1977. During that time, 158 archaeological sites were identified, representing occupation of the areas involved by a wide cultural and temporal range of prehistoric and historic occupants.

During the later stages of the survey, Museum personnel worked closely with representatives of Arizona Public Service and the United States Forest Service in order to develop strategies for the avoidance of archaeologically sensitive areas, to monitor any construction near archaeological sites so that damage to sites could be avoided, and to develop a program of data recovery for the mitigation of information loss associated with unavoidable impacts. Later reports will contain the results of this data recovery study; this report focuses on the results of survey and inventory efforts.

Because data recovery work was begun before completion of the survey itself, no effort has been made in this report to detail site-specific recommendations for protection and data recovery. These are included in a series of interim reports submitted to the United States Forest Service and now on file at the Tonto and Apache-Sitgreaves National Forest offices and at the Arizona State Museum. Instead, this report provides the archaeological information derived from the survey project, as well as results of early (1974) data recovery efforts within the southern portion of the corridor. It is hoped that this report, in conjunction with the later mitigation reports, will provide a coherent account of the results of these studies.

ACKNOWLEDGMENTS

In a project as long and complex as this one, many individuals are involved. The Museum owes a debt of gratitude to many of these, and it is hoped that none of those who have contributed to the completion of the Cholla-Saguaro survey will be omitted here.

We are particularly grateful to Harry Sogan and Bob Bowers of Arizona Public Service, who were most generous with their time and understanding over the years. We deeply appreciate the efforts of Martin McAllister, Archaeologist for the Tonto National Forest, who became involved with the project in 1976 and did much to make the potentially chaotic later part of the project a more orderly and productive undertaking.

From Arizona Public Service, we would also like to acknowledge the assistance of Pete MacDonald and of Tom Thompson, as well as of the many other APS personnel who helped us in coordinating our efforts with those of the construction personnel. Richard Effland, archaeologist for Arizona Public Service, provided assistance and constructive review.

Many Forest Service personnel associated with the Tonto and Apache-Sitgreaves National Forests are also deserving of thanks. Rather than individually list these, we will only note that liason officers as well as others working in the Forests were most helpful. And certainly we cannot omit the careful attention provided to the project by Dee Green, Archaeologist for the Forest Service Southwest Region.

Finally, these acknowledgments would be incomplete without our thanks being offered to Dr. Fred Plog of Arizona State University, who did much to make this project a unique one in the history of the Arizona State Museum. Dr. Plog's concern for the quality of work never waivered, and we only regret that other commitments have prevented us from returning his generous concern and helpfulness.

We must also acknowledge the many people within the Arizona State Museum who have contributed to this project. We will make no effort to list all of the field personnel who have contributed over the years, except to recognize especially the contributions of James N. Spain and Christopher Causey, who served as project field supervisors in 1975 and 1976-77 respectively. We are deeply grateful to R. Gwinn Vivian and Raymond H. Thompson for their support and encouragement.

We would also like to thank John Robertson for his conscientious and excellent editing and Deborah Westfall for her invaluable assistance in making extensive revisions, drafting maps and figures, and contributing significantly to a coherent and readable report. Esther Walker, typist, and Charles Sternberg and Brian Donahue, draftsmen, have been essential to producing this report.

TABLE OF CONTENTS

LIST OF FIGURES

LIST OF TABLES

CHAPTER 1

INTRODUCTION
by Lynn S. Teague

The Arizona Public Service (APS) Cholla-Saguaro 500 kV transmission line corridor is a transect 100.7 m (330 feet) wide extending from Red Rock to Joseph City, Arizona, a distance of 386 km (240 miles). Archaeological survey of the Cholla-Saguaro line was begun by the Arizona State Museum in March, 1974 and continued intermittently through 1977. This survey was conducted in order to comply with federal and state legislation regarding the preservation of cultural resources.

Relevant federal legislation includes the National Historic Preservation Act of 1966 and the National Environmental Policy Act of 1969, which provides that it is the "continuing responsibility of the Federal Government to use all practical means, consistent with other essential considerations of national policy, to improve and coordinate Federal plans, functions, programs and resources to the end that the nation may... preserve important historic, cultural, and natural aspects of our national heritage." Compliance procedures are specified in 36 CFR 800, which provides guidelines for fulfilling the requirements of Section 106 of the National Historic Preservation Act, and in the guidelines of the various federal agencies. These are applicable to this project due to use and modification by APS of federal lands administered by the United States Forest Service (Tonto and Apache-Sitgreaves National Forests) and by the Bureau of Land Management. The Cholla-Saguaro line also crosses lands owned by the State of Arizona and is therefore required to comply with the provisions of the Arizona Antiquities Act.

Initial survey was concentrated within the corridor itself; potential impact areas associated with access roads and other facilities were examined subsequently as their proposed locations were identified by Arizona Public Service. The survey resulted in the identification of 159 sites. Prehistoric sites were identified as Salado, Hohokam, Mogollon, and Anasazi. Historic sites included Anglo ranches and mines as well as remains of recent Apache occupation.

Project Objectives

In order to comply with the pertinent legislation and procedural guidelines, basic project objectives included the identification of all cultural resources within the impact areas associated with this project, evaluation of these resources in terms of their public and scientific importance, and formulation of recommendations for their preservation and protection. In order to provide an adequate evaluation, it is essential that the sites be put into an archaeological context that reflects their relationship to a broader area and their potential to contribute useful information regarding prehistory and history.

In the case of a linear transect like that represented by the Cholla-Saguaro line, this evaluation is a more complex undertaking than are studies with comparable intent in small, geographically confined areas. The study area crosscuts zones of archaeological remains that, because of traditionally perceived differences in material culture, are attributed to prehistoric groups that have been labelled Hohokam, Salado, Mogollon, and Anasazi. When Arizona State Museum archaeologists began formulating an overall research orientation for the project, this diversity and the resulting potential for study of cultural variability was recognized as an appropriate focus for research and evaluation. A research approach based on the examination of cultural adaptations to the various environmental zones along the transect was accordingly adopted. From this approach a series of sectional research designs was formulated. In March, 1974, Veletta Canouts formulated a design for the northern survey section, from the Cholla Plant to the northern boundary of the Apache-Sitgreaves National Forest. This design dealt with resource exploitation of the survey area, seen here as a cultural border region, by both Anasazi and Mogollon peoples.

The southern section of the line was surveyed within a framework established in a design written by Gay Kinkade in the fall of 1974. Like that of Canouts, this design emphasized study of cultural-environmental relationships. In the spring of 1975, ASM archaeologist James N. Spain formulated a research design for the central survey section of the project, a design used in a series of surveys of the central survey section conducted in 1975 and 1976. Spain's design was more specifically directed towards definition of the potential of environmental settings to contribute to prehistoric subsistence, and included detailed recording of a variety of physiographic and biotic variables.

All of these designs, although differing to some extent in emphasis and methodology, were consistent in their recognition of the crucial importance of cultural and environmental variability as a basis for structuring investigations undertaken by this project. In devising appropriate strategies for consideration of problems related to this variability, two basic limitations of available data are critical. First, while the transect does provide a framework for the study of variability, the local and regional context within which the corridor sites themselves exist can only be defined in terms of previous research in adjacent areas. This research has been minimal in many areas. Where previous research has been relatively intensive, it has often addressed specialized problems involving only a portion of the archaeological record, so that data may be sufficient for some types of sites, or sites of a given period, yet insufficient to provide adequate comparative data for other kinds of sites in the same area.

The nature of survey data itself provides yet another limitation. Study of cultural variability entails consideration of differences in site function, site age, and the cultural affiliation of groups who created particular sites. The level at which these variables can be defined on the basis of survey data is often a very general one. Sites without visible architecture or having artifact assemblages dominated by lithics or ceramic plainwares are often impossible to assign to basic culture-chronological categories on the basis of survey data. Site function can be assessed to some extent through observation of surface artifact and feature classes, as well as by inference from the environmental context of the site, but reliable interpretation often must await data from excavation, systematic surface collection, and detailed laboratory analysis. In areas that are relatively well known, earlier work at comparable sites can provide data that permit inference about unobserved subsurface site characteristics. In the absence of such data, survey can in many respects provide only a basis upon which future research plans can be developed.

During the survey field workers used standard ASM survey forms to record the location, general environmental setting, and observable archae-ological characteristics of sites encountered. This report attempts to provide an assessment of that information derived from the survey itself, integrated with existing information regarding the archaeology of adjacent areas. The role that these sites may fulfill in investigating problems of cultural diversity is examined. It is this evaluation that forms the basis of recommendations for future research.

Structure of the Report

A general overview of the environments within the study area is provided in Chapter 2. This is intended to provide an introductory framework within which individual portions of the transmission line can be related to one another. Chapter 3 reviews the history of the survey itself and the methodologies employed at various times during the project.

For presentation of detailed information, the line has been divided into four environmentally and archaeologically distinct areas:
1) Holbrook-Chevelon, from Joseph City to the Mogollon Rim
2) Q Ranch, the mountainous central portion of the line
3) Tonto-Roosevelt, extending from the mountains south to the southern desert
4) the Southern Desert, extending south to Red Rock.

Each of these areas is treated as a discrete unit in the report. The precise location of the study area, the history of previous research, a synthesis of existing data, survey results and their interpretation, and the potential for further research are dealt with independently in each of these units.

This approach was adopted in order to organize coherently a complex body of data. This organization also corresponds to that of the research subsequently conducted to mitigate adverse effects of construction. Thus, this survey report provides a background, in terms of data and in terms of evaluation of research problems, for the mitigation study.

The discussion of the Southern Desert does provide an exception to this general organizational structure, in that mitigation data from research conducted in 1974 is incorporated within discussion of the survey proper. Artifact collections and test excavations were initiated in this area prior to completion of the survey and three years prior to mitigation on the remainder of the line. This is discussed more fully in the history of the survey and in the section of the report dealing with the Southern Desert.

CHAPTER 2

THE STUDY AREA
by Susan D. Morton

The Cholla line corridor is unique for the archaeological problems
it presents. These derive from its narrow and linear nature and from
its placement, which crosscuts a mosaic of physiographic, environmental,
and culturally diverse zones. This section is included to provide background information concerning its physical placement and to further define
physiographic, environmental, and cultural diversity within it.

The APS Cholla-Saguaro transmission line extends some 386 km (240
miles) from Red Rock, Arizona on the south end to Joseph City, Arizona
on the north. Cutting a narrow swath 100.7 m (330 feet) wide, the corridor crosscuts all of the physiographic provinces that occur in the State
of Arizona, three major environmental life zones, and regions thought to
have been inhabited by different peoples generally known as Paleo-Indian,
Archaic, Hohokam, Salado, Mogollon, Anasazi, and in more recent times,
Western Apache and Anglo.

The discussions which follow are necessarily very general, and are
intended to demonstrate the nature of diversities characteristic of the
Cholla line corridor, diversities which have many implications for
archaeological research along the corridor route.

Physiographic Diversity

The APS transmission line corridor crosscuts all of the physiographic
provinces that occur in the State of Arizona. These include, moving from
the southwest to the northeast, the Basin and Range Province, Mountain
Region, Transition Zone, and Plateau Province (Figure 1).

The southernmost portion of the corridor is situated in the Basin
and Range Province, which is characterized by massive, heavily dissected
mountain ranges surrounded by flat basins of varying size. The ranges
are comprised of erosional remnants of underlying resilient bedrock
resistant to erosional degradation.

The south-central portion of the corridor crosses the Mountain
Region, a subdivision of the Basin and Range Province. The Mountain
Region is characterized by (a) higher mountain regions than those found
in the Desert Region of the Basin and Range Province or the Transition
Zone situated immediately to the north, and (b) the absence of basins.

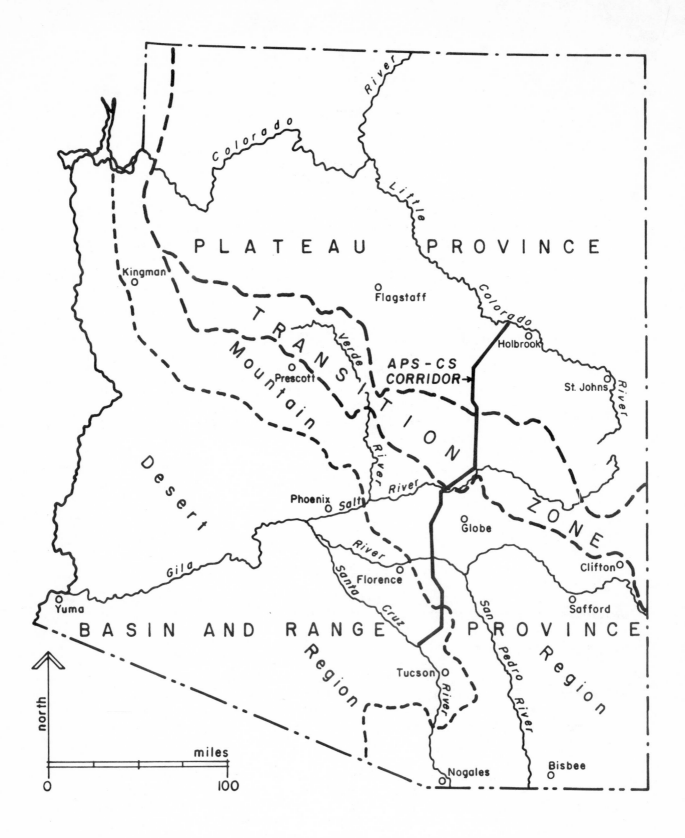

Figure 1. Relationship of APS-CS corridor to physiographic provinces of Arizona

The Transition Zone is marked by extreme diversity in topography depending on the composition of underlying bedrock formations. Down-faulting of bedrock formations in addition to erosion has resulted in the formation of three large river valleys in the Transition Zone: the Verde, the Tonto, and the Chino.

The Plateau Province contains numerous subdivisions. In general, it is characterized by volcanic mountains and many high-topped mesas, more so than any of the other provinces. The major drainage in the Plateau Province is the Colorado River. Of the three subdivisions of the Plateau Province, the transmission line corridor passes through only the Mogollon Slope, which extends from the Mogollon Rim north to Joseph City.

Environmental Diversity

The entire APS corridor bisects the east-central portion of the State of Arizona, and consequently traverses three major environmental life zones offering a wide range of adaptive strategies for prehistoric human groups. As a result, it is expected that the range of adaptive strategies employed by prehistoric groups will be reflected in the archaeological record and that archaeological sites will vary in terms of their environmental settings. This section therefore provides a general overview of environmental diversity in the study region intersected by the transmission line corridor.

The environmental diversity can be defined in the context of major "life zones", of which there are six in Arizona: the Lower Sonoran, Upper Sonoran, Transition, Canadian, Hudsonian, and Arctic Alpine. The Cholla line crosses three life zones: Lower Sonoran, Upper Sonoran, and Transition.

The concept of life zone derives from the observable ecologic distribution of plants and animals as arranged vertically in terms of elevation. Life zones are therefore not equivalent to biotic communities. Instead, a life zone should be considered "generic"--that is, as a higher level of classification which may include one or more major biotic communities.

The following discussion therefore focuses on the higher level of description, the concept of life zones, in order to broadly define environmental diversity.

Lower Sonoran Life Zone

The southernmost portion of the transmission line corridor, extending from the southern terminus at Red Rock, Arizona, to Superior, Arizona, is situated in the Lower Sonoran Life Zone. The vegetation complex associated with the Lower Sonoran Life Zone is termed "Southwestern desertscrub" and extends from an elevation of 100 to 3500 feet. Mean annual precipitation in this zone ranges from 3 to 11 inches, with rainfall distributed biseasonally. Vegetation includes creosote-bush, palo-verde, bur-sage, ironwood, and a wide variety of cacti. The environment is arid to semi-arid (Figure 2).

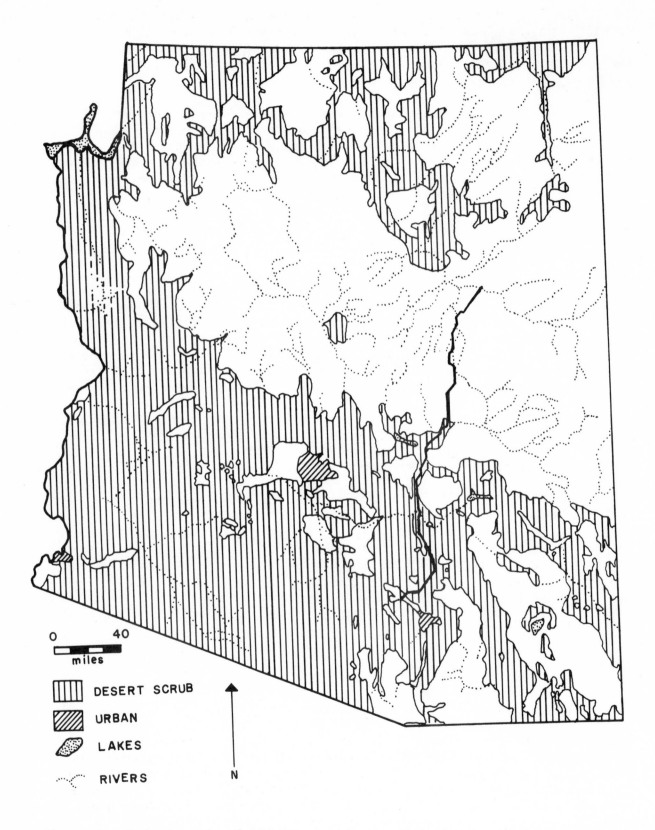

 (legend)

0   40
miles

|||| DESERT SCRUB

//// URBAN

LAKES

RIVERS

N

Figure 2.   Relationship of APS-CS corridor to distribution of desertscrub
            vegetation in Arizona

Upper Sonoran Life Zone

The Upper Sonoran Life Zone consists of four vegetation associations: woodland, chaparral, grassland, and Arizona upland desertscrub. Of these, woodland, chaparral, and grassland are intersected by the transmission line corridor. The Upper Sonoran Life Zone is found mainly at the northern and southern ends of the corridor (Figures 3, 4, and 5).

An area situated between Superior, Arizona and a point approximately 9 miles south of Roosevelt Lake exhibits an extensive chaparral association. Chaparral is usually found at elevations ranging between 4000 and 6000 feet. Precipitation in chaparral zones varies between 13-23 inches annually, with rainfall presently distributed in a biseasonal, winter-summer pattern. The dominant plant in this association is scrub oak. Depending on microenvironmental patterns, manzanita and mountain-mahogany may be found as codominant species. Subdominant species include scarlet sumac, buck-brush, buck-thorn, and Apache-plume. Understory vegetation consists of various species of grama grass, brome, muhly, and awn. The environment is generally semi-arid.

Further north a zone extending approximately 11 km around Roosevelt Lake exhibits Upper Sonoran desertscrub vegetation. This plant association is normally found at elevations from 150 to 3000 feet. Precipitation in desertscrub zones varies between 3 to 12 inches annually. As with the chaparral zone, rainfall is biseasonally distributed, with approximately 60 percent of the annual amount falling during July to September, and the remainder arriving during the January to March period. Overstory vegetation generally consists of creosote-bush, palo-verde, and several species of cacti. Understory vegetation includes a variety of grasses and annual forbs. The climate in this zone is arid.

From an area north of Roosevelt Lake to Young, Arizona is an Upper Sonoran woodland association consisting of pinyon-juniper forest. Pinyon-juniper associations are found between elevations of 4500 to 7500 feet. Precipitation in pinyon-juniper zones varies between 12 and 24 inches annually, with a biseasonal distribution. Overstory vegetation is primarily pinyon, with juniper found in varying densities depending on local conditions. Understory vegetation is much heavier in pinyon-juniper associations in comparison with those associations found at lower elevations. Grasses, forbs, and shrubs form the typical understory vegetation complexes. The climate in pinyon-juniper zones ranges between semi-arid and semihumid depending, again, on local conditions.

Transition Life Zone

Moving northward from Young to Heber, Arizona is a large expanse of Transition Life Zone ponderosa pine vegetation (Figure 6). The Transition Zone is found at elevations of 6000 to 9000 feet, with precipitation

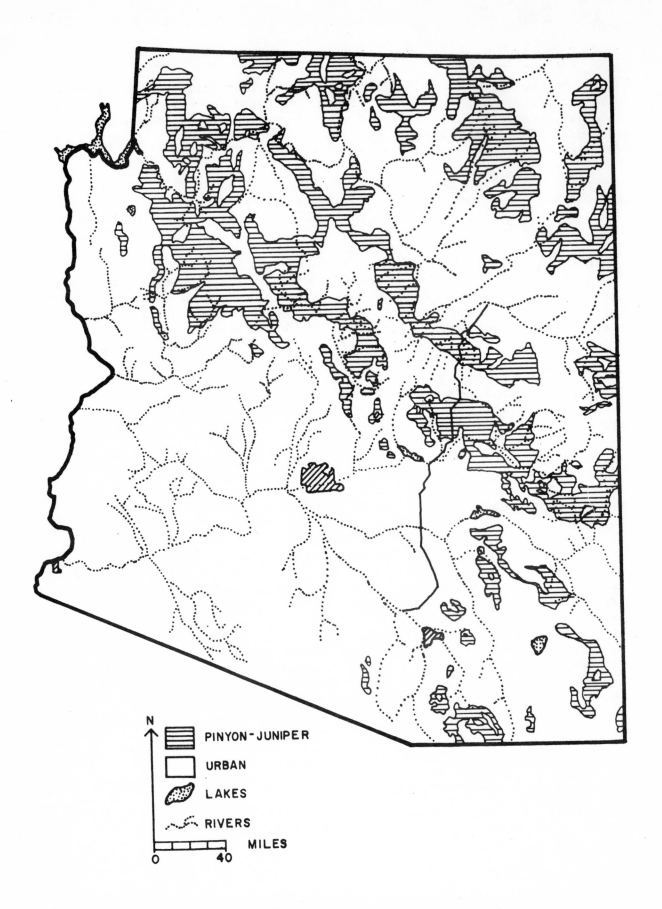

Figure 3. Relationship of APS-CS corridor to distribution of pinyon-
juniper woodland in Arizona

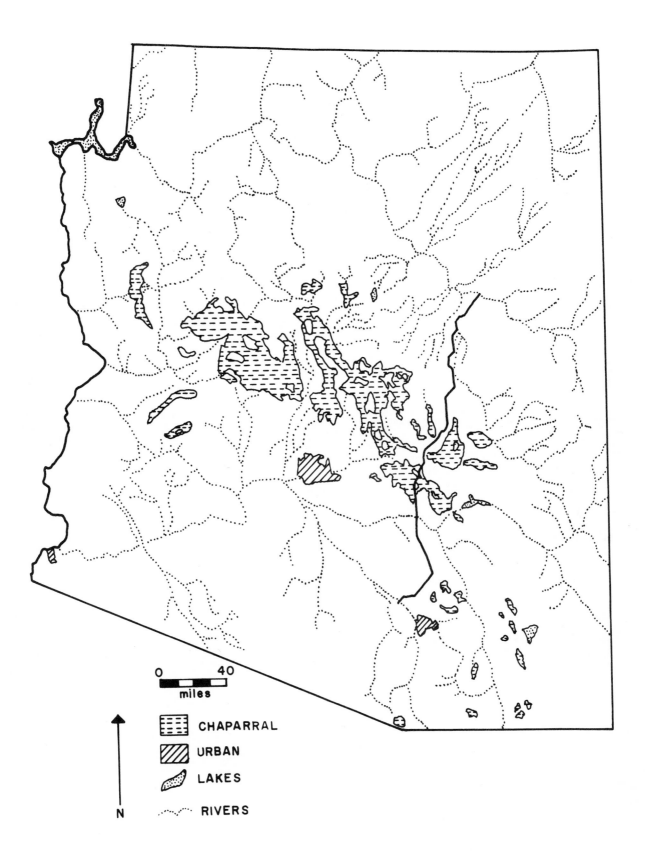

CHAPARRAL

URBAN

LAKES

RIVERS

N

0   40
miles

Figure 4.   Relationship of APS-CS corridor to distribution of chaparral
vegetation in Arizona

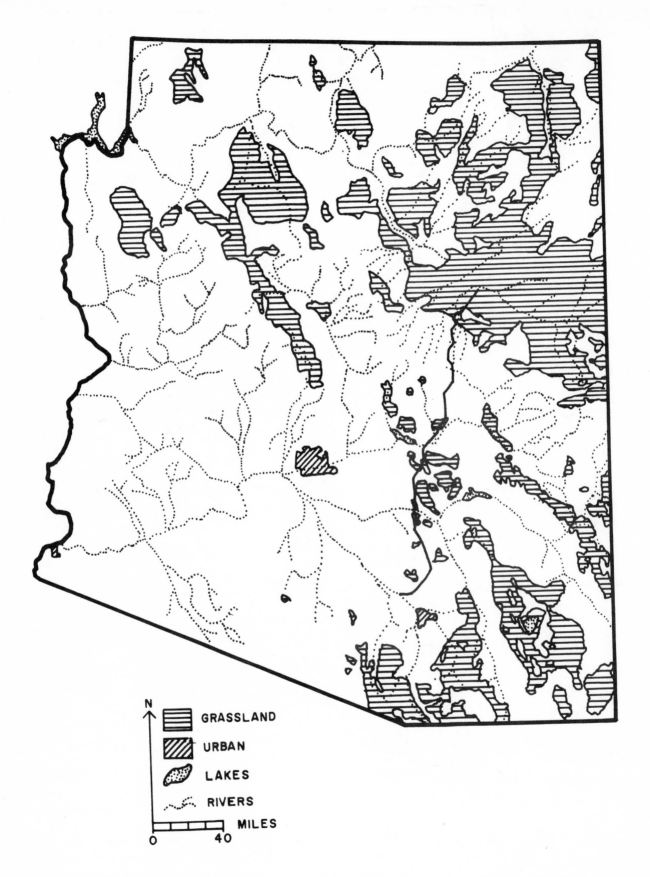

Figure 5.   Relationship of APS-CS corridor to distribution of grassland
vegetation in Arizona

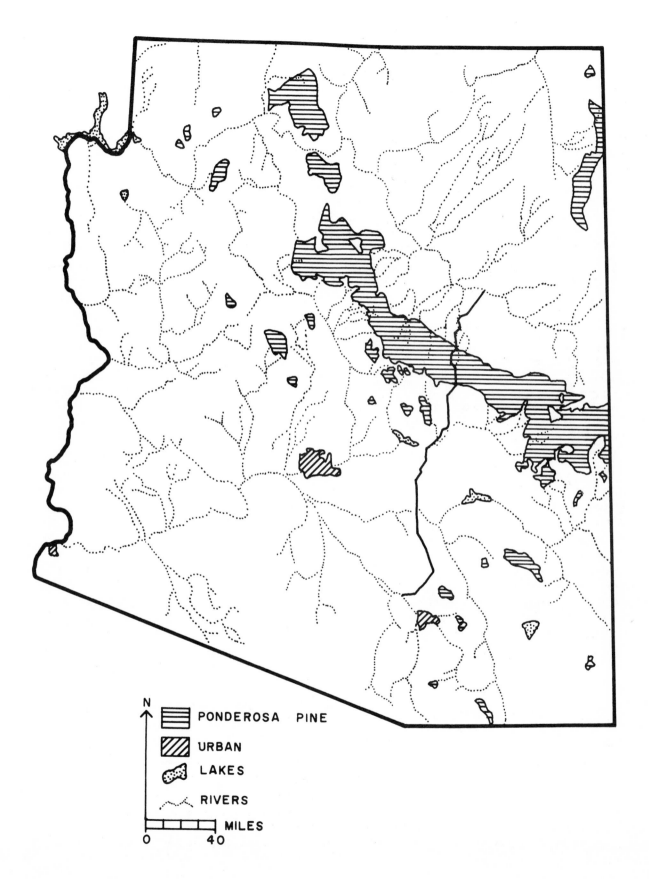

Figure 6. Relationship of APS-CS corridor to distribution of ponderosa
pine forests in Arizona

levels ranging from 20 to 30 inches of rain annually. Unlike the Upper Sonoran Life Zone, the Transition Life Zone receives a greater proportion of rainfall during the winter (primarily from snow). The dominant species in this zone is ponderosa pine, with subdominant species including such varieties as Douglas fir, quaking aspen, Gambel oak, and, at lower elevations, some intermixed pinyon-juniper. The climate in the Transition Life Zone is characteristically semihumid to wet.

Moving further northward from Heber, the corridor again intersects Upper Sonoran pinyon-juniper forest as the elevation decreases. From a zone near the upper reaches of McDonald Canyon to the northern terminus of the corridor at Joseph City, the corridor crosses a zone of Upper Sonoran plains and desert grassland. The plains-desert grassland is normally found at elevations of 4000 to 7000 feet. While plains and desert grassland are actually two separate vegetation associations, they are similar enough to be treated as a single association. Precipitation in these zones varies considerably, with desert grassland receiving between 12 to 15 inches annually, and plains grassland about 11 to 18 inches. Overstory plant species, though they do not usually occur in grassland, are scattered when present and usually consist of isolated pinyon or juniper. Understory species include various species of grama grass. Cacti are often found in areas where the soil is shallow. The climate in grassland zones varies from semi-arid (desert grassland) to semihumid (plains grassland).

Since riparian woodlands generally tend to be localized with respect to water, they crosscut all of the life zones that occur in Arizona. The transmission line corridor intersects riparian woodlands at a number of points, including (south to north) the Salt River, Coon Creek, Cherry Creek, Black Canyon Creek, and the lower Little Colorado River, as well as a large number of unnamed drainages. Riparian woodlands are subdivided into three groups depending on the elevation at which they are found: (1) at elevations of less than 3500 feet, riparian woodlands consist of salt-cedar, mesquite, palo-verde, cottonwood, and other species situated adjacent to ephemeral streams; (2) at elevations between 3500 to 7000 feet, riparian woodlands consist of cottonwood, willow, sycamore, ash, walnut, and other hardwoods found in association with perennial streams; and (3) at elevations greater than 7000 feet, riparian woodlands consist of willow, choke-cherry, maple, and various coniferous species. Annual precipitation varies greatly with elevation; accordingly, these biotic communities cannot be characterized easily as to rainfall received.

This brief introduciton to floral communities intersected by the transmission line corridor indicates the high degree of environmental diversity that is found within the transmission line right-of-way. Of the six life zones found in Arizona, three (the Lower and Upper Sonoran and Transition life zones) are intersected by the corridor. The transmission line corridor further intersects five of the eight vegetation zones that are known for the state. From this it may be seen that archaeological research in the transmission line corridor provides an opportunity to examine prehistoric adaptive strategies over a considerably broader range of environmental variation than that usually available in other archaeological research projects.

Since the present discussion has been confined to the complex of life zones which the corridor intersects, it is not necessary to exhaustively treat all of the faunal resources that are found in all of the environmental zones. Briefly, those animal species of greatest known economic importance include peccary, rabbit, raccoon, mule deer, antelope, and bighorn sheep. Specific questions concerning procurement and use of faunal resources will be addressed when site-specific research designs are developed.

Cultural Diversity

Prehistoric site variability may be examined from a number of aspects. Among these, cultural affiliation, placement in time, functional variability, variation in size, and variability in location constitute those attributes most frequently examined by archaeologists. The purpose of this section of the report is to indicate in a general manner the kinds of site variability that may be found among those sites that will be further investigated in the Cholla line and, further, to indicate the potential for additional variability in archaeological sites in the APS corridor.

While the cultural affiliation of many of the sites remains problematic, the APS corridor extends through at least four of the culture areas known in Arizona (Figure 7). Examples of Hohokam, Salado, Mogollon, and Anasazi sites of varying kinds have been located at various points along the length of the corridor. Many of these sites should provide information on some of these archaeologically defined "cultures".

The placement of archaeological sites in a temporal framework provides some indication of those periods during which particular regions were occupied. Data from sites found within the corridor, when studied in relation to evidence produced from sites adjacent to it, promise to contribute significantly to the current understanding of the temporal sequence of occupation within the regions traversed by the corridor. (Regional phases and associated time periods are indicated in Table 1.)

Owing to the limitations imposed by the nature of data recovered by survey, none of the sites located in the APS Cholla line corridor can as yet be definitively assigned to either the Paleo-Indian (about 10,000 to 5000 B.C.) or Desert Archaic (about 5000 to 100 B.C.) periods. The northern and southern portions of the corridor, in particular, do crosscut regions where Paleo-Indian remains have been recovered. Likewise, Desert Archaic remains are known from the Mogollon, Anasazi, and Hohokam areas, all of which are transected by the corridor.

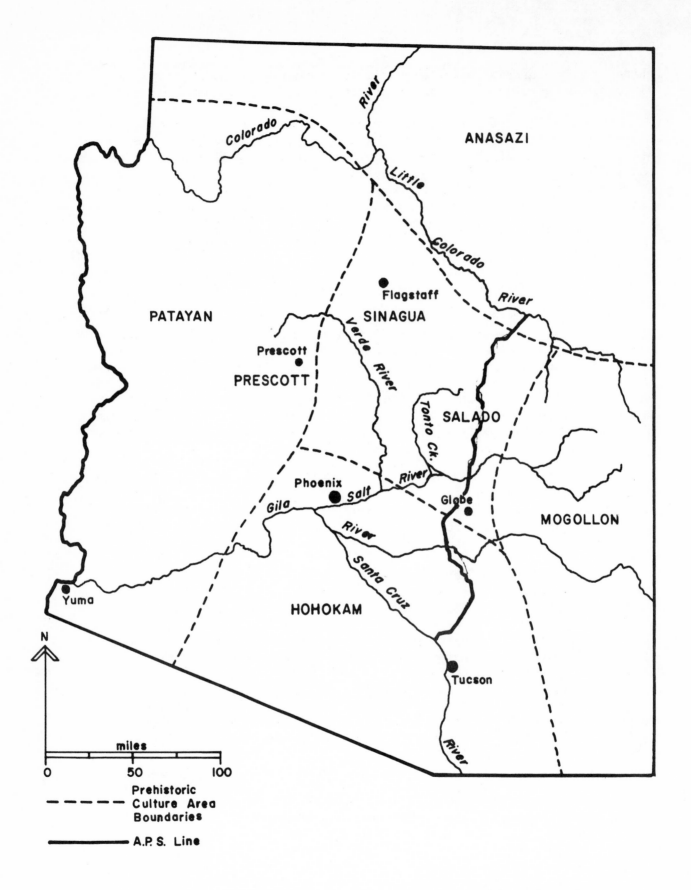

Figure 7. Relationship of APS-CS corridor to major prehistoric culture areas in Arizona

Table 1. Prehistoric cultural sequences in the Southwest (after Gladwin and Gladwin 1935; Breternitz 1960; Doyel 1978)

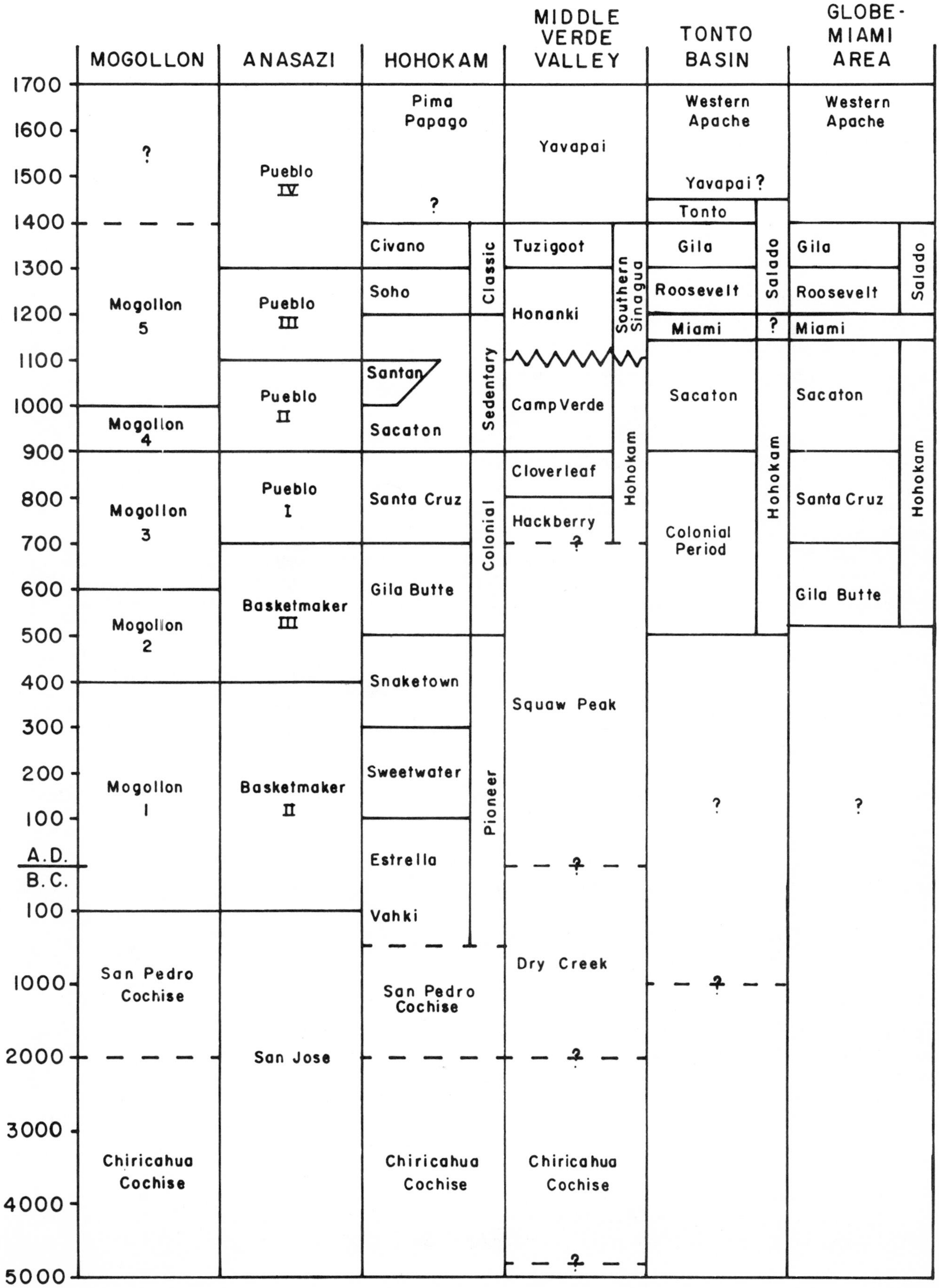

Date	MOGOLLON	ANASAZI	HOHOKAM	MIDDLE VERDE VALLEY	TONTO BASIN	GLOBE-MIAMI AREA
1700	?	Pueblo IV	Pima Papago	Yavapai	Western Apache	Western Apache
1600						
1500			?		Yavapai?	
1400	— — —		Civano	Tuzigoot (Southern Sinagua)	Tonto / Gila (Salado)	Gila (Salado)
1300	Mogollon 5	Pueblo III	Soho	Honanki	Roosevelt	Roosevelt
1200			Santan		Miami ?	Miami
1100		Pueblo II	Sacaton	Camp Verde (Sedentary)	Sacaton	Sacaton
1000	Mogollon 4					
900				Cloverleaf		Santa Cruz
800	Mogollon 3	Pueblo I	Santa Cruz	Hackberry — — ?	Colonial Period	
700			Gila Butte	(Colonial)		Gila Butte
600		Basketmaker III				
500	Mogollon 2		Snaketown	Squaw Peak		
400						
300						
200	Mogollon 1	Basketmaker II	Sweetwater (Pioneer)		?	?
100			Estrella			
A.D.				— — ? — —		
B.C.			Vahki			
100			— — —	Dry Creek		
1000	San Pedro Cochise		San Pedro Cochise		— — ? — —	
2000	— — San Jose — —	San Jose		— — ? — —		
3000	Chiricahua Cochise		Chiricahua Cochise	Chiricahua Cochise		
4000						
5000				— — ? — —		

(Hohokam spans Tonto Basin and Globe-Miami Area columns vertically)

Many sites located within the APS Cholla line corridor exhibit diagnostic architectural and ceramic remains of sufficient quantity and diversity to warrant their (at least tentative) assigning to Anasazi, Mogollon, Salado, or Hohokam cultural groups. The evaluation of these assignments has been tempered by recognition of the fact that, particularly in the case of the Salado culture, no consensus has been reached as regards the degree to which certain architectural or ceramic features are truly diagnostic of any of these cultures.

Of the 45 sites within the Holbrook-Chevelon segment of the APS corridor, as many as two exhibit characteristics suggesting an affiliation with the Anasazi culture, and 16 with the Mogollon, although several sites within these groups possess elements indicating some influence from both cultures.

Fourteen of the 23 sites found during survey of the Q Ranch segment of the corridor exhibit architectural and other remains suggestive of Mogollon and/or Salado cultural affiliation; very few sites in this area of the corridor evidence any Hohokam or Anasazi influence. Most of these 14 sites can be dated roughly to the period A.D. 1000 to 1300.

A considerable extent of the Tonto-Roosevelt segment of the corridor traverses a region generally regarded as a border zone among the Mogollon, Salado, and Hohokam cultures, and as characterized by Salado cultural remains. Of the 71 sites located in this segment, 48 possess architectural remains whose presence suggests a date of A.D. 1100 or later. In this region, sites dated to the period after A.D. 900 have traditionally been interpreted as Salado. However, it is uncertain at present how many of the sites located by the APS line survey can be validly assigned a Salado cultural-temporal affiliation.

Finally, within the Southern Desert segment, the southernmost portion of the corridor, 12 of the 19 sites located can be assigned, with reasonable certainty, a Hohokam or Hohokam-Salado affiliation on the basis of observations made during survey.

A rough approximation of functional variation among sites in this report may be offered. Although detailed artifact collections and analysis were not possible during the survey phase, sites located can be differentiated with regard to the presence or absence of certain artifact classes. These classes include lithics, ceramics/sherds, ground stone, and structures, and are used here in the belief that their presence-absence indicates some differences in the kinds of activities that occurred at any one site, even though the precise nature of those activities cannot be specified.

Sites containing only chipped stone remains (lithics) probably had some kind of a procurement-extraction function. Sites containing lithics, sherds, and ground stone are thought to represent more stable occupations (of varying duration) in which a variety of maintenance-extraction activities may have occurred. Sites containing all of the above artifact classes plus evidence of structures are throught to represent the most stable occupations. As a result, the range of activities that occurred at these sites quite likely was considerably greater than those at other sites.

The discussions in later sections of this report and the site descriptions in the accompanying volume demonstrate that the sites located during survey of the APS Cholla line corridor exhibit a high degree of environmental, cultural-temporal, and functional variability. They accordingly afford the potential for research into a wide variety of topics, an undertaking not often feasible in more regionally and culturally circumscribed projects.

REFERENCES

Breternitz, David A.
   1960   Excavations at three sites in the Verde Valley, Arizona. Museum of Northern Arizona Bulletin 34.

Doyel, David E.
   1978   The Miami Wash Project: Hohokam and Salado in the Globe-Miami Area, central Arizona. Contribution to Highway Salvage Archaeology in Arizona 52.

Gladwin, Winifred and Harold S. Gladwin
   1935   The eastern range of the Red-on-buff culture. Medallion Papers 16. Globe: Gila Pueblo.

CHAPTER 3

SURVEY HISTORY
by Gary T. Cummins and Lynn S. Teague

Introduction

The most efficient method of conducting an archaeological survey
over the route of a linear project such as the Arizona Public Service
Company's Cholla-to-Saguaro 500 kV transmission line is to begin at one
end and follow the corridor to its terminus. The APS Cholla Project,
however, proved to be a case where the most desirable methods were not
feasible. Because the sponsor encountered difficulties in obtaining
right-of-way permission in some cases, certain sections of the line became
available for study before others. In the interest of time, Arizona Public
Service requested the Arizona State Museum to immediately survey those
sections where permission had been obtained. The Cholla-to-Saguaro corridor,
therefore, was surveyed in a 'hopscotch' fashion over a more than two-year
period, from mid-1974 to late 1976. There were three major subdivisions:
the northern section; the central, or United States Forest Service section;
and the southern section. The northern and southern sections were surveyed
as separate projects, while the central section was covered in a series of
shorter surveys. Figure 8 shows the entire route, with the individual
sections marked off.

Corridor Survey

This discussion covers the initial survey of the corridor itself.
This work was conducted primarily in 1974 and 1975; however, completion
of the sequence was achieved only in 1977, when survey of the segment between
Sombrero Peak and Gentry Canyon, previously postponed because the line
had not been flagged, was undertaken.

Field Methodology

Site Definition

The Arizona State Museum Site Survey Manual in use during the
initial corridor survey in 1974 and 1975 stated that three tentative
criteria must be met by an archaeological site: (1) it must exhibit
definable limits in time and space; (2) it must contain more than one
definable locus of past human activity; and (3) it should have an artifact
density of more than five per square meter (Arizona State Museum 1974:3).
Isolated artifacts or artifact concentrations that did not meet the
above criteria were noted as isolated cultural phenomena, but were not
assigned site numbers or recorded in the detail that "sites" were.

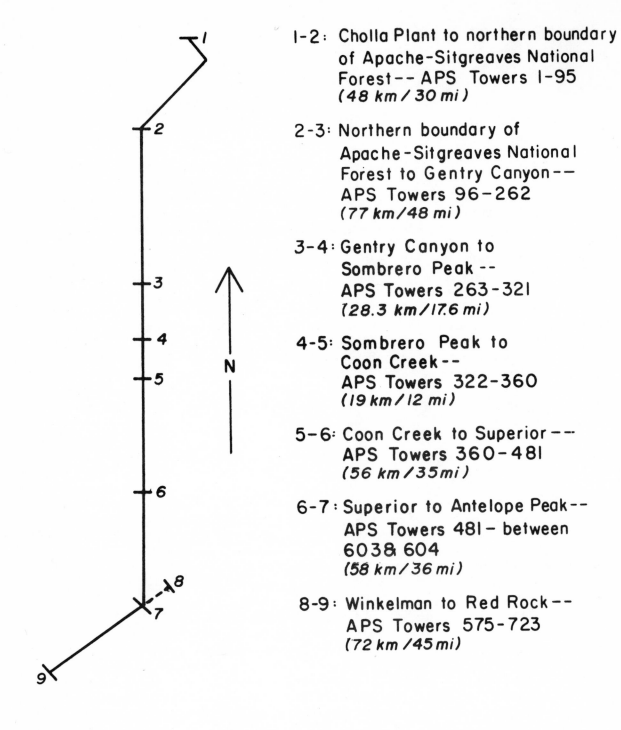

1-2: Cholla Plant to northern boundary of Apache-Sitgreaves National Forest-- APS Towers 1-95 (48 km / 30 mi)

2-3: Northern boundary of Apache-Sitgreaves National Forest to Gentry Canyon-- APS Towers 96-262 (77 km / 48 mi)

3-4: Gentry Canyon to Sombrero Peak-- APS Towers 263-321 (28.3 km / 17.6 mi)

4-5: Sombrero Peak to Coon Creek-- APS Towers 322-360 (19 km / 12 mi)

5-6: Coon Creek to Superior-- APS Towers 360-481 (56 km / 35 mi)

6-7: Superior to Antelope Peak-- APS Towers 481- between 603 & 604 (58 km / 36 mi)

8-9: Winkelman to Red Rock-- APS Towers 575-723 (72 km / 45 mi)

Figure 8. Survey segments of APS-CS corridor

Surface Collections

It is the policy of the Arizona State Museum to exercise restraint in making collections of surface artifacts during the survey phase of a project. This is because of the potential effect on later analysis of the sites when a portion of the artifact material has been removed; the expenditure of time required to properly take surface samples; and the fact that, in many instances, surface artifact material constitutes the only indication of the presence of a site. Removal of artifacts must be justified by the need for information critical for adequate description and interpretation of the resource. During the initial survey of the APS Cholla-to-Saguaro corridor, samples of ceramics considered temporally and culturally diagnostic were sometimes taken. During the survey of the Southern Desert (Winkelman-to-Red Rock) section, samples were taken of ceramics and lithics as mandated by Kinkade's research design emphasis on correlations between artifact type and environmental change (Kinkade 1974:5, 7).

Site Survey Form

All sites located were inventoried and evaluated for research potential through use of the Arizona State Museum site survey form in use at the time. This form was designed to integrate cultural and environmental data in order to answer the following questions (see Kemrer, Schultz, and Dodge 1972:13):

1. What cultural activities are represented at the site?
2. What is the site's cultural and temporal affiliation?
3. Are deposits stratified or superficial?
4. What are the degree and nature of the natural processes and cultural activities affecting the site?
5. How does the site relate to archaeological knowledge of the area?
6. Is the site potentially eligible for National Register of Historic Places status?

The research designs for the Winkelman-to-Red Rock and central survey sections mandated that information of a more detailed nature than provided for in the standard ASM site survey form be collected. Therefore, special forms were designed to supplement the ASM form during these surveys. The Winkelman-to-Red Rock survey special form was designed for surface lithics description, with emphasis on attributes relating directly to subsistence activities (Kinkade 1974:7). The central survey (northern boundary of Apache-Sitgreaves National Forest to Antelope Peak) special form was designed to elicit detailed environmental data concerning vegetation, soils, hydrology, topography, geology, and climate (Spain 1975:1-2). Samples of these supplementary forms are included in the appendix to this report.

Survey Procedures

The APS Cholla Project corridor survey was carried out in sections over a period of more than two years. Although survey procedures differed somewhat in detail from section to section, certain procedures were followed by all crews.

The crews would usually drive to each day's survey location in two vehicles. The first vehicle would be left at the point where the previous day's survey had ended. The entire crew would then proceed along the line to a distance which they felt could be covered during that day's work. Leaving the second vehicle at that point, the crew would then walk back down the line toward the first vehicle, noting archaeological and environmental data. This was usually arranged so that they could walk downhill most of the way. Another advantage was that the crew could walk toward a known point, which helped keep them on line within the corridor.

While carrying out the survey, crew members would align themselves across the corridor in such a manner that complete coverage of the land surface could be achieved. Crew members would often walk in a zigzag pattern along the corridor to achieve total coverage.

Arizona Public Service surveyors attempted to mark the corridor for the archaeological survey crews, who nonetheless encountered considerable difficulty in locating the corridor, particularly in rough terrain. The most satisfactory solution to this problem seemed to be in having the APS surveyors work directly with the archaeologists in the field.

The archaeological survey of access road locations was handled differently than was the transmission line survey. An archaeologist would work directly with the subcontractor responsible for access road construction by examining each proposed access road location for archaeological material. If sites were located, the archaeologist would immediately advise the subcontractor to alter the course of the road to avoid the site. No research design was utilized in the access road surveys.

Finally, at the close of each section of the APS Cholla Project survey, an interim report would be prepared, usually by the supervisory archaeologist for that section. These interim reports noted the area surveyed, names of all crew members, survey procedures followed, problems encountered, brief descriptions of all archaeological sites located, and recommendations for the management of these sites. The data contained in these reports form the basis of the contents of this final report.

Site Recording

In general, all crew members participated in site recording, thus allowing this portion of the survey to proceed faster and ensuring that all data were adequately noted. In some cases, an entire line segment would be surveyed, and all sites noted; later, the crew would return to formally record the site. This procedure permitted survey time to be accurately planned, and made it possible to relate sites to each other in the descriptions. The crews assigned field numbers to all sites, flagged the sites, and placed a wooden lath stake at each site, with a metal tag bearing the field number. Permanent Arizona State Museum site numbers were assigned later.

Survey Data

The following pages include several sections, each of which describes one of the individual surveys which was part of the overall APS Cholla Project transmission line survey. Each of these sections notes the names of Arizona State Museum personnel involved, the areas surveyed, distances, general physiography and vegetation as they were relevant to survey methods, logistics, methodologies, problems, and a tabulated summary of all sites located. Site descriptions are to be found in the volume accompanying this report.

Northern Survey Section: Cholla Plant to Northern Boundary of the Apache-Sitgreaves National Forest

Introduction. The intensive field study of the northern section of the APS Cholla Project survey was carried out by Arizona State Museum archaeologists from March 16 through 21, 1974. The field crew consisted of Veletta K. Reid (Project Supervisor) and Assistant Archaeologists Linda L. Mayro, David A. Phillips, Jr., and Steven Sessions.

Scope of Survey. The survey of this section was conducted from the APS Cholla Plant near Joseph City, Arizona to Wildcat Canyon, a point on the northern boundary of the Apache-Sitgreaves National Forest (Figure 8). The linear distance was approximately 48 km (30 miles) from APS Tower locations 1 to 95, and the corridor was 100.7 m (330 feet) wide. The corridor was designed to extend 100 feet to either side of a center line for the APS transmission line, plus an additional 39.7 m (130 feet) to the west for a proposed Salt River Project transmission line. A total of 486 ha (1200 acres) was thus surveyed in this section.

Terrain. The northern survey section lies within the Colorado Plateau physiographic province, characterized in this area by nearly flat to gently rolling topography, incised by 20 to 40-foot-deep canyons in the southern portion. This area is mostly covered by grassland from APS Tower locations 1 to 20, at which point the grasslands give way to juniper-grass savannahs from APS Tower locations 20 to 95. From APS Tower locations 95 to 96, the land is covered by heavy juniper woodland growth, and the terrain becomes more mountainous. The elevation rises from north to south.

The Cholla Plant is 5000 feet above sea level, while Wildcat Canyon, on the northern boundary of the Apache-Sitgreaves National Forest, is at 6160 feet elevation (Canouts and Phillips 1974:6).

Methodology. The standard survey methodology was followed during this survey. The crew used two vehicles to drive to the site of the survey; they worked together by walking a line abreast across the corridor, zigzagging to ensure complete coverage; and all crew members participated in site record-ing. They took ceramic sherd collections at all sites located, as well as at two isolated sherd clusters, since the ceramics found exhibited certain attributes which required identification and analysis not possible in the field. The general lack of archaeological knowledge about this area made this analysis especially important (Canouts and Phillips 1974:9).

The crew marked all sites with blue and white flagging tape to enable Arizona Public Service construction crews to avoid them. They also marked each site with a lath stake bearing the respective field number.

This section required a total of 368 person-hours (288 for ground survey and site recording and 80 for analysis and report preparation) (Canouts and Phillips 1974:4).

Problems. The overriding problem encountered during survey of this section was that of the crew's staying on line in the corridor. The centerline had been marked only occasionally with scraps of orange flagging tape. Moreover, the tower locations from numbers 1 to 82, although staked and flagged, occurred at intervals averaging one-quarter mile, a distance beyond the range of field binoculars. The line was especially difficult to survey in rugged terrain. Neither towers nor the centerline were marked at all from tower location numbers 82 to 96. The crew, there-fore, had to rely on truck tracks and brush-cutting evidence left behind by the Arizona Public Service survey crews. These, of course, were not always in straight lines, and the archaeologists had to resort to aerial photos to determine the corridor location. This procedure required sub-stantially more time than would have been the case had the corridor been adequately marked.

Access roads and construction facility locations were not marked in any manner, and were therefore impossible to survey at this time (Reid 1974:6).

Survey Results. Eight archaeological sites and several isolated cultural phenomena were recorded within this survey section. The Arizona State Museum has recommended that all of the archaeological sites be preserved through avoidance of them during construction and protection of them from all associated aspects of the transmission line construction.

Table 2 lists the sites located during the survey of this section of the APS Cholla transmission line project. More detailed information on these and all sites located during the APS Cholla Project survey may be found in the site descriptions accompanying this report.

Table 2. Sites in northern section of APS Cholla-Saguaro survey

ASM Number	Field Number
AZ P:3:6	CS-1
AZ P:3:7	CS-2
AZ P:3:8	CS-3
AZ P:3:9	CS-4
AZ P:3:10	CS-5
AZ P:6:1	CS-6
AZ P:6:2	CS-8
AZ P:6:3	CS-9

Central Survey Section: Northern Boundary of Apache-Sitgreaves National Forest to Gentry Canyon

Introduction. The Arizona State Museum began the archaeological survey of the APS Cholla Project transmission line corridor portion from the northern boundary of the Apache-Sitgreaves National Forest to Gentry Canyon (between APS Tower locations 96 and 262) on September 29, 1975, and completed it on November 24, 1975. The four-person crew consisted of Supervisory Archaeologist Randall McGuire and Assistant Archaeologists Patricia Fall, Susan Morton, and Barry Richards.

Scope of Survey. This survey section (Figure 8) was 77 km (48 miles) long, with a corridor width of 100.7 m (330 feet), thus comprising a total area of 778 ha (1920 acres). The APS transmission line corridor was 61 m (200 feet) wide, with an additional 39.7 m (130 feet) added to the west side to accommodate a proposed Salt River Project transmission line.

Portions of both the Apache-Sitgreaves and Tonto National Forests were included in this survey.

Terrain. Physiographically, the area included in this survey contains portions of the Transition Zone and the Plateau Zone of the Basin and Range Province. The area between Gentry Canyon and the Mogollon Rim generally lies within the Transition Zone, and is characterized by high

mountains, steep-walled and deep canyons, and rugged terrain. The area
north of the Mogollon Rim is high (above 5000 feet) and flat, incised
with canyons, and surmounted in areas by volcanic mountain ranges (Wilson
1962:86, 96).

The survey crossed both montane conifer forest and juniper-pinyon
woodland vegetation communities (Lowe 1964).

Methodology. The research orientation for this survey section was that formulated by James N. Spain, who emphasized the definition
of subsistence adaptations to different environments. This necessitated
frequent, detailed, and systematic observations and recordings of cultural
and environmental phenomena.

The crew began the survey of this section at the northern boundary
of the Sitgreaves National Forest (Wildcat Canyon), and from there worked
south along the corridor. They used the same methodology as had been used
in other surveys: walking abreast across the line, and zigzagging to
ensure total coverage. They would often walk through areas, noting sites,
then return later to fill out the ASM and supplementary site forms.

Randall McGuire remained with the project as Supervisory Archaeologist until November 1, 1975, when he left to work on a highway salvage
project. The survey was completed by the three remaining archaeologists.

The crew expended a total of 1468 person-hours on this survey
section, including 904 hours in the field and 564 hours for laboratory
analysis and report preparation.

Problems. During survey of this section, locating the corridor
and staying on line did prove to be major difficulties. This was due in
large part to the nature of the terrain. On the plateau, because the
topography was fairly level and APS had cut a line through the relatively
heavy juniper growth, the centerline was easy to find. However, when the
crew descended into the Transition Zone south of the Mogollon Rim, the
topography became much more rugged, and locating the centerline increased
in difficulty, due to inadequate flagging. Tower locations had not been
plotted by APS prior to this survey, and thus were not marked.

Survey Results. During this survey, the ASM crew located ten
archaeological sites and three isolated cultural phenomena. Table 3
lists these archaeological sites.

Table 3.   Sites in central section of APS Cholla-Saguaro survey: northern boundary of Apache-Sitgreaves National Forest to Gentry Canyon

ASM Number	Field Number
AZ P:6:5	CS-81
AZ P:6:6	CS-68
AZ P:6:7	CS-66
AZ P:6:8	CS-58
AZ P:6:9	CS-60
AZ P:6:10	CS-62
AZ P:6:11	CS-64
AZ P:6:12	CS-56
AZ P:6:13	CS-54
AZ P:6:14	CS-52

Central Survey Section: Gentry Canyon to Sombrero Peak

Introduction. Because of delays in flagging this portion of the line, archaeological survey was not carried out until late in the project, and was eventually integrated with access road survey. Survey work in this section was carried out intermittently between December 27, 1976 and April 22, 1977. The survey crew at this time consisted of Christopher Causey, Robert Hard, Steven Danziger, Neal Ackerly, Michelle Behr, Steven Lensink, and David Gregory. Christopher Causey acted as field supervisor.

Scope of Survey. This corridor segment (Figure 8) extends from APS Tower location 263 to Tower location 321, a distance of 28.3 km (17.6 miles). The APS transmission line corridor was 61 m (200 feet) wide, with an additional 39.7 m (130 feet) added to the west side to accommodate a proposed Salt River Project transmission line. The area surveyed thus comprised 285 ha (704 acres). This segment is entirely within the Tonto National Forest.

Terrain. This area lies within the Transition Zone of the Basin and Range Province. The topography of this zone is more rugged than that of the adjacent Plateau Province and Sonoran Desert Zone. While the Transition Zone is predominantly lower in elevation than is the Plateau Province, it does contain mountains higher than those of the Plateau Province rim. Mountains vary in their appearance depending upon rock composition. In general, mountains of metamorphic rock types tend to be more steep and rugged than those of sedimentary and crystalline rock composition. Steep canyons are numerous in this area.

Methodology. This portion of the survey was the only one within the central section of the APS Cholla Project transmission line survey that was not conducted using the research design developed by Spain. This was a consequence of the delay in surveying this segment and difficulties that had become apparent in applying some of the environmental information solicited by his design. While the standard ASM survey form was used and environmental and cultural variables recorded, there was no systematic sampling of artifacts, soils, and vegetation.

The structure of the field crew varied, depending upon the number of personnel involved at any point during the survey. As was noted previously, this segment was integrated within the later phase of the project, in which personnel were very mobile and responded on a daily basis to priorities established by Arizona Public Service. For further discussion of field methodologies, see the later discussion of access road and tower survey.

Problems. Problems in this survey segment were largely the result of rugged topography and dense vegetation. There were no difficulties of any significance associated with tower and line marking, in contrast to earlier phases of the project.

Survey Results. The survey crews found and recorded a total of 13 sites in this corridor segment. Detailed site descriptions may be found in the volume accompanying this report.

Table 4. Sites in central section of APS Cholla-Saguaro survey: Gentry Canyon to Sombrero Peak

ASM Number	Field Number
AZ P:13:12	CS-277
AZ V:1:8	CS-243
AZ V:1:11	CS-245
AZ V:1:12	CS-248
AZ V:1:13	CS-249
AZ V:1:14	CS-250
AZ V:1:15	CS-251
AZ V:1:16	CS-252
AZ V:1:17	CS-253
AZ V:1:22	CS-258
AZ V:1:23	CS-259
AZ V:1:24	CS-261
AZ V:1:25	CS-262

Central Survey Section: Sombrero Peak to Coon Creek

Introduction. Between July 9 and 25, 1975, Arizona State Museum archaeologists surveyed a portion of the APS Cholla Project transmission line between Sombrero Peak and Coon Creek, Arizona. Eight crew members participated in this survey: James N. Spain and David Doyel, Supervisory Archaeologists, and Assistant Archaeologists Francine Bonnello, Patricia Fall, Randall McGuire, Cherie Scheick, Carla Van West, and Richard Wilk. Spain acted as overall supervisor of field operations (Wilk and Scheick 1975:4).

Scope of Survey. This survey segment, located within the Tonto National Forest, extended for about 19 km (12 miles) between APS Tower location 322 and Tower location 360 (see Figure 8). The corridor was 100.7 m (330 feet) wide--30.5 m (100 feet) on either side of the APS centerline, with an additional 39.7 m (130 feet) on the west side of the APS corridor to accommodate a proposed Salt River Project transmission line. The crew members thus surveyed an area of 194 ha (480 acres) (Wilk and Scheick 1975:2).

Terrain. The survey area is located in the Transition Zone of the Basin and Range Province. This zone is characterized by a more rugged topography than that of the adjacent Plateau Province and Sonoran Desert Zone, and is lower in elevation than the Plateau Province, although it contains some mountains whose peaks are higher than the rim of the Plateau Province. The mountains tend to be flat-topped where they are of sedimentary rock, sharp and rugged where metamorphic rock is dominant, and rugged to rounded when the rock is crystalline. These mountains are often separated by deep, steep-walled canyons and valleys (Wilson 1962:96). Elevations decreased from north to south in this survey segment, from 4200 feet at APS Tower location 322 to 2760 feet at APS Tower location 360.

This survey segment crossed three major vegetation zones: the Arizona upland (palo-verde-–cacti association), desert grassland (scrub-grass association), and the lower borders of the pinyon-juniper community (juniper-grassland association).

Methodology. The research orientation for this survey segment was the same as that developed by Spain for the entire central section of the APS Cholla transmission line survey, and involved an attempt to define pre-historic subsistence adaptations to different environments. This required the field crew to pay close attention to both cultural and environmental variables. Crew members made observations of all aspects of both, and took samples of artifacts (ceramics), soils, and vegetation on a systematic basis. Information was recorded on both the standard ASM site form and supplemental forms designed for this project (Spain 1975:1-2).

The archaeological crew was divided into two teams: Team One, headed by James N. Spain, and including Patricia Fall, Randall McGuire, and Carla Van West; and Team Two, headed by David Doyel, and including Francine Bonnello, Cherie Scheick, and Richard Wilk. Spain's team began work at the northern end of the survey section at APS Tower location 322, near Sombrero Peak, and proceeded south. Doyel's team began its survey at APS Tower location 360, near Coon Creek, and proceeded north. Each team was assisted by an Arizona Public Service surveyor, who preceded the archaeologists by a few hundred feet, flagging the APS centerline at regular intervals.

The members of each crew spaced themselves evenly across the 100.7-m-wide corridor and walked along it, marking all sites located. Both teams decided to make an initial walk-through of the corridor to mark sites, and to then return to record them. This was feasible due to the relatively easy access to the corridor via a good road through most of the Cherry Creek drainage, and further permitted the teams to better budget their time (Wilk and Scheick 1975:5-6).

The teams assigned field numbers to all artifact locations. Permanent Arizona State Museum site numbers were later given to those artifact locations which qualified as archaeological sites. The teams also flagged each site with blue and white tape, and set a wooden stake into the ground, to which was attached a metal tag with the site number stamped on it (Wilk and Scheick 1975:7-8).

Survey of the Sombrero Peak-to-Coon Creek segment required a total of 1747 person-hours: 642 for field work and 1105 for laboratory analysis and report preparation.

Problems. The crew encountered more problems along this survey segment than in the earlier Antelope Peak-to-Superior portion of the line; these problems generally involved difficulties in field orientation. There were often discrepancies between topographic line locations as indicated on the maps and the actual line location in the field. The topographic maps that the crew used were often several years out of date; land modifications carried out since their publication created problems in identifying locations.

The irregular terrain characteristic of this survey segment caused problems in finding the centerline and staying on it. The presence of an APS surveyor with each of the two teams was beneficial, and helped resolve some of the difficulties of location and orientation in a relatively short amount of time (Wilk and Scheick 1975:48-9).

It should be noted that this survey was carried out before Arizona Public Service had plotted any of the tower locations. However, the locating of sites within the corridor and the subsequent reporting of that information to APS and the Forest Service allowed APS engineers and planners to later plot the tower locations so that sites located by ASM could be avoided. These locations could be plotted with the full knowledge that they would not have to be moved later, or that archaeological sites would not be subject to mitigative excavation with its additional costs.

Survey Results. The Arizona State Museum archaeologists found and recorded a total of 25 artifact concentrations during the course of the Sombrero Peak-to-Coon Creek survey. Six of these were very light scatters of sherds, lithics, or both, and did not meet the Arizona State Museum site criteria. The remaining 19 manifestations include 17 pre-historic and two historic sites. Table 5 lists these sites. More detailed site descriptions may be found in the volume accompanying this report.

Table 5. Sites in central section of APS Cholla-Saguaro survey:
Sombrero Peak to Coon Creek

ASM Number	Field Number
AZ V:1:5	CS-45
AZ V:5:11	CS-27
AZ V:5:12	CS-29
AZ V:5:13	CS-30
AZ V:5:14	CS-31
AZ V:5:15	CS-32
AZ V:5:16	CS-33
AZ V:5:17	CS-34
AZ V:5:18	CS-35
AZ V:5:19	CS-36
AZ V:5:20	CS-38
AZ V:5:21	CS-39
AZ V:5:22	CS-40
AZ V:5:23	CS-41
AZ V:5:24	CS-42
AZ V:5:25	CS-43
AZ V:5:26	CS-47
AZ V:5:34	CS-44
AZ V:9:103	CS-46

Central Survey Section: Coon Creek to Superior

Introduction. From September 2 to 24, 1975, an Arizona State Museum archaeological crew surveyed the APS Cholla Project transmission line segment between Coon Creek and the Superior-Globe Highway. The crew consisted of Supervisory Archaeologist Randall McGuire and Assistant Archaeologists Patricia Fall, Susan Morton, and Barry Richards.

Scope of Survey. This survey segemnt (Figure 8) was 5.6 km (35 miles) long, with a corridor width of 100.7 m (330 feet). The APS corridor was 61 m (200 feet) wide, with an additional 39.7 m (130 feet) added to the western side to accommodate a proposed Salt River Project transmission line. The crew thus surveyed an area of 567 ha (1400 acres). The survey began at the northern end, near APS Tower location 360, and proceeded south, stopping at APS Tower location 481 (at U.S. Highway 60-70). The survey took place largely within the Tonto National Forest.

Terrain. The northern end of this survey segment falls within the Transition Zone of the Basin and Range Province, while the larger southern portion falls within the Mountain Region. The Mountain Region is characterized by numerous, high, rugged mountain ranges with wide valleys which contain broad, plain-like floors. The Transition Zone contains steep canyons and rugged mountains (Wilson 1962:93-96).

This survey segment contained the most difficult terrain of the entire APS Cholla Project transmission line survey. Access was so difficult that, on two occasions, a helicopter was required to ferry the crew to survey sites.

This segment of the corridor crossed four vegetation communities: chaparral, desert grassland, pinyon-juniper woodland, and the Arizona upland division of the Sonoran desertscrub. Elevation varied from 2760 feet at APS Tower location 360 to 4140 feet at APS Tower location 485.

Methodology. James N. Spain's research design, emphasizing subsistence adaptations to different environments, was used during this portion of the survey.

The archaeologists normally went into the field with two vehicles, parking one at the stopping point of the previous day's survey, then driving the other to a point farther down the line, parking it, and walking back along the line to the first vehicle. Access to the line was particularly difficult during the survey of this segment. An Arizona Public Service helicopter ferried the crew to Barnes Peak on September 9 and 10. Use of the helicopter in this terrain permitted a survey that would have taken four days to be done in two.

The crew began its survey of this segment of the APS Cholla-Saguaro transmission line at the northern end and proceeded south. While on the line, the crew aligned themselves across the corridor and walked in a zigzag pattern. An Arizona Public Service surveyor assisted the crew by going ahead of them, flagging the right-of-way. This and further assistance from the United States Forest Service, which provided Randall McGuire with "blue line" copies of maps of the area, allowed the crew to avoid many of the orientation problems which had plagued other portions of this survey.

The crew required a total of 781 person-hours for this survey segment, of which 426 were spent in the field, and 355 for laboratory analysis and report preparation.

Problems. The availability of a competent APS surveyor alleviated many of the field orientation problems encountered by earlier survey crews on the project. Better maps were also available. The most serious problems affecting the crew during the Coon Creek-to-Superior survey were posed by nature: extremely rough terrain, high temperatures, and difficult access. These problems tended to reduce efficiency toward the end of each day.

Survey Results. A total of 22 artifact concentrations were located and recorded by the ASM field crew during the survey of this segment. Of these, 18 were of a nature to qualify them as archaeological sites (Table 6). More detailed information may be found in site descriptions accompanying this report.

Table 6. Sites in central section of APS Cholla-Saguaro survey: Coon Creek to Superior

ASM Number	Field Number
AZ U:12:30	CS-67
AZ U:12:31	CS-63
AZ U:12:32	CS-75
AZ V:5:23	CS-41
AZ V:5:29	CS-50
AZ V:5:30	CS-61
AZ V:5:31	CS-57
AZ V:5:32	CS-59
AZ V:5:33	CS-70
AZ V:9:100	CS-53
AZ V:9:101	CS-55
AZ V:9:102	CS-51
AZ V:9:103	CS-46
AZ V:9:104	CS-48
AZ V:9:105	CS-49
AZ V:9:116	CS-69
AZ V:9:117	CS-73
AZ V:9:118	CS-71

Southern Survey Section: Superior to Antelope Peak

Introduction. Between June 23 and July 8, 1975, the Arizona State Museum carried out an intensive archaeological survey of a newly designated segment of the APS Cholla Project transmission line: Superior to Antelope Peak. This was the third archaeological survey carried out by ASM for the APS Cholla Project, and the first to involve land controlled by the U. S. Forest Service (Tonto National Forest). The Arizona State Museum crew consisted of Supervisory Archaeologists James N. Spain and David Doyel, and Assistant Archaeologists Francine Bonnello, Patricia Fall, Randall McGuire, Cherie Scheick, Carla Van West, and Richard Wilk. Mr. Spain acted as overall supervisor of the field operations.

Scope of Survey. The ASM crew surveyed a corridor 61 m (200 feet) wide that extended 58 km (36 miles) from APS Tower location 481, adjacent to U.S. Highway 60-70, 5.6 km (3.5 miles) northeast of Superior, Arizona, to approximately midway between APS Tower locations 603 and 604, at Rabbit Ranch near Antelope Peak (see Figure 8). An area of 354 ha (873 acres) was thus covered in this survey.

Terrain. The Superior-to-Antelope Peak survey section lies within the Mountain Region of the Basin and Range Province. The Basin and Range Province is characterized by numerous, rugged mountain ranges which rise steeply from broad valleys. The Mountain Region contains the highest and widest of these ranges (Wilson 1962:91-96).

The survey corridor crossed three major vegetation communities: the plains and desert grassland, the chaparral-interior chaparral, and the Arizona upland division of the Sonoran desertscrub community. Elevation ranged from 4157 feet at APS Tower location 481 to 3800 feet at APS Tower location 604.

Methodology. James N. Spain's research design formed the basis for the research orientation for this as well as for all surveys done in the central or U.S. Forest Service section of the APS Cholla-Saguaro transmission line. As in other survey segments within the central section, the crews paid close attention to both cultural and environmental variables. Observations of both were made on the standard ASM and supplemental site forms, and samples of artifacts, soils, and vegetation were taken on a systematic basis (Spain 1975:1-2).

The crew was divided into two teams. The first, supervised by James N. Spain, also included Patricia Fall, Randall McGuire, and Carla Van West; the second, supervised by David Doyel, included Francine Bonnello, Cherie Scheick, and Richard Wilk. The corridor between Antelope Peak and the Gila River was divided into two sections. Spain's team began survey from the southern end and worked north, while Doyel's team began survey at

the Gila River and proceeded south. The section of the corridor north
of the Gila River was not further divided, however, and the two teams
surveyed it from south to north, working in proximity to each other
(Canouts 1975:5).

Both teams followed the same survey technique of spacing themselves
within the right-of-way boundaries and walking parallel to the centerline,
often zigzagging to make certain that coverage of the corridor was complete
(Canouts 1975:5).

The crew for this survey segment required a total of 1276 person-
hours, including 704 person-hours in the field, and an additional 572
person-hours for laboratory analysis and report preparation.

Problems. Serious problems encountered by the crew during survey
of this segment essentially involved difficulties of orientation in the
field. The archaeologists found it difficult to locate sites on USGS
7.5-minute-series topographic maps, and often had problems in locating
the APS centerline in the field. Arizona Public Service was unable to
provide large-scale aerial photographs before the survey began, which
forced the crew to rely upon the small-scale USGS maps. Many of these
maps were out of date, and recent changes to the landscape thwarted attempts
to read them. The crew attempted to remedy this situation by employing
7.5-minute-orthoquad aerial photographs of the survey area, obtained from
Arizona Resources Information Systems; however, this measure proved to be
only partly successful (Canouts 1975:17).

Although APS survey crews preceded the archaeologists along the
corridor, flagging the centerline, their efforts proved inadequate in
rough terrain. Also, without aerial photographs of the corridor, it was
difficult to locate archaeological sites in relation to the centerline.
Additional problems of this nature were avoided by having the APS and ASM
crews work closely together (Canouts 1975:17).

Survey Results. The Arizona State Museum archaeological survey
crew located eight sites during this survey. Three of these had been
located earlier by the Museum, while one site (AZ U:16:138) could not
be relocated (Canouts 1975:6). Table 7 lists these sites. More detailed
information may be found in the volume of site descriptions accompanying
this report.

Table 7. Sites in southern section of APS Cholla-Saguaro survey:
Superior to Antelope Peak

ASM Number	Field Number
AZ BB:1:12	CS-23
AZ BB:1:13	CS-25
AZ U:12:26	CS-26
AZ U:16:27	BR-1-19
AZ U:16:116	CS-37
AZ U:16:128	CS-242
AZ U:16:182	CS-24
AZ V:5:20	CS-38

Southern Survey Section: Winkelman, Arizona to Red Rock, Arizona

Introduction. During the period of June 10 to 28, 1974, the
Arizona State Museum conducted an intensive field study of the Arizona
Public Service Cholla Project transmission line corridor from Winkelman
to Red Rock, Arizona. A four-person crew consisting of Gay Kinkade,
Supervisory Archaeologist, and Assistant Archaeologists Patricia Fall,
Patricia Gilman, and Michael McCarthy participated in the survey (Kinkade
and Gilman 1974:2, 4).

Scope of Survey. The survey began at APS Tower location 575, south
of Winkelman, Arizona, and concluded at APS Tower location 723, at the
Arizona Public Service Saguaro Power Plant, southeast of Red Rock, Arizona
(Figure 8). The crew surveyed a corridor 72 km (45 miles) long and 100.7 m
(330 feet) wide for a total coverage of 729 ha (1800 acres) (Kinkade and
Gilman 1974:4).

Subsequent to this survey, the right-of-way for the transmission
line corridor was realigned. As a result, the original corridor area
between original Tower location 575 and Tower location 598 was no longer
within the APS right-of-way. However, no sites were located during survey
of this 10.9-km (6.75-mile) stretch. The Superior-to-Antelope Peak and
Winkelman-to-Red Rock sections of the survey connect at the location of
Tower 598 (see Figure 8).

Terrain. The entire Winkelman-to-Red Rock section lies within
the Sonoran Desert Region of the Basin and Range Physiographic Province.
The terrain in this region is characterized by mountain ranges with low,
rugged peaks separated by broad, flat basins (Wilson 1962:96). Vegetation
in this region consists mostly of salt-bush, cacti, palo-verde, mesquite,
and bur-sage.

Methodology. Standard ASM survey procedures were followed during
this survey. The crew drove to the location of each day's survey segment
and used the "leapfrog" technique of leaving one vehicle at the starting
point, driving to the end-point, and then walking back down the corridor

to the first vehicle. Crew members stayed together during the survey, aligning themselves across the corridor, and often zigzagging to ensure complete coverage. The crew frequently examined areas immediately adjacent to the corridor for archaeological sites which might potentially be indirectly affected by transmission line construction. The supervisory archaeologist walked directly along the centerline at all times, taking frequent sightings on flagged tower locations with a Brunton compass and binoculars. Other crew members were then able to use his position to keep on line (Kinkade 1974:4-5).

In accordance with the research design for this survey section, the crew gave particular attention to the artifactual, environmental, and research-potential aspects of each site in order to record data useful in understanding relationships between variability in subsistence assemblages and environmental diversity. They used ceramic chronologies and, when possible, architectural features to assign dates and cultural associations to all sites. They collected sherd samples at each site, but did not make intensive collections of all artifacts. Moreover, all surface lithics were recorded on specially prepared supplementary forms which emphasized those attributes relating directly to subsistence activities (Kinkade 1974:7).

The crew also plotted all sites on USGS topographic maps and aerial photographs provided by Arizona Public Service. Field numbers were assigned to all sites located until permanent Arizona State Museum numbers could be allotted. In addition, all sites were marked with wooden stakes bearing metal tags stamped with the respective field numbers, and flagged with blue and white flagging tape so that APS construction crews could avoid them (Kinkade 1974:6).

The Winkelman-to-Red Rock survey required a total of 500 person-hours for field work.

Problems. The principal problem encountered by the survey crew during this section of the survey was that of staying on line, despite the fact that the tower locations and centerline were better marked than in the previous section. APS surveyors had erected masts with white flags, which were of considerable help. In addition, they placed orange flagging at some stations between the white flags, marked fences with flagging where the line crossed them, placed stakes in roads where the line crossed, and marked the tower sites with large quantities of orange flagging. However, when knocked down or obscured by vegetation or topography, these flags were of little or no use. The centerline stations and fence and road crossings were marked with too little flagging which was not placed high enough to be of use at any distance. The supervisory archaeologist had to use the Brunton compass to determine corridor boundaries, a very time-consuming operation. The crew also attempted to follow the tire tracks left by the APS surveyors, but found that, instead of driving along the right-of-way, they had driven down ridgetops from access roads to reach the tower locations, thus leaving the area between the tower locations unmarked. As the towers were spaced 400 m (about one-quarter mile) apart, visibility was severely limited in hilly terrain (Kinkade 1974:29-31).

Problems such as these can result in serious losses of time and consequently increased costs. They can also lead to later problems in determining the relationship of sites located during the survey to the actual project route.

Survey Results. Arizona State Museum archaeologists found a total of nine sites and nine isolated cultural phenomena during this survey. Table 8 lists the archaeological sites. More detailed information and site descriptions are to be found in the volume accompanying this report.

Mitigation. Between July 15 and August 9, 1974, an Arizona State Museum crew consisting of Gay M. Kinkade, Supervisory Archaeologist, and Assistant Archaeologists Patricia Fall, Patricia Gilman, and Michael McCarthy carried out a program of mitigative field work on nine archaeological sites located during the earlier Winkelman-to-Red Rock survey. This field work involved the intensive collecting on a sampled basis of artifactual and nonartifactual material from all sites, and the intensive recording of features and environmental data. In addition, the crew undertook a single test excavation at site AZ BB:1:8 (field number APS-CS-11). As a result of this field work, they were able to recommend archaeological clearance for all six sites on December 8, 1975.

Table 8.   Sites in southern section of APS Cholla-Saguaro survey:
Winkelman to Red Rock

ASM Number	Field Number
AZ AA:8:6	CS-16
AZ BB:1:8	CS-11
AZ BB:1:9	CS-12
AZ BB:1:10	CS-13
AZ BB:1:11	CS-19
AZ BB:5:21	CS-14
AZ BB:5:22	CS-15
AZ BB:5:23	CS-18
AZ BB:5:24	CS-17

Corridor Resurvey

As a result of survey inadequacies identified in the Holbrook-Chevelon portion of the corridor, it was decided at a meeting on October 4, 1976, that portions of the corridor should be reexamined in order to determine whether sites had been missed in other areas and, if so, to correct these deficiencies by recording any sites not previously located.

Field Methodology

In general, resurvey procedures were designed to ensure that problems identified in the initial corridor survey were not repeated. While initial survey had employed a single pass of the corridor, with personnel moving in a zigzag pattern to cover the corridor, resurvey was conducted in two passes along the corridor.

Site Definition

Isolated artifacts and some very light scatters were not recorded as sites, but were noted and marked on field maps. These locations, in addition to site locations, have been provided to APS and the Forest Service on project maps.

Surface Collections

Some diagnostic artifacts such as sherds, lithic tools, and projectile points were described and drawn on site survey forms. Materials examined were replaced in the locations in which they were found.

Site Survey Form

Resurvey employed a survey form adopted by the Museum in order to elicit more specific information than that required by older forms and to facilitate integration of survey records with ASM computerized site files. The kinds of information required by this form are similar to those found in previous forms.

Survey Procedures

Two passes were made over each corridor segment. Generally, the APS corridor was surveyed first. One individual walked south on the APS centerline with two people to the east and one person to the west. About midday, the survey stopped at the nearest tower in order to begin the return pass along the Salt River Project corridor. The crew supervisor then walked north on the Salt River Project (SRP) centerline with two people to the west and one person to the east. In this way, four people were covering 50.3 m (165 feet) (half the 110.7-m corridor width) at any one time.

All site perimeters were flagged with blue and white flagging tape, and a site stake marked with a site field number (for example, APS-CS-225) was driven into the ground within the site area. Isolated artifacts and very light scatters were not flagged or given a field number.

Survey Data

The following pages describe briefly the individual resurveys conducted. These descriptions differ somewhat from those provided previously. Terrain is not described here; the reader may refer to the discussion of the same area provided under "Corridor Survey". Methodology was usually consistent in all segments and will not be reviewed further, other than to note exceptions to the procedures discussed earlier. Finally, some of the problems described in the discussion of the initial survey had been largely eliminated by this stage of the project. Corridor and tower location flagging was generally adequate. Difficulties due to terrain and vegetation did not differ appreciably from those discussed in the review of the corridor survey.

APS Tower Locations 96-123

Introduction. Resurvey between APS Tower locations 96 and 120 was conducted during November, 1976 by Christopher Causey, Linda Mayro, Robert Hard, and Sharon Urban. An area encompassing 24 towers (8 miles or 12.9 km of corridor) was surveyed, including both the APS and SRP lines. Approximately 172 person-hours were spent surveying this area, recording sites, and driving to and from the survey area. A second crew consisting of Christopher Causey, Linda Mayro, Robert Hard, and Richard Effland surveyed the corridor between APS Tower locations 120 and 123 and between SRP Tower locations 121 and 124 during early December, 1976. A total of three tower spans (1 mile or 1.6 km of corridor) was surveyed. A report on this survey was submitted to Arizona Public Service by Linda Mayro on July 1, 1977.

Survey Results. A total of 27 sites was identified in the segment between APS Tower locations 96 and 123. Of these sites, ten were identified during the initial survey and 17 during the resurvey of the corridor and access roads. These sites are listed in Table 9.

Table 9.   Sites located between APS Tower locations 96-123

ASM Number	Field Number
AZ P:6:5	CS-81
AZ P:6:6	CS-68
AZ P:6:7	CS-66
AZ P:6:8	CS-58
AZ P:6:9	CS-60
AZ P:6:10	CS-62
AZ P:6:11	CS-64
AZ P:6:12	CS-56
AZ P:6:13	CS-54
AZ P:6:14	CS-52
AZ P:6:15	CS-200
AZ P:6:16	CS-210
AZ P:6:17	CS-211
AZ P:6:18	CS-212
AZ P:6:19	CS-213
AZ P:6:20	CS-214
AZ P:6:21	CS-215
AZ P:6:22	CS-216
AZ P:6:23	CS-217
AZ P:6:24	CS-218
AZ P:6:25	CS-219
AZ P:6:26	CS-220
AZ P:6:27	CS-221
AZ P:6:28	CS-222
AZ P:6:29	CS-225
AZ P:6:30	CS-224
AZ P:6:31	CS-265

APS Tower Locations 139-156

Introduction. Resurvey between Tower locations 139 and 156 was
conducted from October 5-8, 1976, by a crew consisting of Lynn Teague,
Linda Mayro, Christopher Causey, and Carol Coe. A span encompassing
17 towers (6 miles or 9.7 km of corridor) was surveyed, including both the
APS and SRP lines. Approximately 116 person-hours were spent surveying
this area, recording sites, and driving to and from the survey area. A
report on this survey was submitted to Arizona Public Service by Linda
Mayro on January 7, 1976.

Survey Results. A total of four sites was recorded in the vicinity
of the corridor segment between Tower locations 139 and 156. One of these
is located east of the corridor itself. These sites are listed in Table 10.

Table 10. Sites located between APS Tower locations 139-156

ASM Number	Field Number
AZ P:9:2	CS-206
AZ P:9:3	CS-207
AZ P:9:4	CS-208
AZ P:9:5	CS-209

APS Tower Locations 156-167

Introduction. Resurvey between Tower locations 156 and 167 was
conducted during the period of October 24-27, 1976, by Linda Mayro,
Christopher Causey, and Robert Hard. A span encompassing eleven towers
(approximately 3.5 miles or 5.6 km of corridor) was surveyed, including
both the APS and SRP lines. Because the crew consisted of only three
persons, it was decided that field procedures would be modified to ensure
adequate coverage. The survey began at Tower location 156 and proceeded
south to Tower location 167. The corridor was surveyed systematically
and intensively by walking 90-degree transects through it at approximately
10 to 15-meter intervals. A report was submitted by Linda Mayro to
Arizona Public Service on November 8, 1976.

Survey Results. No archaeological sites were found in this corridor
segment. One site, AZ P:9:5 (APS-CS-209), at APS Tower location 156, had
been identified earlier during survey between Tower locations 139-156.

APS Tower Locations 167-184A (SRP Tower Locations 167-185)

Introduction. Resurvey between APS Tower locations 167 and 184A (SRP 67-185) was conducted during the period of November 10-11 by Linda Mayro, Christopher Causey, Robert Hard, and Steven Danziger. A total of 23 tower spans (approximately 5.5 miles or 8.8 km of corridor) was surveyed, including both the APS and SRP lines. Due to extremely rough terrain in the Canyon Creek drainage between Tower locations 178 and 179, this span was not resurveyed. A report on this resurvey was submitted to Arizona Public Service by Linda Mayro on November 30, 1976.

Survey Results. One previously recorded site, AZ P:9:1 (APS-CS-201), was found on resurvey between Tower locations 170-171. This is the possible site of the Camp Verde-to-Fort Apache military road, commonly referred to as General Crook's Road.

APS Tower Locations 184A-258 (SRP Tower Locations 185-258)

Introduction. Resurvey between APS Tower locations 184A and 258 was conducted during the period of March 7-11, 1977, by Christopher Causey, David Gregory, Steven Danziger, Michelle Behr, and Steven Lensink. A total of 38 spans (approximately 11 miles or 17.7 km of corridor) was surveyed, including both the APS and SRP lines. The methodology employed in this survey differed slightly from that used in other segments in that the corridor was surveyed by five people covering the corridor in one pass. The crew supervisor walked north on the APS centerline with one person to the east and three people to the west. All personnel, with the exception of the supervisor, walked in a zigzag pattern to ensure adequate coverage. Coverage was made more difficult by extremely dense vegetation.

Survey Results. As in the initial survey, no archaeological sites were found in the corridor segment between APS Tower locations 184A-258 and SRP Tower locations 185-258.

Other Survey Operations

Construction of a transmission line requires construction of roads into tower sites when these do not already exist. In addition, ground disturbance within the corridor is not confined to tower locations, but includes wire-tensioning locations and, in heavily forested areas, line segments in which higher trees must be felled and removed. The Tonto National Forest established specific procedures for survey of these areas (McAllister 1976). These specified that access roads and a buffer zone of 50 feet (15.25 m) on each side of the road, tower sites and a buffer zone within a 200-foot (61-m) radius of the tower hub, and tensioning sites and a buffer zone within a 500-foot (15.25-m) radius would be surveyed. Prior to establishment of these procedures, access road buffer zones consisted of only 10 feet (3.05 m) on either side.

This work was often carried out by crews also engaged in monitoring and reflagging. The presence of an archaeologist during periods of construction was required by the agencies when work was planned sufficiently close to sites to represent a potential danger to them. Reflagging of sites became necessary when construction followed a year or more after archaeological survey, since weather and animals tended to remove the flagging tape.

Access Roads

Because the access road survey was a continuing effort over a period of several years, many personnel were engaged in this work, which began on September 1, 1975, and was completed in November, 1977. Thirteen individuals participated in this portion of the survey. Results were reported to Arizona Public Service and to the United States Forest Service in a lengthy series of interim reports. Table 11 provides information on these surveys; interim reports are on file at the Arizona State Museum.

The table reflects the somewhat erratic nature of this survey. In a single week, surveyors often found themselves traveling much of the length of the line, surveying roads as their locations were determined. The table also reflects the repeated visits often necessary to survey and resurvey roads, since alignments were altered due to the presence of sites or other nonarchaeological difficulties.

Field Methodology

Access road surveys were conducted according to the same principles as was the corridor survey itself, encountered the same problems of terrain and vegetation, and employed the same field-recording and site-flagging procedures. The method of walking the area itself did necessarily differ. Prior to the fall of 1976, when road buffer zones were only 10 feet (3.05 m) wide, the road was surveyed by a single individual walking the length of the road. After that time, when buffer zones were expanded to 50 feet (15.25 m) in accordance with procedures outlined (1976) by Martin McAllister, the roads were usually surveyed by a crew of two persons. With two crew members, two passes were made on the road, each crew member walking in a zigzag pattern. With a crew of three persons, only one pass was made made along the road, with one person walking the centerline and one person on either side. In this way, the road alignments were surveyed to a width of 34.8 m (114 feet). In addition, tower sites, including a buffer zone of 61-m (200-foot) radius from the center hub, were intensively surveyed after roads had been surveyed.

Tensioning Sites

Wire set-ups, sleeve locations, and pulling stations were surveyed during the period February-July, 1977 by Christopher Causey. In general, bull wheels, pulling stations, and snub locations were all examined. Sleeve locations, construction at which involves only the use of rubber-tired vehicles, were checked whenever previous surveys indicated that there was potential conflict with an archaeological site.

Tensioning-site survey included a 500-foot (15.25-m) buffer zone, as required by the Forest Service (McAllister 1976). These locations, and therefore all sites encountered, are within the corridor.

Site Reflagging

Reflagging was carried out in November and December, 1976, primarily in those portions of the line where survey substantially predated line construction. A total of 19 person-days were spent in this activity by Causey, Hard, and Danziger. Procedures consisted of identifying sites previously located on maps, finding those sites within the corridor itself, and remarking boundaries with blue and white flagging tape.

Table 11. Survey of access roads and related facilities

Survey Dates	Towers and Roads	Personnel	Site Numbers
9/1/75- 12/15/75	APS 483, 723	Gregory	AZ BB:1:14 (JR-1) AZ BB:1:15 (JR-2) AZ BB:1:16 (JR-3) AZ U:12:26 (CS-26)
5/3 - 14/76	APS 403-424 SPR 399-412, 414, 416-417, 419-421	Ahlstrom	None
5/17 - 28/76	APS 96-98, 113, 388-402, 413, 420, 425-426, 475-480, 461 SRP 383-398, 416, 422-423, 459	Morton McClellan Ahlstrom	AZ V:5:35 (CS-125) AZ V:5:37 (CS-128) AZ V:9:107 (CS-126) AZ V:9:110 (CS-127)
6/1 - 11/76	APS 101-102, 104, 111, 431-442, 451-456 SRP 104, 111, 428-438	Hammack	None

Table 11. Survey of access roads and related facilities (continued)

Survey Dates	Towers and Roads		Personnel	Site Numbers
6/7 - 25/76	APS	99-114, 117-137, 431-436, 438-440, 442, 451-456	Morton	None
	SRP	104-114, 117-120, 122-137, 433-438, 435-437		
6/14 - 27/76	APS	140-144, 146-148, 150-154, 156-157, 325-336, 338-358, 360-376, 441	Morton Hammack	AZ V:5:14 (CS-31)
	SRP	326-336, 338-357, 359-374, 428, 439		
6/28-7/30/76	APS	104-106, 114-117, 120, 158-163, 427A-430, 436-437, 444-446 449-450, 459-460	Morton	AZ U:12:31 (CS-63)
	SRP	104-106, 114-117, 121, 158-163, 424-427, 434, 439, 440-442, 444-453, 457-458		
8/2 - 6/76	APS	138A-139, 145, 149-150, 164-167, 171-178	Morton Causey	None
	SRP	138A-139, 145, 149-150, 164-167, 171-178		
8/9 - 9/24/67	APS	119-120, 167-171, 178A-186, 193-213, 217-218, 253-270, 447-448,457-458,485	Causey	AZ P:6:15 (CS-200) AZ P:13:10 (CS-202)
	SRP	120-212, 167-171, 178A-215, 219-221, 253-269, 443-444, 454-456		

Table 11. Survey of access roads and related facilities (continued)

Survey Dates	Towers and Roads	Personnel	Site Numbers
11/3-12/17/76	APS 214-216, 253-262, 325-327, 351-352, 480-481 SRP 216-218, 253-262, 325-327, 350-351, 480-481	Causey Hard	AZ V:1:4 (CS-28) AZ V:5:17 CCS-34) AZ V:5:38 (CS-226) AZ V:5:39 (CS-227)
12/27/76- 4/22/77	APS 263-286, 291-294, 297-324, 328-351, 355-359, 361-369, 373-375, 377-385, 475 SRP 263-285, 291-293, 295-299, 301-324, 328-349, 352-355, 357-358, 360-367, 370-373, 375-381, 419 Also, USFS Road 202 and 203 Bypass	Causey Hard Danziger Ackerly Behr Lensink Gregory	AZ P:13:11 (CS-260) AZ V:1:7 (CS-241) AZ V:1:9 (CS-244) AZ V:1:10 (CS-246) AZ V:1:19 (CS-255) AZ V:1:20 (CS-256) AZ V:1:21 (CS-257) AZ V:5:41 (CS-229) AZ V:5:42 (CS-230) AZ V:5:44 (CS-232) AZ V:5:45 (CS-233) AZ V:5:46 (CS-234) AZ V:5:47 (CS-236) AZ V:5:48 (CS-237) AZ V:5:49 (CS-238) AZ V:5:50 (CS-239) AZ V:5:51 (CS-240) AZ V:5:52 (CS-247) AZ V:9:111 (CS-279)
7/18-9/20/77	APS 114-115, 123, 287 SRP 106-108, 286 Also, 3 batch plants and USF Road 202 Realignment east of Q Ranch	Causey *Davidson *Danziger *Hard *Perrine	AZ P:3:13 (CS-266) AZ P:3:14 (CS-267) AZ P:3:15 (CS-268) AZ P:3:16 (CS-269) AZ P:6:5 (CS-81) AZ P:6:8 (CS-58) AZ P:6:23 (CS-217) AZ P:6:24 (CS-218) AZ P:6:25 (CS-219) AZ P:6:29 (CS-225) AZ P:6:32 (CS-273) AZ U:12:33 (CS-300) AZ U:12:34 (CS-301) AZ U:12:35 (CS-305)

Table 11. Survey of access of roads and related facilities (continued)

Survey Dates	Towers and Roads	Personnel	Site Numbers	
			AZ U:12:36	(CS-306)
			AZ U:12:37	(CS-303)
			AZ U:12:38	(CS-307)
			AZ V:1:18	(CS-254)
			AZ V:5:53	(CS-275)
			AZ V:5:54	(CS-276)
			AZ V:5:55	(CS-274)
			AZ V:5:56	(CS-278)
			AZ V:9:108	(CS-263)
			AZ V:9:109	(CS-264)
			AZ V:9:112	(CS-270)
			AZ V:9:113	(CS-271)
			AZ V:9:114	(CS-272)

*Intermittent

REFERENCES

Arizona State Museum
1974   Preliminary manual for use with ASM site survey record.
         MS. Arizona State Museum, University of Arizona, Tucson.

Canouts, Veletta (editor)
1975   An archaeological survey of the Arizona Public Service
         Cholla to Saguaro 500 kV transmission line proposed
         route. Interim report: Antelope Peak, Arizona to
         Superior, Arizona. Arizona State Museum Archaeological
         Series 81.

Canouts, Veletta, and David A. Phillips, Jr.
1974   An archaeological survey of the Arizona Public Service
         Cholla to Saguaro 345 kV transmission line proposed route.
         Interim report: Joseph City: Cholla plant site to
         Sitgreaves National Forest boundary. Arizona State
         Museum Archaeological Series 43.

Kemrer, Sandra, Sandra Schultz, and William Dodge
1972   An archaeological survey of the Granite-Reef aqueduct.
         Arizona State Museum Archaeological Series 12.

Kinkade, Gay M.
1974   Arizona Public Service Cholla to Saguaro transmission line
         project. Research design for mitigation: Winkelman,
         Arizona to Red Rock, Arizona: Saguaro plant. MS. Arizona
         State Museum, University of Arizona, Tucson.

Kinkade, Gay M. and Patricia A. Gilman
1974   An archaeological survey of the Arizona Public Service
         Cholla to Saguaro 500 kV transmission line proposed route.
         Interim report: Winkelman, Arizona to Red Rock, Arizona:
         Saguaro plant. Arizona State Museum Archaeological Series 54.

Lowe, Charles
1964   Arizona's natural environment. Tucson: University of
         Arizona Press.

McAllister, Martin
1976   File letter in reference to 2720 Special Uses/2360 Special Interest
         Areas. October 13, 1976. Arizona State Museum,University of Arizona,
         Tucson.

Spain, J. N.
1975   APS research design. MS. Arizona State Museum, University
         of Arizona, Tucson.

Wilk, Richard and Cherie Scheick
    1975   An archaeological survey of the Arizona Public Service
            Cholla to Saguaro 500 kV transmission line proposed
            route. Interim report: Coon Creek drainage to Sombrero
            Peak, Arizona. MS. Arizona State Museum, University of
            Arizona, Tucson.

Wilson, E. D.
    1962   A résumé of the geology of Arizona. Arizona Bureau of
            Mines Bulletin 171.

CHAPTER 4

THE HOLBROOK-CHEVELON STUDY AREA
by Alan H. Simmons

Introduction

Forty-five sites and 19 artifact occurrences (that is, isolated sherds and/or lithics) on both private and federal lands were recorded in the Holbrook-Chevelon area (see Table 12). For heuristic purposes, we refer to this study area as the Chevelon Region, following F. Plog's (Plog, Hill, and Read 1976a) similar usage. The following discussion deals with the previous research, culture history, problem orientation, environment, the survey data and interpretation of those data, and, finally, conclusions. However, it is first necessary to define the Chevelon Region in terms of the APS transmission line.

The area of interest here includes sites located between the beginning of the APS 500 kV transmission line at Tower location 1 and Tower location 185. In geographical terms, this includes the area immediately south of Joseph City and continuing south through the Apache-Sitgreaves National Forest to the edge of the Mogollon Rim (Figure 9). Approximately 75 km (59 miles) are covered.

Although the transmission line itself forms a corridor only 100.7 m (330 feet) wide, a transect in essence, we are of course dealing with a larger area in terms of prehistoric occupation. This area, defined by the Chevelon drainage, closely parallels that investigated by F. Plog and colleagues over the past several years. The environmental characteristics of the region will be discussed in detail in a subsequent section.

A few words need be said of general methodology and problem orientation. Appropriate research problems, both those posed by the overall line research design and those posed by previous research in the area, will be addressed. It should be noted, however, that the major thrust of this document is descriptive. A problem-oriented strategy will be employed in the APS Mitigation Report, when more site-specific data have been obtained. Methodological problems will be discussed as they appear.

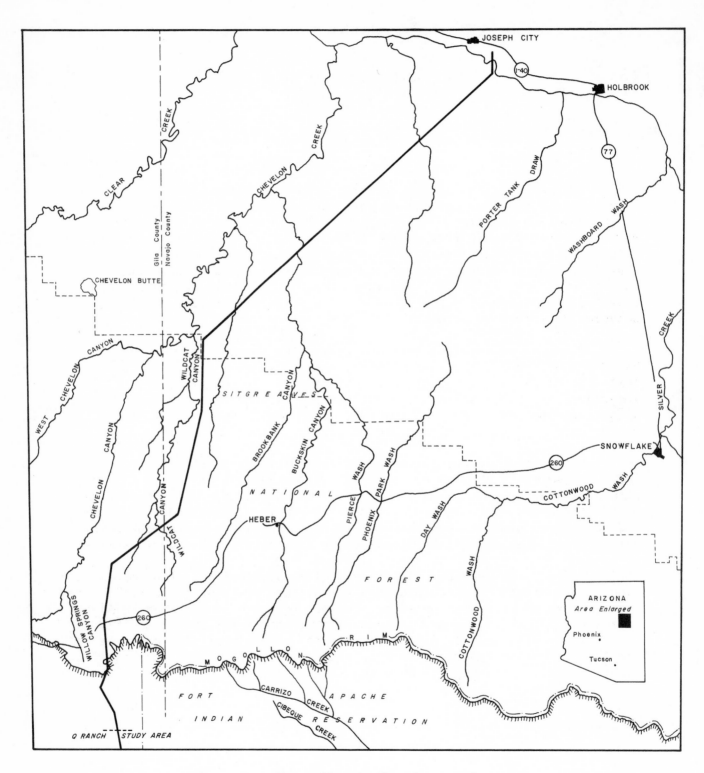

Figure 9. The Holbrook-Chevelon study area

55

Table 12. Archaeological sites in the Holbrook-Chevelon segment of the Cholla-Saguaro corridor

ASM Number	Field Number	Cultural-temporal Affiliation	Site Type	Approximate Size (m²)	USGS Quad	Elevation (feet)
AZ P:3:6	CS-1	Prehistoric(?) (unknown) Historic: Anglo	Structure with artifact scatter	825	Joseph City 15 min.	5020
AZ P:3:7	CS-2	Prehistoric: Anasazi(?) (A.D. 700-1450?)	Artifact scatter	68,750	Joseph City 15 min.	5000-5015
AZ P:3:8	CS-3	Prehistoric (unknown)	Artifact scatter	125,000	Joseph City 15 min.	5060
AZ P:3:9	CS-4	Prehistoric (unknown) Historic: Anglo (post-1900)	Feature with artifact scatter	150	Joseph City 15 min.	5180
AZ P:3:10	CS-5	Prehistoric: Anasazi(?) (A.D. 725-1125)	Artifact scatter	1600	Joseph City 15 min.	5600
AZ P:3:13	CS-266	Prehistoric (unknown)	Features with artifact scatter	9750	Joseph City 15 min.	5380
AZ P:3:14	CS-267	Prehistoric (unknown)	Artifact scatter	16,800	Joseph City 15 min.	5320-5360
AZ P:3:15	CS-268	Prehistoric (unknown)	Features with artifact scatter	9450	Joseph City 15 min.	5620
AZ P:3:16	CS-269	Prehistoric (unknown)	Features with artifact scatter	10,450	Joseph City 15 min.	5620
AZ P:6:1	CS-6	Prehistoric: Mogollon(?) (A.D. 300-1150(?))	Features with artifact scatter	500	Potato Wash Northeast 7.5 min.	5850

Table 12. Archaeological sites in the Holbrook-Chevelon segment of the Cholla-Saguaro corridor (continued)

ASM Number	Field Number	Cultural-temporal Affiliation	Site Type	Approximate Size (m²)	USGS Quad	Elevation (feet)
AZ P:6:2	CS-8	Prehistoric: Mogollon(?) (A.D. 1065-1375)	Artifact scatter	1254	Potato Wash Northeast 7.5 min.	6115
AZ P:6:3	CS-9	Prehistoric: Mogollon (?) (A.D. 1050-1200(?)) Historic: Anglo(?)	Structures with artifact scatter	1088	Potato Wash North 7.5 min.	5970
AZ P:6:5	CS-81	Prehistoric (unknown)	Artifact scatter	28,800	Potato Wash South 7.5 min.	6820
AZ P:6:6	CS-68	Prehistoric (unknown)	Artifact scatter	2000	Potato Wash South 7.5 min.	6790
AZ P:6:7	CS-66	Prehistoric (unknown)	Feature with artifact scatter	1200	Potato Wash South 7.5 min.	6760
AZ P:6:8	CS-58	Historic (unknown)	Structure	16	Potato Wash South 7.5 min.	6590
AZ P:6:9	CS-60	Prehistoric: Mogollon(?)	Artifact scatter	2250	Potato Wash South 7.5 min.	6670

Table 12. Archaeological sites in the Holbrook-Chevelon segment of the Cholla-Saguaro corridor (continued)

ASM Number	Field Number	Cultural-temporal Affiliation	Site Type	Approximate Size (m2)	USGS Quad	Elevation (feet)
AZ P:6:10	CS-62	Prehistoric (unknown)	Structures with artifact scatter	10,500	Potato Wash South 7.5 min.	6700
AZ P:6:11	CS-64	Prehistoric (unknown)	Feature with artifact scatter	12,000	Potato Wash South 7.5 min.	6660
AZ P:6:12	CS-56	Prehistoric: Mogollon(?) (A.D. 1050-1200(?))	Feature with artifact scatter	2000	Potato Wash South 7.5 min.	6210
AZ P:6:13	CS-54	Prehistoric: Mogollon(?) (A.D. 1050-1200(?))	Artifact scatter	15,400	Potato Wash South 7.5 min.	6200
AZ P:6:14	CS-52	Prehistoric: Mogollon (A.D. 1110-1250)	Artifact scatter	11,235	Potato Wash North 7.5 min.	6180
AZ P:6:15	CS-200	Prehistoric (unknown)	Artifact scatter	Unit A-1750 Unit B-3000	Potato Wash South 7.5 min.	6700
AZ P:6:16	CS-210	Prehistoric: Mogollon	Artifact scatter	24,050	Potato Wash North 7.5 min.	6180
AZ P:6:17	CS-211	Prehistoric (unknown)	Artifact scatter	7000	Potato Wash South 7.5 min.	6230

Table 12. Archaeological sites in the Holbrook-Chevelon segment of the Cholla-Sagaro corridor (continued)

ASM Number	Field Number	Cultural-temporal Affiliation	Site Type	Approximate Size (m2)	USGS Quad	Elevation (feet)
AZ P:6:18	CS-212	Prehistoric (unknown)	Artifact scatter	6825	Potato Wash South 7.5 min.	6220
AZ P:6:19	CS-213	Prehistoric (unknown)	Features with artifact scatter	6300	Potato Wash South 7.5 min.	6200
AZ P:6:20	CS-214	Prehistoric (unknown)	Features with artifact scatter	2925	Potato Wash North 7.5 min.	6190
AZ P:6:21	CS-215	Prehistoric (unknown)	Features with artifact scatter	3850	Potato Wash North 7.5 min.	6220
AZ P:6:22	CS-216	Prehistoric (unknown)	Artifact scatter	1000	Potato Wash South 7.5 min.	6280
AZ P:6:23	CS-217	Prehistoric: Mogollon(?)	Artifact scatter	1225	Potato Wash South 7.5 min.	6440
AZ P:6:24	CS-218	Prehistoric: Mogollon(?)	Artifact scatter	4500	Potato Wash South 7.5 min.	6440
AZ P:6:25	CS-219	Prehistoric: Mogollon	Features with artifact scatter	4200	Potato Wash South 7.5 min.	6660

59

Table 12. Archaeological sites in the Holbrook-Chevelon segment of the Cholla-Saguaro corridor (continued)

ASM Number	Field Number	Cultural-temporal Affiliation	Site Type	Approximate Size (m²)	USGS Quad	Elevation (feet)
AZ P:6:26	CS-220	Prehistoric: Mogollon(?)	Features with artifact scatter	10,000	Potato Wash South 7.5 min.	6660
AZ P:6:27	CS-221	Prehistoric: Mogollon(?)	Artifact scatter	9900	Potato Wash South 7.5 min.	6660
AZ P:6:28	CS-222	Prehistoric: Mogollon(?)	Feature with artifact scatter	6700	Potato Wash South 7.5 min.	6670
AZ P:6:29	CS-225	Prehistoric (unknown)	Artifact scatter	4000	Potato Wash South 7.5 min.	6820
AZ P:6:30	CS-224	Prehistoric (unknown)	Structures with artifact scatter	33,000	Potato Wash South 7.5 min.	6790
AZ P:6:31	CS-265	Prehistoric: Mogollon(?)	Structures with artifact scatter	18,750	Potato Wash South 7.5 min.	6820
AZ P:6:32	CS-273	Prehistoric: Mogollon	Structures with artifact scatter	5200	Potato Wash South 7.5 min.	6740
AZ P:9:1	CS-201	Historic: Anglo (post-1870)	"General Crook's Road"	unknown	Woods Canyon 15 min.	7640

Table 12. Archaeological sites in the Holbrook-Chevelon segment of the Cholla-Saguaro corridor (continued)

ASM Number	Field Number	Cultural-temporal Affiliation	Site Type	Approximate Site (m2)	USGS Quad	Elevation (feet)
AZ P:9:2	CS-206	Prehistoric (unknown)	Lithic quarry	2400	Woods Canyon 15 min.	7160
AZ P:9:3	CS-207	Prehistoric (unknown)	Lithic quarry	16,500	Woods Canyon 15 min.	7160
AZ P:9:4	CS-208	Prehistoric (unknown)	Lithic scatter	18,000	Woods Canyon 15 min.	7420
AZ P:9:5	CS-209	Prehistoric (unknown)	Lithic scatter	14,250	Woods Canyon 15 min.	7420

Environment

Introduction

The Chevelon drainage, including Chevelon Creek and its tributaries, exhibits a triangular form some 2300 square kilometers in area (Plog 1978:53) and falls within both the Transition and Plateau physiographic provinces (Wilson 1962:96-7). Emphasis here is on the area in its broader aspects, since a detailed discourse on specific microenvironmental diversities would involve far more space than is available. Although the Cholla-Saguaro transmission line actually traverses an area a few kilometers to the east of Chevelon Creek, the environmental characteristics of the immediate canyon area are fairly representative of the entire region. One should note that the Chevelon Creek drainage is characterized by a high degree of environmental diversity, with a wide range of heterogeneity apparent in both geography and biotic associations. This diversity has, in fact, been used to suggest that Chevelon Canyon is of a quite unique nature (Aitchison and Theroux 1974:1).

Beyond generalized descriptions of the natural environment of Arizona (see Lowe 1964), several Chevelon-specific references are available, including Aitchison and Theroux (1974) for the immediate Chevelon Canyon vicinity, Acker (1973), Satterthwait (1976), and portions of F. Plog (1978).

Topography

The study area under consideration lies within the southern part of the Colorado Plateau. The Colorado Plateau Province extends from the southern Rocky Mountains to the Basin and Range Province of southern Arizona and western Utah. Three convenient subdivisions exist within the Colorado Plateau: the Grand Canyon region, the Navajo County region, and the Mogollon Slope or Plateau (Wilson 1969:97). The last is the specific area of concern here. The majority of the following discussion is derived from Sellers (1972), Satterthwait (1976), Hunt (1956), Wilson (1962), Heindl and Lance (1960), and Wilson (1969).

The ground surface of the Mogollon Plateau dips gradually to the north and northeast towards the Black Mesa Basin. The highest points are near the Mogollon Rim in the south, at elevations of nearly 8000 feet above sea level. The lower elevations of the Plateau occur in the north near the Little Colorado River. Elevations here are about 5000 feet.

The topography of the northern and northeastern portions of the Chevelon drainage is generally flat and unbroken, although south of the Little Colorado the terrain includes rolling sandstone hills and ridges with sandy washes and shallow canyons between them. Near the confluence of Chevelon Creek and the Little Colorado, several gravel terraces are present, as are fairly extensive sand dunes (Wilson 1969:194). In the south, the terrain is considerably more variable and rugged. Several canyons and washes, many with marked relief, cut the ground surface. Chevelon Canyon is one of the more marked of these, as is Wildcat Canyon, near which many of the sites recorded by the APS Cholla Project survey are located. Interspersed with these are several nearly level ridges. As one moves south towards the Mogollon Rim, the terrain becomes increasingly mountainous. To the west, towards Clear Creek and Chavez Pass, the landscape is gently rolling, with sandstone remnants and occasional mesas providing the major relief. These mesas frequently rise 600-700 feet above the surface and are basalt-capped.

The surface geology of the region is relatively simple. Sedimentary rocks, primarily Permian and Triassic limestones and sandstones, predominate. The uppermost strata of these include red shales and sandstones of the Lower Triassic Moenkopi Formation. Eroded remnants of the Moenkopi Formation are also exposed on mesa slopes and on the eroding hills south of the Little Colorado. Underlying the Moenkopi Formation is the Kaibab limestone, which forms the ground surface and upper several hundred feet of bedrock, except in those areas where basalt flows exist. Occurring below the Kaibab limestone is the Coconino sandstone, dating to the Middle Permian. Finally, sandstone and shales are represented below the Coconino sandstone. These occur in the upper Pennsylvanian Supai Formation. Both Kaibab limestone and Coconino sandstone are displayed in the deeper canyons.

To the west of the study area, extensive lava flows of Late Tertiary or more recent age occur. This is of interest to the archaeologist since cinder deposits are frequently associated with such flows. The presence of cinders is important due to the presence of cinder-tempered pottery, which occurs as far east as East Clear Creek, west of Chevelon Canyon (Wilson 1969:194-195).

Other sources of raw material, especially for lithic manufacture, occur locally within the Chevelon. Green (1975) has studied patterns of variation in various lithic raw materials and has determined, on the basis of samples taken during F. Plog's recent research in the area, that three broad categories of raw material are represented among the lithic assemblages recovered: volcanic, quartzite, and chert. Of the volcanic material, most is basalt, which is not available locally. Obsidian is present at some sites, but is not locally available. Findlow, DeAtley, and Hudson's (1976) analysis of obsidian indicates a major source of this material to be Government Mountain, some 80 km (50 miles) west of the Chevelon. The other two materials noted by Green occur locally. Thus, it appears that raw materials for lithic manufacture and certain materials needed for ceramic manufacture were easily obtainable in the area. Unfortunately, little information exists on the location of clay that could have been used in ceramic manufacture.

Climate

As might be expected in an area with a 300-foot range in elevation, the climatic regime of the Chevelon is marked by diversity. Elevation would, in fact, appear to be the prime regulating factor of climatic conditions. Following the Kippen and Geiger climatic classifications, the higher area to the south belongs to the BSkf type (Russell 1931; Goode 1939)-- a cold dry steppe with an intermediate precipitation regime. This falls into Sellers' (1972:88) cold highland designation. The area of lower elevation near the Little Colorado River falls into the BWkfw type, which designates a cold, dry desert climate with a strongly summer-dominant rainfall pattern (Russell 1931; Goode 1939). This falls within what Sellers (1972:88) terms a cold steppe climate.

Precipitation is summer-dominant and frequently occurs as thunderstorms and severe showers. This precipitation originates primarily in the Gulf of Mexico. As with most of Arizona, winter precipitation is less intense than that of the summer. Winter precipitation is dependent on the location of the middle latitude storm track and is therefore extremely variable from one year to the next. The northern portion of the Chevelon, a cold steppe, is one of the driest areas in Arizona (Sellers 1972:87-91). Table 13, modified from Satterthwait (1976:9), who compiled the data from Smith (1945), summarizes climatic data for the greater Chevelon area.

As can be seen from Table 13, most of the Mogollon Slope receives between 10-20 inches (25-50 cm) of precipitation per year. The 10-inch isohyet occurs about 16 km (10 miles) southwest of the Little Colorado River (Wilson 1969:198-199).

Table 13. Climatic data from the Chevelon (compiled from Satterthwait 1976:9)

	Southern Chevelon (Heber)	Northern Chevelon (Winslow)
Elevation	6484 feet	4880 feet
Temperature		
Extremes: highest	97° F (35.8° C)	107° F (41.3° C)
lowest	-27° F (-32.5° C)	-19° F (-28.1° C)
Mean maximum	64.5°F (17.9° C)	71.0°F (21.5° C)
Mean minimum	30.0°F (-1.1° C)	38.4°F (3.5° C)
Mean annual temperature	47.3°F (8.4° C)	54.9°F (12.6° C)
Length of growing season (days)	118	172
Average number of days with 0.01 inches of precipitation or more	56	47
Annual precipitation (inches)	18.90 (48 cm)	8.10 (20.6 cm)
Snowfall (inches)	42.1 (106.9 cm)	11.0 (27.9 cm)

Soils

Soils clearly affect both the floral and faunal distributions within a given region as well as availability of arable land. Unfortunately, detailed information on soils in the Chevelon is lacking, although a few generalizations can be made.

Most of the Chevelon is covered with light-colored loamy and calcareous soils. In the northern portion of the area, however, shallow reddish soils occur, as does loamy soil. Reddish clay soils occur near the Mogollon Rim and extend into the extreme southern portion of the Chevelon (Satterthwait 1976:8).

Soil in the Chevelon differs greatly over short distances according to the parent bedrock material (Wilson 1969:196). This has also been pointed out by Acker (1973:13) in relation to pH variance and bedrock geology. It would appear, based on her sample, that high ($\bar{x} = 7.52$) or alkaline pH values occur with the white or pink limestone-like bedrock. Neutral pH values ($\bar{x} = 6.94$) occur with reddish sandstone.

In areas of basalt coverage, soils generally have clay loam or clay surface soils underlain by well-developed clay or heavy clay loam subsoils. Most have abundant basalt stones or cobbles on the surface. If cinders occur, the soils are frequently redder in color and less clayey. In sandstone areas, sandy loam is the major surface soil with sandy clay loams and clays forming the subsoils. These may be relatively deep. The northern part of the Chevelon has soils characterized as shallow to very shallow, well-drained, and medium to fine-textured. These are usually gravelly and stony soils developed from limestone (Wilson 1969:196; Meurisse and Williams 1966; Buol 1966).

Drainage-Hydrology

Just as soil is a significant factor in determining floral and faunal distributions, water resources are equally important, especially in relation to man's use of the Chevelon. Again, specific drainage data are lacking for the Chevelon region, but a few general statements may be made.

The availability of water in any locality depends on that area's geohydrologic systems, including climate, terrain, and geology. These are the controlling factors that determine the occurrence of water and the fashion with which it enters, moves through, and leaves an area. Precipitation, the ultimate source of water, is dependent upon climate. The occurrence of surface or groundwater is determined primarily by terrain and geology (Ligner and others 1969:471).

Arizona is divided into three water provinces: the basin and range lowlands, the central highlands, and the plateau uplands. The Chevelon falls within the last, specifically within the Little Colorado area, whose most productive tributary streams are Showlow, Chevelon, and Clear creeks, with unit runoffs of 98 acre-feet/square mile, 133 acre-feet/square mile, and 174 acre-feet/square mile, respectively. (An acre-foot is the quantity of water required to cover one acre to a depth of one foot.) These figures provide a useful measure of the flow characteristics of the area (Ligner and others 1969:472-490).

In general, consolidated sedimentary rocks comprise the aquifers of the plateau uplands province. Most of the groundwater of this province occurs in multiple acquifer systems--that is, aquifers that include more than one stratigraphic unit. Groundwater in Navajo County, in which the Chevelon is located, is drawn primarily from the Coconino sandstone south of the Little Colorado River, the Navajo sandstone in the Kayenta area, and the Dakota sandstone and Toreva Formation in the Black Mesa area. Groundwater is present in the alluvium along the Little Colorado and its tributary drainages, including Chevelon Creek. Of concern to the study area is the Coconino sandstone, occurring north of the Mogollon Rim to the Little Colorado (Ligner and others 1969:548-551).

Although the wide and sandy washes typical of the Southwest are present in the northern part of the Chevelon, by far the most common drainage pattern is one which is channeled through a series of deep and narrow canyons which flow northward into the Little Colorado River. These canyons, Chevelon Canyon principal among them, are frequently up to 152 m (500 feet) deep with side slopes of 40 to 80 degrees. Principal drainages in the area include Canyon Diablo, Jack's Canyon, East Clear Creek, and Chevelon Creek. Perennial streams include East Clear Creek, Barbershop Canyon, and Leonard Canyon. Most of the flow from these comes from numerous springs near the heads of the canyons. It is important to note, however, that below their headwaters the principal drainages flow only after heavy rainfall. Perennial water is also available from potholes located along East Clear Creek and Chevelon Creek. In addition, a few springs exist elsewhere. Finally, a series of both permanent and ephemeral lakes, fed by runoff, exists in the western portion of the Chevelon region. Below the high pine area, surface water is only available on a seasonal basis (Wilson 1969:196-7).

In attempting to measure water availability, Plog (1978:57-8), following the SARG (Gumerman 1971) strategy, employs drainage rank. Using this method, he determined that highly ranked areas correspond to the confluence of Chevelon, West Chevelon, and Wildcat creeks, to

Brookbank and Black Canyon creeks, and to Chevelon Creek and the Little Colorado River. Low-ranked zones primarily correspond to the upland surfaces on which primary drainages occur.

A final water source is, of course, rainfall, which affects both runoff in streams and ground moisture. Annual precipitation amounts for various areas within the Chevelon have already been noted. What is important to reiterate here is that precipitation is heaviest during the summer, with much of it produced by thunderstorms and cloudbursts. Winter precipitation is considerably lower than that of summer.

Biotic Resources--Flora and Fauna

Flora

Most of the Mogollon Slope is covered by vegetation characteristic of the Upper Sonoran Life Zone, although the higher portion of the Chevelon drainage also exhibits flora of the Transition Life Zone (Lowe 1964:36-69). Although "life zones" usually refer to fully biogeographic systems, there is a certain lack of consistency in finer breakdowns relating to specific vegetational communities. Thus, Plog (1978:57), using Kuchler's vegetation zones, notes four relevant communities in the Chevelon: pine forests, pinyon-juniper woodland, open woodland or savannah, and short-grass grassland. Satterthwait (1976:9-14) also notes four major vegetation types: pine forest, dense juniper woodland, open juniper woodland, and grassland. He also notes a limited incursion of Great Basin sagebrush desert into the northern reaches of the Chevelon as well as various riparian communities. Thus, Plog's and Satterthwait's distinctions are comparable, with only minor semantic differences.

Aitchison and Theroux (1974:37-48), however, speaking specifically of Chevelon Canyon, employ a slightly different terminology. Following Lowe (1964), they note three major vegetational formations and their associations or subformations: the coniferous forest formation, with the spruce-fir and ponderosa pine forest associations; the evergreen woodland formation, with the pinyon-juniper association; and the plains grassland formation, with the short-grass plains association. These formations intergrade in the open area surrounding Chevelon Canyon. Within the canyon itself, however, a more complex situation exists, with three further associations present: the riparian woodland association, including the tamarix floodplain of the Little Colorado River; the interior chaparral association; and the oak woodland association (Aitchison and Theroux 1974:39-40).

Finally, Lowe (1964:36-62) includes woodland, chaparral, grassland, and Great Basin desertscrub within the Upper Sonoran Life Zone. He also includes riparian woodlands and mountain grasslands as occurring within, but not restricted to, the Upper Sonoran Life Zone. The best example of well-developed mountain grasslands occurs in the White Mountains, several kilometers to the east of the Chevelon (Lowe 1964:48).

Table 14 and Figure 10 summarize the various vegetation communities within the Chevelon. It is readily observable that the various terminologies used for the most part reflect differences that are more apparent than real.

Within the Chevelon region specifically, the Little Colorado River Basin is primarily a barren wasteland of Great Basin desertscrub. Salt-bush and sage are the dominant forms of vegetation. Some grasses are also present. Precipitation in the area is low and the temperature high (Satterthwait 1976:12; Wilson 1969:200).

South of the Little Colorado Basin, trending in a southwest direction, is a belt of short-grass vegetation which covers much of the lower portion of the Chevelon drainage. Grama and other grasses are the dominant vegetation forms, although low shrubs such as snake-weed, salt-bush, and Russian-thistle are also present. The presence of these latter forms may, however, be due to historic overgrazing. Yucca and Cholla also occur, as do isolated junipers. Annual precipitation ranges between 10-14 inches (25-36 cm) (Satterthwait 1976:12; Wilson 1969:200).

Pinyon-juniper woodland occurs as far south as Heber and extends several miles east to McDonald Canyon and west to around Chevelon Butte. As elevation increases, density of these plant types does also. Plog's (1978:57) open woodland and pinyon-juniper woodland regions merge here, the open woodland occurring north of the denser pinyon-juniper woodland. Aitchison and Theroux (1976:43) further support this, placing both the dense juniper woodland and the open juniper woodland into the evergreen woodland formation. Two species of juniper occur in addition to pinyon. Other common forms include snake-weed, grama grass, yucca, cholla, and several other species. The pinyon-juniper zones can be considered as constituting a transitional or ecotonal area separating the hotter, drier grassland from the cooler, wetter forest zones. Annual precipitation ranges between 12-15 inches (30-39 cm) (Satterthwait 1976:12-13; Wilson 1969:200-201).

The forest zone commences near Heber at an elevation of about 7000 feet and extends south to the Mogollon Rim. Most of this area is within the Transition Life Zone (following Lowe 1964:63-69), which is equivalent to the ponderosa pine forest. At higher elevations, Douglas-fir replaces ponderosa pine as a dominant species. Several other trees as well as grasses and shrubs occur in this area. Temperatures here are the coolest and precipitation the greatest, between 18-26 inches (46-66 cm) annually, in the entire Chevelon (Satterthwait 1976:13-14; Wilson 1969:201).

Finally, riparian or deciduous communities occur along washes, draws, and canyon bottoms. The densest riparian community in the Chevelon is found within the coniferous forest formation (Aitchison and Theroux 1974:42), although similar if less dense communities occur in other areas. Although the areal extent of such communities is limited, the variety of floral forms within them is quite large. Common species include sedge, cottonwood, walnut, ash, and brush thickets. Tamarix is quite abundant in the more northern riparian communities near the Little Colorado River (Satterthwait 1976:14; Wilson 1969:201-02).

Table 14. Various classifications of vegetation zones within the greater Chevelon area

Lowe 1964	CARP (Satterthwait 1976)	CARP (Plog 1978)	Aitchison and Theroux (1974)
Great Basin Desertscrub	Desert	Short-grass grassland	Plains grassland 1. short-grass
Grassland	Grassland	Open woodland	Evergreen woodland 1. pinyon-juniper
Chaparral	Open-juniper woodland	Pinyon-juniper woodland	Interior chaparral
Woodland			
Riparian	Dense juniper woodland	Pine forest	Oak woodland
Mountain grassland	Riparian		Coniferous forest 1. spruce-fir 2. ponderosa pine
	Pine forest		Riparian

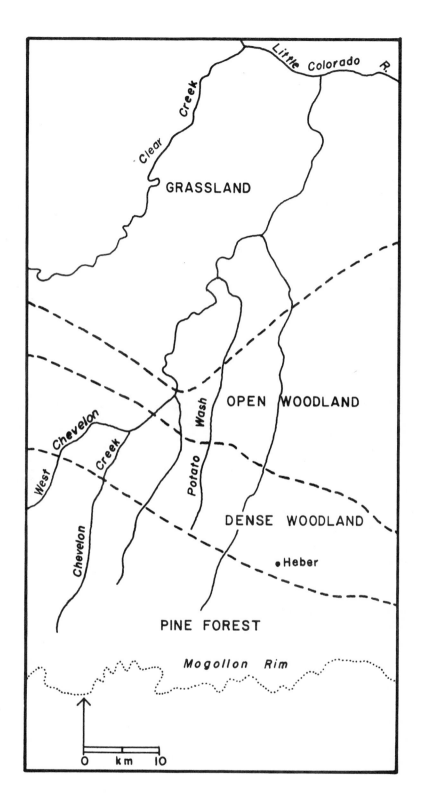

Figure 10. Vegetational communities in the Chevelon (from Plog 1978:57)

Fauna

Biotic provinces, unlike life zones and biomes, are usually delineated
according to faunal characteristics. They are continuous geographic areas,
but, as with vegetation zones, precise definitions and associations are
equivocal. The Chevelon region falls within the broad Navajonian biotic
province (Lowe 1964:93-6), characterized by pinyon-juniper woodlands.
The lowest life belt of the Navajonian is characterized as an arid grassland and the highest as the Alpine Life Belt (Dice 1943:39). Lowe (1964:96-8)
regards faunal areas as distinct from biotic provinces, but frequently con-
fused with them. "Faunal areas... are geographic areas or regions where
the distributional ranges of several animal species are similar, and where
they reach their maximum occurrence. Within the region there are usually
a number of the species which are characteristic of other 'foreign' faunal
areas" (Lowe 1964:97-8).

The most detailed inventory of vertebrate fauna in the Chevelon
drainage is presented by Aitchison and Theroux (1974). Native fauna in
the area are as varied as are the vegetational associations. Before modern
incursions, mammal species within the forest zone included elk, mule deer,
bear, turkey, antelope (in open areas), mountain lion, bobcat, porcupine,
beaver, squirrel, and numerous rodents. Antelope was the most abundant
large mammal in the woodlands, although mule deer, coyote, bobcat, fox,
porcupine, cottontail rabbit, jackrabbit, skunk, badger, and rodents were
also present. As one moves north to the more arid grasslands, the variety
of faunal elements decreases. Antelope, elk, and deer are still present,
as are jackrabbit and cottontail, wolf, coyote, badger, and prairie dog
(Wilson 1969:202; Satterthwait 1976:12-13). Riparian communities also exhibit
specific faunal communites (Aitchison and Theroux 1974:54-5).

Several species of fish occur within the Chevelon area, although
many have been introduced. For Chevelon Creek specifically, 12 species
are presently known, although only three are native (Aitchison and
Theroux 1976:19-21). Ninety-two native species of avifauna are noted
for the area by Aitchison and Theroux (1976:27-31).

In summary, the floral and faunal elements of the Chevelon are
quite diverse. More detail on specific species can be found in Sellers
(1972); Gloyd and others (1972); and Lowe (1964). Certainly
the most detailed check list, covering vascular plants, vegetational
associations, ichthyofauna, herpetofauna, avifauna, and mammalofauna, is
to be found in Aitchison and Theroux (1974).

Economic Potential for Prehistoric Utilization of Biotic Resources

Clearly, the Chevelon offered prehistoric occupants a diversified
and abundant resource base. It is equally clear that, given the extreme

climatic variations in the area, scheduling of resource procurement strategies (see Flannery 1968) would have been an important adaptive response.

Throughout the prehistoric occupation of the Chevelon, subsistence strategies undoubtedly relied upon hunting, gathering, agriculture, and mixed economies. However, more detailed study of these strategies requires specific ecological data to verify hypotheses. To date, such data have been sparse indeed (Plog 1975:7), with the best-preserved materials coming from one cave (Briuer 1976).

Lack of specific ecological data has hampered the generation of economic models. Such models are always difficult to deal with, since the archaeological manifestations used to substantiate them are frequently ephemeral. It is easy to know that prehistoric man collected floral resources and hunted faunal ones, and consumed both. However, articulating the specific elements of such activities is both time-consuming and difficult.

As regards agricultural activities, more evidence fortunately exists, mostly in the form of agricultural features such as check dams or terraces. To posit an agricultural subsistence base, however, one must know how much arable land was available. Although arable land is present in the Chevelon, the rough topography of many such areas probably restricted extensive areal coverage. In areas of open expanse, the climate was usually drier, and the land accordingly less susceptible to dry-farming. Thus a strategy of maximizing available resources on a seasonal basis was likely employed. Several interesting problems present themselves in attempting to investigate these past subsistence strategies, and some preliminary attempts have been made towards their solution. Initial work by F. Plog and his colleagues (Plog, Hill, and Read 1976b:148; Plog 1975) indicates that site locations on the most fertile reddish soils in the area were preferred. In addition, the research by Acker (1973) has investigated the relationship of soil moisture, acidity, and other variables to site location. Initial interpretations indicate that, even in the better reddish soils, exhaustion of nutrients would have occurred within 75 years, forcing abandonment of particular areas. F. Plog (1978) has also attempted to correlate specific environmental variables with site locations. Although publication of his results is only in a preliminary stage, efforts are being made to produce realistic explanations for site locations as well as for various other current archaeological problems.

With an orientation towards viewing the Chevelon as a resource base from which its occupants drew their subsistence, powerful explanatory models can be generated. The Chevelon, as a fairly unique environmental situation, offers an ideal natural laboratory within which to test such models.

Environmental Restrictions

Finally, this section would be incomplete without reference to certain environmental restrictions and implicit assumptions that need to be considered. Principal among these is simply that existing environmental data are inadequate to precisely monitor the quality and nature of past environmental change and fluctuation. It is a mistake to assume that the environment has remained unchanged unless there is direct evidence for this. Even minor environmental fluctuations could have caused major changes in the distribution of plants and animals, as well as variation in the growing season. This can be controlled for to a certain degree, and archaeologists can make reasonable statements regarding the past environment. But the possibility of change must always be kept in mind. Certainly, minor change might in many instances have been insignificant over the long term. Furthermore, one can make basic assumptions that are likely to be true: for example, that the pine forest area of the Chevelon was never an arid desert, at least during human occupation of the region. As long as assumptions are clearly stated, reasonable interpretations may be derived.

Another major point to consider is seasonality, especially among animals. Specific species are not restricted to specific zones on an annual basis. Several of the species in the Chevelon may well have practiced migratory behavior. This is something that prehistoric man would have been aware of, and it would have affected site distribution. Archaeologists should also be aware of this possibility (see Simmons and Ilany 1977). Aitchison and Theroux (1974:25) have noted the seasonality of avifaunal resources in the Chevelon area. Certainly, many of the large mammals in the region migrated on a regular basis.

Finally, one must note the presence of flora and fauna introduced into the region. Aitchison and Theroux (1976), in their check list of biotic resources in Chevelon Canyon, noted several such species. Inclusion of these in a prehistoric economic reconstruction would greatly bias interpretations. In addition, the composition of native fauna and flora has clearly been altered by hunting, competition from livestock, reduction by predators, and destruction of natural habitats (Wilson 1969:202).

Previous Research and Current Problems

Introduction

Although archaeological investigations in the area surrounding the Chevelon have been fairly intense, little research has actually been conducted within the drainage itself until recently. Detailing the history of previous research in the wider plateau area would entail far more space than is available here, and would be of only peripheral interest. Therefore the following discussion will mention these other areas but briefly, and will instead focus mainly upon previous investigations specifically within the Chevelon, a concise reconstruction of the cultural history of the area, and a discussion of current research problems.

Previous Research: Peripheral Areas

Over the last several years, intensive investigations in the regions to the north and northeast of the Chevelon have revealed an intensive occupation of these areas by peoples whose material cultures reflect a blending of Anasazi and Mogollon cultural groups. Principal research efforts have focused on regions near the Little Colorado River drainage and in areas such as Hay Hollow and Vernon. Although the quantity and quality of published results of this research are sporadic, several publications are available. For the northern and northeastern area, syntheses by Gumerman and Skinner (1968) and Gumerman and Olson (1968) exist. Much of the research here was conducted by the Museum of Northern Arizona. More directly to the east, the Field Museum of Natural History has spent years investigating the area (see, for example, Martin and others 1962, 1964, and 1975, and Martin, Longacre, and Hill 1967 for specific case reports, and Longacre 1962:148-67, and 1964:201-15 for summaries). In addition, recent investigations have been conducted in the area of the White Mountains (Donaldson 1975; Doyel: in preparation). Investigations in these areas have revealed complex and interesting problems not of direct concern here. For the purposes of this discussion, it is significant to note that a different cultural adaptation seems to have occurred in the Chevelon, a mere 80 km (50 miles) to the west (Plog, Hill, and Read 1976b:149-51).

To the west of the Chevelon, research efforts have been more sporadic and less intense, until one reaches the Flagstaff area or drops off the Mogollon Rim. Wilson's (1967, 1969) research on the Sinagua "hinterland" investigated some of these western regions, specifically areas near Clear Creek (on the western boundary of the Chevelon), Meteor Crater, Chavez Pass, Anderson Mesa, and upper Canyon Diablo. The results of this work will be discussed in more detail below. The Museum of Northern Arizona also conducted a survey in the Clear Creek vicinity for the Wilkens Reservoir Project (Lindsay and others 1970). Surveys such as Kelly's (1961) in the Payson Basin have added to our knowledge of previous occupations in the region, although, as Olson (1963:94-5) points out, this area is relatively unknown despite the fact that it is located among known cultural groups, including the Salado, Sinagua, and Mogollon.

A limited amount of archaeological activity has been conducted to the southeast of the Chevelon. The majority of this work is unpublished, and what has been published (Haury and Hargrave 1931) needs updating.

It is important to note the presence in this area of fairly large pueblos, such as the Pinedale and Bailey Ruins. It is equally important to note, however, that the results of a recent (albeit limited) survey suggest the existence of a definite past bias towards locating larger sites in the Pinedale area. Although the survey recorded one large pueblo of about 75 rooms, the investigator feels that large pueblos are not as frequent as the limited sample might suggest (S. Plog 1977:98-102).

Research immediately south of the Mogollon Rim has also produced significant results. Since this area is traversed by the Cholla-Saguaro line, detailed information on past research in this area is provided later in this report.

Previous Research: the Chevelon

Archaeological research specifically within the Chevelon drainage has been limited. Only in the past few years have intensive investigations been conducted. Previous work in the area has primarily been salvage-oriented, and specific sites were located and excavated in the absence of any regional research design.

The area has certainly been known for years. The largest ruin, and one certainly atypical of the region on the basis of recent research, is Chevelon Ruin (NA1026), in the northern area of the drainage. Fewkes excavated at this site and produced vague descriptions of his work (Fewkes 1898,1904). Spier (1918) also briefly visited Chevelon Ruin. Hough (1903:302-305) excavated at a medium-sized pueblo near McDonald Canyon, again at the northern extent of the drainage. In addition, surveys and tests by Gila Pueblo were conducted early in the century, but the results of this work are largely unpublished and work in the area appears to have been scant (Gladwin 1957:154).

In more recent years, investigations in the vicinity have been carried out by Vivian (1969), Wilson (1967, 1969), and Grebinger and Bradley (1969). Vivian worked on five sites, one which was of ephemeral occupation (Webb Site), two of which it was felt contained pit houses (Thomas and Aunt Lottie sites), and two of which had surface architectural remains (Roubicek and Turkey Track sites). One of the three rooms at the Turkey Track Site was open to the east, a point to be discussed later (Vivian 1969:13).

Wilson (1967, 1969) conducted a nonsystematic survey over much of the wider Chevelon area. He located 82 sites as well as ten previously recorded ones. Small surface-masonry dwellings and pit houses were the most common site types encountered. Of the areas investigated, only the Heber and McDonald Canyon localities occur specifically within the Chevelon.

In the Heber locality, eight sites with eight components were located: two small pueblos of three to ten rooms, a medium-sized pueblo of 16-19 rooms, four "seasonal" sites of one to four rooms, and one sherd scatter. Of the "seasonal" sites, several were apparently open to the east; Wilson has referred to these as "multiple carports" (Wilson 1969:247-50).

In the McDonald Canyon locality, six sites with a total of eight components were located. Two are "seasonal", of one or two rooms; three contain one to three pit houses; two are small pueblos of three to ten rooms; and one is a medium-sized pueblo of 18-20 rooms, with a possible associated kiva (Wilson 1969:243-6).

The site excavated by Grebinger and Bradley (1969) is located between Heber and Overgaard, and is a limited-activity site with two distinct components. Such sites are important in that they have frequently been ignored by previous investigators. Many of the APS-CS sites are of a similar nature.

Several sites have been located in the Chevelon as a result of archaeological investigations directly related to the construction of the APS -CS transmission line. Forty-six were located by the Arizona State Museum and form the data base of this section. Brief reports listing some of the sites have already been produced. The area from Joseph City to the northern boundary of the Apache-Sitgreaves National Forest is discussed by Canouts and Phillips (1974). Sites on National Forest land are reported by Mayro, Causey, and Hard (1977), Mayro and Causey (1976), and Mayro (1976a,b). Investigations have also been carried out on the Salt River Project portion of the transmission line by the Museum of Northern Arizona (Hartman 1978).

Finally, the most intensive archaeological activities in the Chevelon have been those conducted by F. Plog and his colleagues as part of the Chevelon Archaeological Research Project (CARP). Plog's investigations have been the only ones with a strong research basis. Although several of CARP's models remain untested and many of its hypotheses unverified, CARP's work to date is certainly the most systematic in the Chevelon region. Although much is yet unpublished, several summary works are available, the principal ones being F. Plog, Hill, and Read (1976a), F. Plog (1972, 1974, 1975, 1978), F. Plog and McAllister (1978), and S. Plog (1976a, b, c, 1977). In addition, several theses directly relevant to CARP's research have been generated, as have numerous unpublished student papers.

Since 1971, CARP has surveyed large portions of the Chevelon and located over 1000 sites. Excavations have been carried out at over 40 sites. Perhaps the most significant factor to emerge during CARP's investigations is that the Chevelon appears to be culturally distinct from surrounding regions (Plog, Hill and Read 1976b;149-151). This is most clearly evident in post-A.D. 1000 architectural types. Apparently, the most common form consists of double-coursed dry-laid masonry structures

open on one end, usually to the east. Overall, such sites are small
(three rooms or less) and frequently consist of but one room. Larger
sites are also present, consisting of either single blocks of five to
eight rooms or several blocks of similar size. Large pueblo sites of
50 or more rooms are, however, generally lacking. Although this is a
distinct variation from other areas of the Southwest, F. Plog feels that
this difference may be more apparent than real; that is, previous
researchers may well not have recognized or described smaller complexes
(Plog 1978:55). Nonetheless, F. Plog (1972, 1974) has estimated the
average number of rooms per site for the entire drainage to be three.

Although the small sites described above are the most common types,
larger sites, including those with kivas, do occur (Slatter, Plog, and
Plog 1976). In fact, F. Plog has informed the author that great kivas
may well be present roughly within every 2-4 square kilometers. In
addition, pit houses are present as are smaller limited-activity sites
with no architectural features (Slatter, Plog, and Plog 1976).

Regarding settlement distribution, F. Plog (1975; Plog, Hill, and
Read 1976b:148) has noted a striking correlation between habitation sites
and the distribution of red sandstone-derived soils. This correlation
has been supported by Acker's (1973) more specific studies of site location and soil types. It is interesting to note that, in the west, the
area between Clear and Chevelon creeks is apparently devoid of sites,
prompting Wilson to designate this area as a cultural boundary. To the
east, southeast, south, and north, the just-described type of settlement
pattern as well as house construction appears to end abruptly at the
end of the drainage. Sites in these areas seem to be larger, more agglom-
erated settlements (Plog 1975:9).

Finally, an important point to note is that there apparently is
a distinct preference for locating sites in the pinyon-juniper woodlands.
Site density is low in the grasslands and even lower in the high ponderosa
pine forests, while sites of all types are very densely distributed throughout the pinyon-juniper woodlands. Sites within the ponderosa pine zone
are apparently rare and found only along canyon bottoms. Finally, within
the pinyon-juniper woodlands, site density appears to increase from north
to south (Plog, Hill, and Read 1976b:148; S. Plog 1977:29-30).

Culture History

Prehistoric

Evidence for very early occupation of the Chevelon is scant indeed.
Although there is evidence for aceramic occupation of the Little Colorado
Valley, it is equivocal at best (Gumerman and Skinner 1968:187). Clovis
and Folsom projectile points have been located in the general area
(Agenbroad 1967; Sims and Daniel 1967), but little systematic research
effort has been expended on these early occupations.

Even more problematic are sites felt to represent the "Tolchaco Complex" (Bartlett 1943). These sites remain undated, and little problem-oriented research has been conducted upon them. In fact, the authenticity of the artifacts themselves has been questioned (Ascher and Ascher 1965). Nonetheless, "Tolchaco" sites are constantly cited in the literature; it is best to regard such sites as problematic until further detailed analyses are conducted upon the assemblages. Furthermore, although these sites have traditionally been considered as early, the little systematic work that has been done on them suggests specific functional interpretations that crosscut thousands of years and involve occupations ranging from aceramic to puebloan (Keller and Wilson 1976).

There is slightly better evidence for Desert Culture, or Archaic, occupation of the area. Although the Desert Culture is regionally expressed as the Concho Complex (Wendorf and Thomas 1951; Martin and Rinaldo 1960) by many, there are again problems with cultural definitions. Thus, it might not be accurate to immediately subsume Desert Culture materials under the rubric of the Concho Complex. The Museum of Northern Arizona's recent work in the northern portion of the Chevelon will hopefully yield more data on the problem.

In the Chevelon itself, there is some evidence for related early occupations. This comes primarily from a cave site (CARP Chevelon Survey 191). Charcoal from the bedrock floor of this cave yielded a radiocarbon date of 4224 B.C. ± 120 (UCLA-1676) (Briuer 1976). In addition, other sites dating from 6000 B.C. to the time of Christ are known both from caves and on alluvial fans located on the rim of Chevelon Canyon (Plog 1978:55).

In regions away from Chevelon Canyon proper, occupation appears to have been ephemeral until about A.D. 200-300. During this time, isolated pit houses or small pit house villages occur. Around A.D. 500 to 700, larger pit house villages occur, some associated with semicircular rows of surface units. From about A.D. 800 to 1050, small sites with either shallow pit houses (in general, earlier pit houses are deeper than later ones) or slab houses are common throughout the drainage. At the end of this period, walled sites built on high areas along Chevelon Canyon occur; White (1976) provides an initial discussion of these supposed "defensive" sites. From about A.D. 1100, sites occur primarily in the pinyon-juniper woodland. Site size is variable at this time, with both large and small structures occurring. The drainage was apparently abandoned in the late 13th and early 14th centuries. At the very end of this period, some rooms and even entire sites are of pure masonry construction. Chevelon Ruin, the occupation of which may extend into the 15th century, appears to have had only incidental relationship to the majority of sites in the drainage. Its northern location and late date link it more closely with similar large sites near the Little Colorado River (Plog 1978:55-6; Plog, Hill, and Read 1976:149-50).

As regards settlement location, few data are available to explain site location in the drainage prior to A.D. 850. It was during this time that people apparently moved into the drainage. Habitation sites occur primarily in the pinyon-juniper woodland; limited-activity sites occur close to these, as well as along Chevelon and West Chevelon canyons and in the grasslands. A mixed hunting-gathering and horticultural economic system is indicated. Preferred site locations appear to have been on flat areas of low relief, although there is generally a fairly random location of sites throughout the drainage. Between A.D. 850-1050, many site areas were reoccupied by later groups. Population appears to have shifted southward and was densest in the Wildcat Canyon area, although habitation sites still occur throughout the drainage. Limited-activity sites continue to be important, and were concentrated both near Chevelon Canyon and in the grasslands. Sites also tend to occur in areas of high resource potential. The economy is similar to that of the previous period. From A.D. 1050-1125, sites continue to occur in the pinyon-juniper woodland and in areas of high relief. Population appears to have been concentrated in a relatively few walled sites located along Chevelon Canyon. Economic activities were now aimed towards horticulture. Finally, the period from A.D. 1125-1275 witnessed high population density in the vicinity of Bitumal Tanks and along Brookbank Canyon, although habitation sites occur in other areas of the drainage. Limited-activity sites again occur throughout the drainage, excepting Chevelon Canyon. There is a continued eastward shift of population, which may partially reflect the limited agricultural potential of soils in the area. Most of the sites in the drainage date to this period (Plog 1978:68-70).

The dating sequence as well as cultural affiliation for sites in the Chevelon are yet to be worked out to general satisfaction. Ceramics have formed the core of these sequences. Although Wilson's (1969) work in the area employed ceramic groups as dating devices, his principal interest was in Sinagua ceramics, and the Chevelon area is too far east to be directly related to this "group." CARP's efforts have thus provided the most complete knowledge of ceramics in the drainage. In terms of traditional Southwestern definitions, the Chevelon would be considered a Mogollon area, with the possible exception of some sites dating to around A.D. 600-800 in the northern portion of the drainage; these latter sites would be considered Anasazi. The assignment of sites in the drainage to the Mogollon culture is based on the types of corrugated and plainware ceramics present. Throughout the entire period of occupation, the predominant plain and corrugated types are the red-colored Mogollon brownwares as opposed to the Anasazi Tusayan Gray Wares (S. Plog 1977:31). Painted ceramics include Tusayan, Little Colorado, and Cibola whitewares.

Eschewing the "Colton" typology in favor of a simpler one based on attributes observable on all decorated sherds, F. Plog (1976:59-78; 1978:55) has developed a typology for black-on-white ceramics that considers surface color, surface treatment, temper, and paint. Although

Plog recognizes the usefulness of the Colton typology as a starting point, he also sees it as cumbersome. He further notes that design elements are not used in CARP's typology, these being reserved for later analysis. Briefly, Plog has derived three clusters or combinations, based on the considerations noted above: PSO--polished surface, sand temper, and organic paint; SShO--slipped surface, sherd temper, and organic paint; and PGM--polished surface, gray temper, and mineral paint. These groups represent nonoverlapping categories, and, in fact, correspond quite nicely with the traditional Southwestern ceramic classification--that is, PSO corresponds to Tusayan White Ware. Thus, CARP's classification in essence provides corroborative evidence in support of both the traditional Colton typology as well as that employed by Wilson (1969)(F. Plog 1978:55; F. Plog 1976:59-78; S. Plog 1977:33-5).

Problems do, however, arise when the above scheme is used as a dating device. Implicit in CARP's typology is that early occupations can be related to high proportional occurrences of Tusayan White Ware (PSO), intermediate occupations to Little Colorado White Ware (SShO), and late occupations to Cibola White Ware (PGM). This assumption is not totally verified. Nonetheless, the most recent dating scheme proposed by CARP for the Chevelon is given in Table 15.

The Chevelon dating scheme is further supported by available tree-ring dates (S. Plog 1977:35). F. Plog has informed the author that, while there may well be some problems with the methodology he has used, his scheme does, in fact, appear to work quite well in the Chevelon. (He does state that a similar methodology might not work elsewhere.) He further notes that 80 to 90 percent of the Cibola White Ware in the area would, according to the Colton typology, tentatively be composed of Reserve and Tularosa types. Approximately 80 percent of the Little Colorado White Ware is composed of Holbrook Black-on-white materials, while 10 percent are Walnut or Flagstaff black-on-whites. Finally, much of the Tusayan White Ware is composed of Black Mesa and Sosi black-on-whites.

It is clear that until more absolute dates are available and more ceramic information is published and specific correlations attempted, the precise dating of ceramics-producing occupations in the Chevelon will remain problematic.

- - - - - - - - - -

Table 15. Chronological scheme for the Chevelon (from Plog 1978:58)

A.D. 1200-1275:	predominantly Cibola White Ware
A.D. 1125-1200:	relatively even mixture of Cibola and Little Colorado whitewares
A.D. 1050-1125:	predominantly Little Colorado White Ware
A.D. 850-1050:	predominantly Tusayan White Ware (Black Mesa Black-on-white, Sosi Black-on-white)
A.D. 500-850:	predominantly Tusayan white/graywares (Kana'a Black-on-white, Lino Black-on-gray)

- - - - - - - - - -

Synthesis

A brief outline of the prehistoric culture history of the Chevelon was presented above. Although it is beyond the scope of the present work to attempt to tie in adjacent areas to the Chevelon proper, a few comments may be made in order to achieve a regional perspective. The apparent distinctiveness of the Chevelon has been noted by CARP (Plog, Hill, and Read 1976b:149-151). One must remember, however, that much of the Chevelon's distinctiveness may well be due to the fact that this area has been intensively surveyed on a regional basis. The detail with which all prehistoric sites were noted is a possible skewing factor, particularly when one attempts to correlate cultural events in the Chevelon with those in other areas not as intensively or as systematically surveyed. A further problem rests in the simple fact that when a region is subjected to intensive research, investigators frequently become immersed with the problems of that region rather than problems of a broader scale. Nonetheless, a few major trends and differences may be observed in the Chevelon.

The delineation of chronology is usually a first step in determining the nature of human occupations within any given area. The chronology of the Chevelon has already been discussed, and although problems do occur in the sequence, it at least offers a starting point for comparisons. Table 16 illustrates the relationships of the Chevelon sequence, as derived from Plog (1978), to the sequences of adjacent areas. It is immediately apparent that no major discrepancies occur within the Chevelon sequence. The equivalent of Basketmaker II is quite poorly represented, but after that time the Chevelon sequence is not unlike the standard Pecos classification, except that it is finer. The major difference lies in the Pueblo I Period, where the Chevelon sequence does not distinguish between Basketmaker III and Pueblo I. The A.D. 850-1050 "phase" fits fairly comfortably within a Pueblo II designation. Distinctions within Pueblo III occur in the Chevelon as well as in adjacent plateau areas. Some confusion is also evident in the later Pueblo IV Period throughout the plateau. Most of the Chevelon, however, appears to have seen but sporadic occupation after about A.D. 1275.

In terms of settlement patterns and implied population movement, several trends are observable in the Chevelon. Plog (1974) has addressed this point, noting several differences between the Chevelon (the Purcell-Larson locality) and the Hay Hollow Valley further to the east. These include a more stable rate of population growth in Purcell-Larson than in Hay Hollow, symmetrical site clusters in Purcell-Larson as opposed to either a nonsymmetrical or asymmetrical situation in Hay Hollow, and different integrative patterns between the regions (Plog 1974:88-90). Furthermore, in the Chevelon itself, there appears to be a long-term trend involving movement into the pinyon-juniper woodland, reflected in an initial southern and then eastward distribution of sites (Plog 1978:68-71).

Table 16. Comparative Chronologies of the Chevelon and adjacent areas

Standard Pecos Classification (compiled from Gumerman and Skinner 1968:187)	Chevelon (compiled from Plog 1978:55-8)	East Clear Creek* (compiled from Wilson 1969: Table 2)	Upper Little Colorado (compiled from Longacre 1964: 203-210)	Central Little Colorado (compiled from Gumerman and Skinner 1968:187)	Puerco Valley (compiled from Gumerman and Olson 1968: 116-125)
				Early man	Early man (Clovis)
"Desert Culture"				Tolchaco (?) Pinto	San Pedro Cochise
Basketmaker II (A.D. 100-600)	A.D. 200-300		Phase I (about 1500 B.C.-A.D. 300)	BM II (Black Creek(?))	BM II (Black Creek Phase)
Basketmaker III (A.D. 600-800)	A.D. 500-350	Group I (A.D 700s)	Phase II (A.D. 300-500)	BM III	Lupton and La Plata phases (about A.D.400/500-about 750)
Pueblo I (A.D. 800-900)			Phase III (A.D. 500-700)	P I	White Mound Phase (A.D. 750-850)
		Group II (A.D. 800s)	Phase IV (A.D. 700-900)		Kiatuthlana Phase (A.D. about 850-900)
Pueblo II (A.D. 900-1100)	A.D. 850-1050	Group III (A.D. 900-1050)	Phase V (A.D. 900-1100)	P II (Holbrook Phase: A.D. 1075-1100)	Red Mesa Phase (A.D.about 900-975)
		Group IV (A.D. 1050-1100)			Wingate Phase (A.D.about 975-1050)
Pueblo III (A.D. 1100-1250)	A.D. 1050-1125	Group V (A.D. 1100-1200)	Phase VI (A.D. 1100-1300)	P III (McDonald Phase: A.D. 1100-1250)	Houck Phase (A.D.about 1070-1250)
	A.D. 1125-1200	Group VI (A.D. 1200-1300)			
Pueblo IV (A.D. 1250-about 1350)	A.D. 1200-1275			P IV (Tuwiuca Phase: A.D.1200-1300 and Homolovi Phase: A.D.1300-about 1400)	Kintiel Phase (A.D. 1225/50-about 1300)
			Phase VII (A.D. 1300-1450)		

*Includes Wilson's survey areas west of East Clear Creek. Sites to the east (in the Heber and McDonald Canyon vicinities) fall only within groups 5 and 6 (Wilson 1969: 244-8).

As noted previously, the greater Chevelon was for all intents and purposes abandoned during the late 13th and early 14th centuries (Plog 1978:56). Prior to this period, toward the end of the 12th century, a preference for walled sites built on rincons along Chevelon Canyon is noted. The implication is that these sites are defensive. After these sites were abandoned, there is little evidence for occupation in Chevelon Canyon proper, although smaller habitation sites continued elsewhere in the drainage. An important question to investigate is how these defensive sites relate to other large sites occupied in adjacent regions. It is important to note that throughout its occupation, the Chevelon never exhibited the "large" pueblos that were common elsewhere in the Southwest at the same time. Was the construction of defensive sites in Chevelon Canyon at a relatively early date a precursor of the later large sites such as that at Chavez Pass or Chevelon Ruin itself? Later sites in the plateau area are frequently large, representing large populations incorporated within single settlemnts. This pattern certainly appears to be in evidence in the central Little Colorado Valley (Gumerman and Skinner 1968:195-6), including Chevelon Ruin. One model for the explanation of such aggregations may be that when areas such as the Chevelon were abandoned, these populations moved a few kilometers to the north and, for reasons yet unknown, adopted an adaptive strategy involving a different sort of settlement system, one requiring substantial populations concentrated at large sites.

Yet another problem within the Chevelon is simply its cultural affiliations. The area does, as previously noted, have an overall Mogollon character to it, but there is certainly a distinctive blend of Anasazi elements, at least as revealed in many of the decorated ceramics. The question of Mogollon-Anasazi interrelationships is certainly complex and is not restricted to the Chevelon (see, for example, Gumerman and Skinner 1968:197). Perhaps the investigation of this culture-lending in an area with as distinctive an adaptive pattern as that evidenced in the Chevelon would shed some light on these interrelationships. Not to be overlooked is the possibility that the Chevelon existed as a boundary between distinct cultural groups (Wilson 1967:167).

Historic

Little is known of the historic occupation of the Chevelon. A brief synthesis compiled from Wilson (1969:257-71) is presented here. The determination of specific Native American occupations is complicated by the fact that Navajo, San Carlos Apache, and Northern Tonto Apache tribes all claim to have occupied portions of the Chevelon area as well as other regions, and have placed claims before the Indian Claims Commission. Linking specific archaeological occurrences to specific Indian groups is even more difficult.

Archaeological evidence does indicate that at least two historically known Indian groups inhabited the greater Chevelon area: the Apache and the Navajo. Remains located by Wilson's (1969) survey were inadequate for dating and determining the functions and intensity of occupation at these sites. Six other sites near Heber and three in the central Chevelon Creek drainage are referred to as Apache by Schroeder (1974), although Littell (1966:48-55) prefers to designate them Navajo or unknown. Most of these sites consist of brush shelters and possess few diagnostic features. Considering the lack of archaeological evidence, documentary and ethnographic data are of considerable help in determining the historic occupation of the area.

Havasupai groups have been noted near the Little Colorado River by both Hodge (in Coues 1900:473) and Colton (1918:21-2). Several Spanish expeditions in the area between 1583 and 1605 encountered groups they called "Cruzados" and "Tacabuyes". The terms "Napao" and "Tasabuest" were used to refer to groups living in the general area in 1775 and 1776. Schroeder (1974) provides evidence indicating that all these groups were Yavapai and/or Havasupai.

Anglo occupation of the area produced a bewildering variety of terms for specific native groups. Once again, Schroeder (1974) concludes that all these terms refer to Yuman speakers who were in most cases Yavapai, as well as "Tonto Apaches". With the displacement of Indian groups, confusion as to which specific tribes were present became even greater. Apparently, Athabaskan speakers were also present as well as Yuman speakers and "Tonto Apaches", thus introducing a possible third group. Still uncertain, however, are the extent and disposition of Navajo and Apache occupation.

Cibecue groups of the Western Apache are known to have ranged up to above the Mogollon Rim, hunting in the pine forest country as well as collecting juniper berries and pinyon nuts on a seasonal basis. The Canyon Creek band of the Cibecue group travelled as far north as Chevelon Fork or Chevelon Butte. Apparently, these groups did not range further north for fear of encountering Navajo groups (Goodwin 1942:18, 21-3).

It is significant that intensity of occupation was quite variable. If one requires an "occupation" to be of a permanent, sedentary nature, it would appear that the Chevelon in fact saw little intensive occupation by historic Indian groups. Much more likely, rather, is the occurrence of sporadic, seasonal incursions into the area by these groups (see Wilson 1969:264-5). As indicated above, the Cibecue group travelled into the region, including the Pinedale and Heber areas, on a frequent basis (Goodwin 1942:21-2). It appears highly likely that other native groups used the Chevelon region for similar purposes.

There is little disagreement that both Navajo and Western Apache groups occupied the area south of the middle Little Colorado River to the Mogollon Rim. The problem lies in determining when this occurred. Does it predate 1860 and the Navajo confinement at Fort Sumner? If the

Navajo were not living south of the middle Little Colorado until 1858-59, then the southern Mogollon Slope was either unoccupied or used seasonally by the Western Apache. Schroeder's (1952) summary of source materials indicates that the Apache entered the country north of the Gila River around 1700 or later. If this is true, the Apachean occupation of the rim country should postdate 1700 (Wilson 1969:268-9).

As mentioned earlier, several Spanish expeditions were in the area between 1583 and 1605. Some of the more notable of these that probably passed through or near the Chevelon included the expeditions of Oñate (1598, 1604-05), Farfan (1598), and Espejo (1582)(Bolton 1916). Other Spanish incursions into the general vicinity during the late 1700s included those of Dominguez and Escalante (1776), Garcés (1776), and Cordero (1796). Most of these, however, skirted the Chevelon proper and passed through Navajo land further to the north (Wilson 1969:262).

Early American-period expeditions were frequent in northern Arizona during the latter 1800s. This was a turbulent period in Arizona's modern history, and several U.S. military expeditions passed through the area. Reports noting native groups were made by the Whipple (1853), Ives (1858), Shepard (1859), Carleton (1865), Hughes (1863-64), and Chavez (1864) groups, to name but a few (Wilson 1969: 261-5). Of particular interest are the activities of General George Crook: between 1873 and 1876 his group constructed a trail between Camp Verde and Camp Apache that passes directly through the Heber vicinity (Jacobs 1977).

Finally, late historic Anglo use of the area has been virtually unrecorded archaeologically. We know more of the major military activities in this area simply because they have been documented in historic records, not because of archaeological investigations. The "unimportant" Anglo events are largely undocumented in historic records, but their presence is known. Several such sites were located on the APS-CS survey. Basque sheep herders have also been present in the area for several years, as well as the more permanent Anglo settlers.

Current Research Problems

Introduction

As pointed out earlier, CARP's work in the Chevelon has been the only truly problem-oriented research in the area. Accordingly, the following discussion will focus on some of CARP's research questions, its success in answering them, and directions that further research efforts in the Chevelon should follow. Finally, the relevance of the APS-CS survey to CARP's research orientation will be discussed. The specific research design for the overall APS-CS survey has been discussed elsewhere in this volume. The following discussion will seek to articulate APS-CS survey information with CARP's research and to point out additional avenues of investigation.

CARP's Research Orientation

Broadly stated, the initial focus of CARP's research in the Chevelon was based on two considerations: a desire to investigate the adaptive patterns of prehistoric groups in an area of varied environmental situations, and a desire to study an area in which little previous archaeological investigation had been conducted. The Chevelon drainage met both of these considerations. Intertwined with these was a wish to apply the SARG research design to a specific area. The principal question posed by this design is: "Why are sites located where they are?" (Gumerman 1971). The success that CARP's research has had in focusing on the SARG research design is addressed by F. Plog (1978). In specific terms, many of CARP's research problems have already been alluded to in the previous discussion.

CARP's overriding research problem has been twofold: 1) the explication and explanation of patterned variation in the adoption of innovations, and 2) the explication and explanation of organizational change. CARP's initial research in the Chevelon has indicated a cultural trajectory that appears different from that of adjacent regions. Distinctive patterns of both organizational change and settlement distribution appear in the Chevelon (Plog, Hill, and Read 1976b:147-153; 1976c:2). In the initial Chevelon survey, data were insufficient to investigate these patterns, for several reasons: 1) no settlement pattern data were gathered in the initial survey, which was not formulated to provide these types of data; 2) intrasite data are generally lacking; 3) functional interpretations of the organization of activities within and between sites have not been reached; 4) the explanation of so-called "defensive" sites is unclear; and 5) changes in the natural environment and patterns of its exploitation are unclear (Plog, Hill, and Read 1976b:149-151).

Realizing these limitations, the most recent efforts of CARP have been directed towards two questions: 1) what are the dynamics of organizational change in the Chevelon and how can they be explained, and 2) why does the evolutionary trajectory of this area differ so significantly from that of adjacent areas (Plog, Hill, and Read 1976b). The approach CARP has chosen to follow in investigating these questions employs models of change. Of importance in generating such models is the development of typologies and chronologies. Major models chosen include growth models, homeostatic and morphogenic models, and variety and selection models. Growth models have distinct components consisting of questions regarding population, organization, specialization, and resource exploitation. For more elaboration of these models and their testing, the reader is referred to Plog, Hill, and Read (1976b).

In summary then, CARP's major research problems have included, at varying times, the following:
1) patterned variation in adoption of innovations
2) explanation of organizational change
3) investigation of the apparently different cultural trajectory of the Chevelon

4) development of local typologies and chronology
5) testing of the SARG research design of determining why sites are located where they are.

CARP's Progress

To date, how has CARP fared in isolating, describing, and explaining the problems above? Detailed typological and chronological studies have been done, if not fully published. Documentation of the Chevelon's uniqueness has been provided, although as Plog (1978:55) implies, this may be more apparent than real. Investigations of site location in relation to environmental variables (Plog 1978; Acker 1973), of "defensive" sites (White 1976), of ceramic variability (S. Plog 1977), of raw material procurement (Green 1975), and of the nature of "small" sites (F. Plog and McAllister 1978) have all been initiated if not completed.

Thus it is readily apparent that CARP investigations are now in various stages. In some cases, progress is being made. Perhaps the major criticism of CARP that can be raised is that at present principally interpretive work, rather than data, has been published. Detailed models of site location, for example, have been presented that are based on samples of samples. If all the data were provided, one might see potential alterations in the proposed models. In sum, the Chevelon drainage has provided a laboratory for the investigation of several important archaeological questions. What remains to be seen is how the problems posed will be resolved.

APS-CS Survey

The research strategy for the APS-CS transmission line survey is discussed elsewhere. What is of concern to the present discussion is the degree to which data provided by the sites located on the survey correspond to those that might be expected on the basis of models. Specific site data are presented and discussed in the next section. At this point it is sufficient to note that the APS survey data both support and contradict interpretations offered by CARP researchers.

Problems in assessing the similarity of CARP and APS-CS results lie in research orientation. The APS-CS survey and, even more strongly, the subsequent APS-CS Mitigation Project (to be reported upon in a later volume) are primarily oriented toward settlement and subsistence studies. Thus, settlement patterns become a significant factor in interpretation. It has been noted above and elsewhere (Plog 1974) that CARP's principal orientation was not towards the elucidation of subsistence-settlement models. Thus, comparability of CARP and APS-CS may in many cases be difficult to achieve. Fortunately, when dealing with site-specific data, this problem diminishes, and the only problems that then occur are in interpretation.

Another very major problem in terms of comparison is that, in most cases, no collections were made by the APS-CS survey group in the Chevelon. Thus, specific ceramic and lithic data are not as reliable as one would wish since most identifications were made in the field. As Plog (1978:55 and in a personal communication) has noted, paint type and decoration, features critical to a preliminary typology of ceramics, are frequently quite unclear in the field in the Chevelon due to the nature of the soil matrix. Only after the results of the 1978 APS-CS Chevelon Mitigation Project are analyzed will detailed ceramic and lithic information become available.

Of course, the most basic limitation of the APS-CS survey's data is derived from the fact that the survey was restricted to a transmission line corridor. This has probably not provided a representative sample of the types of sites and their environmental concomitants throughout the Chevelon. CARP's investigations were based on many sample designs (Read 1976:19-27; Plog 1978:53-4); one may be certain that their sample of sites is more representative than is that produced by the APS-CS survey.

With these precautions and limitations fully in mind, attention can now be turned to specific APS-CS site survey data.

APS-CS Site Survey Data

Introduction

The following discussion will deal with the sites recorded by the APS-CS survey in terms of data limitations, the methodology employed here in describing and analyzing these sites, and the interpretation of the APS-CS sites in light of previous research, notably CARP's. In conclusion, suggestions will be offered regarding future research in the area.

Data Limitations

Major data limitations alluded to in previous sections include the noncollection of cultural materials; the possible nonrepresentativeness of a transmission line survey; and the APS-CS survey's basic settlement-subsistence research orientation, a goal not shared by CARP, increasing the potential for data incompatibility between the two projects. Thus, one must constantly be aware of the possibility of skewed interpretations when looking at the APS-CS data alone. These data allow only initial approximations of the composition and nature of recorded sites. Only those sites that were directly impacted by construction activities will be subject to excavation. It is undoubtedly from these sites that the most significant behavioral interpretations will be derived.

Methodology and Results

The APS-CS survey recorded 45 separate sites in the greater Chevelon area. One site had a clear historic as well as prehistoric component; thus, the total number of discrete cultural entities is 46. Although several of the prehistoric sites undoubtedly possess multiple components, the survey data do not accurately reflect this. In addition, 19 artifact occurrences were recorded. These typically consist of but a few sherds and/or lithics. Detailed site-by-site data will be presented in the companion volume to this work; thus, the information presented below is in summary form, and little discussion will be devoted to intrasite problems.

Table 17 lists the site-type distribution of all sites located by the APS-CS survey. Although the majority of these types are self-evident, a few words need be said regarding some of the categories. Sites in the "single (noncontiguous) structure" class simply consist of one structure often open to one side, although this information is not consistent. The "several (noncontiguous) structures" class consists of sites exhibiting two or more discrete, noncontiguous structures, many of them, again, open on one side. The "contiguous structure" category is composed of two classes: "large" and "small" sites. Only two large sites occur, one of them clearly possessing over ten rooms, and the other less well defined, containing a block of between four and eight rooms plus several probably associated single units. The "small" class simply consists of sites with more than two and less than ten rooms. All of these structures might be considered pueblos, if one employs the term loosely. Most are constructed of cobbles rather than true masonry, although one of the "large" sites does exhibit the latter technique of construction.

A principal question to be asked is how representative are these few sites in relation to the more than 1000 sites recorded by CARP? Comparisons are difficult, since specific total site distributions have not yet been published by CARP. Some comparisons can, however, be made. The major monograph on CARP (Plog, Hill, and Read 1976a) contains a listing of all the sites recorded during the 1971 survey (Slatter, Plog, and Plog 1976:29-40). Although only 358 sites are listed, F. Plog has informed the author that, for the overall Chevelon drainage, he feels these are fairly representative. Thus, it is possible to compare the APS-CS sites with those from the 1971 CARP survey.

Table 17 also lists all of the CARP sites by specific class. Again, a few words of clarification are necessary. This portion of Table 17 is compiled from data presented by Slatter, Plog, and Plog (1976). To ensure a degree of compatibility with the APS-CS data, some reorganization was necessary. In most cases, there was no problem,

but when considering "pueblos" (Slatter, Plog, and Plog's apparent terminology for all surface structures), some difficulty presented itself.
"Large" pueblos were considered so if they consisted of ten rooms or
more. Ten is not a magic number, but is simply a useful heurisitic
device. Since only four sites fall within this category, no real analytical or methodological problems are presented. The majority of CARP's
pueblos are much smaller, frequently consisting of single rooms. F. Plog
(1972, 1974) has noted that the average number of rooms per site is three.
Thus, the classification used in Table 17 for sites with surface architecture is simply: 1) single rooms; 2) multiple rooms; and 3) large
pueblos, consisting of ten or more rooms. As it proved impossible to
distinguish between several single or contiguous rooms, these were all
included within the multiple-room category.

A casual perusal of Table 17 demonstrates that the APS-CS survey
did not encounter any of the more specialized sites noted by CARP. These
include agricultural features such as check dams and terraces as well as
more exotic features, such as pictographs. The "Other" category in
Table 17 consists of sites such as rock circles and granaries. Finally,
one should note that CARP did not record historic sites; thus, the distinction in this class between APS-CS and CARP is more apparent than real.

Table 17. Site-type distribution for APS-CS survey and 1971 CARP survey

	APS-CS		CARP *	
	Number	Percent	Number	Percent
Historic	5	10.9	0	0
Lithic and sherd scatter	17	37.0	151	42.2
Litnic scatter	4	8.7	55	15.4
Sherd scatter	2	4.3	11	3.1
Other	0	0	12	3.4
Check dam, water control	0	0	16	4.5
Pictograph	0	0	3	0.8
Pit house	6	13.0	13	3.6
Single structure	5	10.9	38	10.6
Single structure-several	2	4.3	55	15.4
"Small" pueblo	3	6.5		
"Large" pueblo	2	4.3	4	1.1
Total	46	99.9	358	100.1

*CARP data compiled from Slatter, Plog, and Plog (1976).

To statistically compare the APS-CS sites with those of CARP, a Kolmogorov-Smirnov test was conducted on a restricted classification of sites from the two surveys. The Kolmogorov-Smirnov two-sample test is a test of whether two independent samples have been drawn from the same population (or from populations with the same distribution)(Siegel 1956:127). The null hypothesis to test is then simply: Ho: APS-CS and CARP sites have <u>not</u> been drawn from the same population. The classes and number of sites per class are presented in Table 18. Again, this table is self-explanatory. Classes for which there are no data from one or the other surveys were dropped from the analysis. Sites with surface architecture were simply grouped according to their being composed of either one structure or several. A distinction between large and small pueblos was not made since the number of large sites from both surveys is quite small.

Even without benefit of statistical comparison, it is obvious that most classes do not significantly differ. Only lithic scatters and pit houses demonstrate marked percentage differences. The results of the test indicate that, at the .01 level of significance, we can reject Ho, since a critical value of 6 or greater (Siegel 1956:Table L, 278) is required to do so. As can be discerned from Table 18, the maximum difference between cumulative percentages is 11.8, easily rejecting Ho.

Site distribution in relation to vegetation community is indicated in Tables 19 and 20. Also given in Table 19 is the approximate percentage of the transmission line crossing each vegetation zone. A word of caution is necessary here. The line of demarcation between open and dense juniper woodland is not a clear one; in fact, many of the sites fall quite close to it. They were placed in what appeared to be the most appropriate category, with the realization that they may well represent ecotonal locations. Finally, no attempt was made to isolate those sites occurring in riparian communities, since this information was variable on the site-survey forms.

What is immediately apparent is that over 50 percent of the sites occur in the dense juniper woodland. When sites occurring in the open juniper woodland are added, this figure jumps to over 70 percent. These zones comprise less than 40 percent of the total area covered by the line survey. Thus, there does indeed appear to be a marked preference for settlement in the juniper area, at least in relation to the transmission line corridor, which of course does not necessarily provide a reflection of representative archaeological sites. Considering that the APS-CS and the CARP survey data are, however, not markedly distinct in terms of site types, a fairly representative sample of sites in the area may in fact have been obtained by the APS-CS survey, assuming of course that CARP's data are representative.

Many of the sites with structures located on the survey occur on ridgetops or other prominent locations. Although previous research in the Chevelon has indicated that many habitation sites, especially the supposed "defensive" ones (White 1976), occur in high areas, more recent analysis suggests that topographic variables may not be as sensitive as initially thought (Plog 1978:67). This consideration also extends to measurements of arable land, which Plog (1978:67) feels are simply too crude at this point to be very significant. Thus, it is difficult to relate the APS-CS sites to specific topographic features in a meaningful comparative sense.

Little can be said regarding specific cultural affiliations. Since no collections were made, no detailed ceramic data are available. Field impressions always have a certain amount of subjectivity to them. Nonetheless, these are the only sources of information at present possessed. Table 21 summarizes the supposed affiliations.

Clearly such information has little interpretive value. One would certainly expect mixtures of both Anasazi and Mogollon occupations in this area, and that appears to have been the case.

Table 18. Restricted site typology for Kolmogorov-Smirnov statistical test

| | APS-CS | | | CARP | | | |
	Number	Percent	Cumulative Percent	Number	Percent	Cumulative Percent	K_D*
Lithic and sherd scatter	17	41.4	41.4	151	46.2	46.2	4.8
Lithic scatter	4	9.8	51.2	55	16.8	63.0	11.8
Sherd scatter	2	4.9	56.1	11	3.4	66.4	10.3
Single structure	5	12.2	68.3	38	11.6	78.0	9.7
Multiple structures	7	17.1	85.4	59	18.0	96.0	10.6
Pit houses	6	14.6	100.0	13	4.0	100.0	0
Total	41	100.0		327	100.00		

*K_D = maximum difference between cumulative percentages

Table 19. Distribution of all sites by vegetational community

Vegetational Community	Number	Percent	Approximate Percentage of Line Coverage
Grassland	9	19.6	35.9
Open juniper woodland	7	17.4	19.2
Dense juniper woodland	25	52.2	20.5
Pine forest	5	10.9	24.4
Total	46	100.1	100.0

Table 20. Distribution of sites by class within vegetational communities

Vegetational Community	HIST Number	Per-cent	LS Number	Per-cent	LSS Number	Per-cent	SS Number	Per-cent	PH Number	Per-cent	SSt Number	Per-cent	SSt-several Number	Per-cent	CONT St Number	Per-cent
Grassland	2	40.0	0	0	5	29.4	0	0	0	0	0	0	2	100	0	0
Open juniper woodland	1	20.0	0	0	4	23.5	0	0	1	16.6	0	0	0	0	1	20.0
Dense juniper woodland	1	20.0	0	0	8	47.1	2	100	5	83.4	5	100	0	0	4	80.0
Pine forest	1	20.0	4	100	0	0	0	0	0	0	0	0	0	0	0	0
Total	5	100.0	4	100.0	17	100.0	2	100	6	100.0	5	100	2	100	5	100.0

Note: HIST=historic; LS=lithic scatter; LSS=lithic/sherd scatter; SS=sherd scatter; PH=pit house; SSt=single structure; SSt-several=single structure, several; CONT St= contiguous structures.

Table 21. Summary of supposed cultural affiliations of sites
located by the APS-CS survey

	Number	Percent
Historic	5	10.7
Anasazi	10	21.7
Mogollon	12	26.1
Unknown prehistoric	15	32.9
Undated lithic scatters	4	8.7
Total	46	100.1

- -

Table 22. Gross ceramic composition of the 37 ceramic-bearing
sites located by the APS-CS survey

Plainwares	brown, orange, "Salado Red", Kana-a Gray, Alma Plain, neck-banded, polished brown
Corrugated wares	graywares, obliterated, indented
Black-on-white	Lino, Black Mesa, Pinedale, Kayenta, Holbrook, Snowflake, Showlow, Walnut, Tularosa
Black-on-red	present; Salado wares?

Thirty-seven of the sites contained ceramics. Although a specific site-by-site description of the ceramics noted could be given, this would provide little in the way of useful information and might in fact be misleading; the data available are inadequate but for the most simplistic statistics. Thus, it must suffice at present to indicate the gross classes of ceramics noted for the sites overall. This information is given in Table 22. Note that type names are given when available; otherwise, general descriptive labels are employed. Again, the reader is cautioned not to rely too much upon these estimates.

Unfortunately, the survey data available on the lithics are so general as to be virtually useless except as an indicator that lithics are present. It is hoped that the APS-CS Mitigation Report will partially remedy this. Of the four sites that contain only lithics, two are too ephemeral to provide functional data. The other two are believed to have been loci of quarrying activities.

Interpretation

Several precautionary remarks have already been made regarding the interpretation of the APS-CS sites. What would appear to be the most profitable avenue of discussion is to determine how, on a general level, the APS-CS sites add information on the research questions posed by CARP.

Before this is done, however, two additional research questions can be posed. It has been seen that, in general, the APS-CS sites are fairly representative of sites reported by CARP. Perhaps the most significant additional insights, however, are provided by the higher percentage of pit house sites located by the APS-CS survey, and by the presence of sites in the ponderosa pine forest.

The presence of several pit house sites poses interesting research questions. Since the Chevelon appears rather unique, particularly in its later prehistory, it would be informative to determine if this uniqueness extends into earlier periods. At present, the relationship of pit house sites to those with surface architecture is poorly understood. It is tacitly assumed that the pit houses represent earlier occupations, although this is frequently undemonstrated. Moreover, the identification of pit houses from surface remains poses a definite problem.

The APS-CS survey data have indicated that there may in fact be a higher density of pit house sites in the area than previously suspected. This could simply be due to sampling error. Nonetheless, the distribution of these sites is interesting; of the six such sites located, five occur in the dense juniper woodland, while one is situated farther north in the juniper woodland and is, in fact, quite close to the grassland zone. This site was undoubtedly functionally different from those in the more heavily wooded area to the south. Markedly different microenvironments occur between these two areas, along with variations in resources. The northern site is not large, and may contain only one pit house and several associated storage pits. It is probably much more closely related to similar sites occurring even farther north, such as those excavated by the Museum of Northern Arizona in association with the Salt River Project. (Hopefully, the results of this excavation will be published in the near future.) This site may well have Anasazi affiliations, although it has been included in the "unknown prehistoric" category in Table 21. The ceramic remains are not particularly informative; brownwares, possibly Mogollon, are present as well as black-on-white types.

The five pit house sites in the south appear more substantial. Three of them are, in fact, portions of the same site (depending upon how one defines the vague concept "site", an issue discussed elsewhere in this volume). Several pit houses, possibly as many as 30, occur at these three sites, and are found in association with surface units, including one of the "large" sites. A very important question here lies in determining the relationship of these earlier (pit house) to the later (surface unit) sites. The available ceramic evidence at least tentatively indicates that the pit houses are earlier than the surface units. It is clear that at least two components are represented at this large site. In fact, three may be present, since at least one of the pit houses appears to be of some depth while the others appear to be quite shallow. F. Plog has informed the author that earlier pit houses tend to be deeper than late ones. If, then, there are gaps in the occupation, why was this specific spot chosen for reoccupation? Obviously it is a preferred area, but the reasons for this are unclear. If the reasons are economic, then a catchment analysis study (see Vita-Finzi and Higgs 1970) might provide information on resource potential within the immediate vicinity.

The other two sites in the dense juniper woodland may also represent small pit house "villages." One contains apparently four to six pit houses and the other at least one pit house associated with several artifact clusters. More pit houses may be present. Directly associated with this latter site is another contiguous site containing the remnants of a small surface unit. Again the question of "siteness" is at issue. All of these sites were investigated in the summer of 1978 by the APS-CS Chevelon Mitigation Project, and results are being prepared for publication.

The lithic scatter sites pose equally interesting problems. Although only four were recorded, a fifth is located in the far northern extent of the survey area. It contains a small amount of ceramics and was therefore listed as a sherd and lithic scatter. The ceramics, however, appear to be late and probably represent a later component. The remainder of the site is again reminiscent of some excavated by the

Museum of Northern Arizona in association with the Salt River Project. This scatter is relatively dense and may represent a fairly early or long-term, recurrent occupation. It, too, was investigated during the summer of 1978 by the APS-CS Mitigation Project.

The four other lithic sites are more interesting in relation to CARP in that they occur in the ponderosa pine forest, where, according to CARP, only a few sites exist. If four sites were located in this zone within a narrow transmission line corridor, the possibility of additional sites is intriguing. As noted previously, all the sites are ephemeral, even the quarrry sites, and as such have low archaeological visibility. This is compounded by the fact that the ground surface in this zone is covered by pine duff, thus making small sites even more difficult to locate. This precaution should be noted by those intending to do additional research in such areas. Thus, the supposed scarcity of sites in the ponderosa pine forest may be more apparent than real.

It is difficult to determine the functional nature of these sites, particularly in the absence of any systematic collections. Since the high pine forests clearly could have witnessed only seasonal occupations, these sites may represent the remains of small groups of hunters and/or collectors who occupied the area only briefly. The two quarry sites are located at chert outcrops. However, in light of the fact that such outcrops are present at lower elevations, it would appear strange that anyone would travel to the highlands to obtain a resource that was locally available. It is possible that the quality of chert in the highlands was better, but few data are available to support this interpretation. It appears more likely that these outcrops were opportunistically exploited by groups already in the area performing specific tasks.

The interpretation of the remainder of the APS-CS sites falls fairly well within CARP's models and explanations. The sherd and lithic scatters are ubiquitous within the area. The small surface structures appear to be one of the most common site types; larger pueblos are rare. It is interesting to note that the APS-CS survey did not locate any specialized activity sites, such as granaries or petroglyphs, while the CARP survey did.

One further point of interpretation may be noted. A continuing question for archaeologists concerns the seasonality of sites, particularly of those sites containing a small number of structures and little occupational debris. Many of the Chevelon sites appear to be of this type. Interpreting seasonality is, however, a complex issue whose resolution is not facilitated by a lack of excavation data. S. Plog (1977:95-129), in a detailed discussion of this topic, concludes that the Chevelon sites were not seasonally occupied (1977:125). Further data will undoubtedly be required to investigate the seasonality question.

For example, it has been stated that most sites in the Chevelon generally lack middens and that surface materials occur in low densities (S. Plog 1977:126). One of the goals of the APS-CS Mitigation Project will be to test such assumptions on specific sites selected for excavation. Initial impressions, however, do not tend to support these assumptions, and suggest that local ground conditions may easily obscure smaller artifacts on the surface. Regardless of such considerations, it is obvious that the apparent lack of substantial structures at many of the Chevelon sites would have made occupation during the harsh winters rather difficult, at least at the more northern sites.

By way of summary, it is difficult to relate the APS-CS sites to specific problem areas within the CARP research design. However, a few general points can be made. First, the presence of "small sites" has been, as noted above, reaffirmed by the APS-CS survey. Such sites appear to represent a major adaptation within the Chevelon drainage. It is equally likely that early Southwestern researchers simply did not deal with small sites. F.Plog and McAllister (1978) have specifically dealt with this issue in the Chevelon, and it is heartening to see the increased interest in small-site archaeology, as exemplified in the volume edited by Ward (1978).

Second, the APS-CS survey can add no further information regarding the so-called "defensive" sites in the region. Only one site, a "large" pueblo, appears to have a compound wall around it, and it is difficult to conceive of this wall as defensive. The entire issue is a complex one that requires further investigation. It would be a mistake, however, to consider all sites with surrounding walls located on high points to be defensive without considering alternative explanations.

Third, the overwhelming presence of sites in the pinyon-juniper woodlands appears supported by the APS-CS data. This in itself poses additional problems. Grassland and pine forest areas need to be more consistently surveyed. It is clear that a great many of the sites located by CARP's survey fall within the pinyon-juniper woodlands, especially if one lumps dense and open woodlands (Plog 1978:54, 57, Figure 1). Thus, it is not entirely surprising that the APS-CS survey located even more sites in this area.

Fourth, the various models of cultural change posed by CARP are virtually impossible to apply to the APS-CS survey data. Evaluation of models of growth, population, and organization requires investigation of several variables that the survey data simply provide no information on. Potential data for studying intrasite growth and organization may, however, exist at sites such as that discussed above, which consists of pit houses and surface units. These as well as other questions were investigated during the 1978 APS-CS Chevelon Mitigation Project.

Finally, the APS-CS survey has provided additional data for the investigation of this area. Some of these data complement those of CARP, others do not. No conflict is seen here. If archaeology is to develop a scientific approach, it must build on previous work. Errors are bound to occur at all levels of analysis and interpretation. This is simply part of the game plan. With all of the data that have been gathered for the Chevelon in the past ten years, it is hoped that a fairly clear picture of the prehistoric occupation of the area will emerge when all of the results of this research are published.

Conclusions and Suggestions for Future Research in the Chevelon

Several points already made regarding the direction that future research in the Chevelon should take may, by way of summary, be reiterated here.

First, although a large portion of the area has been surveyed using various techniques, more of an emphasis on specific settlement-subsistence patterns is needed. Representative coverage of all vegetation zones is also required.

Second, if we are trying to apply models of organization, growth, and population, two types of data are minimally required: the settlement-subsistence information noted above, and more data on intrasite variability. Emphasis on the site as an analytical unit has not been apparent in previous research. Although variation between sites is important, variation within sites is equally critical.

Third, the concept of "site" must be dealt with in a more satisfactory fashion. Indeed, the majority of sites in the Chevelon are small, but if each individual surface unit , for example, is considered a site, what becomes important is the spatial relationship between these units. If only 30 meters separate two units, should they be considered separate sites? "Small" sites obviously imply occupation by small groups of people. After all, only so many people will fit into a single-room structure as opposed to a large pueblo. But how different is a 15-room contiguous pueblo from a site area composed of, for example, ten individual units? These are problems that need to be investigated. Clearly, questions of organization are significant here.

Fourth, although a preference for specific environmental zones seems indicated by the available data, more discussion on specific micro-environmental diversity is necessary. Thus, there is evidence to indicate that people did occupy the pine forest. Why and to what degree are as yet unanswered. As another example, little is known of riparian communities.

Settlement in these zones, even within a harsh surrounding environment, is quite possible and perhaps even desirable. Such zones should be investigated more thoroughly.

Fifth, although it is anathema to discuss it in current archae- ological circles, more excavation is required. There is only so much information that surface collection and observation can provide. Deposi- tional history and intensity as well as nature and duration of occupation can only rarely be determined on the basis of surface materials alone. Furthermore, the definition of some sites might be more precise if at least limited testing were conducted. This is especially true regarding pit houses, since these structures, in the Chevelon at least, are difficult to identify and define purely on the basis of surface indications.

Sixth, detailed artifact analyses of ceramics, lithics, and other artifact categories are necessary. At some point, "hard" data of this kind become necessary in interpreting a site and its relationship to others.

Finally, specific paleoeconomic concerns need to be investigated. Paleoeconomy has lately been of prime interest to many archaeologists both in the Old and New Worlds, although actual applications of paleo- economic theory have, to date, been rather limited and disappointing. Perhaps the forerunner of recent developments was the work of the late Eric Higgs (1972, 1975). A thorough discussion of the implications and assumptions underlying paleoeconomy would be out of place here, but may be found in the Higgs volumes just cited. Suffice it to say that an economic approach to prehistory is considered both desirable and necessary if archaeologists are to derive behavioral explanations from their data. This is particualrly true regarding settlement and subsistence models.

Summary

As part of the APS-CS 500 kV transmission line construction, the Arizona State Museum was contracted to conduct an intensive survey along the right-of-way corridor. A portion of this corridor passes through the greater Chevelon drainage of north-central Arizona. Forty-five archaeo- logical sites and 19 artifact occurrences of both prehistoric and historic date were located and recorded in the area. The prehistoric sites range from small, ephemeral artifact scatters to pueblos. The majority of sites with structures are small, frequently consisting of but one or two rooms. The cultural affiliation of the prehistoric sites is predominantly Anasazi and Mogollon, or a blending thereof. Temporal span is difficult to determine from survey data alone, but a considerable depth of cultural deposition is indicated. At least one site may represent an Archaic occupation. The presence of pit houses and surface units at other sites indicates later occupations.

Previous archaeological investigations in the region have been minimal, except for the recent work of the Chevelon Archaeological Research Project (CARP). The APS-CS sites were compared to those recorded by CARP, and it was determined that the former are fairly representative of the latter. A few marked discrepancies do, however, exist within the APS-CS data. These include the presence of small lithic scatters in the pine forest vegetation zone, an area that CARP's research had indicated was little utilized, and the disproportionately large number of pit house sites located by the APS-CS survey in comparison to those located by CARP. Finally, the close spatial proximity of many sites may indicate regional populations in the Chevelon as large as in adjacent regions, but practicing a dispersed habitation mode; that is, in the place of large pueblos, specific groups might well have occupied noncontiguous surface units, several of which, in a behavioral sense, would have comprised a "site." Some of these questions have been more intensively investigated by the APS-CS Chevelon Mitigation Project, conducted in the summer of 1978. The results of this research are currently being prepared for publication.

The APS-CS survey has provided yet more data for an area that has until recently been uninvestigated. The Chevelon region appears to exhibit a cultural development significantly distinct from those in adjacent Southwestern areas. Through the combined efforts of all the institutions involved in conducting archaeology in this interesting area, we might be able to investigate at least some of the reasons for this apparent uniqueness.

REFERENCES

Acker, C.
1973   Soil and environment in the explanation of settlement pattern.
        MS. Department of Anthropology, University of California,
        Los Angeles.

Agenbroad, L.
1967   The distribution of fluted points in Arizona.
        The Kiva 32: 113-120.

Aitchison, Stewart W. and Michael E. Theroux
1974   A biotic inventory of Chevelon Canyon, Coconino and Navajo
        counties, Arizona. Museum of Northern Arizona, Department
        of Biology. Submitted to Soil Conservation Service and
        Sitgreaves National Forest. Order No. 6202-11-73.

Ascher, R. and M. Ascher
1965   Recognizing the emergence of man. Science 147: 243-50.

Bartlett, Katherine
1943   A primitive stone industry of the Little Colorado Valley,
        Arizona. American Antiquity 8: 266-268.

Bolton, Herbert E. (editor)
1916   Spanish explorations in the Southwest, 1542-1706.
        New York: Scribner's Sons.

Briuer, Frederick L.
1976   Preliminary report of biological remains recovered from
        the Chevelon survey. In Plog, Hill, and Read, pp. 112-124.

Buol, S.
1966   Soils of Arizona. University of Arizona Agricultural
        Experiment Station Technical Bulletin 171.

Canouts, Veletta and David A. Phillips
1974   An archaeological survey of the Arizona Public Service
        Cholla to Saguaro 345 kV transmission line proposed route.
        Interim report: Joseph City: Cholla plant site to
        Sitgreaves National Forest boundary. Arizona State
        Museum Archaeological Series 43.

Colton, H.
1918   The geography of certain ruins near the San Francisco
        Mountains, Arizona. Bulletin of the Geographical Society
        of Philadelphia 16 (2) 37-60.

Coues, Elliott (editor)
1900   On the trail of a Spanish pioneer: the diary and itinerary
        of Francisco Garcés. Vol. II. New York: Francis P. Harper.

Dice, Lee R.
    1943   The biotic provinces of North America. Ann Arbor:
            University of Michigan Press.

Donaldson, Bruce R.
    1975   An archaeological sample of the White Mountain Planning
            Unit, Apache-Sitgreaves National Forest, Arizona. USDA
            Forest Service, Southwestern Region, Archaeological Report 6.
            Albuquerque.

Doyel, David E. (compiler)
    In preparation
            Prehistory in Dead Valley, east-central Arizona: the TG&E
            Springerville Project. Arizona State Museum Archaeological
            Series.

Fewkes, J.
    1898   Preliminary account of an expedition to the pueblo ruins
            near Winslow, Arizona, in 1896. Smithsonian Annual Report
            for 1896, pp. 517-539. Washington.

    1904   Two summers' work in pueblo ruins. Twenty-second Annual
            Report of the Bureau of American Ethnology, Part 2.
            Washington.

Findlow, F., S. DeAtley, and L. Hudson
    1976   Source analysis of obsidian artifacts from the Chevelon
            drainage, northeast Arizona: interim report. In Plog,
            Hill, and Read, pp. 107-111.

Flannery, Kent V.
    1968   Archaeological systems theory and early Meso-America.
            Anthropological archaeology in the Americas, edited by Betty
            Jane Meggers,   pp. 67-87. Anthropological Society of
            Washington.

Gladwin, Harold S.
    1957   A history of the ancient Southwest. Portland, Maine:
            Bond-Wheelwright.

Gloyd, Howard K., Lyle Sowls, Charles H. Lowe, and Floyd Werner
    1972   Animal life. In Arizona: its people and resources, by
            members of the Faculty of the University of Arizona.
            Rev. second edition, pp. 169-182. Tucson: University
            of Arizona Press.

Goode, John P.
    1939   Goode's school atlas. New York: Rand McNally and Company.

Goodwin, Grenville
    1942   The social organization of the Western Apache. Chicago:
            University of Chicago Press.

Grebinger, Paul, and Bruce Bradley
    1969   Excavations at a prehistoric camp site on the Mogollon Rim,
            east central Arizona. The Kiva 34: 109-123.

Green, M.
    1975   Patterns of variation in chipped stone raw materials for
            the Chevelon drainage. MS. M.A. thesis, Department of
            Anthropology, State University of New York at Binghamton.

Gumerman, George J. (editor)
    1971   The distribution of prehistoric population aggregates.
            Prescott College Anthropological Reports 1. Prescott, Arizona.

Gumerman, George J. and A. Olson
    1968   Prehistory in the Puerco Valley, eastern Arizona.
            Plateau 40: 113-127

Gumerman, George J. and S. Skinner
    1968   A synthesis of the prehistory of the central Little Colorado
            Valley, Arizona. American Antiquity 33: 185-199.

Hartman, Dana
    1978   Archaeological investigations: Salt River Project-
            Coronado-Silverking transmission line- 2 3/4 mi. segment
            of APS-SRP common corridor, federal land, Navajo County,
            Arizona. MS. Museum of Northern Arizona, Department of
            Anthropology, A-77-154.

Haury, Emil W. and L. Hargrave
    1931   Recently dated pueblo ruins in Arizona. Smithsonian
            Miscellaneous Collections 82 (11).

Heindl, L. and J. Lance
    1960   Topographic, physiographic, and structural subdivisions of
            Arizona. Arizona Geological Society Digest 3: 12-18.

Higgs, Eric (editor)
    1975   Paleoeconomy. Cambridge: Cambridge University Press.

    1972   Papers in economic prehistory. Cambridge: Cambridge
            University Press.

Hough, W.
    1903   Archaeological field work in northeastern Arizona: the
            Museum-Gates expedition of 1901. Annual Report of the
            U.S. National Museum for 1901, pp. 279-358. Washington.

Hunt, C.
    1956   Cenozoic geology of the Colorado Plateau. U.S. Geological
            Survey Professional Paper 279. Washington.

Jacobs, Mike
1977   Historic significance of General Crook's Road. In
        Research proposal for APS-CS-2091, an archaeological site
        to be affected by construction of the Arizona Public
        Service Cholla-Saguaro 500 kV transmission line, pp. 7-13. MS.
        Cultural Resource Management Section, Arizona State Museum,
        Tucson.

Keller, D., and S. Wilson.
1976   New light on the Tolchaco problem. The Kiva 41: 225-239.

Kelly, R.
1969   An archaeological survey in the Payson Basin, central Arizona.
        Plateau 42: 46-65.

Leaf, Murray J.
1974   Frontiers of anthropology: an introduction to anthropo-
        logical thinking. New York: D. Van Nostrand.

Ligner, J., N. White, L. Kister, and M. Moss
1969   Water resources. In Mineral and water resources of Arizona.
        Arizona Bureau of Mines Bulletin 180, Part II, p. 471-569.

Lindsay, A., J. Mueller, S. Carothers, R. Johnson, and G. Billingsley
1970   The archaeological, biological and geological resources of
        the proposed Wilkens Reservoir locality. National Park
        Service Bureau of Reclamation, Order No. 931-21.

Littell, N.
1966   Proposed findings of fact in behalf of the Navajo tribe of
        Indians in San Carlos--Northern Tonto overlap (Dockets
        22-D and 22-J). Before the Indian Claims Commission.
        Multilithed.

Longacre, William A.
1962   Archaeological reconnaissance in eastern Arizona.
        In Martin and others, pp. 148-167.

1964   A synthesis of upper Little Colorado prehistory, eastern
        Arizona. In Martin and others, pp. 201-215.

Lowe, Charles H.
1964   Arizona's natural environment. Tucson: University of
        Arizona Press.

Martin, Paul S., William A. Longacre, and James N. Hill
1967   Chapters in the prehistory of eastern Arizona, III.
        Fieldiana: Anthropology, Vol. 57. Chicago.

Martin, Paul S. and John B. Rinaldo
    1960   Excavations in the upper Little Colorado drainage, eastern
            Arizona. Fieldiana: Anthropology, Vol. 51 (1). Chicago.

Martin, Paul S., John B. Rinaldo, William A. Longacre, Constance Cronin,
    Leslie G. Freeman, Jr., and James Schoenwetter
    1962   Chapters in the prehistory of eastern Arizona, 1.
            Fieldana: Anthropology, Vol. 53. Chicago.

Martin, Paul S., John B. Rinaldo, William A. Longacre, Leslie G. Freeman, Jr.,
    James A. Brown, Richard H. Hevly, and M. E. Cooley
    1964   Chapters in the prehistory of eastern Arizona, II.
            Fieldiana: Anthropology, Vol. 55. Chicago.

Martin, Paul S., Ezra B. W. Zubrow, Daniel C. Bowman, David A. Gregory,
    John A. Hanson, Michael B. Schiffer, and David R. Wilcox
    1975   Chapters in the prehistory of eastern Arizona, IV.
            Fieldiana: Anthropology, Vol. 65. Chicago.

Mayro, Linda
    1976a   An archaeological resurvey of the area between towers
            156 and 167 on the proposed Cholla-Saguaro 500 kV
            transmission line (Arizona Public Service), crossing the
            Apache-Sitgreaves and Tonto national forests, Arizona.
            MS. Cultural Resource Management Section, Arizona State
            Museum, Tucson.

    1976b   An archaeological resurvey of the area between towers
            APS 167-184A and SRP 167-185 on the proposed Cholla-
            Saguaro 500 kV transmission line (Arizona Public Service),
            crossing the Apache-Sitgreaves and Tonto national forests,
            Arizona. MS. Cultural Resource Management Section,
            Arizona State Museum, Tucson.

Mayro, Linda and Christopher Causey
    1976   An archaeological resurvey of the area between towers
            139-156 on the proposed Cholla-Saguaro 500 kV trans-
            mission line (Arizona Public Service), crossing the
            Apache-Sitgreaves and Tonto national forests, Arizona.
            MS. Cultural Resource Management Section, Arizona State
            Museum, Tucson.

Mayro, Linda, Christopher Causey, and Robert Hard
    1977   An archaeological resurvey of the area between towers 96
            and 123 on the proposed Cholla-Saguaro 500 kV transmission
            line (Arizona Public Service), crossing the Apache-
            Sitgreaves and Tonto national forests, Arizona. MS.
            Cultural Resource Management Section, Arizona State
            Museum, Tucson.

Meurisse, R. and J. Williams
    1966   Soil management report, Winslow Ranger District, Coconino
            National Forest. USDA Forest Service, Southwestern
            Region, Division of Watershed Management. Alburquerque.

Olson, Alan P.
  1963   Some archaeological problems of central and northeastern
          Arizona. Plateau 35 (3) 93-106.

Plog, Fred T.
  1972   Explaining variability in the distribution of prehistoric
          settlements. MS. Department of Anthropology, Arizona State
          University, Tempe.

  1974   Settlement patterns and social history. In Leaf, pp. 68-91.

  1975   The Chevelon Archaeological Research Project. Paper presented
          at the 40th Annual Meeting of the Society for American
          Archaeology, Dallas.

  1976   Ceramic analysis. In Plog, Hill, and Read, pp. 58-78.

  1978   An analysis of variability in site locations in the Chevelon
          drainage, Arizona. In Investigations of the Southwestern
          Anthropological Research Group: an experiment in archaeological
          cooperation, edited by Robert C. Euler and George J. Gumerman,
          pp. 53-71. Flagstaff: Museum of Northern Arizona.

Plog, Fred T., James N. Hill, and Dwight W. Read (editors)
  1976a   Chevelon archaeological research project, 1971-1972.
          Monograph II of the Archaeological Survey. Department
          of Anthropology, University of California, Los Angeles.

Plog, Fred T., James N. Hill, and Dwight W. Read
  1976b   Future research plans. In Plog, Hill, and Read, pp. 146-167.

  1976c   Introduction to the research. In Plog, Hill, and Read, pp. 1-5.

Plog, Fred and Shirley Powell McAllister
  1978   Small sites in the Chevelon drainage. In Ward, pp. 17-23.

Plog, Stephen
  1976a   The inference of prehistoric social organization from
          ceramic design variability. Michigan Discussions in
          Anthropology 1: 1-47.

  1976b   Measurement of prehistoric interaction between communities.
          In The early Mesoamerican village, edited by Kent V. Flannery,
          pp. 255-272. New York: Academic Press.

  1976c   Relative efficiencies of sampling techniques for archaeo-
          logical surveys. In The early Mesoamerican village, edited
          by Kent V. Flannery, pp. 136-158. New York: Academic Press.

Plog, Stephen
 1977   A multivariate approach to the explanation of ceramic
         design variation. Ph.D. dissertation, University of
         Michigan. Ann Arbor: Microfilms Press.

Read, Dwight W.
 1976   The use and efficacy of random samples in regional surveys.
         In Plog, Hill, and Read, pp. 18-27.

Russell, R.
 1931   Dry climates of the United States. I. Climatic map.
         University of California Publications in Geography 5(1)1-41.

Satterthwait, L.
 1976   The Chevelon Creek area: environmental characteristics.
         In Plog, Hill, and Read, pp. 6-17.

Schroeder, A.
 1952   Documentary evidence pertaining to the early historic
         period of southern Arizona. New Mexico Historical Review
         27: 137-167.

 1974   A study of the Apache Indians. (Vols. 1,4). New York: Garland.

Sellers, William D.
 1972   The climate. In Arizona: its people and resources, by
         members of the Faculty of the University of Arizona.
         Revised second edition, pp. 87-92.

Siegel, S.
 1956   Nonparametric statistics for the behavioral sciences.
         New York: McGraw-Hill.

Simmons, A. H. and G. Ilany
 1977   What mean these bones? Behavioral implications of
         gazelles' remains from archaeological sites.
         Paleorient 3: 269-274.

Sims, Jack R., Jr. and D. Scott Daniel
    1967   A lithic assemblage near Winslow, Arizona. Plateau 39: 175-188.

Slatter, E., Fred T. Plog, and Stephen Plog
    1976   Chevelon site data. In Plog, Hill, and Read, pp. 28-40.

Smith, H.
    1945   The climate of Arizona. University of Arizona Agricultural
            Experiment Station Bulletin 197.

Spier, Leslie
    1918   Notes on some Little Colorado ruins. American Museum of
            Natural History Anthropological Papers 18 (4). New York.

Vita-Finzi, C. and Eric Higgs
    1970   Prehistoric economy in the Mount Carmel area of Palestine:
            site catchment analysis. Proceedings of the Prehistoric
            Society 36: 1-37.

Vivian, R. Gwinn
    1969   Archaeological salvage on the Pinedale and Clay Springs
            sections, Payson-Showlow highway, State Route 160: a
            preliminary report. MS. Cultural Resource Management
            Section, Arizona State Museum, University of Arizona, Tucson.

Ward, Albert C. (compiler and editor)
    1978   Limited activity and occupation sites: a collection of
            conference papers. Contributions to Anthropological
            Studies 1. Center for Anthropological Studies, Albuquerque.

Wendorf, F. and T. Thomas
    1951   Early man sites near Concho, Arizona. American Antiquity 17: 107-114.

White, C.
    1976   Prehistoric warfare in the Chevelon Creek area: an eco-
            logical approach. In Plog, Hill and Read, pp. 126-145.

Wilson, Eldred D.
    1962   A résumé of the geology of Arizona. Arizona Bureau of
            Mines Bulletin 171.

Wilson, J.
    1967   Another archaeological survey in east-central Arizona:
            preliminary report. Plateau 39: 157-168.

    1969   The Sinagua and their neighbors. Unpublished Ph.D.
            dissertation, Department of Anthropology, Harvard University.

CHAPTER 5

THE Q RANCH STUDY AREA
by Richard S. Ciolek-Torrello
and Richard C. Lange

Introduction

The central portion of the APS Cholla-to-Saguaro 500 kV Transmission Line Project traverses the mountain belt of central Arizona. Archaeological sites within this traverse (the Mogollon Rim to APS Tower location 325) appear distinct in their environmental and cultural characteristics from sites in other portions of the transmission line corridor. A broad study area has been defined around the central portion of the line in order to enhance our understanding of these sites (Figure 11a). This region, the Q Ranch, encompasses areas within four USGS quadrangles (15-minute series): Young (1961), Chediski Peak (1961), McFadden Peak (1949), and Blue House Mountain (1946) (Figure 11b).

Environment and Physiography

Physiography

The region lies in the Transition Zone, an area characterized by close groupings of eroded mountain ranges and marked altitudinal varia-tions. It is south of and topographically below the Mogollon Rim, and north of the Salt River. Thus, it lies between the Colorado Plateau to the north and the desert areas to the south. North of the Mogollon Rim, water flows into the Little Colorado River. Most runoff from the Transi-tion Zone eventually flows into the Salt River (Harris 1974:6).

The study area is bounded by several major physiographic features: on the north, Naegelin Rim and Carrizo Ridge; on the east, Cibecue Creek and Cibecue Ridge; on the south, the Salt River, Mustang Ridge, and Sombrero Peak; and on the west, Cherry Creek and the Sierra Ancha (Figure 11a). There are five main types of physiographic features in this study region: plateaus, mountains (a category which also includes major ridges and large mesas), smaller ridges and mesas, basins, and canyons.

In Permian times, the study area was probably a single plateau. Subsequent structural changes dating from this period on, such as faulting, uplifting, and erosion, created a series of smaller plateaus. These are

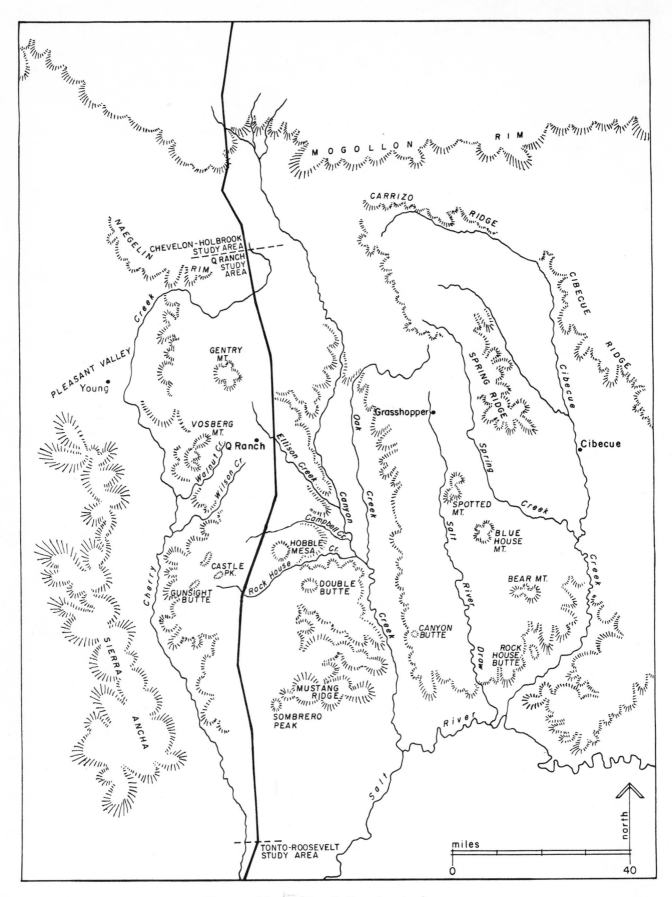

Figure 11a. The Q Ranch study area

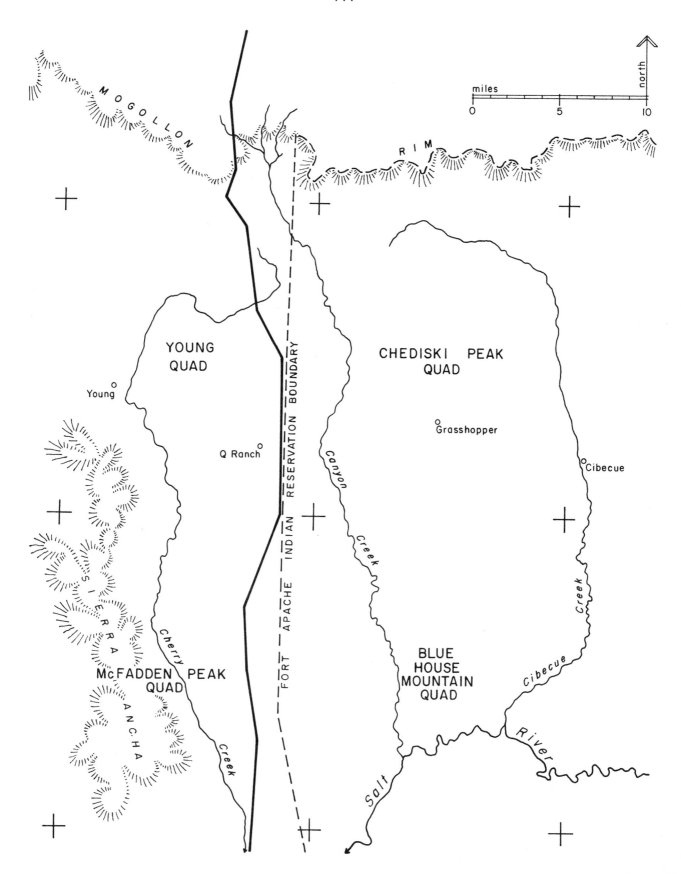

Figure 11b. The Q Ranch study area, with location of USGS quadrangles

more properly referred to as blocks, but will be referred to below as plateaus to be consistent with the existing archaeological literature. The study region contains two such plateaus, here designated the Q Ranch Plateau, lying between Cherry and Canyon creeks, and the Salt Draw Plateau, lying between Canyon and Cibecue creeks.

The higher elevations within these plateaus (mountains, large mesas, and ridges) represent surfaces which have survived the erosional processes altering the original character of the plateaus. Examples of these features in the region include: Spotted, Blue House, and Bear mountains on the Salt Draw Plateau; and Vosberg and Gentry mountains (actually large mesas), Mustang Ridge, Sombrero Peak, Castle Peak, and Gunsight Butte on the Q Ranch Plateau.

The smaller ridges and mesas, though topographically less prominent, are still important features in that they serve to further divide the larger plateaus and influence accessibility to the major features. Deep dissection, particularly in the southern portion of the plateaus, has created hundreds of these minor ridges. In this category are the numerous unnamed ridges and mesas, and named features such as Hobble Mesa, Rock House Butte, and Canyon Butte.

Numerous basins occur at middle to high elevations in the plateaus, although these are structurally somewhat different between the two plateaus. The basins are shallow depressions with low gradients defined by the major and minor physiographic features discussed above. Examples of these features are the Rock House Creek, Walnut Creek, Q Ranch-Ellison Creek, and Salt Draw basins.

The last features typical of the study area are the canyons. These range from deep, steep-walled cuts into the plateaus to less rugged, narrow drainages. The two plateaus are separated and defined by the major canyons in the area, along Cherry, Canyon, and Cibecue creeks. These drainages form natural communication routes from the Mogollon Rim to the Tonto Basin. Numerous smaller canyons have been cut by the drainages which flow into these three perennial north-south streams. The nature of these feeder canyons provides an interesting starting point for a comparison of the two plateaus.

The Q Ranch Plateau

The Q Ranch Plateau is bordered by the steep canyons containing Cherry and Canyon creeks. Across the creeks from the plateau, the canyon walls rise above the plateau, obviously to a much greater extent on the Sierra Ancha side. The Q Ranch Plateau drains bidirectionally into Cherry and Canyon creeks. Thus, the higher elevations are concentrated toward the center of the plateau. The plateau can generally be characterized as heavily dissected.

More major subcanyons or drainages (a mile or more in length) enter Cherry Creek from the east than from the west (at a ratio of almost two to one). Cherry Creek also has a greater number of these (22) than do the other major drainages. The nearly vertical eastern face of the Sierra Ancha range is the limiting factor in developing larger drainages to the west.

Drainages entering Canyon Creek present a mirror image to those of Cherry Creek. Canyon Creek has 16 major subcanyons or drainages roughly evenly divided between entering from the east or west. However, the drainages entering from the west are much bigger, deeper, and longer than those on the east. A vertical face east of Canyon Creek limits the length of major drainages in a manner similar to the Sierra Ancha range west of Cherry Creek.

Because of heavy dissection, flat land on the Q Ranch Plateau is limited to small pockets and several basins. These are relatively small (less than 10 square miles each) and occur frequently at the headwaters of drainages where multiple smaller streams come together. They are defined by watersheds and various combinations of the physiographic features in the region. A large amount of flat land may be available along the bottoms of the long canyons penetrating the Q Ranch Plateau. Accessibility to the interior of the plateau is also enhanced by these numerous deep canyons.

The Salt Draw Plateau

To the east of Canyon Creek is the Salt Draw Plateau, the second major block in the region. This plateau is bounded on the north by mountains and a series of ridges just south of the Mogollon Rim. On the south it is bounded by steep canyons cutting down to the Salt River. In contrast to the Q Ranch Plateau, the Salt Draw Plateau is topographically much less dissected.

As noted above, the Salt Draw Plateau is penetrated on the west by fewer relatively short canyons or drainages. On the east, Cibecue Creek has even fewer subcanyons (13) than either of the other two creeks. The longer canyons enter predominantly from the west side of Cibecue Creek.

The shorter and narrower canyons penetrating the Salt Draw Plateau create three important considerations. First, the Salt Draw Plateau is less accessible from the south, east, or west through canyons. Second, "flat" areas on the plateau are concentrated above the canyons. Third, canyon bottom land is much reduced in comparison with the Q Ranch Plateau.

The Salt Draw Plateau is also slightly higher on the western edge and is folded in the center. This produces a situation in which runoff flows into a single north-south trending drainage, the Salt River Draw.

The draw, however, drains a very limited area. Little runoff is received from the mountains or Mogollon Rim to the north since these are drained to the west by Canyon and Oak creeks and to the east by Spring, Salt, and Cibecue creeks. In addition, the basins of the Salt Draw Plateau are merely subdivisions of a large valley paralleling the course of the Salt River Draw. Thus, in contrast to the Q Ranch Plateau, these are not headwater basins, but flat flanks along a single drainage.

Thus, while the two plateaus are similar in size and type of physiographic features, several important differences are apparent. These differences include the degree of dissection, the ratio of canyon bottom land to plateau top "flat land", length and number of major sub-canyons, direction of drainage from the plateau, and basin position with respect to watersheds. These similarities and differences should have significant implications for the prehistoric occupation of the area.

Elevation

Elevations in the study region range from under 3000 feet above mean sea level at the juncture of the major drainages with the Salt River (Cherry Creek-2480 feet, Canyon Creek-2905 feet, and Cibecue Creek-3163 feet) to over 7000 feet on the higher mountains and ridges. In general, the two plateaus average between 5000 and 6000 feet in elevation.

Geology

Geologically, the Q Ranch Plateau and the Salt Draw Plateau are considerably different. Data for the following descriptions were derived from Harris (1974), Moore (1968), Tuggle (1970), Wilson (1928), and Wilson (1962). Represented in the study region are exposed surfaces dating from Precambrian to Quaternary times. The Q Ranch Plateau is presently primarily Precambrian, while the Salt Draw Plateau is largely Paleozoic. However, due to shifting of these major blocks relative to one another, these plateaus are similar in elevation while being dissimilar in their exposed strata.

The major shift of the blocks occurred along Canyon Creek, a drainage which follows an identified major north-south fault. Cherry Creek is probably also along a major fault, although Douglas Shakel has informed the author that sufficiently detailed mapping has not yet occurred in the area to identify the fault as such. This interpretation is possible because the Sierra Ancha range, while stratigraphically similar to the Q Ranch block, is topographically higher.

The Q Ranch Plateau is composed largely of Younger Precambrian, Apache Group Mescal limestone. An intrusive Precambrian to Tertiary diabase is also prevalent as sills and dikes. Higher topographical features in the west-central portion of the plateau also show some undivided Younger Precambrian, Cambrian, and Devonian sandstone and quartzite. Scattered Quaternary and Tertiary sand, silt, gravel, and conglomerate occur as isolates in the central and north-central portions of the plateau, and as a more expansive formation in the northwestern part of the plateau (Pleasant Valley). Older Precambrian granite and related crystalline intrusives also occur in the Pleasant Valley area.

Older Precambrian granite and related crystalline intrusives; Older Precambrian diorite porphyry; Tertiary gravel, sand, and conglomerate; and Tertiary dacite occur in the southern portion of the plateau. In addition, there are anomalous occurrences of Quaternary-Tertiary basalt in the southeastern section of the plateau.

Carboniferous and Devonian strata (limestone, shale, and sandstone) west of Canyon Creek are limited to the extreme northern portion of the plateau, above the Naegelin Rim, and atop the high peaks of the Sierra Ancha.

The Salt Draw Plateau contains many of these same strata. In the northwest section, along the Canyon Creek fault, and to the south where the plateau has been heavily dissected, the Mescal limestone, intrusive diabase, and undivided sandstone and quartzite are present. However, the major portion of the plateau is composed of Carboniferous and Devonian limestone, shale, and sandstone (which includes the Naco Formation) and the Permian Supai Formation (siltstone, sandstone, and limestone). On higher topographical features, such as Blue House and Bear mountains, Tertiary sandstone, shale, and conglomerate and Quaternary-Tertiary basalt are also present.

Lithic Resources

The geological differences noted in the plateaus produce obvious differences in rock and mineral resources which were immediately available. Building materials on the Q Ranch Plateau are usually diabase or quartzite cobbles or limestone slabs; sandstone is rare. On the Salt Draw Plateau, sandstone and limestone are both available in quantity. Basalt, though present on the Salt Draw Plateau, was not used for grinding purposes. Metates from sites on the Q Ranch Plateau are often of sandstone.

Asbestos and, by association, serpentine and soapstone are part of the Mescal Limestone Formation. These, of course, are more accessible on the Q Ranch Plateau where the stratum is most widely exposed. Some asbestos occurs in Pinal County, but the principal Arizona deposits are in Coconino (Grand Canyon area) and Gila counties. Rock House and Sloan creeks were both centers of major mining operations in recent times (1920s-1950s) because of the high-quality asbestos available there. Logical sources for much of the serpentine and soapstone used in central Arizona prehistorically, as suggested by Harris (1974), are the exposures in Gila and Pinal counties, particularly in the areas around Rock House and Sloan creeks.

Turquoise occurs in small quantities in the Dripping Springs quartzite in lower Canyon Creek; this was exploited prehistorically. Salt occurs in only one major deposit in the study region. Near the mouth of Salt Draw are some small saline springs which have deposited a mantle of salt as the water runs into the Salt River. This salt bank "contributes materially to the salinity of the Salt River" (Wilson 1928:34). Salt is also known from the Supai Formation in south-central Navajo and Apache counties, 97 to 113 km (60 to 70 miles) from the center of the study region.

Known metalliferous deposits in the region are mostly restricted to the Q Ranch Plateau. These include deposits of zinc, copper, lead, and silver on the Naegelin Rim; copper south of Shell Mountain and along Cherry Creek; and gold, silver, and copper south of Sombrero Peak. Iron and copper are noted for the Salt Draw Plateau, occurring in the northwestern portion of the plateau.

Climate

Climate in the region has been characterized as typified by cold, moist winters; warm, dry springs; and hot, moist summers (Chenhall 1972:17). Frost-free days average about 160 per year. Temperatures (averaged for the four reporting stations closest to the plateaus: Payson, Young, Sierra Ancha, and Cibecue) range from a minimum of 22 degrees F (-5.6 degrees C) to a maximum of 93 degrees F (34.2 degrees C). Days with temperatures below 32 degrees F (0 degrees C) average 140 per year, and days with temperatures in excess of 90 degrees F (32.5 degrees C) average 70 per year (although Young itself averages 111 per year).

Precipitation is strongly biseasonal, occurring mostly in winter and late summer. Rains are most often associated with brief but severe storms and average 55.9 cm (22 inches) per year. The Sierra Ancha, on the western edge of the study region, receives some of the heaviest rainfall in the state, but the storms are usually less severe after they have passed over into the plateaus to the east (Chenhall 1972:17).

Similarily, to the north, the high face of the Mogollon Rim serves to block moisture from reaching the Colorado Plateau. Comparisons of yearly averages from Cibecue (south of the rim = 48.3 cm (19 inches) per

year) and Holbrook (north of the rim = 22.9 cm (9 inches)per year) show
that the areas to the south receive much greater rainfall due to the
rain shadow effect of the rim (Peirce 1967:7).

Water Resources

Water resources in the study area center around the perennial
streams--Cherry, Canyon, and Cibecue creeks. Coinciding with the precipitation regime are two flood periods--spring, from the snowpack melt,
and late summer. Within the major land blocks, available water is limited
to perennial and seasonal springs or seeps and the intermittent streams.

Springs and seeps are perhaps more prevalent in the Q Ranch block
because the numerous minor faults would seem to create more possible
situations for underground reservoirs. This seems to be borne out by
U.S. Forest Service maps showing spring locations in the four quadrangles
of the study region. However, there are no definite correlations between
faults and springs in this area; that is, no formal study has been done,
and the USFS plots may reveal only the more commonly known springs.

The intermittent streams run for only two or three days following
major storms, but numerous natural catch basins will hold water for weeks
afterwards.

Agriculture

Agricultural potential in the region appears generally to be
good. Although some soils are extremely sandy and thus poor, many soils
have sufficient balances of nutrients, silt, clay, and appropriate
particle size to be adequately productive. These soils are derived
from decay of the local geological formations, including diabase, shale,
siltstone, sandstone, quartzite, and limestone. Slope angle, facing,
and water availability also determine the agricultural potential of a
particular locale.

The short average growing season, necessitating rapidly maturing
crops, and a general lack of water during the early growth stages are
both problems that had to be overcome by early agriculturalists. Solutions could have been found in planting practices and in water control.
Deep planting of seeds would have permitted early planting with some
insulation against minor frosts or brief freezes, and also have provided
access to groundwater supplies (Cartledge 1976:147-8). Check dams and
other water-control features would have served to retain or channel water,
thus maximizing what few sources there may have been during the early part
of the growing season (Rodgers 1970).

Flora and Fauna

The study area contains a highly varied set of biological communities. Generally, the region shows a mixed association of grassland,
chaparral, woodland, and pine forest (Cartledge 1976:138). Plants
representative of the Lower Sonoran palo-verde community; of the grassland, chaparral, and woodland (evergreen and riparian) communities of
the Upper Sonoran Life Zone; and of the ponderosa pine forest of the
Transition Zone exist at various locations, dependent upon several factors.

Cartledge (1976:139) qualifies the value of regional indices
such as precipitation and growing season because of the aggregate effect
of such factors as elevation, slope facing, slope angle, water availability, and soil composition on vegetational patterns in a specific
locale. In a heavily dissected environment such as that of this region,
combinations of these factors interact to form infinite variations of
the major biotic communities.

Given this great variety, the easiest approach to presenting a
biological description of the region is to provide brief floral and
faunal lists for the "pure" form of each major community.

The Lower Sonoran palo-verde community occurs along the Salt
River. It extends up Cherry Creek to the vicinity of Banning Wash,
at which point it merges with an Upper Sonoran desert grassland com-
munity. This also applies to Canyon Creek up to the vicinity of Mustang
Ridge. The Lower Sonoran palo-verde community has as its typical vege-
tation little-leaf palo-verde (Cercidium microphyllum),blue palo-verde
(C. floridum), saguaro (Cereus giganteus), teddybear cholla (Opuntia
Bigelovii), ocotillo (Fouquieria splendens), Canotia holacantha,crucifixion-
thorn (Holacantha Emoryi), mesquite (Prosopis juliflora), and catclaw
(Acacia Greggii)(Lowe 1964:24-6).

The Upper Sonoran desert grassland community consists of sotol
(Dasylirion Wheeleri), fluff grass (Tridens pulchellus), prickly-pear
(Opuntia Engelmannii), white-thorn (Acacia constricta), and occasional
mesquite (Prosopis juliflora) and one-seed juniper (Juniperus monosperma)
(Lowe 1964:40-5). It occurs between 3500 and 5000 feet, with its best
development between 4000 and 5000 feet. Pockets of this community occur
quite far up the major drainages at lower elevations.

The Upper Sonoran chaparral community in the region often occurs
as an understory for other communities. It generally occurs between
4000 and 6000 feet and includes various evergreen and deciduous shrubs:
shrub live oak (Quercus turbinella), manzanita (Arctostaphylos pungens;
A. Pringlei), turpentine-brush (Aplopappus laricifolius), cliff-rose
(Cowania mexicana), buck-thorn (Rhamnus spp.), squaw-bush (Rhus trilobata),
mountain-mahogany (Cercocarpus spp.), Apache-plume (Fallugia paradoxa),
and wait-a-bit (Mimosa biuncifera)(Lowe 1964:49-50; Chenhall 1972:25).

Most of the region is classified as Upper Sonoran woodland. This community has riparian and evergreen components typically occurring between 5500 and 7000 feet. The evergreen component in central and northern Arizona is essentially a pinyon-juniper woodland. Below 6500 feet, the plant community is often that of a juniper-grass savanna. Common species include: pinyon pine (Pinus edulis), Utah juniper (Juniperus osteosperma), one-seed juniper (J. monosperma), alligator juniper (J. deppeana), shrub live oak (Quercus turbinella), Emory oak (Q. Emoryi), Palmer oak (Q. Palmeri), various grasses including blue grama (Bouteloua gracilis), Arizona fescue (Festuca arizonica), and mountain muhly (Muhlenbergia montana) and other species such as cliff-rose (Cowania mexicana), prickly-pear (Opuntia polyacantha), and rabbit-brush (Chrysothamnus nauseosus) (Lowe 1964:56-60).

The riparian woodland component consists of Arizona walnut (Juglans major), Pacific willow (Salix lasiandra), velvet ash (Fraxinus velutina), netleaf hackberry (Celtis reticulata), southwestern choke-cherry (Prunus virens), and canyon grape (Vitis arizonica) (Chenhall 1972:26).

The Transition Zone ponderosa pine forest usually occurs between 6000 and 9000 feet. The dominant vegetation is, of course, ponderosa pine (Pinus ponderosa), although, in the study area, this rarely occurs in pure stands. The understory often consists of woodland and chaparral shrubs and grasses: buck-thorn (Rhamnus spp.), manzanita (Arctostaphylos spp.), mountain yucca (Yucca Schottii), scarlet sumac (Rhus glabra), Arizona fescue (Festuca arizonica), mountain muhly (Muhlenbergia montana), and blue grama (Bouteloua gracilis). Various species of oak, as well as pinyon, occur frequently in association with the ponderosa in most of the study area (Chenhall 1972:24; Lowe 1964:63-8).

The following list, far from comprehensive, notes several of the animals typically found within the study area: lizards (including horned lizards), rattlesnakes, blue heron, red-tail hawk, owl, dove, quail, wild turkey, skunk, ground squirrel, jackrabbit, cottontail rabbit, javelina, mule deer, elk, coyote, mountain lion, and bear.

Thus, the Q Ranch area is extremely diversified in terms of the biotic and abiotic resources available to a prehistoric human population. This variety of resources and situations would have permitted a number of solutions for coping with the environment and its fluctuations, given a primitive technology.

Previous Archaeological Research

Early archaeological research in the Q Ranch and nearby regions has primarily been both brief and sporadic. Serious investigations began early in the 20th century through a series of reconnaissances by Hough (1903, 1919, 1920) and Spier (1919) in the large region between the Mogollon Rim and the Salt River. Hough (1920, 1935) followed upon his earlier work with exploratory excavations at the Grasshopper Ruin on the Salt Draw

Plateau. Reconnaisance within this large region was continued in the
early 1930s by the newly established Gila Pueblo research group. The
activities of this group resulted in the location of cliff sites in the
Sierra Ancha and several ruins in the vicinity of Young, Q Ranch, and
Grasshopper.

The first intensive investigations in the region were begun by
Emil Haury under the auspices of Gila Pueblo. Following the earlier
work of Gila Pueblo, Haury (1934) carried out an intensive study of cliff
ruins found in the canyons surrounding the Q Ranch region on the west,
south, and east. Most of the sites investigated were on the eastern
slopes of the Sierra Ancha, with several additional sites on Mustang Ridge
and a branch of Canyon Creek. Among the latter was the Canyon Creek
Ruin, where investigation involved intensive excavation and produced the
first complete description of any archaeological remains in the region.

A 30-year hiatus in archaeological research followed these early
studies. This situation changed in the 1960s with the inception of intensive, long-term research programs by the University of Arizona and
Arizona State University. The University of Arizona Archaeological Field
School began work on the Salt Draw Plateau in 1963. Like the earlier
work of Hough, the focus of the Field School's work was on the Grasshopper
Ruin (Thompson and Longacre 1966; Longacre and Reid 1974). In 15 seasons
of work to date, the ruin's architectural boundaries have been outlined
and about 20 percent of its more than 400 ground-floor rooms have been
excavated. Additionally, excavation has included a great kiva and tests
in two plazas, corridors, and other outdoor areas. In recent years,
interest has expanded to include excavations at a nearby small pueblo
(the Chodistaas Site) predating the large ruin (Robertson 1977, 1978)
and further dendrochronological studies of Canyon Creek Pueblo and Red
Rock House, a small cliff ruin in a tributary canyon of Oak Creek.

Regional research has also played a major role in the Field School's
recent research. In 1969, H.D. Tuggle (1970:4, 34) surveyed for his dissertation research an extensive, 25-percent random sample of the region
between Canyon and Cibecue creeks. This was followed in 1974 with the
beginning of an intensive survey of the area within a 3-mile (4.8 km)
radius of the Grasshopper Ruin. Tuggle also returned in 1977 to conduct
a survey of the escarpment that separates the Salt Draw Plateau and Canyon
Creek. Together, these surveys have located over 300 sites in the area
bounded by Canyon Creek, Carrizo Ridge, Cibecue Creek, and the Salt River.

Just 19 km (12 miles) west of the Grasshopper Ruin, the Arizona
State University Archaeological Field School maintained an intensive
research program from 1967 through 1971 in the upper reaches of Walnut
and Wilson creeks on the Q Ranch Plateau. During these four years, test excavations were carried out at several sites in the Vosberg district, the headwater basin of Walnut Creek. These tests produced archaeological materials
from different time periods in the prehistoric occupation of the area

(Morris 1969, 1970, personal communication; Chenhall 1972; Cartedge 1976; A.E. Dittert, personal communication; Harris 1974). In addition to these excavations, an intensive survey of the Walnut Creek and Wilson Creek areas was carried out (Chenhall 1972). Cartledge (1976) supplemented this work in 1974 with transect samples of the Vosberg district. Together these surveys located 87 sites within this small area.

Additional contributions to our understanding of the prehistory of the Q Ranch region have been provided by several short-term projects. The Arizona Highway Salvage program conducted a series of small-scale excavations in the mountainous transition zone of east-central Arizona. One of these excavations is of interest to this review, in that it involved the excavation of eleven burials associated with a large, late prehistoric pueblo near Young, Arizona (Harrill 1969).

Finally, surveys by Kelly (1969) and Wells (1971) provide limited information about the Payson area and lower Cherry Creek on the western and southern peripheries of the Q Ranch region, respectively. Archaeological investigations to the north and south of the Q Ranch study area are discussed in other sections of this volume.

Culture History

The Q Ranch region, though generally placed within the archaeologically defined Mogollon area (Bullard 1962; Johnson 1965), exhibits numerous elements typical of what are referred to as Salado and Hohokam material cultures. The area is definitely a cultural border zone and displays a mixture of cultural elements throughout the period of prehistoric occupation.

Table 23 summarizes the two major chronologies (Chenhall 1972; Tuggle 1970) of the Q Ranch region, and compares them with the more widely used chronology of the Forestdale Branch of the Mogollon (Haury and Sayles 1947; Haury, personal communication).

Archaic

The earliest prehistoric occupation of the Q Ranch region is attested by sites in several areas. These early sites are characterized by projectile points similar to those found in early horizons in the Petrified Forest (Wendorf 1953) and by an absence of ceramics and definable structures. They have been located in the Vosberg district (Chenhall 1972) and, according to Michael Graves, near the Grasshopper Ruin. Those sites in the Vosberg district have been interpreted as sparse and scattered evidence of early hunting camps predating A.D. 700 (Chenhall 1972).

Table 23. Chronologies for the Q Ranch region

CHENHALL (1972:52-55)	TUGGLE (1970)	HAURY (1947)	DATE
ANGLO	APACHE	SHOW LOW (ANGLO) / (APACHE) ALCHESAY	A.D. 1200 TO PRESENT
(APACHE)		SKIDI (APACHE)	A.D. 1700
			A.D. 1600
			A.D. 1500
ABANDONMENT	ABANDONMENT	ABANDONMENT	A.D. 1400
CERAMIC GROUP V LARGE MASONRY PUEBLOS	LATE MOGOLLON III LARGE MASONRY PUEBLOS	CANYON CREEK	A.D. 1300
ABANDONMENT		PINEDALE	A.D. 1200
CERAMIC GROUP IV BOULDER-COBBLE-JACAL STRUCTURES	LATE MOGOLLON II SMALL COBBLE-JACAL PUEBLOS	LINDEN	A.D. 1100
	LATE MOGOLLON I PIT HOUSES	CARRIZO	A.D. 1000
ABANDONMENT			
CERAMIC GROUP III PIT HOUSES		DRY VALLEY	A.D. 900
CERAMIC GROUP II PIT HOUSES	EARLY MOGOLLON	CORDUROY	A.D. 800
CERAMIC GROUP I PIT HOUSES		FORESTDALE	A.D. 700
PRECERAMIC HUNTING CAMPS		PIT HOUSES	A.D. 600
		COTTONWOOD	A.D. 500
			500 B.C.
		HILLTOP	

Early Villages

Small pit house villages of generally five to eight houses are characteristic of the Q Ranch region and nearby areas from A.D. 700-1000 (Chenhall 1972). On the Salt Draw Plateau, they occur slightly later, from A.D. 950-1100 (Tuggle 1970). These villages are often found at relatively low elevations on terraces and ridges above drainages (Tuggle 1970; Wells 1971).

During this period, the Q Ranch Plateau and Cherry Creek areas are characterized by considerable communication and, possibly, population exchange with areas farther to the north and south. Although local indigenous plainwares are the dominant pottery types, a variety of early Hohokam red-on-buff and early Anasazi black-on-white wares predominate among the decorated types in both Vosberg and lower Cherry Creek. In contrast, an early variety of Snowflake Black-on-white is the dominant decorated type on the Salt Draw Plateau (Tuggle 1970). This might indicate closer ties of the latter area to other Mogollon areas. This same variety of Snowflake, however, may also be present among the black-and-white types in Vosberg (Chenhall 1972:47).

Excavations in Vosberg also uncovered pit houses exhibiting both Hohokam and Anasazi-style architecture in the same village (Morris 1969, 1970). Morris interprets this pattern as a reflection of Hohokam-Anasazi cohabitation in the mountain zone. This proposition, however, conflicts with our understanding of the traditional subsistence base of the Hohokam, which involved the intensive agricultural exploitation of broad riverine valleys.

Early Pueblos

During the period A.D. 1000-1250, greater similarities are seen between the plateaus that make up the Q Ranch region. Sites are small, with architecture consisting of boulder or cobble-outline structures in the forms of single rooms and multiroom blocks of up to 30 rooms. The superstructures of these rooms appear to be made of jacal (Cartledge 1976). Excavations in Vosberg suggest that these houses were dug into shallow pits (Cartledge 1976; A.E. Dittert, personal communication). Most sites during this period are found on ridges at relatively higher elevations than during the previous period.

The decorated ceramic assemblage of this period is primarily composed of Snowflake Black-on-white, early White Mountain Red Wares, and early Salado polychromes. Among the plainwares, brown indented corrugated types are predominant, with Salado Red plainwares also occurring. In Vosberg, a crude brown plainware predominates over the corrugated wares in the early part of this period.

These data suggest a correspondence of developments in the Q Ranch region with those in other Mogollon areas and a divergence from developments in areas to the south and west during this period. Architectural techniques and site arrangement change radically in the lower Cherry Creek area after A.D. 1150. Masonry walls replace those of jacal, and many sites are surrounded by low walls (Cartledge 1976:44-5; Wells 1971). These sites are also located closer to the drainages than in earlier periods. This may also have been the period of maximum population in lower Cherry Creek (Wells 1971). Ceramics also present a contrast. Although brown corrugated and Salado redwares are present, Tonto Red is the dominant utility ware in this area. Decorated wares are similar to those from the plateau areas.

Similarly, the upper Tonto Creek and Payson areas present a contrast with the Q Ranch region. As in the case of the lower Cherry Creek area, Tonto Red is the predominant utility ware (Kelly 1969), while corrugated wares are virtually absent (Cartledge 1976). Although extremely low frequencies of decorated ceramics are reported for the Payson area, White Mountain Red Wares are the predominant polychromes, with Salado polychromes also reported (Kelly 1969).

Together, these data indicate widespread similarities between the Q Ranch and Salt Draw plateaus; these areas appear most similar between themselves than to other areas during this period. Some form of regional diversification appears to emerge, although the degree of extensive communication appears to remain about the same between most areas in east-central Arizona.

Aggregated Pueblos

The final period of prehistoric occupation, from A.D. 1250-1400, witnesses the aggregation of population into large pueblos and the development of a complex settlement system. In the plateau areas, this is associated with rapid population growth and what appears to be the occupation of virtually every topographic zone (Tuggle 1970:35). On the Salt Draw and Q Ranch plateaus, large, multistoried, coursed-masonry pueblos of 100-500 rooms are constructed in high meadows or flats in the headwater basins of major tributaries of the Salt River. Smaller sites (40-80 rooms) often occur in similar basins at those points where the drainages drop off into the canyons at the edges of the plateaus. Sites of even smaller size (10-20 rooms) are found scattered along ridges above canyon areas. The first major occupation of the canyon areas around the plateaus is indicated by the location of relatively large sites (20-80 rooms) in the cliffs above Canyon, Cibecue, and Cherry creeks. As a concomitant of these patterns, an increase in distance between villages has been observed (Tuggle 1970:40). Together, these patterns fit the general model of late Mogollon settlement systems (Bluhm 1957, 1960; Danson 1957).

Aggregation occurs in other areas immediately adjacent to the Q Ranch region. In contrast, however, these areas are characterized by a slow population increase or, in one case, a possible population decline. The Cibecue Creek area to the east of Salt Draw, for example, appears underpopulated, with a total population several times smaller than that on the plateau (Tuggle 1970:35). This differs markedly from the historic population distribution. A similar situation may hold true for the Young area immediately west of the Q Ranch Plateau.

The decorated ceramics of this period are essentially the same throughout the entire region. Pinedale Black-on-white and the late White Mountain Red Wares predominate. Late Salado polychromes, however, also occur in extremely large frequencies. Excavations at Grasshopper have revealed the development of the first local indigenous polychromes (Whittlesey 1974; Mayro, Whittlesey, and Reid 1976). Alfred E. Dittert has informed the author that similar ceramics occur at the Q Ranch Ruin. These data suggest a continuation of trends begun in the preceding period, involving the development of localized regional specialization but the maintenance of interregional contacts.

Abandonment

The period of population expansion and aggregation was followed by the complete abandonment of the entire region between the Mogollon Rim and the Salt River. Abandonment may have begun as early as A.D. 1350. By A.D. 1400, no significant population aggregates are known anywhere in the region. The region remained abandoned for several hundred years until the arrival of Athabaskan groups, possibly as early as the 17th century.

Historic Occupation

Athabaskan groups continued to occupy the Q Ranch region into the historic period. In this period the region was occupied by the Western Apache, specifically the Canyon Creek and Cibecue bands of the Cibecue group and several semibands of the Southern Tonto (Goodwin 1942:4-5). The Cibecue band farmed sites primarily along upper and middle Cibecue Creek, with additional farms along Salt and Spring creeks (Goodwin 1942:21). They ranged north to the Pinedale-Heber area above the Mogollon Rim and south to the Black River in hunting and gathering expeditions. Their western boundary, somewhere along the Salt Draw Plateau, was shared with the closely related Canyon Creek band (Goodwin 1942:21-2). The latter band farmed sites on Oak Creek, upper Canyon Creek, and Cherry Creek east of the Sierra Ancha. The Canyon Creek band also traveled north to Chevelon Butte, north of the Mogollon Rim, and south to the Salt River. Their western boundary was formed by the east edge of Pleasant Valley and the east slopes of the Sierra Ancha. Pleasant Valley and the western slope of the Sierra Ancha were used by the Southern Tonto group (Goodwin 1942:23).

Initially, habitation was in small temporary camps indicated today by stone circles (Haury's Skidi Phase), commonly found in association with prehistoric Mogollon or Salado sites. The Apache often reused building stone or even built their habitations within prehistoric rooms. Today most of the Apache are concentrated within a few large settlements (Haury's Alchesay Phase) such as Cibecue within the White Mountain Indian Reservation. The modern area of the reservation lies between the Mogollon Rim and the Salt River, and extends west to the east edge of the Q Ranch Plateau and east to the White Mountains.

The date of the first Anglo occupation of the Q Ranch region is not known. Pleasant Valley on the northwest periphery of the Q Ranch Plateau was permanently settled by 1882 (Forrest 1950:3), shortly after the establishment of the reservation boundaries to the east. By the turn of the century, several ranches and numerous small homesteads were scattered throughout the area west of the reservation. This early Anglo occupation was relatively intensive and is associated with the well-known Pleasant Valley War (Forrest 1950; Ellison 1968:14). Today ranching, mining, and lumbering are the major activities in the Q Ranch region. Thus, the region has been neatly bisected in recent times and occupied by two distinct ethnic groups: Canyon Creek, the Salt Draw Plateau, and parts east are occupied by the modern representatives of the Western Apache, while the Q Ranch Plateau, Cherry Creek, the Sierra Ancha, and areas to the west are occupied by Anglos.

Relevant Research Problems

The following discussion reviews the specific past research conducted in the Q Ranch region. All past research in the region is not considered or equally treated. Rather the discussion is organized according to particular problem domains that are deemed most relevant to a regional survey perspective. The aim of this discussion is to identify specific research problems relevant to the Q Ranch region and appraise the contributions of individual research efforts. This should provide a background for the examination of regional survey data and ultimately provide a foundation for the development of a regional research design.

Locational Studies

Like archaeologists working elsewhere, those in the Q Ranch region have shown a great interest in the identification of environmental factors influencing settlement location. Tuggle is the first to have addressed this problem in the region.

Tuggle (1970) proposed that elevation was an important factor in site location during the prehistoric period onthe Salt Draw Plateau. He observed that sites were clustered at different elevations during each time period. Most pit houses, for example, are located on terraces or benches 12 m (40 feet) to 73 m (240 feet) above and to either side of the Salt Draw. All of these sites are below the 6000-foot elevation contour. In the next period, most sites are located on small hills or bluffs in the more rugged zone above 6000 feet in the northern part of the Salt Draw Plateau. This pattern was not duplicated in the adjacent Cibecue area to the east or in the Oak Creek Valley to the west.

Additional locational information has been provided by analysis of Tuggle's data by members of the University of Arizona Archaeological Field School. Izumi Shimada has informed the author that these studies indicate that geology and soil types appear to be significant factors in altering site location through time. The earliest and latest sites on the Salt Draw Plateau are located on the Naco Formation, while intermediate-period (LM II) sites are on the Supai Formation. Intermediate-period sites also differ in being located on soils less susceptible to erosion. During this period sites appear most clustered and are characterized by the shortest intersite distance recorded; in the following period (LM III), this distance is the maximum for the entire prehistoric period (Shimada, personal communication; Tuggle 1970).

Other locational data have been provided by the initial work for the 3-mile survey project around the Grasshopper Ruin (Spain 1976). Spain points out that no large pueblos occur west of the Salt Draw within this area. Many pueblos, however, are found east of the draw. Spain interprets this dichotomy as a product of differential activity performance. Most of the sites found on the west side are interpreted as loci of specialized agricultural activities. Both habitation and specialized-activity loci are found on the east side, however. Spain proposes a research design relating land-capability classes and the location of agricultural features to population growth on the Salt Draw Plateau in order to explain this dichotomy.

The research proposed by Spain was inspired by the previous work of Rodgers (1970), Chenhall (1970), and Cartledge (1976) in the nearby Vosberg district. Rodgers classified architectural features, with inferred agricultural functions, located in the district. He identified eight distinct types of features which, in various combinations, serve as the "elements" of four agricultural systems. System A is composed of a single element, check dams, which function to conserve water and prevent soil erosion. Systems B, C, and D are diversion systems that differ in their complexity of elements and the type of topography and edaphic conditions involved. Rodgers (1970:11) observed particular patterning in the chronological placement of these systems. No architectural devices were employed prior to A.D. 1000, when alluvial areas on gentle slopes were apparently utilized. After A.D. 1050, perishable and permanent structures were built in these same areas. By A.D. 1100, cultivation of colluvial areas is dominant and associated with the construction of a variety of agricultural elements. This pattern continues until A.D. 1300, when the alluvial areas are again cultivated and permanent agricultural elements constructed. Rodgers (1970:12) proposes that this patterning reflects attempts by the local inhabitants to cope with changing environmental conditions.

In his examination of sampling strategies in archaeological surveys, Chenhall (1972) also focuses on the cultural relevance of particular environmental factors. He (1972:127) emphasizes a significant relationship between settlement locations and microenvironments, and concludes that there is a high probability that sites in the Vosberg district are located, regardless of temporal placement or function, within the pinyon-juniper-oak-manzanita-catclaw vegetation zone and on slopes facing (proceeding clockwise) between a southeastern and western direction. Slope angles of under 10 percent also appear to be significant characteristics of sites (Chenhall 1972:141-2). However, most land in the Vosberg district may be included within these microenvironments. The above vegetation zone, for example, is probably the most common one in the district. Chenhall does not attempt to control for size of zones in estimating probability of site occurrences.

Cartledge's (1976) research into changing coresidence patterns in the Vosberg district avoids the latter problem by the calculation of densities of cultural phenomena. Cartledge defines eight land-capability classes according to range of agricultural potential and then estimates the land area per class. He tests the proposition that population concentration should be associated with agricultural potential by correlating room counts and land-capability classes. Only after conversion of these counts to a density measure does he find a significant positive correlation between agricultural potential and number of rooms. Cartledge also investigates the temporal dimension of this pattern, with inconclusive results. Finally, employing Rodgers' data, Cartledge correctly predicts that agricultural systems were more numerous, larger, and more elaborate during the later periods of occupation in the Vosberg district. This conclusion, like those of Rodgers, suffers from the difficulty of assigning temporal placement to agricultural features, which are rarely associated with large quantities of datable material.

Population Growth and Aggregation

The concern with settlement location has often coincided with an interest in the expansion and concentration of population in the Q Ranch region. Again, Tuggle was among the first to approach this problem from a regional perspective. Tuggle (1970:34-5) observed that population size, for example, increased rapidly in the period of A.D. 1000 to 1400. He estimated an increase on the order of 50 to 75 percent during the Late Mogollon II period and a further doubling or tripling of population by A.D. 1350 on the Salt Draw Plateau.

This last period (LM III) has been of special interest due to the concentration of efforts at the Grasshopper Ruin by the University of Arizona Archaeological Field School. Tuggle suggests that the Salt Draw Plateau was characterized by a complex settlement system, aggregation, and overpopulation during the Late Mogollon III period. Virtually every topographic zone, including the canyons to the west and southwest, was occupied (Tuggle 1970:35). Six large pueblos ranging in size from 40 rooms to the 500-room Grasshopper Ruin, the largest prehistoric site in the region, are scattered throughout the Salt Draw Plateau during this period (Tuggle 1970:33). In addition to these are numerous small sites of three to 20 rooms each on the plateau and, for the first time, several cliff dwellings, including the Canyon Creek Ruin of more than 50 rooms (Tuggle 1970:33-4). In contrast to this situation, Tuggle (1970:35) suggests that the lower Cibecue area to the east experienced only moderate growth during this period and was relatively underpopulated. He points out (1970:35-6) that this is the opposite of both the general Mogollon trend towards occupation of lower elevations and major streams and the location of modern Apache settlements.

Longacre (1975, 1976), following Reid (1973), focuses his attention on the growth of the Grasshopper Ruin. He estimates the sizes of the site's founding and peak populations using the sequence of room construction combined with a standard abandonment rate of 25 percent and Hill's estimates of the number of people occupying a pueblo room (Hill 1970:75-7). The results of a simulation program modeling annual population growth and immigration rates suggested to Longacre (1976:183) that the peak population could only be accounted for by immigration from other settlements. The source of these immigrants is unknown. It is possible that local populations in the Grasshopper area aggregated at the large pueblo. This does not seem probable, however, given the relatively small number of habitation sites preceding the appearance of the large pueblo on the Salt Draw Plateau.

Most recent studies present some conflicting information. A recent study of room function at Grasshopper suggests a higher rate of room abandonment and remodeling than that predicted by Longacre (Ciolek-Torrello 1978). If all else is held constant, this would produce a lower peak population estimate. In addition, all the large LM III pueblos on the Salt Draw Plateau may not have been contemporaneous in construction and occupation. It is possible that some of these may have preceded Grasshopper in construction by 25 years or more. If so, these could have been occupied for a short time and then contributed their populations to the larger pueblo, obviating the need for locating immigrants from other regions to account for the growth of Grasshopper. It is more likely, however, that these pueblos were occupied slightly later than the Grasshopper Ruin and absorbed migrants from that ruin.

The population dynamics of the Q Ranch Plateau are much less well understood. Most efforts have concentrated on the small Vosberg locality without any attempt to synthesize the scattered survey data for the entire plateau. This constricted view produces major problems in viewing long-term population dynamics. The pattern of population growth at Vosberg, for example, initially appears to contrast with that of the Salt Draw Plateau. Cartledge (1976:117) argues that the period A.D. 1050-1250 (roughly equivalent to Tuggle's LM II) was the time of major occupation of the Vosberg area. Clearly, most sites occur in this time period. The distribution of room counts from sites seriated by ceramics indicates to Cartledge (1976:132-5) that population growth during this period was exponential. In contrast, only one large site of about 40 rooms is found in the locality after A.D. 1300. This suggests to Cartledge that population growth leveled off after A.D. 1250.

Cartledge and other investigators in Vosberg ignore the large Q Ranch Ruin of 250 to 300 rooms, located less than a mile outside of the Vosberg locality. This ruin is contemporaneous with Grasshopper. Many inhabitants of Vosberg may have migrated to the Q Ranch Ruin after A.D. 1250, but continued to utilize land in the adjacent Vosberg area. The Q Ranch Ruin and several other large contemporaneous pueblos known for the Q Ranch Plateau suggest a settlement pattern quite similar to that of the Salt Draw Plateau. The developments in the Vosberg area can be seen as part of a larger pattern within which similar events would have occurred in any equal-sized area on the Salt Draw Plateau.

Aggregation in Vosberg supports this assertion. Cartledge (1976:133-4) observes that large sites generally occur late in the occupation sequence in Vosberg, and that late small sites are larger than early small sites. These data suggest to Cartledge a gradual trend towards the aggregating of population within larger pueblos. Thus, the movement of Vosberg residents to the Q Ranch Pueblo can be seen as the logical conclusion of this trend.

Seriation

Population dynamics and other issues to be discussed point to the importance of chronological inference as a research problem in the Q Ranch region. For the most part, ceramic seriation has been the sole basis of such inference. Only at the intensively investigated Grasshopper and Canyon Creek ruins have other means of dating (tree rings) been available.

The seriation of ceramics from surface collections has proven to be a difficult problem, however, in this region. Decorated ceramics, for example, are rare from surface collections, especially from sites predating A.D. 1250. The most common decorated wares--the black-on-whites-- evidence a confusing mixture of design styles and technological traits that defy traditional classification. This problem has been encountered in both Vosberg (Chenhall 1972:46; Cartledge 1976:125) and the Salt Draw Plateau

(Tuggle 1970; Reid, personal communication; Whittlesey, personal communication) and may characterize the entire region south of the Mogollon Rim.

Another problem involves the dating of the Salado polychromes, which are also common in the Q Ranch region. Both Chenhall (1972:49) and Cartledge (1976:36) agree that these types are all intrusive in the Vosberg area. Chenhall, however, maintains that Gila and Pinto polychromes start at Vosberg no later than A.D. 1100, at least 100 years earlier than suggested by Breternitz (1966:77, 88) on the basis of tree-ring-date associations. In the case of Gila Polychrome, Chenhall's estimate is 200 years earlier than the appearance of such pottery in well-dated archaeological contexts in the vicinity of Vosberg. The reasoning behind Chenhall's estimates is not clear.

Cartledge avoids the entire issue in his seriation of Vosberg sites by restricting analysis only to the more common locally produced plainwares. This strategy, however, presents a new set of problems since plainwares are not nearly as sensitive to temporal changes as are the decorated wares. Furthermore, crossdating with locally produced and consumed wares is next to impossible. Thus, Cartledge's seriation of sites is subject to question and limited in utility. Clearly, there is a great need for considerable work in regard to regional ceramics and temporal inference.

Environmental Stress and Population Pressure

Archaeologists commonly attribute changes in settlement patterns to stresses brought about by changes in resource availability or by an increased population sharing a limited set of resources. On the Salt Draw Plateau, human response to changing environmental conditions has been sought as an explanation of the abrupt changes in settlement patterns. The rapid population buildup on the plateau after A.D. 1300 is seen as a response to favorable environmental conditions relative to other regions in the Southwest (Reid 1973, 1978; Dean and Robinson, in preparation). The relatively underpopulated condition of the Cibecue area during this time may also be attributed to environmental conditions such as flooding or downstream arroyo-cutting (Tuggle 1970:36).

A return to normal or even worse than normal conditions has been offered as an explanation of the abandonment of the area. However, no significant changes have been observed that coincide with this abandonment (Reid 1973, 1978). Recently, a much more sophisticated model has been presented to account for the abandonment problem (Reid 1978).

Environmental deterioration resulting from overexploitation of resources by an overly dense population is an alternative or complementary explanation for regional abandonment. This explanation has been more

popular among archaeologists working in the Vosberg locality. Using
the work of Rodgers (1970), both Chenhall (1972) and Cartledge (1976)
have attempted to demonstrate a relationship between the increasing
number and complexity of agricultural features and the growing population
size in Vosberg. They see this intensification of agricultural practices
as an attempt to increase resources for a growing population.

Similar water-control systems have been observed on the Salt Draw
Plateau (Tuggle 1970; Spain 1976). The presence of these, together with
the work in Vosberg, has inspired Spain (1976) to develop a research
design for investigating the relationship between population size and
agricultural features at Grasshopper. Data derived from this proposed
analysis are expected to provide an explanation for the aggregation of
population in the early 1300s and the eventual abandonment of the region.
In contrast, Reid (1973) sees the abandonment of the region as the eventual
outcome of a gradual process of population dispersion and extensification
of subsistence practices. His model is supported by the abandonment of
Grasshopper Pueblo and the movement of population into the canyons during
the latter part of the 14th century. In the canyons, the previously
aggregated population would have been dispersed into smaller, more isolated
groups practicing a more varied subsistence strategy than on the plateau
itself.

Prehistoric Social Organization

The research problems discussed above have been of
major concern to the individual studies of most investigators in the
Q Ranch region. The remaining topics to be discussed have been of more
restricted interest. One of these is the identification of
prehistoric social groups and the investigation of their changes through
time. This topic has been studied primarily through the examination of
domestic groups (Cartledge 1976; Ciolek-Torrello and Reid 1974; Ciolek-
Torrello 1978; Rock 1974) and mortuary complexes (Clark 1969; Whittlesey 1978).

Domestic groups are identified in the archaeological context from
the distribution of activities and functional room types within larger
architectural units. Ciolek-Torrello (1978) has employed the rich data
base at the Grasshopper Ruin to develop a functional classification of
rooms. Six types are observed: (1) limited-activity rooms, (2) habitation rooms, (3) storage rooms, (4) multifunctional habitation rooms,
(5) manufacturing rooms, and (6) storage and manufacturing rooms. Many
household dwellings are small, consisting of a single habitation room.
However, considerable household variability exists, with the possibility
of large domestic groups utilizing several habitation rooms and one or
more of each of the other types. In addition, a pattern of functional
zoning was observed in this large pueblo. Whether this pattern reflects
normal changes in utilization of space within a community (see Morenon 1977)
or the development of a complex organizational pattern has not been resolved;
the latter, however, is suspected.

Although the data base is not quite as secure, Cartledge has also attempted to reconstruct certain aspects of organizational change in the Vosberg area. In contradiction to Chenhall's (1972) conclusions, Cartledge (1976) proposed that site-size variability exhibits a trend towards increasing site size (increasing coresidence) rather than contemporaneous functional variability. Cartledge, however, was unable to find any strong supporting evidence for either viewpoint.

The existence of a large burial population at the Grasshopper Ruin has provided an additional source of data. In an early study, Clark (1969) found considerable variability in burial associations and what he believed to be a nonrandom distribution of the more richly accoutered burials. He interpreted these data as evidence of a stratified society. More recently, however, Whittlesey (1978) has attempted a more comprehensive and methodologically sophisticated study of a much larger burial sample. Results of this are at variance with those of Clark. Although considerable variation in burial treatment is apparent, this cannot be attributed to a system of ranking or stratification.

Interregional Trade and Contact

Another problem that has until now been of interest to a limited number of investigators is that of interregional contacts. This has been treated for both the Vosberg locality (Harris 1974; Morris 1969, 1970) and for the Grasshopper Ruin (Mayro, Whittlesey, and Reid 1976; Whittlesey 1974, 1978).

Harris examined the distribution of nonlocal resources and manufactured goods in Vosberg in order to identify contact with surrounding areas. She also attempted to identify local resources that may have been exchanged with other groups. The most important of the latter resources are steatite and serpentine. Numerous pieces of raw material, blanks, and finished products were found, indicating extensive utilization of these resources. Harris then attempted to locate steatite and serpentine artifacts in collections from other areas in order to identify contact of these areas with Vosberg. The most important sources of these materials in Arizona are located in a narrow strip whose southern limit is near Globe and its northern limit below the Mogollon Rim on the Q Ranch Plateau. No sources are located on the Salt Draw Plateau to the east or in other areas to the west. Although Vosberg is clearly located in the source area, Harris was not able to pinpoint the particular source of specific artifacts in collections from other areas. Overall, the evidence of the exchange of other materials is meager. This, however, may be primarily due to the small collections produced by the limited excavations in the Vosberg area.

Contact of a different nature has been proposed for an early time period in Vosberg. Morris (1969, 1970) argues that during the earliest period of intensive occupation of Vosberg, the area was occupied simultaneously by both Hohokam and Anasazi groups. This proposition is suggested by the presence of both Hohokam and Anasazi-style pit houses at Walnut Creek Village in association with relatively large frequencies of early red-on-buff wares and Anasazi black-on-white wares.

On the Salt Draw Plateau, evidence of interregional contact is restricted to the last occupation period represented at the Grasshopper Ruin. Several sources of evidence concerning trade exist at Grasshopper, including nonlocal ceramics, shell, animals, and various types of minerals and artifacts made from nonlocal resources. The only detailed study, however, has been limited to an investigation of imported ceramics (Whittlesey 1974). An analysis of functional and stylistic attributes of the three polychromes most commonly found at Grasshopper allowed Whittlesey to argue that Grasshopper and Gila polychromes were locally manufactured, while Fourmile Polychrome vessels were probably imported. The conclusion regarding Gila Polychrome was generalized to include other Salado polychromes (Whittlesey 1974:110). Whittlesey also suggests that some of the Salado types may have been imported as well as locally manufactured (1974:111).

This significant Salado presence (in terms of ceramic information) at Grasshopper has been suggested as a reflection of the presence of Salado groups at the pueblo and their manufacture of Salado wares for export (Mayro, Whittlesey, and Reid 1976:92). It has been proposed that this export was part of a regionally specific system involving the exchange of goods in an ecotonal situation among culturally diverse but areally restricted populations (1976:93). This proposition is consistent with conclusions drawn by Tuggle (1970) from his analysis of the distribution of stylistic elements on black-on-white pottery on the Salt Draw Plateau. These conclusions also tend to agree with Morris' notions of interaction during a much earlier period at Vosberg. However, in the latter case, the extent of regional specificity and areal restriction of population was probably much less.

Together, these various notions are consistent with the cultural-boundary nature of the entire study area. The various admixtures and blendings of ceramic information observed independently by different investigators, for example, suggest that the Q Ranch region was a melting pot throughout its prehistoric occupation. Evidence of interaction among various culturally diverse populations is present from the earliest period. Although long-distance exchange is indicated by the presence of macaws at Grasshopper (Olsen and Olsen 1974) and shell at both Grasshopper and Vosberg, this type of exchange appears relatively insignificant in comparison to the more localized regional exchange.

The APS-CS Survey

The APS-CS survey of the Q Ranch region was carried out in the first half of 1977. A transect more than a hundred meters wide was surveyed along the projected course of the transmission line. Proposed access roads for the line's construction were also surveyed. The transect passed through the Tonto Basin along the course of Cherry Creek to Sombrero Peak; it then headed northeast, traversing the eastern half of the Q Ranch Plateau, and finally left the region at the Mogollon Rim west of Canyon Creek (see Figure 11a).

The survey located a total of 21 sites on the plateau (Table 24). These occur in three locales. Eighteen sites are located in the McFadden Peak Quadrangle: five around Rock House Creek and 13 around middle Campbell Creek. Three additional sites are located in the Young Quadrangle in the vicinity of Ellison and Rock creeks. Sites are of three types: lithic scatters, sherd and lithic scatters, and sites with structures. As in the nearby Vosberg area, large quantities of steatite debris and blanks indicative of local manufacturing activities are associated with several sites in the Rock House Creek and Campbell Creek areas.

Sites with structures are primarily of cobble-outline construction similar to that of sites of Ceramic Group IV at Vosberg. The presence of scattered adobe at these APS-CS sites suggests that the latter material was used in conjunction with cobble outlines. Rooms range in number from one to five and are often not contiguous. One site (AZ V:1:16) is composed of several contiguous rooms constructed of three to five courses of slab masonry. The superstructure of these rooms may have been formed by adobe as in the case of the cobble rooms.

The determination of cultural affiliation and dates of occupation for individual sites is difficult, in that, under the Forest Service permit, collections were not permitted at the time of survey. The extensive information collected on ASM site-survey forms was used to provide a detailed description of each individual site (see volume accompanying this report).

Table 24. Archaeological sites in the Q Ranch segment of the Cholla-Saguaro corridor

ASM Number	Field Number	Cultural-temporal Affiliation	Site Type	Approximate Size (m²)	USGS Quad	Elevation (feet)
AZ P:13:10	CS-202	Prehistoric (unknown)	Lithic scatter	875	Young 15 min.	6100
AZ P:13:11	CS-260	Prehistoric (unknown)	Structures with artifact scatter	87,500	Young 15 min.	5600
AZ P:13:12	CS-277	Prehistoric (unknown)	Structures with artifact scatter	8075	Young 15 min.	5560
AZ V:1:8	CS-243	Prehistoric (unknown)	Artifact scatter	8400	McFadden Peak 15 min.	5320
AZ V:1:9	CS-244	Prehistoric (unknown)	Artifact scatter	6000	McFadden Peak 15 min.	5360
AZ V:1:10	CS-246	Prehistoric: Salado	Structure with artifact scatter	600	McFadden Peak 15 min.	5560
AZ V:1:11	CS-245	Prehistoric (unknown)	Structure with artifact scatter	1,440,000	McFadden Peak 15 min.	5200
AZ V:1:12	CS-248	Prehistoric: Salado(?)	Structure with artifact scatter	33,750	McFadden Peak 15 min.	5350
AZ V:1:13	CS-249	Prehistoric (unknown)	Structure with artifact scatter	36,000	McFadden Peak 15 min.	5320
AZ V:1:14	CS-250	Prehistoric (unknown)	Structure with artifact scatter	19,800	McFadden Peak 15 min.	5320
AZ V:1:15	CS-251	Prehistoric (unknown)	Structure with artifact scatter	56,700	McFadden Peak 15 min.	5280

Table 24. Archaeological sites in the Q Ranch segment of the Cholla-Saguaro corridor (continued)

ASM Number	Field Number	Cultural-temporal Affiliation	Site Type	Approximate Size (m²)	USGS Quad	Elevation (feet)
AZ V:1:16	CS-252	Prehistoric (unknown)	Structure with artifact scatter	45,000	McFadden Peak 15 min.	5200
AZ V:1:17	CS-253	Prehistoric (unknown) Historic:Anglo (pre-1912)	Structure with artifact scatter	6175	McFadden Peak 15 min.	5200
AZ V:1:18	CS-254	Prehistoric (unknown)	Structure with artifact scatter	3900	McFadden Peak 15 min.	5160
AZ V:1:19	CS-255	Prehistoric (unknown)	Lithic scatter	2700	McFadden Peak 15 min.	5160
AZ V:1:20	CS-256	Prehistoric (unknown)	Features with artifact scatter	11,250	McFadden Peak 15 min.	5160
AZ V:1:21	CS-257	Prehistoric (unknown)	Artifact scatter	8100	McFadden Peak 15 min.	5180
AZ V:1:22	CS-258	Prehistoric (unknown)	Artifact scatter	1500	McFadden Peak 15 min.	5390
AZ V:1:23	CS-259	Prehistoric (unknown)	Artifact scatter	5250	McFadden Peak 15 min.	5360
AZ V:1:24	CS-261	Prehistoric (unknown)	Features with artifact scatter	5625	McFadden Peak 15 min.	5160
AZ V:1:25	CS-262	Prehistoric (unknown)	Features with artifact scatter	3000	McFadden Peak 15 min.	5120

Not all sites found by the APS-CS survey represent the prehistoric period exclusively. A stone circle about 2 meters in diameter was located at one site (AZ V:1:11), and may represent the remains of an Apache wickiup. It is build on top of a prehistoric artifact cluster within this large site. The materials used in constructing the circle were most likely scavenged from a prehistoric structure in the immediate vicinity.

APS-CS 253 (AZ V:1:17), a historic homestead consisting of a cabin and the remains of outbuildings and corrals, is also superimposed on a light prehistoric sherd and lithic scatter. This site was identified by Phil Smith as the Campbell Creek homestead of Buss Ellison, now of Ellison Ranch on lower Cherry Creek. Smith obtained information at the homestead in an interview with the Ellison family. Pertinent aspects of the interview (a transcript of which was generously provided by Smith) are summarized below.

The area was opened to homesteading by the Forest Service in 1919. Buss Ellison built the present cabin in 1921 and abandoned the homestead in 1929. At some point during this period, a barn and chicken house were also constructed. The former was constructed with the help of Buss' father Perl, who had another homestead in the vicinity of Campbell Creek. Buss Ellison cleared and planted 20 acres in the meadow near the cabin; part of this meadow may be included in AZ V:1:11. The crops planted included hegari (like milo), corn, and cane. Ellison also raised cattle (10-40 head) on the homestead. Problems with dry wells and access across neighbors' land may have precipitated Ellison's departure.

After 1929, the place was occupied for two to three years by a man named Charlie Williams, who added a galvanized tin roof to the cabin. Buss Ellison returned in 1937 and removed the roof and other building material for his new ranch on Cherry Creek. The homestead was also occupied after Ellison by Claude H. Burt, who owned an adjoining homestead while Ellison was at Campbell Creek. The interview indicates that pot hunting at local prehistoric sites had already begun during this early homesteading period.

The following section summarizes the cultural and environmental characteristics of the APS-CS sites and relates them to sites located by other surveys in the Q Ranch region.

Regional Site Survey Data

A regional perspective for research is mandated by the nature of the APS survey, which traverses the Q Ranch Plateau from north to south. Under ideal conditions, analysis would proceed by comparison of APS survey data with the existing body of site information. The existing data recorded by various institutions during the past 50 years, however,

has been collected under a variety of circumstances. Some information
has been collected from the systematic and intensive survey of small
isolated locales. Other information has been derived from unsystematic
coverage of larger areas. The remainder comes from the chance reporting
of sites by ranchers, hunters, and other interested individuals. Added
to discrepancies in the coverage of areas are major inconsistencies in
recording from locale to locale or, in some cases, within the same locale.
As a result, it is not currently possible to conduct a comprehensive
analysis of regional survey data.

Thus, analysis is limited to a descriptive level in which the
existing data are summarized and patterns isolated. The purpose of such
description is to interpret these patterns in terms of gaps and biases
in the data and to generate testable hypotheses. The regional perspective
of this description is intended to complement the specific research projects
discussed earlier. In the process, we will assess the significance of local
patterns for the region as a whole and for areas investigated by the APS
survey.

To achieve this, the APS survey data are coupled with the existing
body of site information recorded by various institutions (Table 25).
All sites are considered, although greater emphasis is placed during the
interpretive process on those sites from the intensively surveyed areas.
A measure of control for differences in environment, survey strategies,
and recording techniques is provided by dividing the total site collection into seven subsets (Table 26). Four sets are composed of those sites
located in each of the USGS quadrangles that encompass the region. Three
additional sets overlap these in membership: the sites located by the
intensive surveys conducted by Arizona State University in the Vosberg
area and the University of Arizona in the Grasshopper area, and the APS-CS
survey sites.

It should be noted that although the areally limited surveys are
considered subsets of the appropriate USGS quadrangle site set, they
often dominate the sample within that quad in terms of numbers of sites.
Thus, while it may be stated during the analysis that a survey reflects
its quadrangle, it must be realized that these limited surveys are in
large part responsible for the archaeological character of an entire
quadrangle.

Cultural and environmental characteristics of all known sites in
the region have been encoded in a format (see Janney and Reid, APS-CS
Mitigation Report, in preparation) amenable to computer analysis. This
limits analysis to those data most consistently recorded by the different
survey systems. Much of the environmental data, however, was obtained,
independently of the survey data, from USGS and Forest Service maps.
Together these data provide information on site function, population size
and aggregation, chronological placement, and cultural affiliation. Figures
for comparison are generated for all quads combined, each individual quad,
and each intensive survey. Environmental characteristics, site characteristics, and culture history are the major headings under which comparisons
will be made.

Table 25.   Sources of information on the total site collection
within the Q Ranch study area

A.   Survey Systems

Name	Number of Sites Recorded
Gila Pueblo (GP)	107
Gila Pueblo/Arizona State Museum (GP/ASM)	5
Arizona State University (ASU)	96
Arizona State Museum (ASM)	227
Arizona State Museum/APS-CS (ASM/APS-CS)	25*
TOTAL	460

B.   Number of sites by quad per survey system

System Name	Young	Chediski Peak	McFadden Peak	Blue House Mountain
GP	25	5	68	9
GP/ASM	2	2		1
ASU	96			
ASM	7	175	3	42
ASM/APS-CS	3		22*	
TOTALS	133	182	93	52

* Four ASM/APS-CS sites included here are located within the Tonto-Roosevelt
study area.

- - - - - - - - - - - - - - - -

Table 26.   Subsets of the total site collection used for analysis

Quadrangle	Number of sites
A. Young (USGS 15-min. series, 1961)	133
B. Chediski Peak (USGS 15-min. series, 1961)	182
C. McFadden Peak (USGS 15-min. series, 1949)	93
D. Blue House Mountain (USGS 15-min. series, 1946)	52
	460

Intensive surveys	Number of sites
E. Arizona State University--Vosberg survey (1971-1974)	96
F. University of Arizona--Grasshopper survey (1969-1978)	72
G. Arizona State Museum--APS-CS survey (1977)	24
	192*

* Sites of E-G are themselves subsets of A-D. Thus, total sites = 460.

Environmental Characteristics

Site Elevation

Sites range in elevation from a minimum of 2800 feet to a maximum of 7600 feet (Table 27). This widest range is found in the McFadden Peak quad (MFP), with the Chediski Peak quad (CP) having the narrowest range. Young is more similar to CP, and the Blue House Mountain quad (BHM) more similar to MFP. The greater range within BHM and MFP reflects the presence of an extensive series of canyons in addition to mountain valleys and basins. Canyons are much less frequent in the Young and CP quads. The three intensive surveys were undertaken in areas exhibiting a much narrower range in elevation, from 5100 feet to 6500 feet. Intensive surveys have been almost exclusively restricted to the high valleys and basins. Of the sites located by these surveys, the Vosberg sites are situated below 5800 feet and the Grasshopper sites are above 5800 feet. The APS-CS sites are concentrated in the lower elevations but span the whole range from 5000-6000 feet.

Table 27. Site Elevations (in feet)

	Young	Chediski Peak	McFadden Peak	Blue House Mountain	All Quads
Minimum	5040	4520	2800	3520	2800
Mean	5379	5677	4876	5399	5333
Maximum	6280	6480	7600	5840	7600
Total sites	133	181	86	52	
Missing cases	0	1	7	0	

	Grasshopper	Vosberg	APS
Minimum	5800	5160	5160
Mean	6046	5393	5352
Maximum	6480	5760	6100

Do these site elevations reflect location selectivity on the part of prehistoric inhabitants? In most cases, site elevations appear to merely reflect the range of elevations in an area. Sites do not occur, however, in the 4000-5000-foot elevation range. This pattern may be due to the fact that potential locations within that range are very few in number or small in area or, because of slope, essentially unusable for human activities. Alternatively, surveys may have avoided areas in this elevation range, which is characterized primarily by canyons and ridges.

Some preliminary tests (see Janney and Reid, in APS-CS Mitigation Report, in preparation) resolve some of these difficulties. A t-test comparing the mean elevation of known sites with the mean elevation of a set of randomly selected points on the maps (see Table 28) indicates that particular elevations were selected from those available for prehistoric activities. This does not, however, resolve the problem of survey bias, since sites may yet be found in the 4000-5000-foot range when additional areas are intensively surveyed.

Topography

Three variables are used to describe site topography: on-site topography (the feature on which a site is located); area topography (site location in a broader perspective); and site-area topography, which combines the two.

Analysis of on-site topography shows a strong tendency for sites in all quads to be located on top of a topographical feature such as a ridge or knoll as opposed to its sides or on bottom lands (Table 29). This tendency is strongest in the Young and Chediski Peak quads and weakest in the BHM and MFP quads, where sites commonly occur in the cliffs and canyons that are prevalent in those two areas.

Analyses of area and site-area topography show a tendency for sites in all quads to be on high topographic features situated among lower types of features, as opposed to being on features which are situated among features of similar size (Tables 30 and 31). Sites tend to occur more often, for example, on ridges or knolls within basins or valleys rather than within larger ridges or knolls. The three more intensive surveys likewise exhibit this tendency for their respective quads.

A simple functional breakdown of sites shows some contrasts in topographic location. Sites with structures occur most often on canyon sides, cliffs, terraces, knolls, and ridges (Table 32). Of these, pit houses are found most often on ridges and knolls, while sites without structures are located most often on bluffs.

A more significant divergence occurs with area topography (Table 33). Sites with structures, including pit houses, occur most often in valleys, basins, and canyons. In contrast, sites without structures occur on higher topographical features such as major ridges and benches.

The site-area topographic variable exhibits a consistent pattern (Table 34). Sites with structures occur on high points within valleys and other relatively low-lying areas, while other sites occur on high points of the higher topographical features.

Table 28. Site elevation (in feet) significance and selection

Comparison of mean elevations of archaeological sites and randomly selected points in each quad. Difference of means test for elevations uses 0.01 level of significance.

	Number of cases	Mean	Standard Deviation	F-Value	2-tail proba-bility	$T_{0.01}$	Variance df	Estimate T-value (2-tail test)	
Quad: Young									
On-site elevation	133	5379	197	8.11	.0001	±2.617	117	-9.96	separate variance
Random point elevation	100	5962	560						
Quad: Chediski Peak									
On-site elevation	181	5677	440	1.76	.001	±2.576	162	-5.83	separate variance
Random point elevation	100	6067	584						
Quad: McFadden Peak									
On-site elevation	86	4876	1039	1.57	.039	±2.576	170	-3.28	pooled variance
Random point elevation	86	5346	829						
Quad: Blue House Mountain									
On-site elevation	52	5399	524	1.64	.081	±2.63	102	6.08	pooled variance
Random point elevation	52	4681	671						

Table 29. On-site topography of Q Ranch area sites by topographic class* (percentages in parentheses)

Topographic Class	Young	Chediski Peak	McFadden Peak	Blue House Mountain	All Quads	Grasshopper	Vosberg	APS-CS
1	86(64.7)	107(58.6)	37(39.9)	20(38.4)	250(54.3)	44(61.2)	70(72.9)	13(61.9)
2	21(15.9)	46(25.1)	15(16.2)	11(21.1)	93(20.3)	16(22.2)	6(6.2)	3(14.3)
3	26(19.6)	27(14.8)	21(22.7)	11(21.1)	85(18.5)	12(16.7)	20(20.8)	5(23.8)
4	0(0)	2(1.1)	20(21.5)	10(19.2)	32(7)	0(0)	0(0)	0(0)
Other	0(0)	0(0)	0(0)	0(0)	0(0)	0(0)	0(0)	0(0)
Missing cases	0(0)	0(0)	0(0)	0(0)	0(0)	0(0)	0(0)	0(0)
Total sites	133	182	93	52	460	72	96	21

* Topographic Classes: 1 = flat, ridge, saddle, hill, mountain, bluff, mesa, knoll
2 = canyon, canyon floor, valley, floodplain, terrace, valley bottom, bench, basin
3 = canyon side, valley side, slope
4 = cliff

- -

Table 30. Area-topography of Q Ranch area sites by topographic class* (percentages in parentheses)

Topographic Class	Young	Chediski Peak	McFadden Peak	Blue House Mountain	All Quads	Grasshopper	Vosberg	APS-CS
1	15(11.4)	20(10.8)	15(16.2)	13(25.0)	63(13.6)	4(5.6)	11(11.5)	1(4.8)
2	104(78.1)	128(70.3)	46(49.5)	20(38.5)	298(64.8)	52(72.1)	81(84.4)	18(85.7)
3	14(10.6)	34(18.7)	30(32.3)	19(36.6)	97(21.1)	16(22.2)	4(4.1)	2(9.5)
4	0(0)	0(0)	1(1.1)	0(0)	1(.2)	0(0)	0(0)	0(0)
Other	0(0)	0(0)	0(0)	0(0)	0(0)	0(0)	0(0)	0(0)
Missing cases	0(0)	0(0)	1(1.1)	0(0)	1(.2)	0(0)	0(0)	0(0)
Total sites	133	182	93	52	460	72	96	21

* Topographic Classes: 1 = flat, ridge, saddle, hill, mountain, bluff, mesa, knoll
2 = canyon, canyon floor, valley, floodplain, terrace, valley bottom, bench, basin
3 = canyon side, valley side, slope
4 = cliff

Table 31. Site-area topography of Q Ranch area sites by combined topographic classes* (percentages in parentheses)

Topographic class	Young	Chediski Peak	McFadden Peak	Blue House Mountain	All Quads	Grasshopper	Vosberg	APS-CS
1 situated on 1	12(9.1)	15(8.0)	9(9.8)	8(15.3)	44(9.5)	4(5.6)	9(9.4)	1(4.8)
1 situated in 2	63(47.4)	64(35.0)	16(17.3)	2(3.8)	145(31.5)	27(37.7)	58(60.4)	11(52.3)
Other	58(43.5)	103(57)	68(72.9)	42(80.9)	271(59)	41(56.7)	29(30.2)	9(42.9)
Total sites	133	182	93	52	460	72	96	21

* Topographic classes: 1 = flat, ridge, saddle, hill, mountain, bluff, mesa, knoll
2 = canyon, canyon floor, valley, floodplain, terrace, bench, valley bottom, basin

Table 32. Site topography and the presence of structures (percentages in parentheses)

Number of sites

Topographic situation	Structures absent	Structures possible	Structures definite	Total
Canyon side	7(32)	0	15(68)	22
Terrace	4(21)	0	15(79)	19
Valley side	15(48)	3(10)	13(42)	31
Valley bottom	21(44)	7(14)	20(42)	48
Cliff	2(6)	0	30(94)	32
Slope	11(34)	7(22)	14(44)	32
Ridge	51(37)	14(10)	74(53)	139
Bluff	11(55)	3(15)	6(30)	20
Knoll	12(20)	13(22)	35(58)	60
Other	34(61)	0	22(39)	56
Totals	168	47	244	459

Missing cases   1

Table 33. Area topography and presence of structures
(percentages in parentheses)

Number of sites

Topographic situation	Structures absent	Structures possible	Structures definite	Total
Canyon	13(18)	3(4)	55(78)	71
Valley	72(41)	21(12)	82(47)	175
Ridge	23(55)	3(7)	16(38)	42
Hill	7(37)	2(11)	10(52)	19
Bench	33(67)	2(4)	14(29)	49
Basin	20(20)	16(16)	65(64)	101
Total of all situations	168	47	242	457
Missing cases	3			

- -

Table 34. Site-area topography and presence of structures
(percentages in parentheses)

Number of sites

Topographic situation	Structures absent	Structures possible	Structures definite	Total
Valley in canyon	6(29)	1(4)	14(67)	21
Valley in valley	36(37)	14(14)	48(49)	98
Slope in valley	10(31)	7(25)	14(44)	32
Ridge in valley	12(19)	6(9)	46(72)	64
Knoll in valley	17(41)	3(8)	21(51)	41
Cliff on valley side	1(4)	0	25(96)	26
Ridge on valley side	14(35)	8(20)	18(45)	40
Knoll on valley side	6(30)	2(10)	12(60)	20
Ridge on ridge	30(62)	3(7)	15(31)	48
Knoll on ridge	18(54)	2(7)	13(39)	33
Other	13(50)	0	18(50)	36
Total of all situations	168	4	244	459
Missing cases	1			

As in the case of site elevations, topographical patterns are subject to certain problems. In the MFP quad, for example, there has been
a bias towards the study of cliff sites and canyons, while studies in the
Young and CP quads have been biased towards basins and valleys, respectively.
The survey biases, however, reflect to a certain degree the major topographical features in each quad; that is, there are more canyons and cliffs in
the MFP quad than in the Young quad.

A more difficult set of problems derives from the specification
of the topographic variable. One problem is best illustrated by an
example: when does a canyon become a valley? Another problem arises
as one stands at a particular site and looks around. What are the focal
limits for specifying site location? If a site is on a ridge which in
turn is on a larger ridge, and both are within a basin, should the site
be coded as being on a ridge within a larger ridge or as on a ridge within
a basin? A further complication is presented by site size. Larger sites
tend to cover larger areas and possibly several topographic features
simultaneously. Different surveys and even individuals within each survey
have most likely not been consistent in assigning these designations.

Vegetation

Differences in the association between sites and vegetation generally reflect the dominant vegetation in each quadrangle and survey area.
The grassland-ponderosa pine forest association, for example, predominates
as the setting for sites in the Young and CP quads (Table 35). The
greater abundance of ponderosa in the CP quad relative to the Young quad
is reflected in larger frequencies of sites associated with that vegetation type in the former quad. Sites in the MFP and BHM quads are usually
associated with pinyon-juniper--chaparral vegetation types, with scrub
or pinyon-grassland being the second most common association. Sites from
the intensive surveys show patterns consistent with their respective quads.
On the whole, the association between vegetation types and sites appears
random or trivial at best.

Little patterning is observable when sites are broken down into
simple functional types. Slight divergences from the general pattern
are suggested by the APS-CS and Grasshopper survey data; these divergences,
however, are contradictory. In the Grasshopper region, sites with structures tend to be located more often in grasslands than in the more common
ponderosa areas (Table 36). In contrast, APS-CS sites with structures
are more often located within pinyon-juniper vegetation areas, while sites
without structures occur more often in grasslands. In all quads, there
appears to be a tendency for sites with structures to be located more
often in grassland or mixed forest and grassland areas, while sites without structures are more common in chaparral and disturbed areas. The
divergence shown by APS-CS sites may be due to an extremely small sample
size.

Table 35. Site occurrence by vegetation zone (percentages in parentheses)

	Young	Chediski Peak	McFadden Peak	Blue House Mountain	All Quads	Grasshopper	Vosberg	APS-CS
Grassland	27(28)	26(14)	0(0)	4(9)	57(16)	3(4)	20(34)	0(0)
Pinyon-juniper	11(12)	8(4)	10(28)	17(37)	46(13)	1(1)	3(5)	9(43)
Pinyon-juniper--grassland	8(8)	8(4)	5(14)	2(4)	23(6)	0(0)	1(2)	5(24)
Ponderosa-grassland	6(6)	22(12)	1(3)	7(15)	36(10)	16(22)	2(3)	1(5)
Ponderosa	24(25)	52(29)	4(11)	8(17)	88(24)	33(46)	21(36)	1(5)
Chaparral	4(4)	16(9)	2(6)	1(2)	23(6)	2(3)	2(3)	1(5)
Other	7% ri-parian 3% pin-yon-juniper mixes	7% disturbed grassland <3% of each: chaparral, grass-land, and pinyon-juniper mixes	14% gen-eral Lower Sonoran <3% others	<4% each: riparian and chaparral mixes	4% dis-turbed grassland, 2% chapar-ral vari-eties and Upper Sonoran grassland 3% ripar-ian	8% dis-turbed grassland <3% each: various pinyon-juniper--chaparral mixes	10% riparian <2% each: Upper Sonoran, oak wood-land, mixed pinyon-juniper, chaparral, and pon-derosa	<5% each: mixed ri-parian, grassland, pinyon-juniper, and pinyon-juniper juniper
Total sites	95	182	36	46	359	72	96	21
Missing cases	38	0	57	6	101	0	38	3

Table 36. Associations of vegetation types with sites with structures
(expressed in percentages)

Vegetation type	Sites with definite structures	Other sites
APS-CS sites (24)		
General Lower Sonoran	4.2	0
Upper Sonoran desert grassland	8.3	4.2
Chaparral	4.2	0
Pinyon-juniper	25.0	12.5
Ponderosa pine	4.2	4.2
Oak woodland-grassland	0	4.2
Pinyon-juniper--grassland	4.2	16.7
Pinyon-juniper--chaparral	0	4.2
Grasshopper sites (72)		
Grassland	2.7	1.4
Chaparral	0	2.7
Pinyon-juniper	1.4	0
Ponderosa pine	13.7	31.5
Disturbed	1.4	4.1
Ponderosa-grassland	16.4	5.5
Disturbed-grassland	1.4	6.8
Ponderosa-chaparral	0	2.7
Disturbed-chaparral	0	2.7
Ponderosa--pinyon-juniper	4.1	0
Disturbed-ponderosa	0	1.4
Vosberg sites (96)		
Grassland	11.5	9.4
Chaparral	2.1	0
Pinyon-juniper	2.1	1.0
Riparian	2.1	4.2
Ponderosa pine	15.6	6.3
Pinyon-juniper--grassland	1.0	0
Riparian-grassland	1.0	0
Ponderosa-grassland	1.0	1.0
Riparian--pinyon-juniper	0	1.0
Ponderosa--pinyon-juniper	1.0	0

Interpretation of vegetation associations is difficult, if not tenuous. The patterning of current vegetation types is the product of a series of ongoing microenvironmental changes. Vegetation communities normally fluctuate in size, location, and composition through time. Added to such fluctuations are more drastic changes produced by long-term changes in climatic regimes and the numerous alterations brought about in the last century by modern man. The latter include ranching (grazing, chaining, pond construction), homesteading, mining, lumbering, and road construction. Fires and, more recently, the control of natural fires have also had significant effects on vegetation communities. Together, these various factors would tend to militate against the existence of any significant, detectable patterns involving prehistoric human activity and modern vegetation communities.

Another cause of trivial site location-vegetation associations may be our current inability to specify the vegetation types that were significant to prehistoric inhabitants in selection of site locations; that is, the gross vegetation categories usually employed, such as grassland or ponderosa pine forest, may be too general to adequately specify the vegetation types selected for by prehistoric people. On the other hand, our categories may be too specific; several may be cross-cut by prehistorically significant types. Thus, the vegetation variable is among the weakest utilized in the analysis.

Site Characteristics

Site characteristics are treated under three main headings: site type, site size, and culture history. The discussion of site type provides basic functional information through consideration of variables such as the presence of structures and other architectural features and type of construction materials. Site size provides additional information concerning site function and higher-level aspects of settlement organization. Finally, culture history is concerned with cultural affiliation and chronological developments as seen through ceramics and other available information.

Site Types

Sites are classified into types on the basis of the presence of structures, sherd scatters, and lithic scatters. Sites with structures are further divided on the basis of the presence of aboveground structures and/or pit houses. The presence of pit houses is usually inferred from nonstructural surficial evidence except where excavations have demonstrated them to exist.

Table 37. Site types and features (percentages in parentheses)

	Young	Chediski Peak	McFadden Peak	Blue House Mountain	All Quads	Grasshopper	Vosberg	APS-CS
A. Site types (not mutually exclusive due to some overlap in coding)								
Sherd scatters	17(13)	78(43)	1(1)	22(42)	118(26)	23(32)	12(12)	0
Lithic scatters	3(2)	15(8)	1(1)	2(4)	21(5)	4(6)	3(3)	1(4)
Sherd and lithic scatters	11(8)	14(8)	8(9)	2(4)	35(8)	13(18)	12(12)	10(42)
Definite structures	85(64)	61(34)	77(88)	23(45)	246(53)	30(42)	60(63)	13(54)
Definite pit houses	35(26)	11(6)	1(1)	4(8)	51(11)	5(7)	31(32)	0
B. Check dams								
Check dams	26(20)	5(3)	4(4)	8(15)	43(9)	2(3)	26(27)	2(10)
Possible structure and check dam	17(13)	2(1)	4(4)	6(12)	29(6)	1(1)	17(18)	2(10)
Definite structure and check dam	2(2)	0	0	0	2(0.4)	0	2(2)	0
Pit house and check dam	7(5)	0	0	0	9(2)	0	7(7)	0
C. Aboveground structures and pit houses								
Definite structure and pit house	18(14)	2(1)	0	0	20(4)	2(3)	18(19)	0

Table 37. Site types and features (percentages in parentheses)
(continued)

	Young	Chediski Peak	McFadden Peak	Blue House Mountain	All Quads	Grasshopper	Vosberg	APS-CS
D. Plazas and compounds								
Plaza	4(3)	1(0.5)	2(2)	1(2)	8(2)	5(7)	2(2)	0
Compound	2(1)	0	1(4)	0	6(1)	0	0	1(5)
E. Cave sites and pictographs								
Cave sites	0	2(1)	20(23)	9(17)	1(7)	0	0	0
Pictographs	0	0	1(1)	3(6)	4(1)	0	0	0
F. Isolated hearths								
	8(6)	0	2(2)	1(2)	11(2)	0	8(18)	2(10)
G. Historic buildings								
	4(3)	11(6)	1(1)	0	16(3)	2(3)	2(2)	1(5)
Total sites	133	182	88	52	460	72	96	24
Missing cases	0	0	5	0	0	0	0	0
H. Construction materials								
Adobe	1(1)	0	0	0	1(0.4)	0	0	1(8)
Cobble	66(78)	4(7)	36(7)	2(9)	108(44)	1(3)	46(64)	8(67)
Slab masonry	31(38)	61(100)	46(60)	23(100)	161(65)	35(97)	26(36)	3(25)
Total sites	85	61	77	23	246	36	72	12
Missing cases	0	0	5	0	0	0	0	0

Sites with structures appear to predominate over sherd and/or lithic scatters (Table 37). The low frequencies of the latter, especially lithic scatters, are probably the result of survey bias. Most surveys tend to ignore or at least downplay such sites. An exception, the APS-CS survey clearly is more focused toward the recognition and recording of sherd and lithic scatters. In contrast, high frequencies of definite structures, especially in the MFP quad, show the strong bias of the Gila Pueblo research group in recording primarily medium to large sites with structures. Such a bias towards the larger, more obvious sites is in keeping with the exploratory nature of the early surveys. It also suggests that at present the region as a whole is relatively poorly known.

Between the extremes of the APS-CS and Gila Pueblo surveys, however, are the intensive Vosberg and Grasshopper surveys. The latter support conclusions that sites with structures occur most commonly and lithic scatters least commonly. If we assume that structures represent relatively permanent habitation activities and that sherd and lithic scatters represent specialized activities, we can then hypothesize that most sites were used for permanent or recurrent temporary habitation activities and that few sites were used solely for specialized activities. Due to the nature of surveys in most of the region, however, the currently available figures most likely are inflated in favor of sites with structures.

The recorded occurrences of pit houses also show survey bias. Pit houses are very common in the Vosberg area and, as a result, are relatively frequent in the Young quad as a whole (see Table 37). These high frequencies are probably due to the fact that the intensive Vosberg survey was coupled with test excavations which provided information allowing better prediction of subsurface structures. On the other hand, it may not be unreasonable to hypothesize that, of the intensively surveyed areas in the region, Vosberg was the most heavily occupied area during the period of pit house construction. The virtual absence of habitation structures in the Walnut Creek Valley later during the period of peak population for the region as a whole (Chenhall 1972; Cartledge 1976) is consistent with the notion of differential population distributions.

Presently there is little discernible association between pit houses and aboveground structures. The two types appear to occur in different topographic locations; in Vosberg, for example, aboveground structures occur largely on ridges and knolls within the basin, while pit houses are found in the bottom lands.

Other architectural features, particularly check dams and other agricultural features, provide functional information. Check dams are reported in above-average frequencies for the Vosberg and APS-CS surveys and the BHM quad. The low frequencies of check dams in the Grasshopper area argue against the possibility of any bias resulting from intensive survey. High frequencies of check dams occur in basins 5000-5500 feet in elevation. There also appears to be a strong correlation between the presence of check dams and definite structures in such areas. The latter pattern is best illustrated with Vosberg data.

In Vosberg, agricultural features are associated with the larger sites exhibiting aboveground structures, but not with pit house sites. This is consistent with Rodgers' (1970) argument that agricultural features occurred later in the occupation span of the area. Thus, it is possible to extend this generalization to other similar basins in the region.

Other architectural features exhibit few interesting patterns. Compounds occur in extremely low frequencies. The surveys indicate that plazas also are uncommon; it is known by the authors, however, that plazas are common among medium and large sites, especially the late sites in the Chediski Peak quad. Pictographs are also uncommon, although, as one would expect, pictographs and caves are more common in the BHM and MFP quads. Though also infrequent, isolated hearths are more common in the Young and MFP quads. This does not appear to be the product of a bias resulting from intensive survey, since this pattern is mirrored in the Vosberg and Grasshopper areas; that is, Vosberg exhibits a high frequency of isolated hearths and Grasshopper a low one. Historic buildings occur in roughly equivalent, generally quite low frequencies in all quads.

An additional source of information, construction materials for aboveground structures, strongly reflects which resources were available in the immediate area of a site. Limestone and diabase are the building materials most commonly available in the western quads, Young and MFP. Limestone and sandstone are the most commonly available materials in the eastern quads, CP and BHM. Limestone and, especially, sandstone lend themselves to shaping and stacking into large walls; diabase, in contrast, occurs exclusively in cobble form. In the Young quad and Vosberg and APS-CS survey areas, cobbles are the predominant construction material in sites with structures. Shaped-slab masonry construction predominates in the CP and BHM quads and in the Grasshopper area.

Regardless of which material was most commonly available, shaped-slab masonry appears to have been preferred for most large structures. The higher frequency of slab construction in the MFP quad relative to the Young quad can be accounted for by the group of large sites reported by Gila Pueblo in the former area. Even though such slabs were not commonly available, shaped-slab masonry construction was used in all areas of the region.

Other construction materials such as adobe or jacal are reported in very low frequencies. The APS-CS survey is an exception in reporting a relatively high frequency of sites with such construction materials present. These materials are often associated with cobble-outline rooms. Thus, one would expect adobe and jacal construction to be more commonly

reported, especially in the western quads, where cobble-outline structures are more common. The reported infrequency of such construction
may then be a function of poor visibility and recording inconsistency
rather than actual occurrences.

Site Size

Site-size variability is measured by the number of rooms per site.
Accordingly, the examination of this variable is limited to sites with
visible rooms. Measurements of site area obtained from the surveys were
found to be too inconsistent and inaccurate for the purposes of this
analysis.

Sites were divided into six size classes, and quads and survey
areas then compared (Table 38). The CP and BHM quads are the most similar in the range and proportions of site sizes. BHM has a higher proportion of medium and large sites (6-19 to 100-500 rooms), while CP contains
the largest site on the Salt Draw Plateau.

Data from the Young quad are heavily weighted in favor of small sites
(0 and one to five rooms), a product of the many small sites in the
Vosberg region. It is interesting to note that, in comparison to the
Grasshopper intensive survey, the Vosberg survey found relatively few
sites without rooms (Grasshopper 50 percent, Vosberg 26 percent). This
is most likely attributable to the better ability of the Vosberg survey
to predict the presence of structures, especially subsurface ones, on
the basis of test excavations.

The Young quad contains the smallest number of large sites, suggesting
that, apart from Vosberg, this quad may be the most poorly known area in
the region. Both Gila Pueblo and the ASM, however, have reported that
few sites are known to exist in the Pleasant Valley area of the Young quad.
Considering the size of the modern population in Pleasant Valley, at
least the large sites should be known by now. Thus, the low frequency
of large sites in the Young quad probably reflects the absence of such
sites in most of those areas of the quad where they would be expected.

In contrast to the Young quad, data from the MFP quad are heavily
weighted toward the medium to large sites. Again, this reflects the
bias of Gila Pueblo toward the large cliff sites and pueblos of the
Sierra Ancha and lower Cherry Creek rather than a true picture of site-
size distributions.

In two cases, data from the intensive surveys tend to reflect
the archaeological assessments of their respective quads or, perhaps more
accurately, to strongly influence those assessments. Grasshopper survey
data reflect the situation in the CP quad, although the higher frequencies

Table 38. Number of rooms per site in each quad and survey area (percentages in parentheses)

Number of rooms	Young	Chediski Peak	McFadden Peak	Blue House Mountain	All Quads	Grasshopper	Vosberg	APS-CS
0	36(27)	117(64)	11(12)	27(52)	191(42)	36(50)	25(26)	10(42)
1 - 5	81(61)	47(26)	34(37)	11(21)	173(38)	30(42)	59(62)	14(58)
6 - 19	6(5)	8(4)	28(30)	7(13)	49(11)	2(3)	5(5)	0
20 - 49	7(5)	6(3)	9(9)	3(6)	25(5)	2(3)	6(6)	0
50 - 99	1(0.8)	1(0.5)	7(8)	2(4)	11(2)	1(1)	0	0
100 -500	1(0.8)	3(2)	4(4)	2(4)	10(2)	1(1)	0	0
Total sites	132	182	93	52	459	72	95	24
Missing cases	1	0	0	0	1	0	1	0

Table 39. Cultural affiliations of sites in Q Ranch study area (percentages in parentheses)

	Young	Chediski Peak	McFadden Peak	Blue House Mountain	All Quads	Grasshopper	Vosberg	APS-CS
Unspecified prehistoric	5(5)	52(31)	20(77)	6(14)	83(24)	20(31)	0	21(86)
Unspecified Mogollon	2(2)	23(14)	0	7(17)	32(9)	10(15)	0	0
Early Mogollon	6(6)**	10(6)**	0	1(2)	17(5)	5(8)	4(4)**	0
Late Mogollon	64(61)**	61(36)**	1(4)	27(64)	153(45)	27(41)	60(65)**	0
Salado	0	2(0.9)	4(15)	0	6(2)	1(2)	0	2(10)
Archaic/unspecified preceramic	1(1)	1(0.6)	0	0	2(0.6)	1(2)	1(1)	0
Anglo	4(4)	1(0.6)	1(4)	0	6(2)	0	2(2)	1(5)
Apache	1(1)	15(9)	0	1(2)	17(5)	1(2)	1(1)	0
Unspecified multicomponent	11(10)	0	0	0	11(3)	1(2)*	12(13)	0
Anasazi/Hohokam	1(1)	0	0	0	1(0.3)	0	1(1)	0
Other	10(9)	3(2)	0	0	13(3)	0	12(13)	0
Total sites	105	168	26	42	341	66	93	24
Missing cases	28	14	67	10	119	6	3	0

* Anglo/Apache multicomponent; ** Salado or Mogollon

of small sites in the former area are indicative of more intensive
survey. Similarly, Vosberg data reflect the situation in the Young quad,
but entirely lack large sites, probably due to the smaller area covered
by the ASU survey. If the Vosberg and Grasshopper surveys were equivalent in size, then the large Q Ranch pueblo would be included in the
former area. Similar to Vosberg but in contrast to its respective quad,
the APS Cholla line survey data exhibit a definite bias toward small
sites. Obviously, the line has avoided the large, costly-to-excavate
sites.

In summary, the CP and BHM quads, more than any others, have provided data which probably most closely approximate the true picture of
site-size variability. If one compares the large sites, for which the
data are most complete, the population in the BHM quad was distributed
among several medium to large pueblos of 50 to 99 or more rooms, while
the CP quad population was concentrated in larger pueblos. Although the
Young quad surveys are biased in favor of small sites, it is believed
that the fewest large sites will be found in this quad. In terms of
population aggregation, however, it is most similar to the CP quad. The
largest known ruin in the Young quad--the Q Ranch Pueblo--is about half
the size of the Grasshopper Ruin but still much larger than any known in
the BHM or MFP quads. Population in the MFP quad was distributed among
numerous medium to large pueblos as in the case of the BHM quad. Thus, population
appears to have been more dispersed in the southern quads and more aggregated
in the northern quads. This difference corresponds with a topographical
difference: the basins, valleys, and canyons in which the large sites
are located are smaller and more distinct in the southern quads, while
in the northern quads basins and valleys are larger and topographical
boundaries between drainages less distinct.

Cultural Affiliation and Chronology

Survey data from all quads demonstrate an interesting aspect of
assigning cultural affiliation in surveys: there is either a fear of
assigning affiliation on the basis of scant data or a real inability to
do this on the basis of survey data.

The summed data for all quads appear to provide a good indicator
of the relative frequencies of various cultural affiliations (Table 39).
Sites in the Q Ranch region are predominantly (66 percent) Mogollon. A
large, unknown Salado component probably exists, but is proportionately
smaller than the Mogollon. There is a very small proportion of preceramic sites and a low frequency of Anasazi and Hohokam manifestations.
Anglo and Apache sites also occur in low frequencies, with Apache sites
the more common.

158

Several problems are presented by the large unspecified categories (up to 30 percent of all sites), which include sites originally described as unknown prehistoric, sites where no information as to affiliation was provided, and multicomponent sites where all components were not specified. The proportion of unspecified sites is so great that patterns could be altered if affiliations were eventually determined. One would expect, for example, larger proportions of Apache, Hohokam, Anasazi, Archaic, and, especially, Salado sites; the Mogollon sites, however, would still probably be in the majority. It may be that Anasazi, Hohokam, and, especially, Salado traits are not differentiated from Mogollon traits in the early periods, but that distinctive patterns emerge later.

If one examines each quad and intensive survey area, the highest proportion of sites with unspecified affiliations comes from the CP and MFP quads and the Grasshopper and APS-CS surveys. In contrast, the low frequencies of such sites for the Young quad and Vosberg survey, where survey was coupled with excavation, support the idea that affiliation is difficult to determine from survey data alone. Test excavations, however, did not aid in the determination of affiliation at multicomponent sites in Vosberg.

The MFP quad is the only one where Mogollon sites are outnumbered by those of another culture, in this case the Salado. This may reflect more extensive Salado occupation of this quad, an expected phenomenon considering that MFP has the easiest access into the Roosevelt Basin. However, the cultural affiliations of 78 percent of the MFP quad sites are unspecified. The absence of Salado sites in the Young quad suggests that the Q Ranch Plateau witnessed little Salado occupation. Salado peoples were most probably concentrated in the southern part of the quad, in the lower Cherry Creek Valley.

The distribution of historic sites reflects the modern political boundaries resulting from the aggregation of various Apache bands within the Fort Apache Indian Reservation in the 1870s. The CP and BHM quads are contained within the reservation, while the Young and MFP quads lie primarily outside the reservation. The Young and CP quads contrast in relative proportions of Anglo and Apache sites: Young is high in Anglo sites and low in Apache sites, while CP shows the opposite pattern. The intensively surveyed areas within each quad exhibit consistent patterns.

Chronological information is provided primarily by the decorated ceramics, with additional information derived from architectural types and, in some cases, tree rings. Decorated ceramics are divided into six classes: black-on-white wares (generally predating A.D. 1300), red-on-buff wares (early varieties such as Santa Cruz and Sacaton), late Salado polychromes (Gila and Tonto), early Salado polychromes, Fourmile Polychrome (White Mountain Red Wares postdating A.D. 1300), and earlier White Mountain Red Wares.

The black-on-white wares are the most commonly found decorated ceramics in all quads and survey areas (Table 40). These ceramics are present at nearly 75 percent or more of the sites reporting ceramics in the MFP and BHM quads and in the Vosberg and APS-CS areas. According to data from the Vosberg and APS-CS surveys, the red-on-buff wares are also relatively common in the MFP quad, but most common in the Young quad. Ceramic information from the many Gila Pueblo sites in the MFP quad was not available for this analysis; thus, the MFP quad is represented almost exclusively by data from the small number of APS-CS sites located there. The early White Mountain Red Wares are also most common in the Young and MFP quads, while early Salado Polychromes are most common in the Young quad.

The early ceramic varieties are least common in the BHM quad, which instead has the highest percentage of late Gila, Tonto, and Fourmile polychromes. The CP quad has moderate percentages of both early and late ceramics, especially White Mountain Red Wares.

It can be inferred from these data that the MFP and Young quads have the largest proportion of early sites, that the BHM quad has the largest proportion of late sites, and that the CP quad has relatively high proportions of both.

Medium to large sites are almost exclusively associated with post-A.D. 1300 ceramics. These inferences are consistent with the earlier observations that population was relatively high in the Young quad during earlier periods of occupation and higher in the CP quad during the later periods.

There are, however, serious problems in this analysis. In the first place, ceramic information has been reported for only a small fraction of the sites known in the region; admittedly, many sites with unspecified cultural affiliations do not have associated ceramics. In addition, a considerable bias in favor of early sites is apparent in the case of the MFP quad, which is represented by a small number of APS-CS sites; it is known that the many cliff sites in this quad are late and contemporaneous with the associated Fourmile pueblos (Haury 1934). Thus, one would expect the MFP quad to have many more late sites than noted above.

Whereas ceramic information is not usually reported on survey forms, phase/period designations often are noted. As Tables 39 and 41 show, for example, the number of Mogollon sites increases through the early phases up to LM II, then sharply drops off in LM III. This is in accord with the greater number of sites reporting the early ceramic types. A concomitant of the reduction in the number of sites during the LM III period is a tremendous increase in site size (four to ten times as large in the later period). As indicated by ceramic data, almost all large sites postdate A.D. 1300.

Table 40. Presence of ceramic types at sites (percentages in parentheses)

	Young	Chediski Peak	McFadden Peak	Blue House Mountain	All Quads	Grasshopper	Vosberg	APS-CS
Black-on-white	21(60)	106(100)	24(80)	34(74)	185(64)	42(60)	11(69)	19(90)
Gila/Tonto polychromes	1(3)	5(5)	2(7)	3(7)	11(4)	1(1)	1(6)	0
Earlier Salado polychromes	5(14)	5(5)	1(3)	2(4)	13(4)	3(4)	5(31)	0
Fourmile polychrome	1(3)	19(18)	5(17)	22(48)	47(17)	6(9)	1(6)	0
Earlier White Mountain Red Wares	7(20)	18(17)	6(20)	7(15)	38(14)	11(16)	3(19)	1(5)
Red-on-buff	10(29)	0	1(3)	0	11(4)	0	8(50)	1(5)
Total sites*	35	106	30	46	288	70	16	21
Missing cases	98	75	63	6	172	2	80	0

* Total sites = number of sites for which presence or absence of ceramics is reported.

Table 41. Sites of Late Mogollon periods in Q Ranch study area (percentages in parentheses)

	Young	Chediski Peak	McFadden Peak	Blue House Mountain	All Quads	Grasshopper	Vosberg	APS-CS
Late Mogollon I	2(2)	15(9)	0	9(21)	26(8)	3(5)	2(2)	0
Late Mogollon II	55(52)	25(15)	0	3(7)	83(24)	16(24)	55(51)	0
Late Mogollon III	4(4)	10(6)	1(4)	4(10)	18(5)	3(5)	3(3)	0
Unspecified Late Mogollon	1(1)	11(6)	0	11(26)	23(7)	5(8)	0	0
Other sites	44(42)	107(64)	25(96)	15(36)	211(62)	39(59)	33(35)	24(100)
Total sites	146	168	26	42	341	66	93	24
Missing cases	27	14	67	10	119	6	3	0

The individual quads and survey areas also show consistent results. The Vosberg area shows a population loss, as Chenhall (1972) and Cartledge (1976) have maintained. This area may not be representative of the entire quad, however, since much of the population from the Vosberg and other areas could have aggregated at the Q Ranch Pueblo. In contrast, the CP quad exhibits relatively similar frequencies of both LM II and LM III sites. The greatly increased size of LM III sites (on the average, two to ten times larger than LM II sites) clearly shows rapid expansion in the LM III period, as Tuggle (1970) has suggested. The lack of large, late sites in the Young quad argues against the occurrence of an equivalent expansion of population in that area at this time.

Population expansion may also have taken place in the Sierra Ancha and lower Cherry Creek areas, as suggested by the many sites dated by tree rings. However, little evidence concerning early sites in these areas is available. Although the data from Wesley Wells' survey could not be obtained in time for use in this analysis, it is appropriate to return to some of his conclusions. Wells (1971) argues for the virtual abandonment of the lower Cherry Creek area by A.D. 1300 and an overall pattern of population dynamics very reminiscent of the pattern apparent in the Vosberg area. However, the population probably moved to the higher elevations around the creek, such as the Sierra Ancha, Mustang Ridge, and Sombrero Peak. Added to the many large, late, cliff sites in these areas is the Granite Basin Ruin, one of the largest in the region and known to date after A.D. 1300. Thus, the MFP quad seems again very similar to the BHM quad in having both early and late sites as well as a possible expansion of population in the late period.

Summary and Conclusions

What contributions does the examination of regional survey data make to the research questions discussed earlier? Despite the many biases, inconsistencies, and gaps in the data from the various surveys conducted within the larger region, certain significant patterns are discernible. These patterns support many of the conclusions derived regarding the individual survey areas.

Elevation, for example, appears to have been an important factor in site location throughout the region. Areas between 4000 and 5000 feet and above 6000 feet in elevation do not appear to have been inhabited. Sites with structures tend to occur more often at lower elevations within the 5000 to 6000-foot contour than do sites without structures. Tuggle's observation of chronological correlates to site elevation on the Salt Draw Plateau could not be substantiated for the region as a whole, however. The association between agricultural features and late sites proposed by Rodgers (1970) was also corroborated. It is interesting to note, however, that agricultural features are more common in the two southern quads (MFP and BHM).

The rapid aggregation of population on the Salt Draw Plateau after A.D. 1300 (Tuggle 1970) appears to be characteristic of the region as a whole. The Salt Draw Plateau, however, probably experienced the greatest population growth and aggregation in the region during this period. The immediate area within the Vosberg locality does not seem to have experienced population growth during this period, although events on the Q Ranch Plateau as a whole resembled those on the Salt Draw Plateau. Likewise, the population of Cibecue and Pleasant valleys appears to have grown only slightly.

Little information can be contributed to the study of the problems of seriation and environmental stress due to the lack of artifactual material in the survey collections. Regional population increases and an associated increase in the use of agricultural features are suggestive of some sort of population pressure.

Late Sites

It is safe to assume that most masonry pueblos of 50 or more rooms have been located and recorded by one of the institutions that have worked in the Q Ranch region. Large sites in areas untouched by archaeological survey have invariably been found and brought to the attention of archaeologists by ranchers, hunters, and campers. These large sites are primarily late, postdating A.D. 1300 (Tuggle's LM III, Chenhall's Ceramic Group V, Haury's Canyon Creek Phase). Because the set of large, late sites known in the region is probably then a close approximation of the actual number of such sites, several descriptive statements can be made concerning settlement patterns during the late period of occupation in the region. Such statements have important implications for the understanding of subsistence, social organization, and exchange during this period.

Differences in the size and distribution of large, late sites on the Salt Draw Plateau and Q Ranch Plateau correspond with previously described differences in environmental and physiographic conditions. These environmental differences are seen as the source of minor variations in an overall pattern of adaptation to the ecologically diverse, mountainous region between the Colorado Plateau and Basin and Range provinces.

The Q Ranch Plateau has been characterized as more heavily dissected than the Salt Draw Plateau. The former is drained by a series of east-west-coursing streams ending in Canyon and Cherry creeks. The divide between the east and west-coursing drainages is marked by a series of prominent ridges and mesas. This physiographic pattern produces several small basins at the headwaters of one or more of these streams. The basins are isolated from each other by narrow canyons and high ridges.

In contrast, the Salt Draw Plateau is drained by a single stream, the Salt River Draw, and several tributary drainages. This pattern produces a single long valley with several smaller valleys and canyons converging towards its southern half. These branch valleys are roughly equivalent in size to the basins of the Q Ranch Plateau. Unlike the basins, however, each valley opens into the larger valley of the Salt River Draw. Thus, the drainage and morphological patterns of the Salt Draw Plateau facilitate interaction between subareas (valleys), while such patterns in the Q Ranch Plateau tend to isolate subareas (basins).

Large, late pueblos occur in almost every basin and branch valley. The largest pueblos, such as those at Grasshopper and Q Ranch, are centrally located within their respective areas. That basins and valleys were the centers of relatively intensive horticultural activities is suggested by factors of topography, water availability, and vegetation, and by the fact that large, permanent settlements were located within these areas. Of interest here is the observation that the large pueblos of the Salt Draw Plateau are almost twice the size of similar pueblos on the Q Ranch Plateau.

Since the areas contained within these basins and valleys are roughly of equal size, the availability of potentially arable land does not appear to have been the decisive factor in determining the size of settlements. Water availability and vegetation also appear to have been constant. Soils are probably different due to the different geological compositions of the two plateaus; however, the implications of soil differences in regards to horticulture cannot be determined at this time. On the other hand, variation in settlement size does correspond with differences in drainage patterns and topography. Thus, facility of interaction between settlements or of access to different areas of the plateaus appears to have been an important factor in relation to differences in settlement size.

Local interaction between subareas of a plateau must be distinguished from regional interaction involving movement between the plateaus and areas outside the region as defined. In contrast to local interaction, regional interaction does not appear to have affected the observed size differential between settlements in the Q Ranch Plateau and Salt Draw Plateau. A massive escarpment on the east side of Canyon Creek effectively isolates much of the Salt Draw Plateau from areas to the west, while high ridges and mountains separate it from areas to the east. In contrast, a series of gradually ascending canyons penetrate deeply into the Q Ranch Plateau, providing excellent access to this area from the outside. The west side of the Q Ranch Plateau, in particular, is provided with direct access to the Tonto Basin and Pleasant Valley areas via Cherry Creek.

Differences in regional access correspond with differences in the size of cliff sites located in the side canyons of Cherry and Canyon creeks. Although cliff sites as a group are smaller than sites on the plateaus, those on the west side of the Q Ranch Plateau divide are more numerous and larger than those on the east side. The largest known cliff site east of

this divide, the Canyon Creek Ruin, is about half the size of the largest
site west of the divide, AZ C:1:16. This pattern is diametrically opposed
to that of sites in the basins and valleys of the plateaus. The
differences among cliff sites may be due in part to the poorer survey
of the Canyon Creek area. Nonetheless, most of the largest sites should
be known in all areas.

Thus, on the one hand, the size of cliff settlements corresponds
with ease of access to major areas of the region. We may infer then
that a primary function of cliff sites was related to regional interaction.
On the other hand, the size of settlements in the basins and valleys of
the plateaus is related to ease of access to subareas of each plateau,
which suggests that the primary function of the latter settlements involved the exploitation of indigenous resources--probably through horti-
culture--and the local exchange of goods and services.

The number and size of large, late settlements suggest that the
Q Ranch and Salt Draw plateaus were densely populated relative to other
areas and periods. The problem of absolute contemporaneity of late sites
has already been raised. We will assume for the time being that these
sites were contemporaneous during at least part of the late period. Such
an assumption is quite valid, given the fact that the available tree-ring
and ceramic data indicate that the occupation of most sites overlapped
considerably, even if their growth cycles were not absolutely contemporaneous.

If we assume that late sites are contemporaneous, then the settlement distribution reflects a complex organizational pattern. The two
plateaus were similarly organized and probably reflect distinct units.
Each plateau contains a single extremely large pueblo (over 200 rooms)
surrounded by a series of medium-sized sites (20-100 rooms) at a minimum
distance of about 4.8 km (3 miles). On both plateaus, numerous smaller
sites (5-20 rooms) are interspersed among the large and medium-sized
pueblos. The sites on the plateaus are bounded in turn by small to
medium-sized sites in the cliffs of the surrounding canyons. Thus, the
late period in the Q Ranch region is characterized by a settlement system composed of four or more levels of habitation sites, in addition to
specialized-activity loci. The association of such settlement stratification with peak population expansion and aggregation is suggestive of
maximum interaction and exploitation of diverse ecozones.

Earlier Sites

The emergence of this late settlement pattern appears to have been
a relatively sudden phenomemon, although its roots are apparent in earlier
periods. The work done at the sites predating A.D. 1300 indicates a
continuous increase in the number and size of settlements and agricultural features. In fact, a more precise assessment of contemporaneity
of sites may lessen the magnitude of the changes observed in the late
period, although the relative changes should not be significantly affected.

What do we know about the sites predating A.D. 1300? Earlier sites appear to be most common on the Q Ranch Plateau, especially in the Vosberg area, although it must be remembered that there is a strong possibility of survey bias in this instance. Early sites can be assigned to two different periods: a middle period (LM II, Ceramic Group IV) dating from about A.D. 1050-1300, and an early period (LM I; Ceramic Groups I, II, and III) from about A.D. 700-1100. Almost nothing is known about sites predating A.D. 700 in the region. The ceramic assemblage associated with the pit house villages characteristic of the early period includes Hohokam and Anasazi types. These types are especially common in the Vosberg area, which had easy access to Cherry Creek. Cherry Creek, in turn, provides one of the best routes from the Colorado Plateau to the Tonto Basin areas from which the nonlocal ceramic types came. Thus, regional interaction may have been extremely important prior to A.D. 1000, although such interaction was most likely of a nature quite distinct from that after A.D. 1300. During the early period, Vosberg may have served as an important stopover for migrants or travelers moving north-south. Its position along Cherry Creek would have made it an ideal location, since it is among the first well-watered basins along Cherry Creek north of the Tonto Basin. Extended stays of such migrants in Vosberg are suggested by the existence of permanent habitations of Hohokam and Anasazi-style construction. The abundance of steatite at Vosberg and in the Q Ranch Plateau as a whole may have further contributed to the area's attractiveness.

Population continued to grow at a rapid rate throughout the region until A.D. 1300 when the Salt Draw Plateau emerged as the area of densest population. The population of the Q Ranch Plateau probably continued to grow into the late period, although at a slower pace. Several important changes took place between A.D. 1000 and 1300: pit houses were replaced with aboveground structures, sites became larger, site locations changed, an increasing variety and number of agricultural features were constructed, and the range of ceramic variability was narrowed and indigenous types emerged. Although such changes presage the developments of the late period, they do not account for the magnitude of the changes that occurred later.

The changes during the period A.D. 1050 to 1300 can be interpreted as reflecting increasing complexity in settlement systems with minimal stratification in habitation-site size, increasingly intensive horticultural activities, and the development of local traditions. It is significant to note that no sites larger than 20 rooms are found on either plateau, and no cliff sites are known in the region prior to A.D. 1270. This circumstance tends to only accentuate the gap in our knowledge of the transition to the late period.

Regional Research Problems

The conclusions drawn in this study highlight several regional research problems that require examination. One problem concerns occupation of the canyon areas. Several questions require resolution:

(1) precisely when were canyons occupied relative to the aggregation and expansion of the plateau settlements, (2) what functions did cliff sites have in the late regional settlement system, and (3) is there any evidence of exploitation of canyon areas in early periods?

Traditionally, cliff sites have been seen as seasonal habitation loci related to larger settlements and affording access to ecologically diverse areas. The possibility of such seasonal settlements becoming permanent has been interpreted as the product of expansion of population into less desirable niches or the environmental deterioration of plateau areas (Reid 1973, 1978). A contrasting interpretation of the funciton of cliff settlements has been offered in this study. These conflicting interpretations can be explored through locational and chronological studies.

Expansion of dendrochronological analyses of cliff sites and fine-scale seriation of ceramics from other sites can provide valuable informa- tion about the problems of contemporaneity and the timing of population movements in the late period. Locational studies should compare size of cliff sites and their location relative to regional and local resources. Thus, if local subsistence needs were the prime factor in cliff site location, then site size should be related to the local availability of water, arable land, and wild plants and animals. If expansion of popu- lation from plateau basins and valleys was the cause of movement into canyons, we would expect more and larger sites in the more heavily popu- lated Salt Draw area relative to the Q Ranch Plateau area. If regional interaction was more important than local subsistence needs, we would expect more and larger sites in the Cherry Creek area than in the Canyon Creek area.

A second problem concerns the late settlements in the basins and valleys of the plateaus themselves. If the subsistence base of these settlements was horticultural, then we would expect a relationship among site size, water availability, area of arable land, and soil types. It is proposed that the valleys and basins of the plateaus were the prime agricultural areas in the region. If this is true, then a detailed examination of the physiography of the basins and valleys should produce patterns that correspond with observed differences in late settlement size. Application of locational models and site catchment analysis should prove of immense value in such a study.

A third problem involves the forms of interaction during the dif- ferent time periods; in other words, we need to know what was being ex- changed at the local level in contrast to the regional level. A wide variety of commodities could have been exchanged in either circumstance, including information, food, services, raw materials, tools, and status goods. On the other hand, exchange may not have been as important as the actual movement of groups of people from area to area in search of resources. The form of interaction and types of commodities exchanged would be expected to vary from period to period. For example, were people moving from area to area collecting resources themselves in the early periods and collecting local resources and exchanging them with neighbors

for nonlocal resources in the late period? Also, was steatite as important a commodity in the late period as the work at Vosberg suggests for
the early period?

A final problem concerns the middle period (about A.D. 1050 to
1250-1300) in the occupation of the region. It has been noted that
several important events took place during this period. Thus, an
examination of settlement patterns during this period and comparison
with the other periods is essential. Of special significance to regional
analysis is the comparison of stratification in site size and location
of sites relative to environmental features, resources, and contemporaneous sites.

This brief discussion introduces several research problems and
specific questions. These problems reflect the regional focus of research
employing primarily data that can be obtained from maps, survey, or surface collections. This does not imply that other problems or the use of
excavation procedures are irrelevant to our understanding of the region's
prehistory. Rather, examination of problems discussed here should provide
the groundwork for the examination of other problems. It is readily apparent,
however, that survey of the entire region is impractical. It will be more
efficient to identify smaller areas exhibiting specific environmental and
cultural characteristics that require investigation.

One such area in the vicinity of Campbell and upper Rock House
creeks on the Q Ranch Plateau is traversed by the APS-CS transmission line
corridor. Eighteen APS-CS sites occur in this area in addition to a couple
of sites located by Gila Pueblo. Investigation of APS-CS sites, if conducted within a regional perspective, will offer an excellent opportunity
for adding significant information to our understanding of the prehistory
of the Q Ranch region.

APS-CS Sites and the Q Ranch Region

In a strict sense, the sites located by the APS-CS survey are
representative of sites in the region as a whole. APS-CS sites occur
at elevations (5000-6000 feet) and in topographical situations (on low
hills and ridges within basins) characteristic of most sites in the
region. Eighteen of the 21 sites occur in the headwater basins of Campbell
and Rock House creeks at elevations between 5000 and 5400 feet; the remaining sites are located farther north in the vicinity of Q Ranch. The
Campbell Creek and Rock House Creek basins are isolated from the rest of
the Q Ranch Plateau by a series of ridges, mesas, buttes, and canyons. The
basins are similar to the Vosberg Basin in most environmental features,
although they drain into Canyon Creek.

Sites in the three basins are also similar. Most APS-CS sites are
small sites with structures, date to the period around A.D. 1000-1300,
and, on the basis of comparison with sites from the Vosberg and Grasshopper

areas, can be assigned either a Salado or Mogollon cultural affiliation. No pit houses were identified, although their presence is suspected at one or more sites, nor were any large, late sites located by the APS-CS survey, although their existence has been indicated by Gila Pueblo surveyors, who located one such site in the Rock House Creek Basin and another in an adjoining canyon. Aboveground structures appear almost identical in form, layout, and materials to those in Vosberg. In addition, steatite abounds as raw material, manufacturing debris, and finished products in all three basins. Thus, the APS-CS survey area affords an excellent opportunity to study the importance of regional interaction from the vantage point of proximity to Cherry or Canyon creeks.

The location of the Rock House Creek and Campbell Creek basins on the east side of the Q Ranch Plateau also offers an opportunity to expand the study of cliff sites in Canyon Creek. Comparison with the cliff sites on the western escarpment of the Salt Draw Plateau on the other side of Canyon Creek may shed further light on the function of these sites. As noted earlier, the long, gradually descending canyons of the Q Ranch Plateau contrast markedly with the short, precipitous canyons of the Sierra Ancha and Salt Draw Plateau. Differences in water availability, extent of arable land, and other resources should have affected the size and location of settlements. Comparison of Canyon Creek cliff sites as a group with those of the Sierra Ancha should also provide information concerning the importance of proximity to Cherry Creek and access to the Tonto Basin during the late period. Finally, dendrochronological analysis of cliff sites in the Rock House Creek and Campbell Creek areas should expand our knowledge of the timing of settlement in the canyons.

Comparison of the physiography of the Rock House Creek and Campbell Creek basins with that of the Vosberg and Grasshopper areas could provide needed information concerning the relationship of agricultural potential to the size and location of the late sites in the basins. An added benefit would be derived from comparison of this information with the distribution of early sites during the important but poorly understood period from A.D. 1000 to 1300. Such sites are common in the Rock House Creek and Campbell Creek areas and comprise an overwhelming majority of the APS-CS survey sites.

REFERENCES

Bluhm, Elaine
    1957   The Sawmill Site: a Reserve Phase village, Pine Lawn
            Valley, western New Mexico. _Fieldiana: Anthropology_,
            Vol. 47 (1). Natural History Museum, Chicago.

    1960   Mogollon settlement patterns in Pine Lawn Valley,
            New Mexico. _American Antiquity_ 25: 538-546.

Breternitz, David
    1966   An appraisal of tree-ring dated pottery in the Southwest.
            Anthropological Papers of the University of Arizona 10.
            Tucson: University of Arizona Press.

Bullard, William R.
    1962   The Corro Colorado Site and pithouse architecture in the
            southwestern United States prior to A.D. 900. _Papers of_
            the Peabody Museum of American Archaeology and Ethnology,
            Harvard University, Vol. 44 (2).

Cartledge, Thomas R.
    1976   _Human ecology and changing patterns of co-residence in_
            the Vosberg locality, central Arizona. Ph.D. disserta-
            tion, Arizona State University. Ann Arbor: University
            Microfilms.

Chenhall, Robert G.
    1972   _Random sampling in an archaeological survey._ Ph.D.
            dissertation, Arizona State University. Ann Arbor:
            University Microfilms.

Ciolek-Torrello, Richard S.
    1978   _A statistical analysis of activity organization at_
            Grasshopper Pueblo, Arizona. Ph.D. dissertation,
            University of Arizona. Ann Arbor: University Microfilms.

Ciolek-Torrello, Richard S. and J. J. Reid
    1974   Change in household size at Grasshopper. _The Kiva_ 40: 39-47.

Clark, Geoffrey
    1969   A preliminary analysis of burial clusters at the Grass-
            hopper Site, east central Arizona. _The Kiva_ 35: 57-86.

Danson, Edward B.
    1957   An archaeological survey of west central New Mexico and
            east central Arizona. _Papers of the Peabody Museum of_
            Archaeology and Ethnology, Harvard University, Vol. 44 (1).

Dean, Jeffrey and William Robinson
    in preparation
            Dendrochronology of Grasshopper Pueblo. In Multidis-
            ciplinary research at the Grasshopper Ruin, edited by
            William A. Longacre. Anthropological Papers of the
            University of Arizona.

Ellison, Glenn R.
    1968   Cowboys under the Mogollon Rim. Tucson: University of
            Arizona Press.

Forrest, Earle R.
    1950   Arizona's dark and bloody ground. Idaho: Caxton Printers, Ltd.

Goodwin, Grenville
    1942   The social organization of the Western Apache. Chicago:
            University of Chicago Press.

Harrill, Bruce
    1967 Prehistoric burials near Young, Arizona. The Kiva 33: 54-59.

Harris, Myra
    1974   An investigation into trade and contact at Vosberg, Arizona.
            MS. M.A. Thesis, Arizona State University, Tempe.

Haury, Emil W.
    1934   The Canyon Creek Ruin and the cliff dwellings of the Sierra
            Ancha. Medallion Papers 14.   Globe: Gila Pueblo.

Haury, Emil W. and E. B. Sayles
    1947   An early pit house village of the Mogollon Culture,
            Forestdale Valley, Arizona. University of Arizona Social
            Science Bulletin 16,   Vol. 11, No. 4.

Hill, James N.
    1970   Broken K Pueblo: prehistoric social organization in the
            American Southwest. Anthropological Papers of the University
            of Arizona 18.   Tucson: University of Arizona Press.

Hough, Walter
    1903   Archaeological field work in northeastern Arizona: the
            Museum-Gates Expedition of 1901. Annual Report of the
            U.S. National Museum for 1901, pp. 279-358. Washington.

    1919   Archaeological exploration in Arizona, 1918. Smithsonian
            Miscellaneous Collections 70 (2) 90-3.

    1920   Archaeological excavations in Arizona, 1919. Smithsonian
            Miscellaneous Collections 72 (1) 64-6.

    1935   Exploration of ruins in the White Mountain Apache Indian
            Reservation, Arizona. Proceedings, U.S. National Museum 78
            (2856) 1-21. Washington.

Johnson, Alfred E.
  1965   The development of western Pueblo culture. Ph.D. dissertation,
          University of Arizona. Ann Arbor: University Microfilms.

Kelly, Roger E.
  1969   An archaeological survey in the Payson Basin, central Arizona.
          Plateau 42: 46-65.

Longacre, William A.
  1975   Population dynamics at the Grasshopper Pueblo, Arizona.
          In Population studies in archaeology and biological
          anthropology: a symposium, edited by Alan Swedlund,
          pp. 71-76. Memoirs of the Society for American
          Archaeology 40 (2), Part 2. Washington.

  1976   Population dynamics at the Grasshopper Pueblo, Arizona.
          In Demographic anthropology: quantitative approaches,
          edited by Ezra Zubrow, pp. 169-184. Albuquerque:
          University of New Mexico Press.

Longacre, William A. and J. Jefferson Reid
  1974   The University of Arizona Archaeological Field School at
          Grasshopper: eleven years of multidisciplinary research
          and teaching. The Kiva 40: 3-38

Lowe, Charles H.
  1964   Arizona's natural environment. Tucson: University of
          Arizona Press.

Mayro, Linda, Stephanie M. Whittlesey, and J. Jefferson Reid
  1976   The Salado presence at Grasshopper Pueblo. The Kiva 42: 85-94.

Moore, Richard T.
  1968   Mineral deposits of the Fort Apache Indian Reservation,
          Arizona. Arizona Bureau of Mines Bulletin 177.

Morenon, E. Pierre
  1977   Architectural attributes and intra-site variability: a
          case study. Ph.D. dissertation, Southern Methodist University.
          Ann Arbor: University Microfilms.

Morris, Donald H.
  1969   A ninth-century Salado (?) kiva at Walnut Creek, Arizona.
          Plateau 42: 1-10.

  1970   Walnut Creek Village: a ninth-century Hohokam-Anasazi
          settlement in the mountains of central Arizona.
          American Antiquity 35: 49-61.

Olsen, Stanley J. and John W. Olsen
     1974   The macaws of Grasshopper Ruin. The Kiva 40: 67-70.

Peirce, H. Wesley
     1967   Geologic guidebook 2 - Highways of Arizona, Arizona Highway
              77 and 177. Arizona Bureau of Mines Bulletin 176.

Reid, J. Jefferson
     1973   Growth and response to stress at Grasshopper Pueblo, Arizona.
              Ph.D. dissertation, University of Arizona. Ann Arbor:
              University Microfilms.

     1978   Response to stress at Grasshopper Pueblo, Arizona. In
              Discovering past behavior: experiments in the archaeology
              of the American Southwest, edited by Paul F. Grebinger.
              London: Gordon and Breach.

Robertson, Patricia Crown
     1977   Distribution and function of pre-aggregation communities
              in the Grasshopper region. Paper presented at the 42nd
              Annual Meeting of the Society for American Archaeology,
              New Orleans.

     1978   Design variability in the Southwest: new insights from the
              Chodistaas Site. Paper presented at the 43rd Annual Meeting
              of the Society for American Archaeology. Tucson.

Rock, James
     1974   The use of social models in archaeological interpretation.
              The Kiva 40: 81-91.

Rodgers, James B.
     1970   Prehistoric agricultural systems in the Vosberg locality,
              Arizona. Paper presented to a symposium on water control
              systems at the 1970 Pecos Conference, Santa Fe, New Mexico.

Spain, J. N.
     1976   Prehistoric agricultural land-use strategies in the
              Grasshopper region: a research overview. MS. Arizona
              State Museum Library, Tucson.

Spier, Leslie
     1919   Ruins in the White Mountains, Arizona. Anthropological
              Papers of the American Museum of Natural History 18 (5) 363-87.
              New York.

Thompson, Raymond H. and William A. Longacre
     1966   University of Arizona Archaeological Field School at
              Grasshopper, east central Arizona. The Kiva 31: 255-275.

Tuggle, Harold David
     1970   Prehistoric community relationships in east central Arizona.
             Ph.D. dissertation, University of Arizona. Ann Arbor:
             University Microfilms.

Wells, Wesley
     1971   Prehistoric settlement patterns of lower Cherry Creek.
             MS. Department of Anthropology, Arizona State
             University, Tempe.

Wendorf, Fred
     1953   Archaeological studies in the Petrified Forest National
             Monument. Museum of Northern Arizona Bulletin 27.

Whittlesey, Stephanie M.
     1974   Identification of imported ceramics through functional
             analysis of attributes. The Kiva 40: 101-112.

     1978   Status and death at Grasshopper Pueblo: experiments toward
             an archaeological theory of correlates. Ph.D. dissertation,
             University of Arizona. Ann Arbor: University Microfilms.

Wilson, Eldred D.
     1928   Asbestos deposits of Arizona. Arizona Bureau of Mines
             Bulletin 126.

Wilson, Eldred D.
     1962   A résumé of the geology of Arizona. Arizona Bureau of
             Mines Bulletin 171.

CHAPTER 6

THE TONTO-ROOSEVELT STUDY AREA
by David A. Gregory

Introduction

This section of the survey report deals with that segment of the
APS Cholla line corridor between APS Tower locations 320 and 497. This
area will subsequently be referred to as the Tonto-Roosevelt study area.
A total of 71 archaeological sites were discovered and recorded during
the course of the survey of this segment; this inventory of sites forms
the basis for the present discussion (Table 42).

This report is primarily descriptive in emphasis and is organized as follows. A specific description of the location of the Cholla
line is followed by a general summary of the environment and a breakdown and expansion of the corridor into five geographically defined
study units. Previous archaeological research accomplished in the
area is summarized and a critical review and summary of the known culture history of the area presented. Variability among the sites recorded
by the survey is dealt with in terms of a set of empirically defined
site types, and the locational characteristics of the sites by study
unit are briefly discussed. A summary discussion of the survey data
in terms of the known sequence of occupation and current research problems completes this section of the report.

Table 42. Archaeological sites in the Tonto-Roosevelt segment of the Cholla-Saguaro corridor (continued)

ASM Number	Field Number	Cultural-temporal Affiliation	Site Type	Approximate Size (m2)	USGS Quad	Elevation (feet)
AZ U:12:26	CS-26	Historic:Anglo (1930s)	Features with artifact scatter	3.3	Superior 7.5 min.	4000-4140
AZ U:12:30	CS-67 and CS-309	Prehistoric (post-A.D. 1150)	Structures with artifact scatter	6650	Haunted Canyon 7.5 min.	3320
AZ U:12:31	CS-63	Prehistoric:Salado (?)	Structures with artifact scatter	11,640	Haunted Canyon 7.5 min.	3260
AZ U:12:33	CS-300	Prehistoric (unknown)	Features with artifact scatters	6975	Superior 7.5 min.	4040
AZ U:12:34	CS-301	Prehistoric (post-A.D. 1150)	Structures with artifact scatters	16,740	Superior 7.5 min.	4240
AZ U:12:35	CS-305	Prehistoric (unknown) Historic (1930s?)	Features with artifact scatter	13,200	Superior 7.5 min.	4160
AZ U:12:36	CS-306	Prehistoric (post-A.D. 1150)	Features with artifact scatter	187	Superior 7.5 min.	4160
AZ U:12:37	CS-303	Prehistoric (post-A.D.1150) Historic:Anglo (1930s)	Structures, petroglyph, lithic scatter	29,520	Superior 7.5 min.	4000
AZ U:12:38	CS-307	Prehistoric (post-A.D.1150) Historic:Anglo (1930s)	Features with artifact scatter	5280	Superior 7.5 min.	4160

Table 42. Archaeological sites in the Tonto-Roosevelt segment of the Cholla-Saguaro corridor (continued)

ASM Number	Field Number	Cultural-temporal Affiliation	Site Type	Approximate Size (m2)	USGS Quad	Elevation (feet)
AZ V:1:4	CS-28	Prehistoric (unknown) Historic:probably Apache	Features with artifact scatter	40,250	McFadden Peak 15 min.	4040-4080
AZ V:1:5	CS-45	Prehistoric:Salado (?)	Features with artifact scatter	455	McFadden Peak 15 min.	2840
AZ V:1:6	CS-223	Prehistoric (unknown)	Artifact scatter	77,400	McFadden Peak 15 min.	3880-3960
AZ V:1:7	CS-241 and 8a	Prehistoric (unknown)	Artifact scatter	2975	McFadden Peak 15 min.	2840
AZ V:5:11	CS-27	Prehistoric:Salado (?) Historic (1930s)	Features with artifact scatter	9600	Rockinstraw Mtn. 15 min.	2800
AZ V:5:12	CS-29	Prehistoric:Salado (?) (A.D. 1250-1325)	Structures with artifact scatter	600	Rockinstraw Mtn. 15 min.	2780
AZ V:5:13	CS-30	Prehistoric:Salado (about A.D. 1300)	Structures with artifact scatter	3000	Rockinstraw Mtn. 15 min.	2680
AZ V:5:14	CS-31	Prehistoric:Salado (about A.D. 1100-1250)	Features with artifact scatter	3200	Rockinstraw Mtn. 15 min.	2760
AZ V:5:15	CS-32	Prehistoric:Salado (?) (post-A.D. 1150)	Structures with artifact scatter	864	Rockinstraw Mtn. 15 min.	2680

Table 42. Archaeological sites in the Tonto-Roosevelt segment of the Cholla-Saguaro corridor (continued)

ASM Number	Field Number	Cultural-temporal Affiliation	Site Type	Approximate Size (m2)	USGS Quad	Elevation (feet)
AZ V:5:16	CS-33	Prehistoric:Salado (A.D. 1150-1300)	Structures with artifact scatter	unknown	Rockinstraw Mtn. 15 min.	2760
AZ V:5:17	CS-34	Historic:Anglo (post-1930s)	Structures with artifact scatter	12,950	Rockinstraw Mtn. 15 min.	2640
AZ V:5:18	CS-35	Prehistoric:Salado (A.D. 1000-1250)	Structures with artifact scatter	720	Rockinstraw Mtn. 15 min.	2760
AZ V:5:19	CS-36	Prehistoric:Salado (?) (post-A.D. 1150)	Feature with artifact scatter	1875	Rockinstraw Mtn. 15 min.	2680
AZ V:5:20	CS-38	Prehistoric:Salado (?) (post-A.D. 1150)	Feature with artifact scatter	2590	Rockinstraw Mtn. 15 min.	2820
AZ V:5:21	CS-39	Prehistoric:Salado (A.D. 1150-1300)	Structures with artifact scatter	26,400	Rockinstraw Mtn. 15 min.	2680
AZ V:5:22	CS-40	Prehistoric:Salado (?) (post-A.D. 1150(?))	Structures with artifact scatter	312	Rockinstraw Mtn. 15 min.	2720
AZ V:5:23	CS-41	Historic:Anglo (1880-1917)	Features with artifact scatter	495	Rockinstraw Mtn. 15 min.	2680
AZ V:5:24	CS-42	Prehistoric (unknown)	Structures with artifact scatter	1350	Rockinstraw Mtn. 15 min.	2700
AZ V:5:25	CS-43	Prehistoric:Salado (A.D. 1000-1200)	Structures with artifact scatter	525	Rockinstraw Mtn. 15 min.	2680

Table 42. Archaeological sites in the Tonto-Roosevelt segment of the Cholla-Saguaro corridor (continued)

ASM Number	Field Number	Cultural-temporal Affiliation	Site Type	Approximate Size (m2)	USGS Quad	Elevation (feet)
AZ V:5:26	CS-47	Prehistoric:Salado (post-A.D. 1150)	Structures with artifact scatter	54,000	Rockinstraw Mtn. 15 min.	2780
AZ V:5:29	CS-50	Prehistoric (unknown)	Structures with artifact scatter	272	Rockinstraw Mtn. 15 min.	3760
AZ V:5:30	CS-61	Prehistoric:Salado (?)	Structures with artifact scatter	2142	Rockinstraw Mtn. 15 min.	3840
AZ V:5:31	CS-57	Prehistoric:Salado (?) (post-A.D. 1150(?))	Structures with artifact scatter	3685	Rockinstraw Mtn. 15 min.	3800
AZ V:5:32	CS-59	Prehistoric (unknown)	Structures with artifact scatter	100	Rockinstraw Mtn. 15 min.	3800
AZ V:5:33	CS-70	Prehistoric (unknown)	Possible structure	unknown	Rockinstraw Mtn. 15 min.	3680
AZ V:5:34	CS-44	Prehistoric:Archaic (?)	Lithic scatter	2000	Rockinstraw Mtn. 15 min.	3280
AZ V:5:35	CS-125	Prehistoric (unknown)	Feature with sherd scatter	22.5	Rockinstraw Mtn. 15 min.	3900
AZ V:5:37	CS-128	Prehistoric (unknown)	Artifact scatter	52,500	Rockinstraw Mtn. 15 min.	3200
AZ V:5:38	CS-226	Prehistoric (unknown)	Lithic scatter	2600	Rockinstraw Mtn. 15 min.	2640

Table 42. Archaeological sites in the Tonto-Roosevelt segment of the Cholla-Saguaro corridor (continued)

ASM Number	Field Number	Cultural-temporal Affiliation	Site Type	Approximate Size (m²)	USGS Quad	Elevation (feet)
AZ V:5:39	CS-227	Prehistoric (unknown)	Artifact scatter	107,000	Rockinstraw Mtn. 15 min.	2640
AZ V:5:41	CS-229	Prehistoric (unknown	Structure with lithic scatter	100,000	Rockinstraw Mtn. 15 min.	2800-2920
AZ V:5:42	CS-230	Prehistoric (unknown)	Lithic scatter	138,544	Rockinstraw Mtn. 15 min.	2600-2720
AZ V:5:44	CS-232	Prehistoric (unknown)	Possible feature with lithic scatter	103,400	Rockinstraw Mtn. 15 min.	2860
AZ V:5:45	CS-233	Prehistoric (unknown)	Lithic scatter	89,775	Rockinstraw Mtn. 15 min.	3120
AZ V:5:46	CS-234	Prehistoric:Salado (?) (post-A.D. 1150(?))	Lithic scatter	23,800	Rockinstraw Mtn. 15 min.	3160
AZ V:5:47	CS-236	Prehistoric (unknown)	Artifact scatter	9600	Rockinstraw Mtn. 15 min.	2920
AZ V:5:48	CS-237	Prehistoric (unknown)	Artifact scatter	8050	Rockinstraw Mtn. 15 min.	3360
AZ V:5:49	CS-238	Prehistoric:Archaic (?) (6000-3000 B.P.) (unknown)(A.D. 900-1300)	Rock shelter and midden	1500	Rockinstraw Mtn. 15 min.	3380

Table 42. Archaeological sites in the Tonto-Roosevelt segment of the Cholla-Saguaro corridor (continued)

ASM Number	Field Number	Cultural-temporal Affiliation	Site Type	Approximate Size (m²)	USGS Quad	Elevation (feet)
AZ V:5:50	CS-239	Prehistoric:Salado (?)	Rock shelter and artifact scatter	1840	Rockinstraw Mtn. 15 min.	3240
AZ V:5:51	CS-240	Prehistoric (unknown)	Rock shelter and artifact scatter	754	Rockinstraw Mtn. 15 min.	3100
AZ V:5:52	CS-247	Prehistoric:Salado (?)	Artifact scatter	36,372	Rockinstraw Mtn. 15 min.	2800
AZ V:5:53	CS-275	Prehistoric:Salado (post-A.D. 1150)	Structures with artifact scatter	3500	Rockinstraw Mtn. 15 min.	3760
AZ V:5:54	CS-276	Prehistoric:Salado (post-A.D. 1150)	Feature with artifact scatter	5775	Rockinstraw Mtn. 15 min.	3680
AZ V:5:55	CS-274	Prehistoric:Salado (post-A.D. 1150)	Feature with artifact scatter	4320	Rockinstraw Mtn. 15 min.	3820
AZ V:5:56	CS-278	Prehistoric (unknown)	Petroglyphs	225	Rockinstraw Mtn. 15 min.	3120
AZ V:9:100	CS-53	Prehistoric:Salado (post-A.D. 1150)	Structure with artifact scatter	80	Inspiration 7.5 min.	3475
AZ V:9:101	CS-55	Prehistoric:Salado (post-A.D. 1150)	Structure with artifact scatter	72	Inspiration 7.5 min.	3480
AX V:9:102	CS-51	Prehistoric:Salado (post-A.D. 1150)	Structure	28	Inspiration 7.5 min.	4600

Table 42. Archaeological sites in the Tonto-Roosevelt segment of the Cholla-Saguaro corridor (continued)

ASM Number	Field Number	Cultural-temporal Affiliation	Site Type	Approximate Size (m²)	USGS Quad	Elevation (feet)
AZ V:9:103	CS-46	Prehistoric:Salado (?) (post-A.D. 1150)	Structure with artifact scatter	25	Inspiration 7.5 min.	4450
AZ V:9:104	CS-48	Prehistoric:Salado (?) (post-A.D. 1150)	Possible structure with artifact scatter	315	Inspiration 7.5 min.	4150
AZ V:9:105	CS-49	Prehistoric:Salado (post-A.D. 1250)	Structures with artifact scatter	676	Inspiration 7.5 min.	3950
AZ V:9:107	CS-126	Prehistoric:Salado (?) (post-A.D. 1150(?))	Structures with artifact scatter	3432	Inspiration 7.5 min.	4075
AZ V:9:108	CS-263	Prehistoric:Salado (?) (A.D. 1300)	Structures with artifact scatter	1500	Inspiration 7.5 min.	4450
AZ V:9:109	CS-264	Prehistoric:Salado (A.D. 1150-1450)	Structures with artifact scatter	1536	Inspiration 7.5 min.	4675
AZ V:9:110	CS-127	Prehistoric (unknown)	Possible structure with artifact scatter	20,475	Inspiration 7.5 min.	4825
AZ V:9:111	CS-279	Prehistoric:Salado (?) (post-A.D. 1150)	Structure with artifact scatter	1890	Inspiration 7.5 min.	4200
AZ V:9:112	CS-270	Prehistoric:Salado (?) (post-A.D. 1150)	Structure with artifact scatter	4275	Inspiration 7.5 min.	3450
AZ V:9:113	CS-271	Prehistoric:Salado (?) (post-A.D. 1150)	Structure with artifact scatter	168	Inspiration 7.5 min.	3425

Table 42. Archaeological sites in the Tonto-Roosevelt segment of the Cholla-Saguaro corridor (continued)

ASM Number	Field Number	Cultural-temporal Affiliation	Site Type	Approximate Size (m2)	USGS Quad	Elevation (feet)
AZ V:9:114	CS-272	Prehistoric:Salado (?) (post-A.D. 1150)	Structure and possible terrace	12,600	Inspiration 7.5 min.	3475
AZ V:9:116	CS-69	Prehistoric:Salado (?) (post-A.D. 1150)	Structures with artifact scatter	1500	Inspiration 7.5 min.	3625
AZ V:9:117	CS-73	Prehistoric:Salado (?) (post-A.D. 1150)	Structures with artifact scatter	625	Inspiration 7.5 min.	3550
AZ V:9:118	CS-71	Historic:Anglo (1930s)	Check dams and artifact scatter	54,400	Inspiration 7.5 min.	3250-3550

Corridor Location

The location of the Tonto-Roosevelt segment of the Cholla line and its relationship to major physical and urban features are shown in Figure 12. The specific location of the corridor may be described in greater detail as follows.

APS Tower location 320 is located in Gila County, McFadden Peak Quadrangle (USGS 15-minute series), Township 6N, Range 15E, Section 22, SE ¼ of SW¼, at a point just south and west of Sombrero Peak, a prominent landmark located some 7.2 km (4.5 miles) east of Cherry Creek in the middle reaches of that drainage. Moving south from this point, the line generally parallels Cherry Creek to the east until it turns southwest and crosses the creek some 4.8 km (3 miles) above its confluence with the Salt River.

The course of the line then runs in a southwesterly direction, passing out of the Cherry Creek Basin. It crosses Coon Creek and several minor washes as it moves to the north and then west of the large volcanic remnant known as Black Mesa. The line hugs the base of this feature on its northwestern side, and then follows the ridges formed by the washes draining away from Black Mesa toward the Salt River.

The line crosses the Salt River just above the point where the river breaks into the wide floodplain of the Salt River arm of the Tonto Basin, and turns in a more southerly direction. Here it crosses State Highway 88 just to the west of Salt River Peak, and follows a line roughly parallel to and equidistant from Pinal and Pinto creeks. At the point where the line intersects DeVore Wash, a major tributary of Pinal Creek, it turns southwest again, following this wash to its head in the northern end of Granite Basin.

Crossing the watershed between Pinal and Pinto creeks at this point, the line continues in a southwesterly direction until it intersects Pinto Creek itself. It then runs more or less due south, first following the creek and then continuing south out of the Pinto Creek Basin.

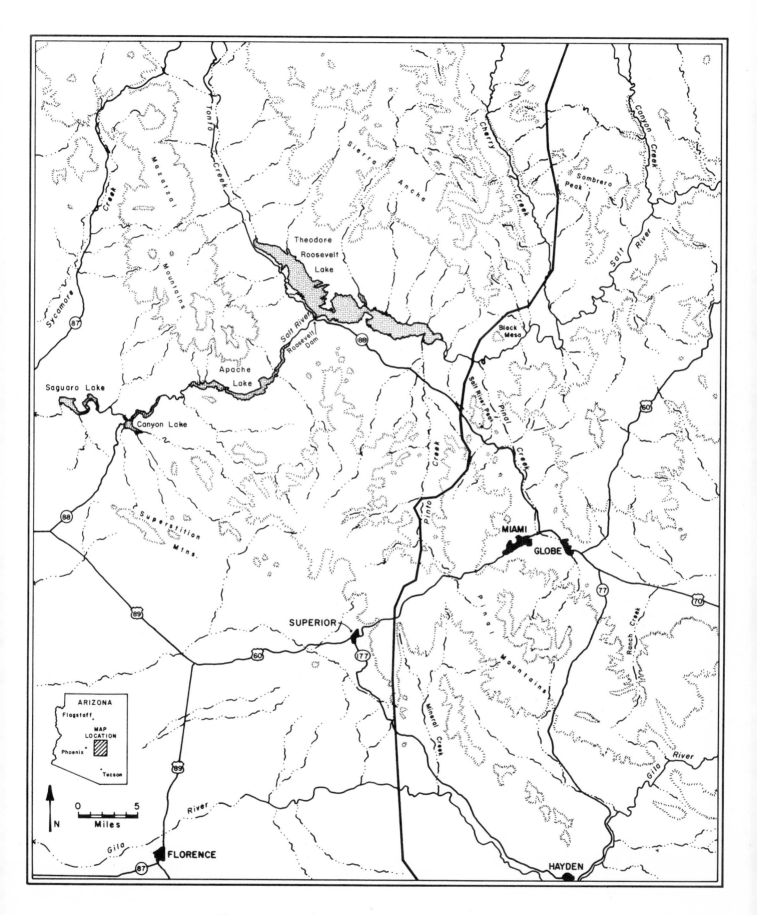

Figure 12.   The Tonto-Roosevelt study area

After passing out of the Pinto Creek drainage and therefore across the watershed between the Salt and Gila rivers, the line makes another slight southwesterly jog and then turns south again, crossing the Miami-Superior highway (State Highway 60) at a point some 5.6 km (3.5 miles) east and south of Superior in the Oak Creek drainage, a tributary of Devil's Canyon and ultimately of Mineral Creek and the Gila River. APS Tower location 497 is located in Pinal County, Superior Quadrangle (USGS 15-minute series), Township 2S, Range 13E, Section 20, NW¼ of NE¼. The segment of the corridor between APS Tower locations 320 and 497 covers a distance of some 80 km (50 miles).

Environment

The Tonto-Roosevelt area is a part of a region that is physiographically and biologically transitional between the desert to the south and the plateau country to the north (Sellers and Hill 1974 ; Wilson 1962; Lytle-Webb 1978). The specific topography, vegetation, fauna, and climate all exhibit transitional characteristics.

Geology

As with the rest of Arizona, the basic physiographic and hydrologic patterns of the region appear to have been established during Miocene to early Pliocene time, and were accentuated or otherwise modified by later events of deformation, volcanism, erosion, and sedimentation (Wilson 1962:89). The specific geologic history and resulting structure of the area are not well documented, except locally (Peterson 1962). A variously alternating sequence of sedimentation, volcanism, uplifting, and folding and faulting extending back to the early Precambrian and occurring as recently as the Pleistocene has been summarized for the Globe-Miami area; it may be expected that the general sequence would be essentially similar for the rest of the area (Lytle-Webb 1978).

Igneous, sedimentary, and metamorphic rocks are all well represented in various strata, and a variety of minerals and geologic exotics are present in the area. Significant mining activity began in the late 19th and early 20th centuries and continues to the present, with the primary emphasis on copper (Wilson 1962:100-1). Locally available minerals including turquoise have been documented in archaeological contexts (Haury 1932; Windmiller 1972b; Doyel 1978). Materials suitable for the manufacture of chipped stone artifacts are abundant but generally of poor quality, consisting primarily of stream cobbles and fine to medium-grained rhyolites and basalts.

Geography and Topography

Owing to the complex geology that underlies it, the topography of the area is marked by extreme and often quite localized variability in elevation, slope, and aspect. Maximum elevations approaching 8000 feet are reached in the Pinal and Sierra Ancha ranges, whereas the Salt River flows through the area at just under 2200 feet, thus producing vertical relief of over a mile.

The principal physical features of the area include the Pinal, Sierra Ancha, and Mazatzal mountain ranges, and the Salt River and its major tributaries. The Pinal and Mazatzal ranges on the south and west and the Sierra Ancha range on the east form the extreme perimeters of the southern end of the Tonto Basin. Like the other two great valleys of central Arizona (the Chino and the Verde), the Tonto Basin was formed as a result of relative downfaulting and subsequent erosion (Wilson 1962:96). The southern end of the basin at its lower elevations has been inundated since the construction of Roosevelt Dam in 1912.

On the north side of the Salt, the southern end of the north-south trending Sierra Ancha range dominates the topography. The nearly vertical eastern face of this range is cut by several deep, steep-sided canyons that plunge precipitously to Cherry Creek, in some places dropping nearly 4000 feet in 2 miles. The eastern tributaries of Cherry Creek drain an upland environment of high, undulating hills and ridges. The western and southern slopes of the Sierra Ancha range are less severe, dropping more gradually toward the Salt River to the south and southwest and toward Tonto Creek to the west. The country here is rugged nonetheless, and sizable canyons are present in many of the drainages. The area is also punctuated by numerous volcanic intrusives and remnants such as the prominent Black Mesa. These features often interrupt the direct path of drainages flowing toward the Salt River, locally affecting their direction and pattern of development.

To the south of the Salt River lie the Pinal Mountains running roughly northwest-southeast and forming the watershed between the Salt and Gila Rivers in this area. Two major tributaries of the Salt River, Pinto Creek and Pinal Creek, flow north away from the Pinals through a rugged terrain of smaller mountains, mesas, buttes, hills, and small basins. Directly north of the southeastern end of the Pinals are situated the low Globe Hills, with their western side drained by tributaries of Pinal Creek. To the east and southeast, the country drops away from these hills and from the Pinals and is drained by the western tributaries of the San Carlos River, principally by Ranch Creek. Mineral Creek, Dripping Springs Wash, and several smaller washes that ultimately flow into the Gila River have their origins on the southern slopes of the Pinals in an area of high hills and mesas and deep canyons.

The overall effect of these topographic features is a variable and extremely rugged country that is difficult of access and prohibitive to travel except along corridors formed by the major drainages of the region (the Salt River, Pinal Creek, Cherry Creek, and Tonto Creek).

Drainage Patterns and Water Availability

As noted above, the drainage patterns of the area are often strongly affected by local geology and are consequently variable in their patterns of development. Pinal and Pinto creeks are fully developed drainages exhibiting essentially dendritic patterns. Cherry Creek and Coon Creek are strongly linear, having a more trellis-like patterning with some minor variations. The courses of the smaller washes in the area of Black Mesa are directly determined by the shape of that feature.

The Salt River is a permanently flowing stream, as is Cherry Creek along most of its length. Pinal Creek is said to have been a permanent watercourse in historic times, and it is likely that Pinto Creek was also. At present, both of these drainages are ephemeral, probably due in part to the lowering of the water table by mining and other recent human activities. Springs are quite numerous in the area and were undoubtedly important water sources prehistorically.

The Salt River arm of the Tonto Basin is the first place where the Salt breaks open into a wide floodplain, and is therefore the first place where the water from the large area drained by this major river would have been available in a situation suitable for canal-aided agriculture. Pinal Creek, Pinto Creek, and Cherry Creek all have sizable floodplains at various places along their lengths, and it is possible that canal irrigation could have been carried out on a more limited scale in these drainages.

Vegetation

In the higher elevations of the area, the ponderosa pine forest of the Transition Life Zone is present, but most of the area falls within either the Upper or Lower Sonoran life zones (Lowe 1964). The distribution of these zones and their constituent plant communities may not, however, be easily sorted out in practice. The marked variability in topography and substrate fostered by the complex geology of the area imposes itself on the typical vertical zonation of vegetation, producing an environment that is in many places truly mosaic in character. Further complexity is introduced by the fact that the Sierra Ancha range is a zone of mixing between northern and southern plant species (Kearney and Peebles 1960:8). The major washes all exhibit more or less continuous riparian communities along their courses, while the smaller tributaries of these washes exhibit pockets or stretches of riparian vegetation at points where the available water is sufficient, usually at or near springs.

The general vertical distribution and characteristic plant communities of the major life zones are shown below in Figure 13, which gives some basic idea of the vegetation present in the Tonto-Roosevelt area. It must be remembered, however, that the distribution of vegetation types is complex and highly dependent on local factors. A more specific picture of the variation in vegetation present along the Cholla line corridor may be seen in Figure 14. The major life zones, communities, and associations recorded in transects taken at one-mile intervals along the corridor are shown in relation to an elevational cross section of the line.

Fauna

The transitional nature of the environment is further illustrated by the fact that the intersection of three of the four major biotic provinces defined for the state occurs within the area (Dice 1943). The concept of biotic province is based essentially on fauna and is "concerned with, and usually...intended to show, subcontinental or smaller regions (often quite small) of faunal differentiation (subspecies, species, genera)" (Lowe 1964:94). As defined by Dice(1943), the Navajonian, Apachian, and Sonoran biotic provinces intersect approximately at Globe.

It is not possible to enumerate all of the species to be found in the area, but various large (deer, bear, mountain lion, coyote, peccary) as well as smaller animal species (rodents, birds, reptiles, amphibians, fishes, insects) are well represented (Lowe 1964; Lytle-Webb 1978). The area is a favored hunting territory for the sportsmen of the state, especially for deer, bear, mountain lion, and quail. Bobcat, pronghorn antelope, and mountain goat remains have been discovered in archaeological contexts (Sparling 1978).

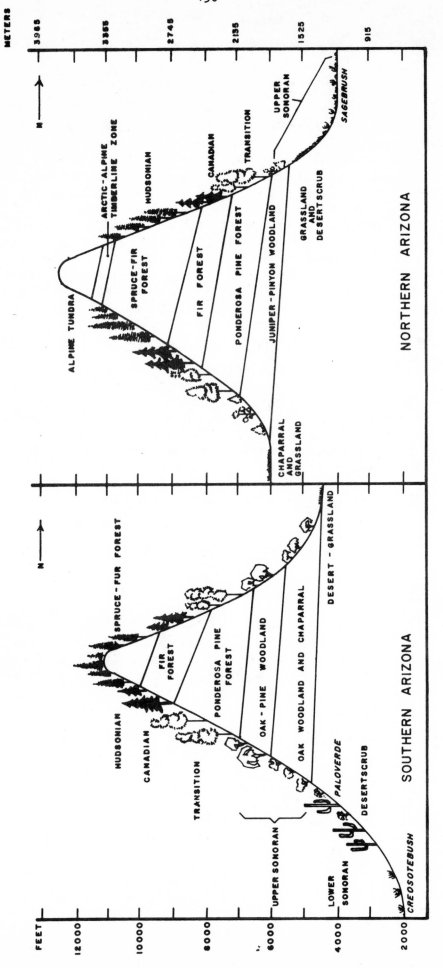

Figure 13. Vertical distribution and characteristics of major life zones (from Lowe 1964:18)

191

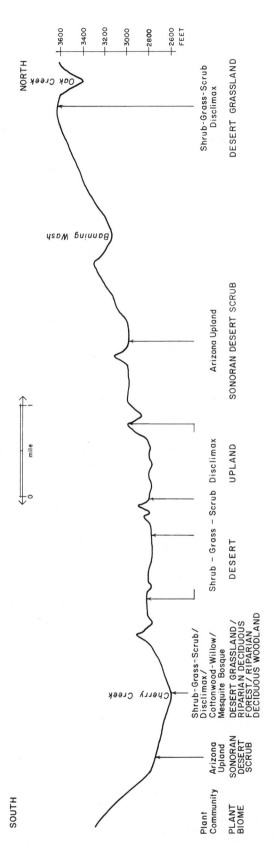

Figure 14a. Vegetation represented by plant transects shown in relation to elevational cross section of transmission line corridor: Cherry Creek area

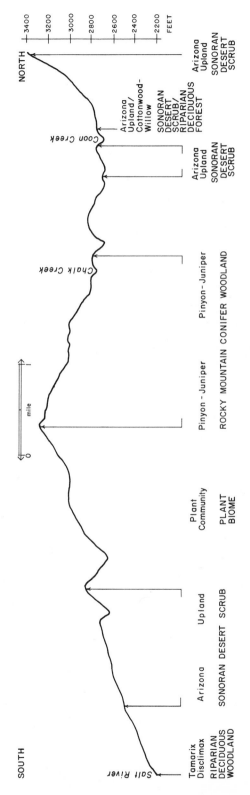

Figure 14b. Coon Creek-Black Mesa area

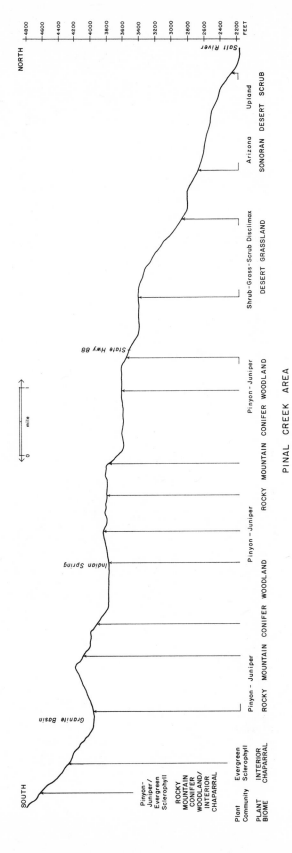

Figure 14c. Pinal Creek area

193

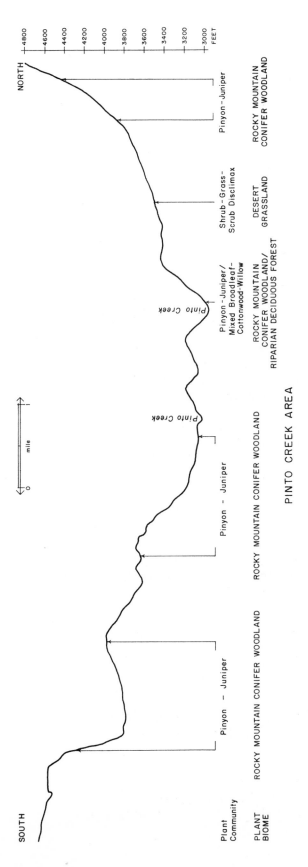

Figure 14d. Pinto Creek area

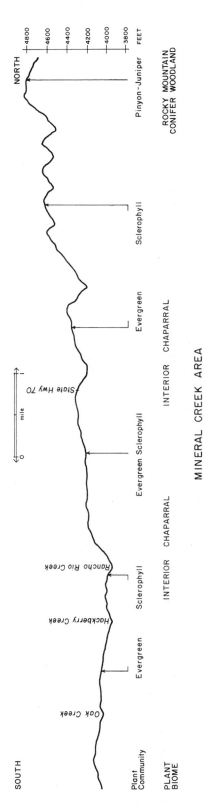

Figure 14e. Mineral Creek area

Study Units

The conceptual and methodological difficulties presented by samples of archaeological materials derived from arbitrary linear transects are many. The overall question of the representativeness of such samples looms large in relation to the archaeological materials discovered and the geographic space intersected (Goodyear 1975). This factor imposes some restrictions on the kinds of problems that may be approached and on the appropriate methodologies that may be employed.

In addition to various difficulties with the samples produced, arbitrary linear transects do not in and of themselves provide an adequate context for the simple description of such variables as site location and related environmental characteristics.

In order to provide a more useful context for the discussion of the Tonto-Roosevelt survey material, the area traversed by the line will be segmented and expanded to form five geographically defined units. With the few minor exceptions noted in the definitions that follow, these units correspond essentially to the drainage basins of the major tributaries of the Salt and Gila rivers that are crossed by the line. These units are defined below and their boundaries may be seen in Figure 15.

Lower Cherry Creek. This area includes the drainage basin south of a line running east-west through Sombrero Peak. Above this line on Cherry Creek the drainage becomes much more restricted and lacks the well-developed floodplain to be found in the lower reaches of the creek. On the east side of the creek, this line corresponds roughly to the boundary between the pinyon-juniper woodland community to the north and the more open Upper Sonoran habitat to the south.

Coon Creek-Black Mesa area. This area includes the drainage basin of Coon Creek and a complex of smaller washes that drain around and away from the prominent volcanic remnant known as Black Mesa. The western boundary of this area is marked by the Meddler Wash drainage. The drain-age patterns of this area are strongly affected by Black Mesa.

Pinal Creek area. This unit is defined as the entire drainage of Pinal Creek.

Pinto Creek area. This unit includes the entire drianage basin of Pinto Creek, and also the Poison Springs Wash drainage, a small un-branched tributary of the Salt River that runs parallel to Pinto Creek in its lower reaches.

Mineral Creek area. This area subsumes the entire drainage basin of Mineral Creek, which, unlike the drainages in the other units, flows to the Gila River instead of the Salt. Although only the extreme upper

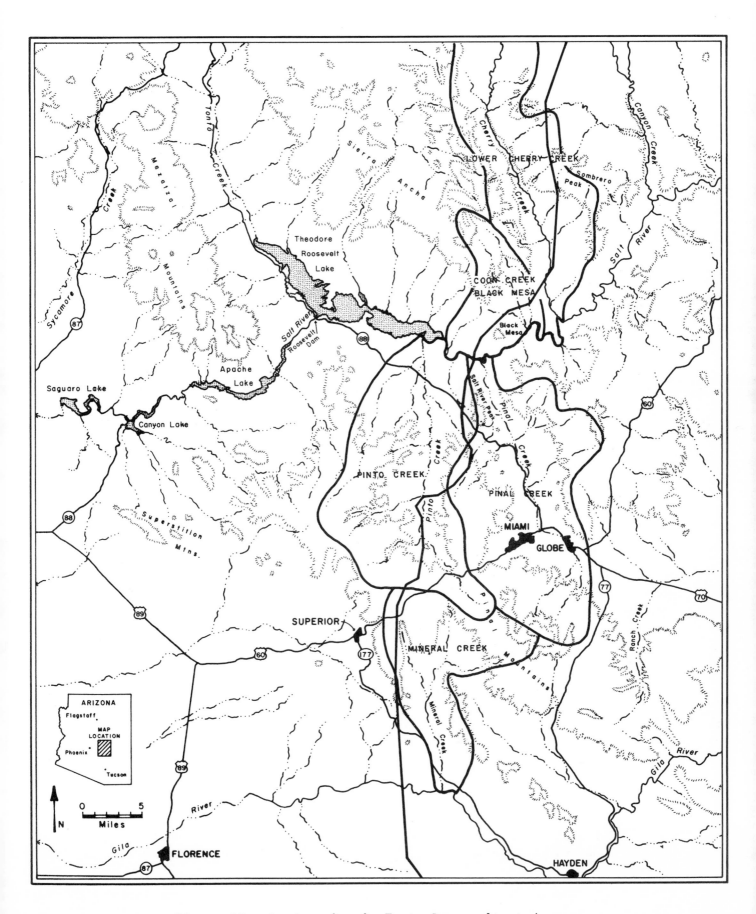

Figure 15. Study units in Tonto-Roosevelt study area

tributaries of this drainage are crossed by the segment of the Cholla line considered here, the entire basin is included to show the relationship between the Salt and Gila watersheds and to make the unit more closely comparable to the other four.

Previous Archaeological Research

Previous archaeological research accomplished in the Tonto-Roosevelt area will be summarized here in chronological order. In order to orient the reader and to illustrate graphically the distribution of past research activities, the locations referred to in the text are designated by arabic numerals on the map in Figure 16. These numbers correspond to the names and references summarized in Table 43. The periods and phases referred to in the text and in Table 43 are defined and discussed in the following section on the culture history of the area. Presented in this way, the sample of archaeological materials that forms the basis for the extant notions of the prehistory of the area may be better conceptualized and understood, and a convenient basis for a subsequent discussion of the culture history and relevant research problems is also established.

Pre-1900

Bandelier's travels of 1883 took him through Globe, down Pinal Creek, over into the valley of the Salt, and ultimately up Tonto Creek and out of the area. His journals and the reports that resulted from them constitute the earliest records of archaeological materials from the area made by a professional archaeologist (Bandelier 1892; Lange and Riley 1966). Although he visited and noted many sites, two observations contained in his accounts are of particular interest. First, Bandelier notes private collections of artifacts shown to him by residents of Globe, giving some idea of the time depth involved in the still-continuing modification of archaeological sites through curio-collecting and vandalism. Second, he observed a large canal (acequia) on the north side of the Salt River in the area now inundated by Roosevelt Lake (1892). Unfortunately, the exact nature, extent, and relative age of this feature and the possible existence of other similar ones are unknown and will likely remain so. His observations may, however, be taken as some evidence that canal-aided agriculture was practiced in the Tonto Basin prehistorically.

Hough's (1907) summary of the antiquities of the upper Salt and Gila drainages simply duplicates Bandelier's notations on ruins in the area and contains nothing concerning the Tonto-Roosevelt area that may not be found in the original report by Bandelier.

1900-1950

During the first half of the twentieth century, archaeological research was carried out in the area by E.F. Schmidt in connection with

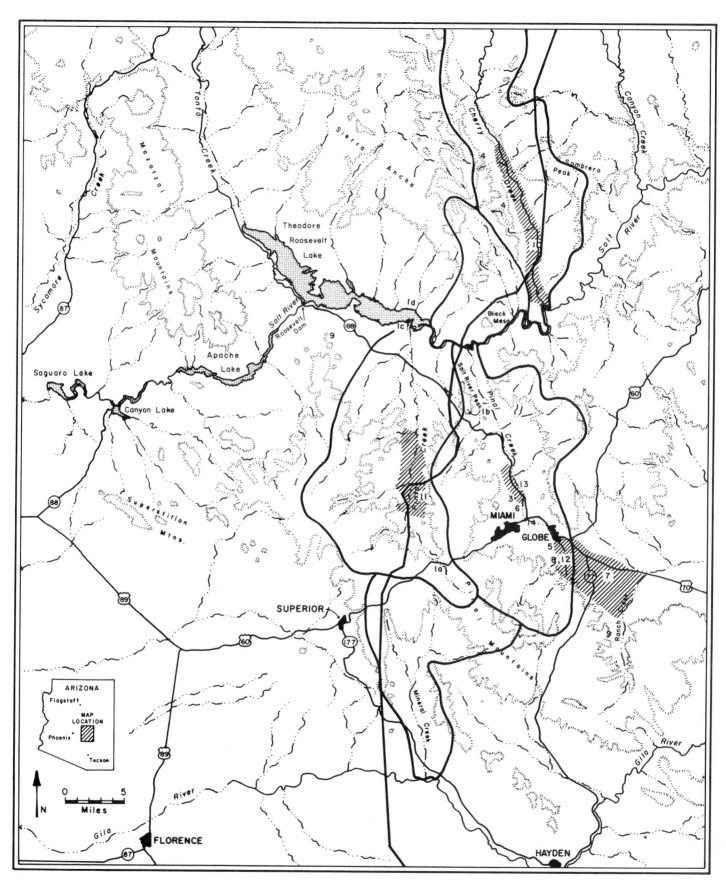

Figure 16. Locations of past archaeological research in the Tonto-
Roosevelt study area

Table 43. Previous archaeological research in the Tonto-Roosevelt area

Site/Area	Type of site	Reference
1a To-get-zo-ge*	Gila Phase Salado pueblo; 100+ rooms	Schmidt 1926,1927,1928
1b Murphy Mesa*	Pueblo with enclosures	Schmidt 1926,1927,1928
1c Spring Creek*	Two-story "black-on-white" ruin	Schmidt 1926,1927,1928
1d Armer's Gulch*	"Communal house" and "courtyard ruin" with Casa Grande-type "temple house"	Schmidt 1926,1927,1928
2 Roosevelt 9:6	Santa Cruz Phase Hohokam pit house village	Haury 1932
3 Bead Mountain Pueblos*	Large Gila Phase Salado pueblos with possible earlier components ("black-on-white ruin")	Hawley 1932; see also Grady 1974
4 Canyon Creek Ruin and the Sierra Ancha cliff dwellings	Pinedale and Canyon Creek Phase cliff dwellings	Haury 1934
5 Besh-ba-go-wah*	Gila Phase Salado pueblo with underlying Roosevelt Phase component; 200 rooms	Vickery 1939
6 Inspiration I*	Santa Cruz Phase Hohokam pit house village with possible earlier component and later Salado component	Vickery 1945
7 Globe area survey	100+ sites; Hohokam, Salado, and Apache manifestations	Brandes 1957a
8 Gila Pueblo*	Gila Phase Salado pueblo; 200+ rooms; single room excavated	Shiner 1961

Table 43. Previous archaeological research in the Tonto-Roosevelt area
(continued)

	Site/Area	Type of site	Reference
9	Tonto cliff dwellings	Gila Phase Salado cliff dwellings	Steen 1962
10	Lower Cherry Creek survey	60+ sites; Santa Cruz Phase Hohokam site and other materials dating A.D. 900-1325	Wells 1971
11	Pinto Creek survey and excavations	Excavated sites represent Hohokam, Salado, and possibly Apache occupations	Windmiller 1971a and b, 1972a and c, 1974a and b
12	Hagan Site (Gila Pueblo)	Gila Phase Salado pueblo; small roomblock associated with main pueblo excavated	Young 1972
13	Miami Wash Project	Excavation of eight small sites; occupations documented from Gila Butte/Santa Cruz through Gila phases and an Apache occupation; Hohokam, Salado, and "mixed" assemblages	Doyel 1974, 1976a, b, and c, 1978
14	Central Heights Site*	Small Gila Phase Salado pueblo with earlier (Santa Cruz/Sacaton Phase) Hohokam component	McGuire 1975

* No published site report

the Mrs. William Boyce-Thompson Expedition of 1925 and 1926 (Schmidt 1926); by the Globe-based Gila Pueblo organization, founded by H. S. Gladwin in 1927; and by Vickery (1939, 1945) and Steen (1962) in conjunction with public works projects begun during the Depression years.

Schmidt's work included the excavation of major portions of To-get-zo-ge, a large, apparently pure Gila Phase Salado pueblo located in the upper reaches of Pinto Creek. Less extensive excavations were carried out at the Spring Creek Ruin (now called Schoolhouse Point), a two-story "black-on-white" ruin located on the south side of the Salt River near the mouth of Pinto Creek; and at Armer's Gulch, described by Schmidt as follows:

> There was a series of ruins near the northeast shore of the lake, all of them below the high-water line. Here once more a burial ground was discovered, situated close to a "courtyard" ruin, which consisted of rectangular plazas enclosed by long rows of stones with a few rooms in the center and at the sides. About 1000 feet south-east of this place was another extensive ruin, composed really of two structures, one a communal house, the other of Casa Grande type. This resembled the courtyard ruins except for an additional "temple building" originally perhaps three stories high (1926:640-1).

The principal decorated ceramic types at these sites were black-on-white wares, with some "Little Colorado" black-on-red sherds recovered as well. Several burials were excavated in which black-on-white and red-on-buff ceramics were directly associated (1928:184). These intriguing sites would therefore appear to represent prepolychrome occupation about which little is known (Gladwin 1957:249).

On the basis of this and further work at sites on the San Carlos Reservation (Rice, Cutter) and near Phoenix (La Ciudad, Pueblo Grande), Schmidt published two articles defining the temporal relations of ceramic types in southern Arizona (1927, 1928). For the time when it was accomplished, Schmidt's work is remarkable in its use of quantitative data, and it is unfortunate that no site reports were ever published.

The work undertaken by the Gila Pueblo organization included extensive survey of the area and excavation of the site of Gila Pueblo, a large Salado pueblo near Globe that became the type site for Gladwin's Middle Gila Phase (Gladwin and Gladwin 1934, 1935). Haury's pioneering work at Roosevelt 9:6 (1932) and at the Canyon Creek Ruin and the Sierra Ancha cliff dwellings (1934) was carried out under the auspices of Gila Pueblo.

With the exception of Haury's reports, the undertakings of Gila Pueblo in the Tonto-Roosevelt area were reported in only the most general and summary fashion (Gladwin and Gladwin 1930, 1934, 1935; Gladwin 1957). This work nonetheless formed the basis for Gladwin's definition and interpretation of the culture history of the area (1957).

Vickery excavated the site of Besh-ba-go-wah in connection with the ERA and WPA programs begun in the 1930s (Vickery 1939). Two hundred rooms and 300 burials were excavated. This site is only a short distance from Gila Pueblo and represents a similar Gila Phase Salado occupation with an underlying component apparently dating to the poorly known Roosevelt Phase (Vickery 1939; Doyel 1976c). Vickery also excavated Inspiration I, a predominantly Santa Cruz Phase pit house village located on the first terrace overlooking Miami Wash from the west side (Vickery 1945). The Hohokam component of the site consisted of 16 pit houses and associated features, and was in part overlain by a later Salado component already largely covered at that time by the tailings pile from the Inspiration Mine. Three rooms of the Salado component were excavated. Neither Inspiration I nor Besh-ba-go-wah was the subject of a full-fledged site report.

Portions of the Tonto cliff dwellings were excavated during the stabilization and restoration of these ruins by CCC crews in 1937 and 1942 (Duffen 1937; Steen 1962), but the material remained unpublished until 1962 (Steen and others 1962). These well-preserved sites also represent the Gila Phase Salado occupation of the area. Due to excellent preservation, studies of materials from the Tonto cliff dwellings have added much to the knowledge of perishable material culture and plant use during the Gila Phase (Borher 1962; Kent 1962; Van Valkenburgh 1962).

Hawley published a short popular article dealing with sites known collectively as the Bead Mountain Pueblos, a series of ruins overlooking Miami Wash just above its confluence with Pinal Creek (1932). No site report exists for this ruin group, but the sites were mapped and subjected to limited testing in 1974 by the Arizona State Museum (Grady 1974). Two rooms at one of the sites were excavated in connection with the Miami Wash Highway Salvage project (Doyel 1978). The sites appear to date primarily to the Gila Phase with possibly earlier components.

1950-present

Since 1950 the bulk of archaeological research carried out in the Tonto-Roosevelt area has been in connection with highway salvage and other contract projects. Projects of a more limited scale have been carried out by various individuals.

Brandes, in conducting a survey of the area south and east of Globe (1957a), recorded 121 sites, including Hohokam, Salado, and Apache manifestations. Wells surveyed the lower portions of Cherry Creek and recorded 56 sites ranging in date from preceramic to the 14th century (1971). Shiner excavated a single room within the main ruin of Gila Pueblo (1961), and Young excavated the Hagan Site (also at Gila Pueblo), a small roomblock associated with the occupation of the main ruin (Young 1972; Windmiller 1972b). The Central Heights Site, a small, late Salado pueblo underlain by an earlier Hohokam component, was excavated in 1966 as a highway salvage project. The site was located near the intersection of State Highways 60 and 88, but has since been destroyed. A report on the excavations now awaits publication (McGuire 1975).

Two projects of a slightly larger scale have contributed substantially to the knowledge of the prehistory of the area. Windmiller conducted survey and excavations in the Pinto Creek drainage in preparation for expansion of mining activities there (Windmiller 1971a, 1972a and c, 1974a). Fifty-one sites were located and recorded during the survey; excavation of several of the sites has revealed both Hohokam and Salado occupations of the area. Possible Apache materials were also noted.

Doyel excavated eight small sites along Miami Wash as a highway salvage project carried out prior to the realignment of State Highway 88. The Miami Wash project uncovered evidence for continuous prehistoric occupation of the area from the Gila Butte Phase of the Colonial Hohokam Period through the Gila Phase Salado occupation (Doyel 1974, 1978). The Apache occupation of the area was also represented in the form of sherds on the surface of several prehistoric sites. On the basis of this work, Doyel has presented the most recent synthesis and revision of the culture history of the area (1978). He defines a newly recognized Miami Phase (approximately A.D. 1150-1200), which appears to be transitional between the Hohokam and Salado occupations of the area, and makes several revisions in Gladwin's scheme for the sequence of occupation in the area.

The U.S. Forest Service has recently conducted surveys in the area, and reports on this work, according to Jon Scott Wood, are now in preparation. The work accomplished in conjunction with the construction of the APS Cholla line constitutes the most recent archaeological research in the area.

Culture History

Although archaeological research has been carried out in the Tonto-Roosevelt area in nearly every decade of the present century, and despite recent work that has added much information, knowledge of the prehistory of the area remains preliminary and somewhat fragmentary (Doyel 1976c:245; 1978). Several factors contribute to this condition.

Because many of the excavations and surveys undertaken in the past have not been fully reported on, a complete record of the overall form and content of the materials represented is lacking. Thus, the detailed information necessary for continuing and systematic restudy, reinterpretation, and comparison is unavailable. This situation is rendered even more frustrating by the fact that several poorly known time periods are represented by, and have been defined and interpreted primarily on the basis of, largely unpublished data.

Another factor limiting the knowledge of the prehistory of the area is well illustrated by the distribution of past research activities seen in Figure 16. The lack of survey coverage is apparent and, with few exceptions, the concentration of previous research has been in areas along major drainages. The combined effect is a skewed and incomplete picture of site variability and distribution through time over space. Further exacerbating this bias is the effective removal from systematic investigation of the large area inundated by Roosevelt Lake. There is every indication that the floodplain of the Salt River was an important focus of prehistoric activity, and any consideration of the sequence of occupation in the area must take into account the sampling bias imposed by this man-made feature (Bandelier 1892; Haury 1932; Schmidt 1926; Fuller, Rogge, and Gregonis 1976; Doyel 1976c). Surveys undertaken by the U.S. Forest Service during the extreme low-water levels experienced in 1977 may serve to partially alleviate these effects, but silting and other effects of inundation have undoubtedly affected the visibility and general condition of sites (Wood and McAllister 1978).

Within the pre-1950 work undertaken in the area may be noted another element of bias, one toward a primary concern with larger, more conspicuous sites. Recent work has done much to counterbalance this earlier emphasis (Doyel 1978; Windmiller 1972b, 1974b; McGuire 1975b). However, the lack of published materials from the earlier work limits the potential for comparative studies of site types.

All of the factors noted above hamper attempts to deal with problems focusing on settlement pattern data and more specifically with the modeling of subsistence-settlement systems, concerns which require large quantities of quality data produced by both excavation and survey (Struever 1971). Although survey data are available from the Arizona State Museum and Arizona State University site files, this information is for the most part not based on systematic sampling procedures and is highly variable in quality. Because of the lack of excavated data from a variety of sites, and the consequent lack of detailed information concerning the relative chronology of the range of site types and ceramic assemblages from the area, surface manifestations can for the most part serve as only crude indicators of chronology and possible function. The apparent pattern of frequent multiple occupations of site locations in the area compounds the problems in dealing with survey data (Doyel 1978; McGuire 1975).

Finally, the very nature of the sequence of prehistoric occupations witnessed by the area renders the interpretation of that prehistory an unusually complex proposition. It is clear that the area was a zone of interaction between various groups, but the chronological aspects and nature of that interaction have yet to be specified and systematically examined. In addition to Salado manifestations, Hohokam, Mogollon, and Anasazi cultural traditions all come into play in an area that is as complex and variable in its prehistory as it is environmentally.

With these general problems in mind, a critical summary of the culture history of the area as it is presently known is presented below.

Preceramic Period

The most conspicuous feature of sites dating to the preceramic period in the area is their virtual absence. No Paleo-Indian remains of any sort have been reported, and only a few Archaic sites are known. The only well-documented preceramic site is the Hardt Creek Site, located near Jake's Corner in the middle reaches of Tonto Creek (Huckell 1973). This site has been interpreted as a specialized-activity area, and dated on typological grounds to the Chiricahua Stage or Amargosa II Period of the southern Arizona Archaic, roughly 7000 to 3000 B.P. (Huckell 1973:192, 196). Huckell notes the presence of a larger Archaic site exhibiting both ground stone artifacts and hearths near the Hardt Creek Site. Wells (1971) reported a single site of possible Archaic date from lower Cherry Creek (AZ V:5:61, ASU). Given the scarcity of data, little can be said concerning the specific nature and extent of the Archaic occupation of the Tonto-Roosevelt area.

This situation raises several questions that are significant to an understanding of the preceramic period, both within the Tonto-Roosevelt area and for the larger region of which it is a part. First, it must be asked whether the absence of sites dating to the preceramic period is real or only apparent. Is the lack of preceramic material a function of overall sampling error, contributed to by poor survey coverage, a combination of geologic factors, and the obscuring effects of later occupations? Are there preceramic sites under Roosevelt Lake or in other situations where they might be deeply buried or otherwise poorly visible? Are some of the lithic scatters that have been recorded in the area representative of preceramic occupations and simply not yet recognized as such due to a lack of comparative material? If further evidence for an Archaic occupation is uncovered, what was the relationship of these earlier populations to the later occupation of the area by sedentary agriculturalists?

Alternately, if the scarcity of preceramic material should prove to be real, there are significant implications for the interpretation of these early occupations. Such a situation would suggest that an area relatively abundant in resources was not being intensively exploited during these time periods, even though adjacent areas with essentially similar resources have been shown to have witnessed Paleo-Indian and Archaic occupations (McGuire 1977; Huckell 1978). This, in turn, may suggest (1) a relatively low population density, or (2) an adjustment by Paleo-Indian and Archaic populations to their environments that was more specific than is now generally conceptualized--that is, that this area was somehow not particularly well-suited to the various forms of the Paleo-Indian and Archaic lifeways that evolved and subsequently developed in surrounding regions. Furthermore, if there were no indigenous populations in the area, then the abundant evidence for later occupations must be accounted for by movement of peoples into an essentially unoccupied territory. Current interpretations maintain that this was in fact the case; the earliest substantial occupation of the area is seen as representing the expansion of Hohokam populations from the Salt-Gila Basin into this and other peripheral areas that were previously unoccupied (Doyel 1974; Wood and McAllister 1978).

The questions raised here are general and of necessity based on little data. The lack of known sites dating to preceramic periods begs interpretation, however, and is significant not only to the prehistory of this area, but of the Southwest in general. The relationship between Archaic populations and later, more easily delimited entities is poorly understood and, with few exceptions, rarely addressed (Sayles 1945; Sayles and Antevs 1941; Irwin-Williams 1967; Haury 1950). The extent and nature of the preceramic period occupation deserves attention in future research carried out in the Tonto-Roosevelt area.

Hohokam Occupation

The Tonto-Roosevelt area is a part of a much larger archaeological region recently defined as the Northeastern Hohokam Periphery (Wood and McAllister 1978). This designation contrasts this region with the Salt-Gila Basin or Hohokam Core Area, where the longer, more substantial, archaeologically definitive Hohokam sequence is well known (Haury 1976). The core-periphery contrast provides a conceptual basis for the investigation of the expansion of Hohokam peoples out of the Salt-Gila Basin. This movement has long been recognized and appears to have occurred primarily during the appropriately named Colonial Period (Gladwin and Gladwin 1935). Several explanations focusing on population pressure and resource availability have been suggested to account for the migratory tendencies of the Hohokam during this period (Haury 1976; Martin and Plog 1973; Plog 1978; Wood and McAllister 1978). Whatever the ultimate reasons behind it, this Colonial Period expansion resulted in the earliest Hohokam materials found in the area considered here (Haury 1976).

Colonial Period (A.D. 500-900)

The earliest well-documented occupation of the Tonto-Roosevelt area occurs during the Gila Butte and Santa Cruz phases of the Colonial Hohokam Period (Haury 1932; Vickery 1945; Brandes 1957a and b; Windmiller 1972c; Doyel 1974, 1976b, 1978; Wells 1971; Wood and McAllister 1978). Some ceramic evidence for a Pioneer Period (Snaketown) occupation exists (Vickery 1945), and future research may reveal additional materials dating to this earlier period. The presence of Pioneer Period materials in other areas outside the Salt-Gila Basin has been documented (Weed and Ward 1970; Franklin and Masse 1976; Wood and McAllister 1978).

The Gila Butte and Santa Cruz phases are represented by village sites as well as by specialized or limited-activity loci (Doyel 1978; Vickery 1945; Windmiller 1972c). A Santa Cruz ball court has been identified, located on Ranch Creek in the San Carlos drainage east of Globe (Brandes 1957a and b; Schroeder 1963a). Village sites appear to be restricted to locations on or very near major drainages, but beyond this little can be said concerning overall site distribution and variability in site types.

The available data suggest that the Colonial Period materials from the Tonto-Roosevelt area are sufficiently similar in form, content, and date to those present in the Salt-Gila Basin to warrant the same period and phase assignments. It has been suggested that these similarities extend to the ecological and organizational aspects of the Core Area populations (Wood and McAllister 1978). Canal-aided agriculture such as that known to have been practiced in the Salt-Gila Basin may have been an important aspect of subsistence activities in the Tonto-Roosevelt area, and the presence of environmental situations suitable to this technology may have played a role in the initial movement of Hohokam populations into the area. Doyel (1978) has suggested that additional exploitative strategies may have been employed in areas where canal-aided agriculture was not feasible.

Interaction at some level with northern non-Hohokam populations is indicated by intrusive black-on-white sherds at all excavated Colonial Period sites, and is further supported by sites in adjacent areas exhibiting contemporaneous Hohokam and Mogollon and Hohokam and Anasazi architecture as well as ceramics (Morris 1970; Haas 1971; Cartledge 1976; Haury 1940). Generalized Mogollon influence on the material culture assemblage at Inspiration I was suggested by Vickery (1945). The exact nature of the relationship formed between the Colonial Hohokam and various other groups that they may have come into contact with is unclear, as is the part these relationships may have played in the initial Hohokam occupation of and subsequent adjustments to the area.

Sedentary Period (A.D. 900-1150(?))

The existence of materials dating to the Sacaton Phase of the Sedentary Hohokam Period has been demonstrated at four excavated sites and by several surveys in the Tonto-Roosevelt area. Doyel discovered three pit houses dating to the Sacaton Phase at sites along Miami Wash, each from a different site, and each differing from the others in form (1976b:248). An archaeomagnetic date of A.D. 1090 was recovered from one of these pit houses. Sacaton Phase materials were also recovered from the Central Heights Site (McGuire 1975). Wells recorded two and possibly three sites in lower Cherry Creek that are dated to an unnamed A.D. 900-1100 time period and exhibit pit house architecture and paddle and anvil plainware ceramics (1971). The possibility of Sacaton materials under Roosevelt Lake has been noted (Doyel 1976b:249), and Wood and McAllister have recently suggested a Sedentary Period occupation of the Tonto Basin on the basis of unpublished survey data (1978; see also Jeter 1978). Immediately adjacent areas to the north and east have also produced evidence for a Sacaton Phase occupation (Brandes 1957a; Morris 1970).

The present sample of materials dating to this period is inadequate as a basis for a discussion and interpretation of site variability and distribution (but see Wood and McAllister 1978). The large pit house villages that characterize the Sacaton Phase in the Salt-Gila Basin have not been reported for the Tonto-Roosevelt area, but it is quite possible that they exist. Determination of the distribution and density of the Sacaton occupation may be made difficult by the prevalent pattern of reuse of site locations that seems to be emerging. This is especially true with respect to the use of survey data. All of the excavated sites producing Sacaton materials thus far have been multicomponent, with the Sacaton component consistently overlain by the remains of later Salado occupations (Doyel 1976b; 1978). An unknown number of the numerous Salado sites in the area may well overlie and obscure Sacaton materials. Intrusive black-on-white ceramics (Snowflake) are associated with the Sacaton materials from all excavated sites, thus continuing the pattern observed in the earlier Colonial Period occupation of the area (Doyel 1978).

The Sacaton Phase is in general poorly known for the Tonto-Roosevelt area, and it should be noted that the materials that have been documented do not duplicate the close similarity to contemporaneous manifestations from the Salt-Gila Basin seen in Colonial Period sites. It remains to be determined whether the apparent differences simply represent a sampling bias, are evidence of a diverging Hohokam adjustment to the area, may involve the influence or presence of non-Hohokam populations, or resulted from a combination of these or other as yet unknown factors. It is clear that a more complete definition of the nature and extent of the Sacaton occupation of the area will be required before these problems can be more specifically formulated and resolved.

Transitional Period (A.D. 1100-1200)

It has long been recognized that by the end of the Sedentary Hohokam Period, changes were occurring in the Tonto-Roosevelt area that resulted ultimately in sites and assemblages that do not warrant the designation "Hohokam" as it is used for the later periods in the Salt-Gila Basin. The Gladwins were the first to use the term Salado to refer to these later manifestations, viewing them as the result of the migration of populations into the area, first from the upper Little Colorado region and later from the Kayenta area (1935:27; Gladwin 1957). These populations were thought to have brought with them and subsequently modified and developed the traits that came to be diagnostic of the Salado complex, including various forms of aboveground cobble-masonry architecture and a ceramic assemblage distinguished by the distinctive Salado polychromes (Gladwin and Gladwin 1930, 1935).

Although the area in and around the southern end of the Tonto Basin is still considered to be the early heartland of the Salado phenomenon, the Gladwin's reconstruction and interpretation of the underlying prehistory has been subject to a variety of criticisms, revisions, and elaborations (Doyel and Haury 1976; Doyel 1976b and c). In particular, the conception of the Salado complex as a suddenly appearing constellation of distinctive elements that represent the in-migration of peoples has been questioned. While full resolution of the multifaceted problem of Salado origins must await further research, it is increasingly clear that knowledge of the period A.D. 1100-1200 will be critical to an understanding of the events and processes that produced the complex of materials referred to as Salado (Doyel 1976c:14).

There is some evidence to suggest the existence of a pre-A.D. 1200 complex exhibiting some of the traits thought of as Salado, but also having affinities to Hohokam assemblages and lacking the diagnostic Salado polychromes. On the basis of materials from a single site located along Miami Wash, Doyel has defined the Miami Phase, provisionally dated between A.D. 1150 and 1200, and representing

> a mixed cultural pattern, with numerous puebloan elements combined with a Classic period Hohokam plainware and redware assemblage. Furthermore, this phase possesses a number of elements traditionally thought to be Saladoan, such as extended burials, cobble masonry, and enclosing walls, suggesting that we will have to redefine what is uniquely Saladoan (1976b:251-2).

The decorated ceramics associated with this phase include Snowflake and Reserve-Tularosa black-on-white types, St. John's Polychrome, San Carlos Red-on-brown, and McDonald Painted Corrugated. The architecture consists of noncontiguous surface structures and "pit-rooms" within the above-mentioned enclosing wall (Doyel 1976b). The phase is presently thought to apply to the Globe-Miami area and possibly the Pinto Creek drainage; it is further noted that the suggested dates for the phase may extend somewhat in either direction (Doyel 1976b; Windmiller 1974a).

While the Miami Phase will require further substantiation and refinement, the existence of roughly contemporaneous materials exhibiting at least some of the characteristics defined for the phase is suggested by other sources. Gladwin himself proposed the existence of a prepolychrome Salado horizon, but never defined the associated complex of materials beyond the mention of small cobble-masonry sites near Globe with an associated ceramic assemblage including Cibola White Wares (Gladwin and Gladwin 1935; Gladwin 1957:249). It may be that Gladwin's briefly defined Cherry Creek Phase in part represents this proposed prepolychrome horizon (Gladwin and Gladwin 1934). The Cherry Creek Phase was placed in a temporal position preceding and in part overlapping the Roosevelt Phase (Gladwin and Gladwin 1934:Figure 5). The phase is defined as exhibiting small pueblo and patio-house architecture accompanied by a ceramic assemblage including Snowflake Black-on-white, Roosevelt Black-on-white, and Salado Red Ware. It is interesting that the type site for the Cherry Creek Phase is located in the Coon Creek drainage, and in Gladwin's comparative phase chart is placed in an intermediate geographic position between the Salado Branch and the Cibola Branch to the east and north (Gladwin and Gladwin 1934).

Employing survey data from lower Cherry Creek, Wells (1971) distinguished two periods, A.D. 1100-1150 and A.D. 1150-1200, both of which are characterized by materials exhibiting some similarities to those of the Miami Phase. The A.D. 1100-1150 period is characterized by a ceramic assemblage of Cibola White Wares (Snowflake, Reserve, Tularosa, and Roosevelt black-on-whites) and Tonto Red in association with rectangular aboveground structures having cobble foundations and occurring in groups of one to 30. The immediately following period is defined on the basis of a similar ceramic assemblage with the addition of Salado Red and a rough, corrugated utility ware (Tonto Corrugated?). Architecture dated to the A.D. 1150-1200 period consists of both contiguous and non-contiguous aboveground rooms built of cobble masonry and often surrounded by enclosing walls (Wells 1971).

The relationship of the Cherry Creek materials and Gladwin's Cherry Creek Phase to those materials defined as characteristic of the Miami Phase is difficult to assess, given the nature of the data. The point to be noted is that several different workers have suggested the existence of a complex consisting in part of aboveground cobble-foundation or masonry structures, sometimes with an enclosing wall, and having a ceramic assemblage with a significant Cibola White Ware component, prior to the appearance of the Salado polychromes. Given the dating of the earliest of these types, Pinto Polychrome, this would mean prior to A.D. 1200 (Doyel 1978). Determination of the validity, nature, and extent of such a complex should be a priority for future research in the area, and will bear on a variety of issues, including the problem of Salado origins and the relationship of the Salado materials to the earlier Hohokam occupation of the area.

Salado Occupation

Roosevelt Phase (A.D. 1200-1300)

The Roosevelt Phase represents the earliest specifically defined Salado occupation of the Tonto-Roosevelt area. As originally defined, it is characterized in part by the presence of Pinto Polychrome and Roosevelt Black-on-white in association with architecture consisting of single-story, cobble-foundation rooms within "compounds" or enclosing walls (Gladwin and Gladwin 1935). The original dating of the phase, between A.D. 1100 or 1150 and 1200, has been recently revised upward to A.D. 1200-1300 on the basis of excavated material and a reconsideration of the dating of Pinto Polychrome (Doyel 1978: 197).

No single-component "compound" of the sort defined as diagnostic of the Roosevelt Phase has ever been excavated, but sites exhibiting this characteristic architecture are known to be quite common in the area. Excavation of sites along Miami Wash produced evidence of a Roosevelt Phase occupation, represented by one to four crude cobble rooms without enclosing walls and a ceramic assemblage including Pinto Black-on-red, Salado Red, St. John's Polychrome, Pinedale Black-on-red, and Roosevelt Black-on-white in addition to Pinto Polychrome (Doyel 1978). The Cedar Basin Ruin, located in the Pinto Creek drainage, may represent a Roosevelt Phase occupation, but no Pinto Polychrome was recovered and the dating is based on intrusive ceramics (Windmiller 1974b; Doyel 1976b). Little is known of the Roosevelt Phase occupation at Besh-ba-go-wah, but the site was apparently a multiroom pueblo during this period (Vickery 1939; Doyel 1976c).

Survey data from lower Cherry Creek indicate a possible Roosevelt Phase occupation, with sites consisting of contiguous and noncontiguous rooms with enclosing walls and a ceramic assemblage including Cibola White Wares, St. John's Polychrome, and Pinto Polychrome, dated between A.D.1200 and 1250. Between A.D. 1250 and 1300, Pinedale Black-on-red is added to the ceramic assemblage, and Wells (1971) suggests that village size increases.

The picture in the lower Cherry Creek drainage is complicated by the fact that the Sierrra Ancha cliff dwellings were built and occupied during the latter part of the A.D. 1200-1300 period. These sites may not properly be called Salado, as the dominant decorated ware represented is Fourmile Polychrome, while the Salado polychromes occur only in small

quantities and not at all sites (Haury 1932 and personal communication;
Gladwin and Gladwin 1935). Further work will be required to clarify the
relationship between the Sierra Ancha sites and the possible Roosevelt
Phase occupation of the lower elevations of the lower Cherry Creek drainage.

Site types occurring during the Roosevelt Phase include function-
ally specialized small sites such as those excavated along Miami Wash
(Doyel 1978) in addition to the diagnostic but poorly known compound sites.
It is assumed that subsistence activities were focused on the cultivation
of domesticates, with supplemental collecting of wild foodstuffs (Doyel 1978).
Much more data concerning all aspects of the Roosevelt Phase are required
for an adequate understanding of the period, and it is imperative that a
Roosevelt Phase compound be excavated and reported on.

Gila Phase (A.D. 1300-1450)

The Gila Phase Salado occupation of the Tonto-Roosevelt area is
perhaps the best documented period in the entire prehistoric sequence.
As presently defined, the phase is an amalgamation of Gladwin's original
Middle Gila and Tonto phases, and is dated between A.D. 1300 and 1450
(Gladwin and Gladwin 1935; Doyel 1976b). The diagnostic ceramic type is
the well-known and widely distributed Gila Polychrome, with Tonto Polychrome appearing later in the phase. Gladwin saw the Gila Phase as a
development resulting from the migration of proto-Hopi peoples into the
area (Gladwin and Gladwin 1935; Doyel 1976b); this hypothesis has yet to
be systematically assessed.

The pattern of aggregation into large sites witnessed in other
areas of the Southwest during this time period is also apparent in the
Tonto-Roosevelt area at such large Gila Phase sites as Gila Pueblo,
Besh-ba-go-wah, and To-get-zo-ge. A diversified settlement pattern is
demonstrated, however, by the existence of smaller pueblos such as the
Tonto cliff dwellings (Steen and others 1962) and the Central Heights
Site (McGuire 1975), and by even smaller, functionally specialized sites
such as those excavated along Miami Wash (Doyel 1976a, 1978). Subsistence
appears to have been concentrated on agricultural pursuits, but was augmented by wild foodstuffs. The Roosevelt Phase component underlying
the larger Gila Phase pueblo at Besh-ba-go-wah suggests some continuity
in site location and construction sequences between the two phases, but
the existence of apparently pure Gila Phase sites such as Gila Pueblo
and To-get-zo-ge provides evidence for the occupation of new site locations, accompanied by major construction episodes occurring entirely
during the phase (Gladwin 1957; Schmidt 1928).

The Sierra Ancha cliff dwellings overlap this and the preceding
Roosevelt Phase; these sites were abandoned by the early decades of the
14th century (Haury 1934). Wells (1971) suggests that lower Cherry Creek

was entirely abandoned by A.D. 1375 and notes that only one or two sites existed in the area after A.D. 1300. No Tonto Polychrome was observed at any of the sites recorded in the area. Again, the possible distinctiveness of the occupational sequence of this area should be noted. The inclusion of the known materials from lower Cherry Creek within the Gila Phase is not warranted at present, especially given the complexities introduced by the non-Salado Sierra Ancha cliff dwellings.

The entire Tonto-Roosevelt area appears to have been abandoned by A.D. 1450. Gladwin hypothesized that the abandonment was due to pressure from Apachean raiders, but this appears unlikely on the basis of present evidence (see below, p. 215). The abandonment of the area by its prehistoric inhabitants was likely the result of complex factors that will only be understood within a regional perspective and through a greatly expanded data base.

Yavapai and Apache Occupations

The area in and around the southern end of the Tonto Basin includes parts of the ethnographically known territories of two groups, the Southeastern Yavapai and the Western Apache (Gifford 1932; 1936; Goodwin 1942). Figure 17 (after Goodwin 1942; Gifford 1932, 1936) shows the ethnographic boundaries and intragroup divisions as they are known to have existed at approximately 1850, and includes the locations to be referred to in the following discussion.

The boundary between the two groups was defined essentially by the crests of the Pinal and Mazatzal mountains, with the Southeastern Yavapai occupying the territory to the west and the Western Apache living to the east. Only the Mineral Creek study area, as defined for this report, lies within the former territory of the Southeastern Yavapai; the remaining four areas fall within what was Western Apache territory in 1850.

Southeastern Yavapai

The Southeastern Yavapai were a seminomadic hunting and gathering people, practicing only limited and incidental cultivation of domesticates. The group was divided into two named, territorial bands. The area north of the Salt River was primarily the domain of the Wikedjasapa band ("chopped-up-mountain-people", "Four Peaks people"), while the territory south of the Salt River was occupied by the Walkamepa band ("Pinal Mountain people"). The boundary between these two groups was by no means hard and fast; both freely visited each other's territory and interacted frequently. Known Yavapai camp sites include Amanyika' ("quail's roost"), located near the confluence of Fish Creek with the Salt River, and Skull Cave, also near the Salt in the same vicinity and

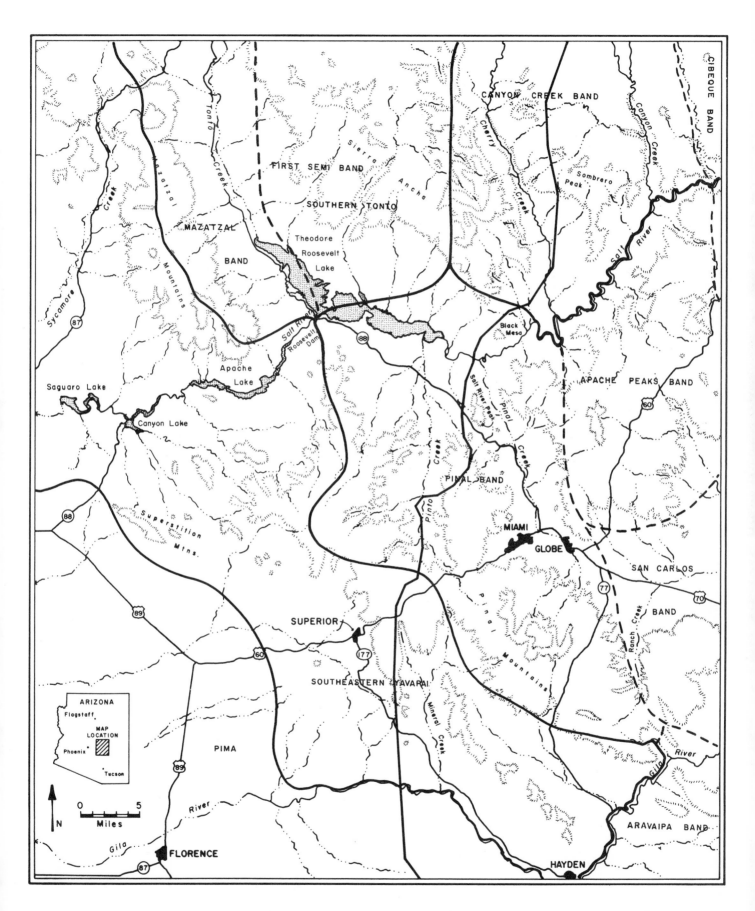

Figure 17. Ethnographic boundaries in the Tonto-Roosevelt area as of 1850

the scene of the 1872 massacre of Yavapai by Anglos (Bourke 1891:188).
Yavapai are said to have wintered in the Tonto cliff dwellings and in a
similar ruin in a nearby canyon (Gifford 1932:180, 203; Steen 1962:7).

Little is known of the prehistory and early history of the Southeastern Yavapai. The closely related Northeastern Yavapai were apparently
in their ethnographically known territory before 1600 (Hammond and Rey
1929; Bolton 1919; Gifford 1932); there is no similar information concerning the southeastern group. Few documented archaeological sites in
the area have been interpreted as being of Yavapai origin, and the nature
of the material culture inventory as described by Gifford (1932, 1936)
indicates that discrimination of Yavapai sites may prove somewhat difficult.
Possible Yavapai mescal pits have been reported in the Queen Creek drainage
near Superior (Wood 1978). Steen suggests that hilltop sites on Valentine
Butte (some 6.4 km or 4 miles north of Roosevelt Dam) and on Black Mesa
(within the area considered here) represent Yavapai occupations (1962:7).
No basis for this assertion is given, however, and some question must be
raised as to its validity. These sites would appear to correspond quite
well to "compounds" of the sort found in abundance in the area and clearly
of prehistoric origin:

> These sites consist of the remains of stone walls which were built
> around the perimeters of rather flat hilltops. The area enclosed
> is sometimes as much as an acre. Rooms were usually built within,
> and adjoining the wall; as many as 20 small rooms may be counted
> at this type of site (Steen 1962:7; compare Gladwin and Gladwin 1935:217-8).

If Yavapai did indeed occupy these sites, it is more likely a case of the
reoccupation and reuse of prehistoric sites rather than Yavapai construction
of them. Gifford's work does not describe any similar features as having
been constructed by the Southeastern Yavapai. Furthermore, the location
of these hilltop sites would appear to contradict an apparent Yavapai pre-
dilection for caves and rock shelters as abodes (Gifford 1932:203). For
the present, the date of initial occupation of the area by the Southeastern
Yavapai and their relationship to archaeologically known populations are
problematic.

Western Apache

Because of the superbly detailed work of Goodwin (1942) and several
other treatments of Western Apache culture, quite specific information is
available concerning the Apache occupation and use of the area just prior
to and immediately following the initial Anglo presence. The Western
Apache relied on a mixed economy of hunting, gathering, and agriculture,
and raided other groups as an economic pursuit as well (Buskirk 1949;
Goodwin 1942, 1971; Basso 1970). The Western Apache were divided into
five major groups that were further subdivided into named bands, each
occupying a specific territory (Goodwin 1942:1-6).

The Tonto-Roosevelt area was the domain of the San Carlos and Cibecue groups, with the first semiband of the Southern Tonto group occupying the west side of the Sierra Ancha range as close neighbors to the north. All of Pinto Creek, most of Pinal Creek, and a small triangular area north of the Salt (including Black Mesa) fell within the territory of the Pinal band (ti s e van, "cottonwoods in gray wedge-shape people") of the San Carlos group, while the remainder of the Pinal Creek drainage and the area in and around the Apache Peaks was occupied by the Apache Peaks band (nada dogulnine, "tasteless mescal people"), also of the San Carlos group. The Cherry Creek drainage west of the crest of the Sierra Ancha range was the domain of the Canyon Creek band (gulkijn, "spotted-on-top people") of the Cibecue group. Goodwin (1942) provides a treatment of the composition of and various social relations that obtained within and between Western Apache groups and bands.

Farming sites of these various groups within the Tonto-Roosevelt area were located on Pinal Creek in the area of Wheatfields and near the confluence of Pinal Creek and Miami Wash. There were also scattered farm sites along the Salt River from the mouth of Pinal Creek to the mouth of Tonto Creek, near the present site of Roosevelt Dam. Additional sites were situated on Coon Creek and in lower Cherry Creek at the base of the Sierra Ancha range (Goodwin 1942:11-4). The use of water-control techniques by the Western Apache has been documented (Griffin, Leone, and Basso 1971; Reagan 1930:299), but it is not known if similar systems were in use at any of the aforementioned locales. In addition to farming, the Western Apache collected, processed, and used a variety of wild foodstuffs, principally mescal and pinyon (Buskirk 1949;Reagan 1929, 1930; Goodwin 1942). Both of these plants are locally abundant.

As with the Southeastern Yavapai, the early history and prehistory of the Western Apache in the area are poorly known. The hypothesis that Apachean raiders were responsible for the Salado exodus from the region was put forth by Gladwin (Gladwin and Gladwin 1935), and Goodwin notes that Apache oral traditions claim three ruins in the region as having been occupied by non-Apache peoples and raided by the Apache (1942:69). This would require an Apache presence in the area by at least 1450 and quite probably earlier. There is little empirical evidence at present to support either of these contentions (Schroeder 1974).

The historical accounts resulting from the journeys of Spanish explorers and missionaries provide little information concerning people that may have been occupying the area during the 16th and 17th centuries. These early expeditions never really penetrated what was in 1850 the principal territory of the Western Apache, skirting it instead to the east, north, and south (Goodwin 1942:67; Schroeder 1974). Apache raids into Sonora began in the 1680s, and Apache raiding forced the abandonment of the San Pedro settlements of the Sobaipuri during the 18th century (Winter 1973:69). However, it is unclear whether the people participating in these raids were Chiricahua or Western Apache. People identified as

Apache were seen in the area north and west of the San Pedro-Gila confluence in 1696, and Apache raids on the Gila River Pima commenced in 1699 (Winter 1973). If the people observed in 1696 and later responsible for the raids on the Gila Pima were in fact Western Apache, this would constitute the earliest record of their presence in their ethnographically known territory. It is interesting in this regard that one of Goodwin's informants referred to a time when the Western Apache were situated east of the Sierra Ancha range and had not yet occupied the Tonto Basin (1942:64; see also Schroeder 1974). There is also a general north-south trend to the movements described in clan origin myths (Goodwin 1942:64-5).

Initial contacts with Anglos came in the mid-1800s, when mountain men traveled through the area and traded with the Apache (Goodwin 1942:95). Prospectors, miners, and ranchers soon followed, and disruption and modification of the aboriginal way of life was well underway by the latter half of the 19th century (Goodwin 1942; Bourke 1891; Ellison 1968; Basso 1970).

The only definitely Apachean archaeological site excavated in the immediate area dates to the late historic period (Vivian 1970), and is located on Ranch Creek in the San Carlos drainage. Here, the remains of an Apache wickiup probably dating between 1900 and 1935 were uncovered, situated in the middle of the Santa Cruz Hohokam ball court mentioned above (Vivian 1970:130). Brandes, who first recorded the site, noted several other possible Apache sites in the general vicinity (1957b). Features of possible Apache origin have been noted by Windmiller (1972c) in Pinto Creek, while Doyel found Apache sherds without associated features on the surface of several sites in Miami Wash (1976b:260-1). These sherds are likely associated with the farming activities of the Pinal and Apache Peaks bands. Several features of possible Apache origin were recorded during the APS Cholla line survey and will be discussed below in the section dealing with the survey material.

Discussion

The Yavapai and Apache occupations of the area deserve attention from archaeologists for several reasons. In order to successfully identify and interpret the full range of archaeological materials to be found, some consideration must be given to manifestations potentially attributable to these ethnographically known groups. Even a cursory review of the relevant literature indicates that in addition to dwellings, such constructions as sweat houses; roasting pits for mescal, pinyon, corn, and meat; shrines; water-control devices; and possibly other features would have produced lasting remains (Buskirk 1949; Reagan 1929, 1930; Goodwin 1942; Griffin, Leone, and Basso 1971). A systematic study of the material culture and known distribution of Yavapai and Apache groups would provide an initial basis for identifying the probable nature and extent of sites produced by the activities of these peoples, and would establish a foundation for

subsequent inferences concerning the origin and possible function of
problematic archaeological remains exhibiting similar characteristics.
This line of reasoning is applied in the discussion of possible Apache
features from the Cholla line survey (p. 237 ff.).

The ability to identify Yavapai and/or Apache sites and distinguish them
from other archaeological materials is a prerequisite for the investigation of a
variety of potential research problems focusing on such data. The questions of the
date of initial occupation of the area by and earlier distributions of
these groups, their relationships to the peoples represented by the known
archaeological sequence, and the nature of precontact subsistence-
settlement systems of Yavapai and Apache groups are all examples of
problems on which data from Yavapai and Apache sites might be brought to
bear.

The problem of chronological control is particularly important.
Although Gladwin's hypothesis of Apache raiders as the cause of the Salado
abandonment of the area is not now widely held, neither has it been
systematically examined using empirical data. As Goodwin long ago noted,
"the date of Western Apache arrival... could be determined if evidence of
their culture was found in definite association with dateable remains from
other peoples" (1942:68).

His statement may be augmented to include the proposition that datable
materials from any demonstrably Apache site would assist in resolving
the problem.

For the moment, the potential contribution of an archaeological
approach to these and other related problems remains undetermined. The
degree to which archaeological data may inform on various aspects of the
Yavapai and Apache occupations of the area depends on 1) the ability to
successfully identify Apache and Yavapai sites, and 2) the determination
of the nature, extent, and content of such sites relative to a specifically
posed set of research questions.

Another archaeologically relevant aspect of the ethnographically
known occupations of the area is the degree to which these peoples may
have modified the existing archaeological record in the course of pursuing
their particular lifeways. In addition to the alterations resulting from
the actual reoccupation and reuse of sites such as the Tonto cliff dwellings and the Ranch Creek Site noted above, Apaches are known to have been
well aware of prehistoric sites in the region and to have routinely
scavenged them, collecting such items as projectile points, turquoise,
shell, and jet (Goodwin 1942:63; Reagan 1930:303). Since scavenging is
a subtractive process, the relative extent and effects of such activities
at any given site would be impossible to determine in the absence of
additional evidence. The possibility of such modifications of sites should
be acknowledged and considered nonetheless, especially in the interpretation
of surface assemblages.

Other modifications of archaeological sites may have occurred as a result of the farming and collecting activities of Apache groups. Features often interpreted as Apache (?) mescal-roasting pits are consistently associated with prehistoric sites (see below, p.237). Additionally, activities associated with the preparation and maintenance of farm plots might be expected to have altered archaeological sites either directly (through plowing or the construction of water-control features) or indirectly (by affecting the pollen rain and therefore the pollen content of sites on or immediately adjacent to farm plots).

The foregoing discussion suggests two general ways in which the Yavapai and Western Apache occupations of the Tonto-Roosevelt area are significant to the archaeologist. First, there is the possibility of studying these occupations through the identification and examination of archaeological remains. Because of relatively incomplete ethnographic data, a low population density and the seminomadic character of their adjustment to the environment, and a rather ephemeral nonperishable material culture assemblage, such an approach may prove difficult with respect to the Yuman-speaking Southeastern Yavapai. On the other hand, the relative abundance of specific ethnographic information, a more substantial population and more localized way of life, and a more elaborate material culture are all factors suggesting potentially fertile ground for an archaeological approach to the Western Apache occupation of the area. The other aspect of the ethnographically known occupations of concern is the nature and extent of modifications of the archaeological record. The possibility of such effects should be considered and their potential impact assessed in the interpretation of archaeological materials from the Tonto-Roosevelt area.

The culture history discussed above is summarized in Figure 18, which divides the cultural chronology of the Tonto-Roosevelt area into three separate phase sequences.

The Mineral Creek study area is shown separately, owing to its position in the Gila rather than the Salt River watershed and due to the lack of previous research upon which to base a summary of the culture history of the area. The Mineral Creek area also differs from the others defined here in that it is the only area that falls into the former territory of the Southeastern Yavapai. The Pinto Creek and Pinal Creek areas form another unit, and the recently defined phase sequence for the Globe-Miami and Tonto Basin areas essentially applies here (Doyel 1976b). The Coon Creek and lower Cherry Creek areas form the final unit, based on the lack of excavated material and the indications noted above that the sequence of occupation in these areas may differ in several aspects from that defined for the Pinto and Pinal Creek areas.

Specific features of the chart presented in Figure 18 should be noted:

1. The possible applicability of the Gila Basin sequence to the Mineral Creek area is indicated but no named phases are included due to the general lack of work in the area. Although the Yavapai occupation of the area is indicated, not even a provisional date is suggested for the initial occupation of the area by the Yavapai due to the absence of evidence.

2. The Sacaton Phase as presently defined is retained for the Pinto Creek and Pinal Creek areas, with a dotted line indicating the indeterminate end date for the phase as noted above (Doyel 1976b). The Sacaton Phase is also included for the Coon Creek and lower Cherry Creek areas, but its provisional status is indicated by a question mark; a dotted line indicates a provisional end date of A.D. 1100 as suggested by Wells' (1971) data.

3. The remainder of the Globe-Miami/Tonto Basin sequence is retained for the Pinto and Pinal Creek areas, and is augmented by the addition of the Apache and Anglo occupations, thus bringing the sequence up to the present. A provisional date of 1650 is suggested for the initial Western Apache occupation of the area, based on the admittedly scanty evidence available. The date nonetheless establishes a position around which evidence may be presented either in support of the suggested reconstruction or in favor of an alternative interpretation.

4. Gladwin's Cherry Creek Phase is included on a provisional basis for the Coon Creek-Black Mesa and lower Cherry Creek areas. Although the characteristics of the phase are poorly defined and will undoubtedly require refinement and reevaluation, his construction is supported to some extent by Wells' survey data and emphasizes the possibility that the sequence of occupation in these areas may have differed from the one presently defined for the immediately adjacent areas to the west and southwest. No named phases are included for the Coon Creek and lower Cherry Creek areas after the Cherry Creek Phase because of the lack of excavated materials. The possibility of a Roosevelt Phase occupation is suggested by survey data, but the presence of the Sierra Ancha cliff dwellings complicates the picture. Only future work will resolve the question. For now, the inclusion of a Roosevelt Phase is not warranted. The Sierra Ancha sites and the Granite Basin Ruin are shown in their proper temporal positions with lower-case letters to indicate a nonphase status. The Apache occupation of the area is included in the sequence for these areas.

5. A dotted line indicates the initial Anglo occupation of the three areas, and should be considered as representing an average date.

DATE	GILA RIVER BASIN	SALT RIVER BASIN	
	MINERAL CREEK	PINTO CREEK PINAL CREEK (TONTO BASIN)*	BLACK MESA LOWER CHERRY CREEK
1900	ANGLO	OCCUPATION	
1800	SOUTHEASTERN YAVAPAI ?	WESTERN	APACHE
1700			
		?	?
1600	SEQUENCE ?		
1500		? ABANDONED ?	
1400		GILA	Granite Basin Ruin ?
1300			Sierra Ancha Sites
1200		ROOSEVELT	
		MIAMI*	CHERRY CREEK
1100	BASIN		?
1000		SACATON	SACATON ?
900			
800	? GILA	SANTA CRUZ	SANTA CRUZ
700			
600		GILA BUTTE	?
500			
		SNAKETOWN ?	
	PRECERAMIC		

*TONTO BASIN SEQUENCE DOES NOT INCLUDE THE MIAMI PHASE

Figure 18. Culture chronologies for the Tonto-Roosevelt area

The APS-CS Survey Sites

Site Variability

Two basic dimensions of variability in the inventory of sites discovered along the Tonto-Roosevelt segment of the Cholla line will be dealt with. First, the sites will be grouped and discussed in terms of their morphological characteristics; and second, the general distributional characteristics of the sites will be presented and discussed in terms of the study areas defined above.

Since systematic surface collections were not taken during the survey, a chronological ordering of the sites based on datable ceramic materials is unfortunately prevented. The generating of inferences concerning the relative temporal position of sites on the basis of architectural features is hampered by the lack of a well-established sequence of architectural variability for the area, except at the most general level. Thus, the chronological control over the recorded sites is painfully poor. Recorded materials that may relate to the temporal position of sites will be selectively referred to.

Site Morphology

Sites will be grouped and discussed here in terms of empirical site types; that is, groupings of sites based on combinations of characteristics that regularly occurred together (Hester and Hobler 1969). The characteristics of the types and internal variability within them will be defined and illustrated with examples.

The groupings of sites presented are designed to impart a more lucid conception of morphological variability than is available from a collection of individual site descriptions. They in no way imply temporal placement, cultural affiliation, or function beyond what is specifically and selectively noted and discussed. While some of the types defined here may prove to have validity beyond the heuristic descriptive categories they are intended to be, others may simply reflect the vagaries of site definition and description based on surface observations.

Through an ordering of sites on the basis of their observable similarities, a foundation for comparison with other reported sites is established and an expanded record of site variability in the Tonto-Roosevelt area made available. The results of excavations of particular site types will provide a means for assessing the relationship between surface configurations and overall site content, and thus establish the relative validity and utility of the types defined here.

Nine separate site types have been isolated: artifact scatters, rock shelters, isolated cobble features, small sites with two to four rooms, compounds, multiroom pueblos, petroglyphs, possible Apache features, and historic sites. In many cases these types are not mutually exclusive. For example, several sites have both historic and prehistoric components, while the possible Apache features all occur in association with other types of features. The coassociation of types is noted in the descriptions that follow.

For more specific information concerning individual sites, the reader is directed to the accompanying volume of site descriptions. For convenience, the numbers of the sites included in each type along with the distribution of site types by individual study area are presented in Tables 44-48.

Artifact Scatters

Sixteen sites consisting of variously composed artifact scatters without observable architectural features were recorded. The areas covered by the scatters range from small (1575 square meters) to quite large (over 100,000 square meters), with the relative density of artifacts highly variable. The great variation in the size of the scatters probably reflects the arbitrary nature of site definition more than the relative intensity or duration of the behaviors that originally produced the remains.

All of the sites had chipped stone materials present, and ground stone artifacts were observed at all but one of the sites. None of the scatters exhibited artifacts clearly diagnostic of an Archaic or Paleo-Indian assemblage. Nine of the 16 sites exhibited sherds in small quantities. One site (AZ V:5:39) had a petroglyph associated with it.

Only one site (AZ V:9:104) showed firm indications of subsurface materials, in the form of areas of darkly stained soil and an atypically high density of artifacts, especially sherds. Aside from this site, all of the scatters appear to be essentially surficial in character.

Work conducted at six of these sites during the subsequent phase of the project should provide a wealth of information concerning this infrequently dealt with site type.

Rock Shelters

Four rock shelters were recorded during the course of the survey. All of the shelters are small and fairly shallow (Figure 19). Three of the sites show interior modification of the natural shelter either through simple clearing of the space or construction of boulder and cobble dividers or walls. In one case, this modification appears as

two crude rooms built up against the slight overhang that forms the
natural shelter (Figure 20). The area immediately in front of two of
the sites appears to have been filled in and leveled off to create additional space, either by the construction of a small retaining wall (at
AZ V:5:51) (Figure 20) or the filling in of natural crevices in the rock
(at AZ V:5:49). Bedrock mortars and metates were present at one site
(AZ V:5:49), and numerous one-hand manos were observed on the surface
of another (AZ V:5:51). Both AZ V:5:50 and AZ V:5:51 are in close proximity
to the artifact scatter designated AZ V:5:46, and all of the sites are
in areas where artifact scatters and other features were recorded. It
may be that these rock shelters were associated with the exploitative
activities represented by these other nearby sites.

AZ V:5:49 was excavated during the subsequent phase of the project;
the report on that work will constitute the first documentation of this
type of site in the area.

Petroglyphs

Petroglyphs were recorded at three sites in association with other
materials, while one instance of isolated rock art (AZ V:5:56) was
observed on two large boulders in the general vicinity of a rock shelter
and a large lithic scatter (AZ V:5:49 and AZ V:5:42, respectively). The
petroglyphs at this site include both geometric and zoomorphic forms, with
the latter interpreted as representing a centipede, a turtle, a scorpion,
a lizard, and mountain sheep (Figure 21). The other three sites with
petroglyphs also exhibit both geometric and zoomorphic forms (Figures 22
and 23).

Only one instance of nonportable art has been reported from the
area, consisting of a "labyrinth" drawn into one of the walls at the
Tonto cliff dwelling while the plaster was still wet (Abel and Van
Valkenburg 1961). In addition to the petroglyphs recorded by the survey, others are known to exist in the lower reaches of Coon Creek and
in Chalk Creek and Dry Creek near Black Mesa.

The possible dating and function of these features is problematic.

Isolated Cobble Foundations

Twenty-one sites were recorded that consist of isolated cobble
features with associated artifact scatters of variable density. Most
of the sites clearly represent the remains of single rooms or two or
three-sided structures having definite cobble foundations with one to
four courses of stone remaining (Figure 24a-e). The foundations probably
once supported perishable superstructures. One site had two "wing" walls
extending from the rectangular foundation (Figure 24d); one site, apparently more ephemeral than the others, consisted of a simple circular

224

Figure 19. AZ V:5:9

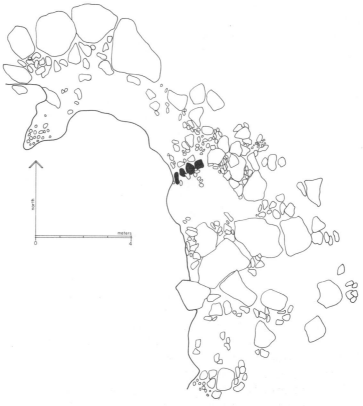

north

meters
0   4

Figure 20. Map of
AZ V:5:51

Figure 21.   Petroglyphs at AZ V:5:56

Figure 22.   Geometric petroglyph from
AZ U:12:34

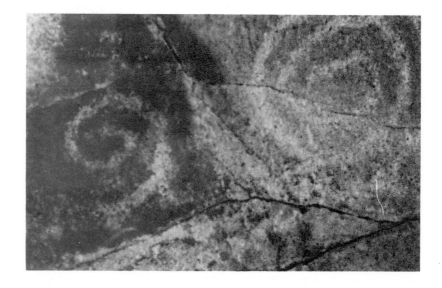

Figure 23.   Zoomorphic
petroglyph from
AZ U:12:34

alignment of fist-sized cobbles rather than a clearly defined foundation (Figure 24e). In many cases, the vegetative cover and general condition of the sites prevented the determination of the original shape of the feature.

Those sites with a clearly rectangular shape that could be measured range from 3 m by 3 m to 6.5 m by 9 m. Most of the sites are smaller than the largest one recorded, typically measuring approximately 4 m by 5 m.

Included in this category are several sites consisting of a number of cobble foundations situated at some distance from one another. At AZ V:5:26, six such features were found over an area measuring 300 m by 180 m and were recorded as a single site.

Similar features have been recorded in the Pinto Creek drainage, in the Globe-Miami area, near Roosevelt Lake, and in lower Cherry Creek (Windmiller 1971a, 1972a; Brandes 1957a; Doyel 1974; Fuller, Rogge, and Gregonis 1976; Haury 1932; Wells 1971). Excavated features of this type show great variability in size, quality of construction, range of internal features, and date (Doyel 1978).

AZ V:5:35 was excavated during the subsequent phase of the project.

Two to Four-room Sites

Sixteen sites were recorded that consist of the remains of two to four rooms grouped in close proximity to one another and sometimes in association with a retaining or enclosing wall. Three variations occur within this type of site:

a. Six sites consisted of two or three contiguous rooms with yet another noncontiguous room situated close by. In two cases, a retaining wall was associated with the features (Figure 25c, d).

b. Eight sites consisted of two or three noncontiguous features situated less than 10 meters apart, in one case associated with an L-shaped enclosing wall (Figure 25e, f).

c. Two sites included two or three contiguous rooms with an attached wall defining a "patio" or plaza area (Figure 25a, b).

These sites may in part represent arrangements similar to that documented by Doyel and dated to the Miami Phase (A.D. 1150-1200). Although the ceramic assemblages observed at the sites are not indicative of any specific temporal range, the presence of polychromes from the White Mountain Red Ware series at two of the sites would suggest a post-A.D. 1100 date. The fact that such small sites may have multiple components has been amply demonstrated; thus, the assumption that all of the architectural features at any given site are contemporaneous may not be made (Doyel 1974, 1978).

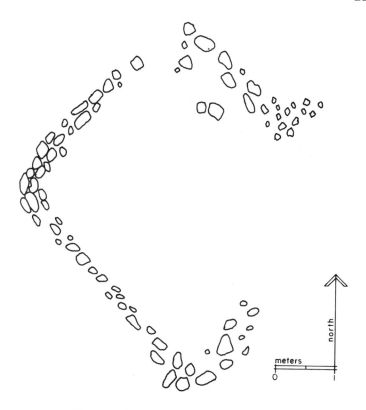

Figure 24a.   Isolated cobble
              foundations -
              AZ V:9:100

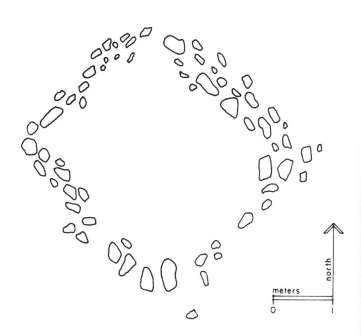

Figure 24b.   AZ V:9:101

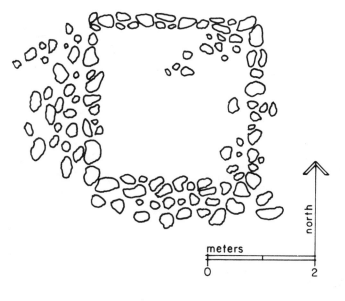

Figure 24c.   AZ U:12:36

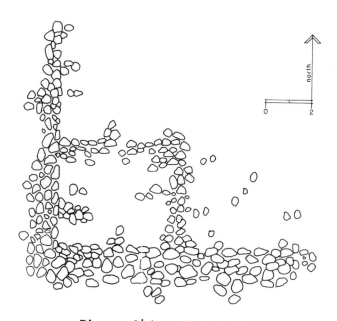

Figure 24d.   AZ V:5:29

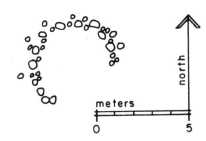

Figure 24e.   AZ V:5:35

Figure 25a. Two to four-room sites - AZ V:9:105

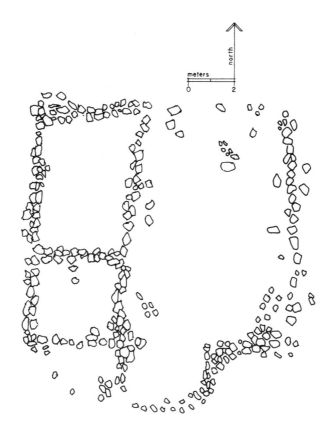

Figure 25b.   AZ V:5:16

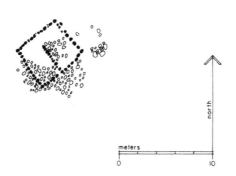

Figure 25c.   AZ V:9:107

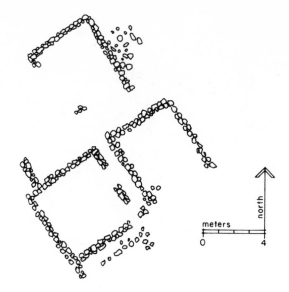

Figure 25d.   AZ V:5:18

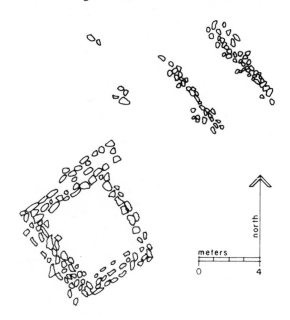

Figure 25e.   AZ V:5:12

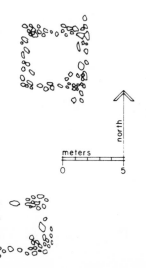

Figure 25f.   AZ V:5:15

Two sites from this category (AZ V:9:107 and AZ V:9:105) were excavated during the subsequent phase of the project.

"Compounds"

Three sites were recorded that appear to correspond essentially to Gladwin's (Gladwin and Gladwin 1935) description of Roosevelt Phase compounds, in that they consist of a rectangular space defined by a cobble foundation wall with rooms variously arranged within and against the wall. The area enclosed by the compound wall is roughly equal at all three sites, being 15 or 20 meters on one side and 20 or 25 meters on the other (Figures 26a-e). The amount of rubble present indicates that the enclosing walls were low, perhaps no more than a meter in height.

Only one site (AZ V:5:21) exhibited a ceramic assemblage that deserves comment, consisting of Salado Red, a redware of the White Mountain series, unidentified black-on-reds and black-on-whites, obliterated corrugated, and brown plainware sherds. Although the diagnostic Pinto Polychrome was not observed, the assemblage is not inconsistent with a Roosevelt Phase date (A.D. 1200-1300).

Unfortunately, none of these sites was subjected to further data recording.

Multiroom Pueblos

Eight sites were recorded that consist of blocks of contiguous, pueblo-like rooms. Similar sites have been recorded in the general area (Windmiller 1971b, 1972b; Brandes 1957a; Wells 1971)(Figures 27a-d).

In general, the construction technique employed at these sites would appear to correspond to that traditionally defined as Salado-- coursed masonry walls of unshaped cobbles with abundant mortar and possible perishable upper walls in some cases. Some variation of this technique is suggested at two sites. At AZ V:5:32, a large pothole had exposed a section of wall composed of well-shaped, coursed masonry. There was no indication of this technique on the surface, suggesting that shaped, coursed masonry may be present at other sites that appear from surface indications to be constructed solely of unshaped cobbles. The lower courses of stone in the two room blocks at AZ V:1:4 also showed the use of shaped stones (Figure 27d).

Because there is so little information concerning variability in room size and the internal composition of Salado pueblos, exact room estimates based on the extent of rubble are hazardous. It may be noted, however, that the area covered by rubble is quite regular for six of the

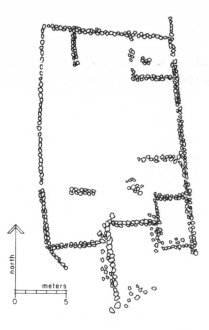

Figure 26a. "Compounds" - AZ V:5:21

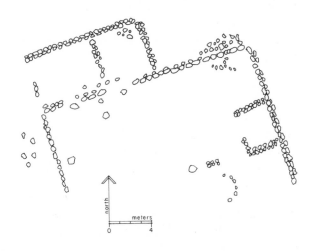

Figure 26b. AZ V:5:25

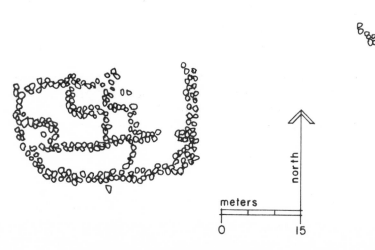

Figure 26c. AZ V:9:112

Figure 27a. Multiroom pueblos - AZ V:5:32

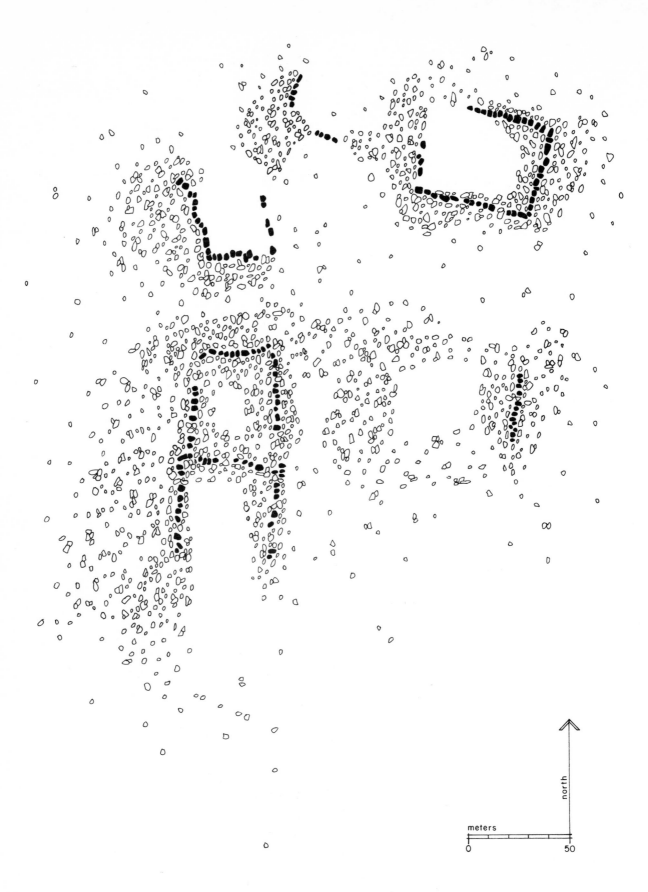

Figure 27b.   AZ V:9:108

north

meters

0   10

Figure 27c.   AZ V:9:109

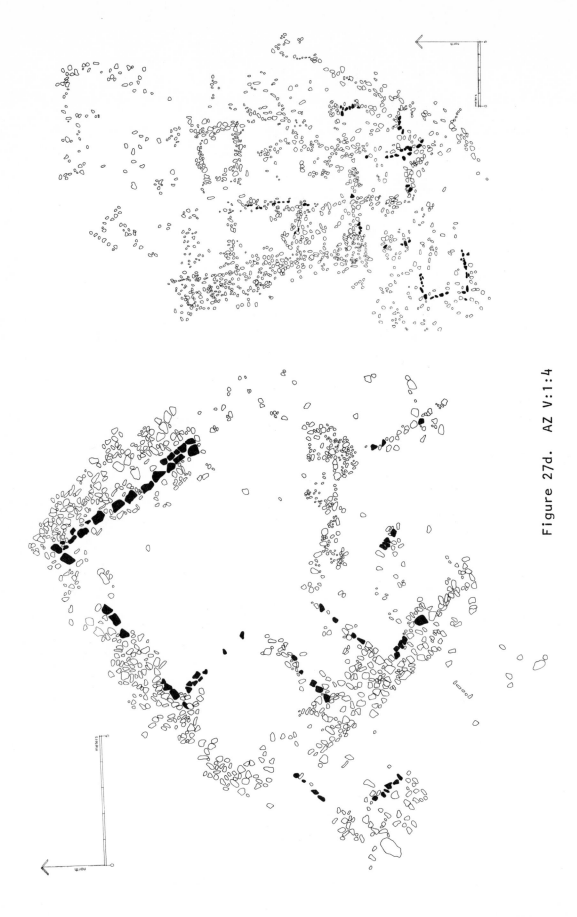

Figure 27d. AZ V:1:4

eight sites, defining a roughly rectangular area of between 400 and 500 square meters. The area covered by the excavated room block at the Central Heights Site was approximately 300 square meters, and there were nine rooms and a ramada area within that space (McGuire 1975). This would suggest the probability of ten or more rooms at the sites discussed here.

One site exhibited an enclosing wall that formed one side of the room block and encompassed it, forming a "courtyard" with a definite entrance (Figure 27a; compare Gladwin and Gladwin 1935). A large circular structure was associated with the room block at AZ U:12:31.

The ceramic materials observed at five of the sites included Gila Polychrome, and thus indicate a Gila Phase occupation dating sometime after A.D. 1300.

All of the sites had been vandalized to some degree. AZ V:1:4 was mapped and surface collected during subsequent data recovery activities.

Possible Apache Features

Three features of possible Apache origin were recorded during the survey, all directly associated with definitely prehistoric materials. These features are discussed separately to emphasize their problematic identity and to suggest that they are as likely Apache as prehistoric.

Two of the features consist of low, crescentic mounds composed primarily of fist-sized cobbles and having a slight depression in the center (Figure 28a). Both are located on multiroom pueblo sites in or abutting discernible rooms (see Figure 27c above), and both are approximately 4 meters across at their widest point. The third feature is a larger circular structure some 10 meters across and having a slight central depression. This feature is located some 30 meters from a prehistoric room block (Figure 28b).

Several lines of indirect evidence suggest an Apache origin of these features. The sites are clearly located within the former territory of the Western Apache. As noted above, these peoples are known to have exploited a variety of wild plant foods, especially mescal and pinyon (Buskirk 1949; Reagan 1929, 1930; Goodwin 1942). The morphology of these features compares well with the remains that would be left from roasting pits for mescal and pinyon that are described in the ethnographic literature; furthermore, they differ in their characteristics from roasting pits discovered in demonstrably prehistoric contexts (see Doyel 1978; Haury 1932). Windmiller (1974b) has suggested that similar features excavated in the Pinto Creek drainage and associated with prehistoric materials may represent later Apache use of the sites.

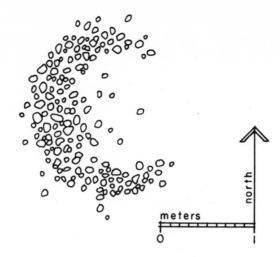

Figure 28a.   Possible Apache features - AZ V:9:108

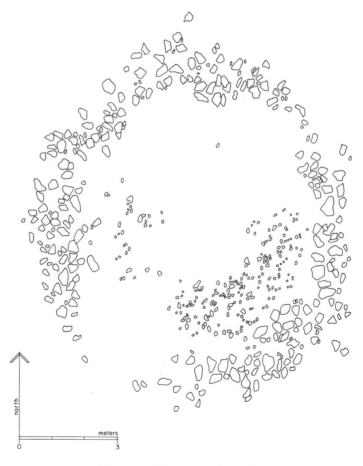

Figure 28b.   AZ V:1:4

The consistent association of these features with the larger and more conspicuous prehistoric sites may be due to two reasons. First, there appears to be an abundance of mescal growing in and around the room blocks at these sites (see Minnis and Plog 1976). It is known that the Apache situated their roasting pits in locations closest to the greatest abundance of the plants to be collected (Buskirk 1949). Second, the relatively loose fill within rooms and in trash areas would make for ease of digging the roasting pits, a significant consideration in this rough and rocky region. The Apache considered the digging of such pits to be men's work and a particularly loathsome task (Buskirk 1949; Reagan 1929, 1930).

Although the origin of these features may not be determined on the basis of existing evidence, consideration should nonetheless be given to the possible Apache origin of these and similar features. The importance of being able to distinguish materials of Apache origin from those produced by other peoples has been discussed above.

None of the three features discussed here was excavated during the subsequent phase of the project.

Historic Sites

Eight of the sites recorded have components clearly datable to the historic period.

Seven of these eight sites represent the remains of various CCC activities in the area. Six sites consist of check dams and other erosion-control features, and are distinguishable from similar prehistoric features by the use of mesh and concrete as construction materials and the presence of historic trash. One site (AZ V:5:17) represents the remains of a CCC camp, and includes the concrete foundations of several buildings and an associated trash deposit.

Another historic site (AZ V:5:23) consists of the cobble foundations of two buildings, an old fence line, and an associated scatter of trash, including glass bottles, cans, horseshoes, and shell casings. Identification of the glass suggests an occupation sometime between 1880 and 1917.

None of these sites was the subject of later data recovery activities.

Site Distribution

The distribution of sites discovered along the Tonto-Roosevelt segment of the APS Cholla line will be presented and briefly discussed in terms of the study areas defined above (see Tables 44-48). Presentation of the sites in terms of these areas allows the location of the transect (and therefore the location of sites discovered along it) to be assessed in terms of the natural geographic units crossed by the line and the range of potential site locations within those units. This method of presentation also facilitates comparison with previously recorded sites.

The lack of chronological control severely limits, except in the most general terms, potential statements concerning the significance of the sites for the interpretation of the occupational sequence of the area. This situation should be remedied somewhat by materials collected during the subsequent data recovery phase of the project, during which 16 sites were investigated.

Lower Cherry Creek

The segment of the Cholla line that crosses the lower Cherry Creek Basin begins well back in the high ridge systems to the east and cuts across these ridges as it moves progressively closer to the creek (Figure 12). After reaching the creek, the line follows it on the eastern side for some 5.6 km (3.5 miles) and then turns southwest and proceeds out of the Cherry Creek watershed.

Seventeen sites were recorded along this segment of the corridor, and eight of the nine site types defined above were observed (Table 44).As is apparent in Figure 3 in the accompanying volume, most of the sites are located on the terraces and ridge tips immediately adjacent to the creek itself; 15 of the 17 sites are so situated. Only two sites (AZ V:1:4 and AZ V:1:6) are located well away from the drainage on the high ridges to the east.

It is clear that the areas immediately adjacent to Cherry Creek were a major focus of prehistoric activity, having the combined attractions of available water and arable land. This is obvious from Wells' 1971 data, and further substantiated by the Cholla line survey material. It is also apparent, however, that some sites were located well away from the creek, at least during some periods, as exemplified by the two sites mentioned above and the Sierra Ancha cliff dwellings. It is also known that a large, late pueblo (Granite Basin Ruin, Gila Pueblo C:1:35) is situated to the east of Cherry Creek in the upper reaches of Banning Wash. Thus, the successful reconstruction and interpretation of the prehistoric occupation of the lower Cherry Creek drainage will require an examination of the distribution of sites known to exist outside the immediate environs of the major drainage.

Coon Creek/Black Mesa

Eighteen sites (Table 45) occurring in two clusters were recorded in the Coon Creek/Black Mesa area (Figure 3 in the accompanying volume). Six of the sites are located on the tips of ridges overlooking and immediately adjacent to Coon Creek near

Table 44. Site types in lower Cherry Creek study unit of Tonto-Roosevelt study area

ASM Number	Artifact scatters	Rock shelters	Petro-glyphs	Isolated cobble foundations	Two to four-room sites	"Compounds"	Multiroom pueblos	Possible Apache features	Historic sites
AZ V:1:4 +							X	X	
AZ V:1:5					X				
AZ V:1:6	X								
AZ V:1:7	X								
AZ V:5:13					X				
AZ V:5:15					X				
AZ V:5:17									X
AZ V:5:19				X					
AZ V:5:20					X				
AZ V:5:21						X			
AZ V:5:22				X					
AZ V:5:23									X
AZ V:5:24					X				
AZ V:5:25						X			
AZ V:5:26				X					

Table 44. Site types in lower Cherry Creek study unit of Tonto-Roosevelt study area (continued)

ASM Number	Artifact scatters	Rock shelters	Petro-glyphs	Isolated cobble foundations	Two to four-room sites	"Compounds"	Multiroom pueblos	Possible Apache features	Historic sites
AZ V:5:38	X								
AZ V:5:39 +	X		X						
TOTALS	4	0	1	3	5	2	1	1	2

+ Sites exhibiting characteristics of more than one type.

Table 45. Site types in Coon Creek-Black Mesa study unit of Tonto-Roosevelt study area

ASM Number	Artifact scatters	Rock shelters	Petro-glyphs	Isolated cobble foundations	Two to four-room sites	"Compounds"	Multiroom pueblos	Possible Apache features	Historic sites
AZ V:5:11 [+]					X				X
AZ V:5:12					X				
AZ V:5:14					X**				
AZ V:5:16					X				
AZ V:5:18					X				
AZ V:5:37	X								
AZ V:5:41	X								
AZ V:5:42	X								
AZ V:5:44	X								
AZ V:5:45	X								
AZ V:5:46	X								
AZ V:5:47	X								
AZ V:5:48	X								
AZ V:5:49		X							
AZ V:5:50		X							
AZ V:5:51		X							

Table 45. Site types in Coon Creek-Black Mesa study unit of Tonto-Roosevelt study area (continued)

ASM Number	Artifact scatters	Rock shelters	Petro-glyphs	Isolated cobble foundations	Two to four-room sites	"Compounds"	Multiroom pueblos	Possible Apache features	Historic sites
AZ V:5:52				X					
AZ V:5:56			X						
TOTALS	8	3	1	1	5	0	0	0	1

** Although the surface remains recorded at AZ V:5:14 warrant its inclusion in the category of two to four-room sites, excavation of the site revealed the remains of five noncontiguous structures. This situation illustrates the potentially variable relationships between surface features and overall site content and should serve as a cautionary tale relevant to the interpretation of survey data from the area.

+ Sites exhibiting characteristics of more than one type.

the point where the corridor crosses that drainage. A permanent spring
near this point provides the supporting moisture for a lush riparian
community that lines the bottom of the creek in this area, and
arable land is present. Several other sites in addition to those recorded
by the survey are known to exist in the immediate vicinity, and it appears
that the spring created a highly desirable situation for the prehistoric
inhabitants. All of the sites in this locality have architectural features,
indicating some degree of permanence.

A second, less concentrated cluster of twelve sites occurs around
the base of Black Mesa. Eight of the 12 sites are artifact scatters
without observable architecture; three rock shelters and a single petroglyph site were also recorded. The area is generally rugged and rocky,
and there is little in the way of arable land in the immediate vicinity.
Springs are present, but the drainages in the area are deeply entrenched
into bedrock and do not support the kind of lush riparian community
observed in Coon Creek.

The sites recorded in the Black Mesa area document the prehistoric
use of "marginal" areas not obviously suited to horticultural pursuits.
The presence of such species as mesquite and prickly-pear may suggest
the nature of the prehistoric use of the area. Six of the artifact
scatters and one of the rock shelters were subjected to further data
recovery and should shed some light on the possible function of these sites.

Pinal Creek

The segment of the Cholla line that traverses the Pinal Creek
Basin follows the upper reaches of DeVore Wash, a tributary of Pinal Creek
(Figure 12). The terrain is rugged, consisting of high hills and ridges
and steep-sided washes, and supports a mixed interior chaparral-juniper-
pinyon woodland vegetative community. The extreme upper reaches of DeVore
Wash drain a basin situation where the terrain is somewhat less severe.

The 17 sites recorded in this area (Table 46) provide an interesting contrast to the well-known prehistoric remains located along Pinal Creek itself
and its major tributary, Miami Wash. The interior portions of the Pinal
Creek drainage were relatively unexplored prior to the Cholla line survey,
and the materials discovered here suggest that these areas witnessed a
significant prehistoric occupation. Five of the eight multiroom pueblos
recorded by the survey are located in the DeVore Wash area, three of them
within one-half mile of each other (AZ V:5:30, AZ V:5:32, and AZ V:5:53).
Nine more of the sites recorded exhibit various architectural features.

Two attributes of the environment may have been significant to the
prehistoric occupation of the area. First, there are numerous springs
in the area to provide water; and second, the basin situation in the
upper reaches of the wash could have supported a considerable amount of
farming activity.

Table 46. Site types in Pinal Creek study unit of Tonto-Roosevelt study area

ASM Number	Artifact scatters	Rock shelters	Petro-glyphs	Isolated cobble foundations	Two to four-room sites	"Compounds"	Multiroom pueblos	Possible Apache features	Historic sites
AZ V:5:29				X					
AZ V:5:30							X		
AZ V:5:31							X		
AZ V:5:32				X					
AZ V:5:33	X								
AZ V:5:34	X								
AZ V:5:35				X					
AZ V:5:53 +				X			X	X	
AZ V:5:54				X					
AZ V:5:55				X					
AZ V:9:103	X			X					
AZ V:9:104	X								
AZ V:9:105					X				
AZ V:9:107					X				
AZ V:9:108 +							X	X	

Table 46. Site types in Pinal Creek study unit of Tonto-Roosevelt study area (continued)

ASM Number	Artifact scatters	Rock shelters	Petro-glyphs	Isolated cobble foundations	Two to four-room sites	"Compounds"	Multiroom pueblos	Possible Apache features	Historic sites
AZ V:9:109							X		
AZ V:9:110				X					
TOTALS	3	0	0	7	2	0	5	2	0

+ Sites exhibiting characteristics of more than one type.

As noted above, the presence of Gila Polychrome materials at several of the multiroom pueblos suggests that the occupation of the area dates in part to the Gila Phase, or post-A.D. 1300. Materials gathered from three sites excavated during the subsequent phase of the project may provide further information concerning the nature and extent of the occupation of areas well away from the major drainages.

Pinto Creek

Two noncontiguous segments of the Cholla line cross the Pinto Creek area as it is defined for this report (Figure 12). The first segment runs from the Salt River along the base of the Salt River Mountains, crossing the area drained by the extreme upper reaches of H-Z and Poison Springs washes, both of which drain directly into the Salt, and Quail Springs and Blevens washes, both legitimate tributaries of Pinto Creek. Only one artifact scatter, located on a ridge overlooking H-Z Wash, was recorded along this segment.

The second line segment included in the Pinto Creek drainage runs southwest from the point where the line leaves the Pinal Creek Basin, crossing an area of high hills and ridges and then turning south to follow Pinto Creek itself. Eleven sites were recorded along this segment of the line (Table 47), five of them on or very near Pinto Creek, and the remaining six on the high ridges and hills to the east of the drainage.

The prehistoric occupation of the Pinto Creek drainage has been documented by Windmiller (1971a, 1972a and c, 1974 a and b), and is further substantiated by the Cholla line survey materials. The range of site types observed compares well with that recorded by Windmiller, and is characterized by architectural features ranging from multiroom pueblos to isolated cobble foundations.

None of the sites in the Pinto Creek area was the subject of later data recovery.

Mineral Creek

The southernmost segment of the Cholla line in the Tonto-Roosevelt area traverses an area drained by the upper tributaries of Mineral Creek, a major wash flowing south toward the Gila River (Figure 12). In this area, the corridor generally parallels Devil's Canyon, a deep, rugged feature that has been cut by the drainage that becomes Mineral Creek somewhat farther south.

Seven sites were recorded along this segment, including one historic site (Table 48). All six of the prehistoric sites documented are located within a mile of one another, and are situated along and between Hackberry Creek and Oak Creek, both of which drain into Devil's Canyon immediately to the east. All of these sites are located in low areas drained by

Table 47. Site types in Pinto Creek study unit of Tonto-Roosevelt study area

ASM Number	Artifact scatters	Rock shelters	Petro-glyphs	Isolated cobble foundations	Two to four-room sites	"Compounds"	Multiroom pueblos	Possible Apache features	Historic sites
AZ U:12:30					X				
AZ U:12:31							X		
AZ V:9:100				X					
AZ V:9:101				X					
AZ V:9:102				X					
AZ V:9:111				X					
AZ V:9:112						X			
AZ V:9:113				X					
AZ V:9:114				X					
AZ V:9:116					X				
AZ V:9:117				X					
AZ V:9:118									X
TOTALS	0	0	0	7	2	1	1	0	1

Table 48. Site types in Mineral Creek study unit of Tonto-Roosevelt study area

ASM Number	Artifact scatters	Rock shelters	Petro- glyphs	Isolated cobble foundations	Two to four-room sites	"Compounds"	Multiroom pueblos	Possible Apache features	Historic sites
AZ U:12:26									X
AZ U:12:33 +		X			X				
AZ U:12:34 +			X				X		
AZ U:12:35 +	X			X					X
AZ U:12:36				X					
AZ U:12:37 +			X	X					X
AZ U:12:38 +					X				X
TOTALS	1	1	2	3	2	0	1	0	4

+ Sites exhibiting characteristics of more than one type.

small, shallow washes which form small valleys between the surrounding steep-sided hills and ridges. A small multiroom pueblo as well as several less substantial architectural features are represented.

It is interesting to note that all of the ceramic materials observed at these sites represent Gila Red, Gila Plain, and unidentified mica-tempered plainwares. This minimal evidence at least suggests the possibility of a Classic Period Hohokam occupation, perhaps similar to that defined for the upper reaches of nearby Queen Creek by Wood (1978). Whatever their temporal placement and cultural affiliation may be, the sites do document the prehistoric occupation of a rugged, out-of-the-way area; this occupation will require further attention and definition.

None of the sites in this area was investigated during subsequent data recovery operations of the project.

Summary

The segmentation and expansion of the area traversed by the Tonto-Roosevelt segment of the Cholla-Saguaro corridor into geographic units have provided a useful context for summarizing and understanding (a) the distribution and character of past research activities, (b) the culture history of the area as it is presently known, and (c) the nature of the Cholla-line survey data with respect to the morphological variability represented within the sample of sites and the sample of geographic space intersected by the corridor.

(a) Previous archaeological research carried out in the Tonto-Roosevelt area has been reviewed. The spatial distribution of that research has been presented in graphic form to emphasize the nature of the sample of materials on which current interpretations of the prehistory of the area are based. The unfortunate dearth of published reports forthcoming from research undertaken in the first half of this century and an earlier emphasis on larger, more conspicuous sites are factors limiting an understanding of the range of site variability to be found within the area and of several critical time periods. More recent research has begun to alleviate the effects of these biases.

The overall sampling problems imposed by the effective removal from systematic investigation of the area inundated by Roosevelt Lake and the implications of the presence of this man-made feature for the interpretation of the prehistory of the area have been noted. The need for more extensive and systematic survey coverage of the area has been emphasized.

(b) Consideration of the existing evidence relating to the sequence of occupation suggests that the prehistory and history of the study units defined here are not uniform from area to area. Specifically, the lower Cherry Creek and Coon Creek-Black Mesa areas do not appear to have participated in the same sequence presently defined for the Pinto Creek and

Pinal Creek areas. Similarly, the upper reaches of the Mineral Creek drainage appear to have witnessed a distinctive occupational sequence. These differences may be seen in the most general terms as resulting from the differential occupation and use of these respective areas by Hohokam, Salado, Mogollon, and, later, Yavapai and Apache populations. The further documentation and determination of the significance of these apparently variable sequences remain to be accomplished.

In addition to emphasizing the potential complexities to be dis- covered in the prehistory of the area, this situation bares some of the weaknesses of the phase and culture-area concepts in dealing with areas that seem to have been zones of interaction. To suggest that the Tonto- Roosevelt area was, at various times, a zone of interaction among Hohokam, Salado, and Mogollon groups is hardly incorrect; but neither is this perspective very informative or useful in the attempt to sort out and interpret the data relating to the variable prehistory of the transitional environment to be found wedged between the mountains and the deserts. It is clear that future approaches to the interpretation of the archaeology of the area will require not only the fundamental chronological and spatial control established through the definition of local sequences, but a more encompassing perspective that will somehow provide an effective and operational conceptualization of dynamic interactions occurring within and beyond the area. Some of the more specific aspects of this problem are touched upon below in the section dealing with directions for future research.

(c) A set of empirical site types has been defined as a means for documenting the variability in the surface morphology of sites encountered within the Cholla-Saguaro corridor and for relating that variability to materials resulting from previous research in the area. While some of the sites appear similar to those already described in the literature, pre- viously undocumented site types have been recorded as well. These include several forms of architectural features, variously composed artifact scatters, rock shelters, and petroglyphs. Furthermore, several site types known to exist elsewhere in the area are absent from the inventory of sites produced by the Cholla-line survey, including any definitively pre-Classic Hohokam sites or large Gila Phase Salado pueblos. The like- lihood of some of the features recorded being of Yavapai or Apache origin has been suggested and the significance of these features discussed.

The site types defined here will provide a basis for an examination of the relationship between surface manifestations and overall site content as revealed by excavated materials recovered during the mitigation phase of this project and by future undertakings in the area. Thus, a firmer basis for the interpretation of survey data may be established.

The distribution of sites by study area has been summarized and discussed. In combination with already known materials, the Cholla-line survey data suggest that areas well away from the major drainages of the region (for example, the interior portions of Pinal and Pinto creeks and the upper reaches of Mineral Creek) witnessed significant prehistoric occupations. The extent and nature of these occupations and the specific time periods that they represent remain to be determined, but they appear to be primarily post-A.D.1150 phenomena. The previously recorded occupation of areas on or near the major drainages of the area is further substantiated by the Cholla-line materials (for example, from lower Cherry Creek, Coon Creek, and Pinto Creek).

The inability of the Cholla-line survey data to sustain an analysis more penetrating than the descriptive summary presented here stems from (1) the nature of the survey data and (2) the general state of archaeological knowledge of the area as it bears on the interpretation of survey data.

(1) The general problems inherent in dealing with samples of archaeological materials resulting from the survey of arbitrary linear transects have been mentioned. Specifically, such samples preclude effective generalization and comparison of the locational and distributional characteristics of sites. Another limiting factor in the survey data is the lack of surface collections of materials upon which inferences of cultural and temporal affiliations might be based. Such critical inferences are thus restricted to a primary reliance upon architecture (or the absence of it) as an indicator of chronological position and cultural affiliation.

(2) The interpretive problems imposed by the nature of the Cholla-line materials are exacerbated by the status of archaeological knowledge of the Tonto-Roosevelt area. This is an area where the interpretation of survey data is severely hampered by a lack of adequately documented, well-defined relationships between the temporal, cultural, and functional variability represented by sites and the variability that may be observed and recorded from surface manifestations. The temporally and culturally diagnostic forms and assemblages thus far defined for the area do not begin to subsume or allow the effective ordering of the variability represented by the Cholla-line survey materials.

In the absence of distinctive ceramic assemblages and diagnostic architectural forms, the label "Salado", for example, is little more than an insinuation based solely on the location of the sites within the geographic area traditionally considered Salado. Even the smaller sites that have been excavated thus far have produced multiple components representing different cultural traditions or admixtures of them (Doyel 1978). The degree to which such multiple components may be discerned from surface materials has yet to be determined.

These and other difficulties that might be noted are but specific forms of the more general problems associated with the interpretation of any survey data and are not peculiar to the Tonto-Roosevelt area. However, in this area, these difficulties are of sufficient magnitude to preclude all but the most general ordering and interpretation of the data at hand;

accordingly, at least for the moment, they significantly restrict the potential of those materials for contributing to the clarification and solution of problems in the prehistory of the area.

As research continues, the data presented here may be subjected to better informed analysis, comparison, and reinterpretation. The Cholla-line survey materials further expand the already wide range of known archaeological phenomena that must be considered and incorporated to achieve a real understanding of the prehistory of the Tonto-Roosevelt area, and stand as a challenge to those who would undertake such an ambitious enterprise.

Directions for Future Research

Examination of the Cholla-line survey data has provided the opportunity to touch upon some of the problems in the archaeology of the Tonto-Roosevelt area that await investigation. It is appropriate to conclude this section with some suggestions for research priorities and questions around which future investigations might be organized. Several general problem domains of major importance may be isolated and briefly discussed in chronological order.

Preceramic Occupation

The dearth of documented Paleo-Indian and Archaic sites raises several questions concerning the occupation of the area during these time periods. Two general problem areas are suggested: (1) What were the nature and extent of the Paleo-Indian and Archaic occupations of the area? Given the present knowledge of these periods, approaches to this question will logically begin with the discovery and documentation of sites dating to these time periods. (2) What were the relationships (if any) between these earlier manifestations and the subsequent occupations of the area? This question involves the significant problem of whether or not the area was essentially unoccupied at the time of the initial Hohokam occupation.

Pioneer and Colonial Hohokam

Although a Colonial Hohokam occupation of the Tonto-Roosevelt area is beyond doubt, more specific information is required concerning the nature of that occupation and the possibility of an earlier Pioneer Period presence. (1) Was there a Hohokam occupation of the area during the Pioneer Period, and what were the nature and extent of that occupation?

(2) Does the Colonial Period occupation of the area simply represent a movement into an area with ecological characteristics similar to those found in the Gila-Salt core area and therefore suitable to the subsistence technology previously known and employed (that is, canal irrigation in the floodplain of the Salt River)? (3) What alternative subsistence strategies were employed by Colonial Period occupants of the area? (4) What was the nature of the relationships formed between the Colonial Hohokam in the Tonto-Roosevelt area and non-Hohokam populations in adjacent areas?

Sedentary Period/Sacaton Phase

As noted above, a more complete understanding of the Sacaton Phase occupation of the area will be important to an understanding of a variety of problems: (1) Are the materials to be found in the Tonto-Roosevelt area and dating to the period A.D. 900-1150 sufficiently similar to those in the Gila-Salt core area to warrant the same period and phase designations? (2) What is the nature of the differences in contemporaneous materials from the two areas, and what factors were responsible for producing them (for example, diverging adjustments to a different environment, the presence or influence of non-Hohokam populations, and so on)? (3) Were Hohokam populations the only occupants of the area during the period A.D. 900-1150, and what were the relationships between those populations and contemporaneous groups in adjacent areas?

A.D. 1100-1300

The period A.D. 1100-1300 is critical to an understanding of the prehistory of the Tonto-Roosevelt area; at present, our knowledge of this period remains preliminary and in need of considerable elaboration.

Many of the problems relating to this time period may be seen as revolving around the Salado concept. As several authors have observed (see Doyel and Haury 1976), the notion of Salado will require elaboration and refinement to insure its continued utility, especially in a direction that moves away from the narrow ceramic and architectural diagnostics that define the concept. As we have seen, the concept in its present form is of little utility in the interpretation of survey data exhibiting a wide range of morphological variability.

A variety of hypotheses have been advanced to account for the origin and character of the Salado phenomenon, but the systematic evaluation of those hypotheses will require much greater temporal and spatial control over the materials than is presently available. The development of a more fully elaborated and empirically based definition of Salado will remain a general goal for some time to come. Research in the Tonto-Roosevelt area will be particularly important to this process, as this area is still considered to be the "heartland" of the Salado. Suggested research questions dealing with the period A.D. 1100-1300 in the area may be phrased in terms of the known sequences of occupation as follows:

(1) Is there a distinctive prepolychrome Salado complex within the area (Gladwin and Gladwin 1935; Gladwin 1957), and how do the materials defined for the Cherry Creek Phase (Gladwin and Gladwin 1934) and the Miami Phase (Doyel 1978) relate to such a complex? (2) Does the Cherry Creek Phase represent a valid phase distinction, and, if so, what are its characteristics and geographic extent? (3) What are the spatial distribution and significance of the complex of materials defined for the Miami Phase? (4) What is the relationship of the Cherry Creek and Miami phases to the Sacaton (?) Phase occupation of the area; more generally, what part did Hohokam populations play in the emergence of the Salado complex? (5) What are the nature and extent of the Roosevelt Phase, and how does it relate to earlier manifestations? (6) Beyond the diagnostic "compound" form, what was the range of settlement types present during the Roosevelt Phase? (7) To what degree was the emergence of the Salado complex an autochthonous development, and to what degree was it the result of influences (through migration, exchange networks, and other factors) from outside the Tonto-Roosevelt area?

Gila Phase

The period from A.D. 1300 to 1450 in the Tonto-Roosevelt area is the best documented period within the prehistoric sequence, and a variety of fairly specific research questions relating to this period may be posed: (1) What was the structure of Gila Phase subsistence-settlement systems, and what differential exploitation of the natural environment is suggested? (2) To what degree do Gila Phase subsistence-settlement systems reflect continuity of or divergence from those of the preceding Roosevelt Phase? (3) What were the relationships existing between large Gila Phase sites (such as Gila Pueblo, Besh-ba-go-wah, and To-get-zo-ge) and centers of population aggregation found in other areas during this time period (such as the Grasshopper Ruin, Granite Basin Ruin, and Rye Creek Ruin)? (4) To what degree was the location of these major sites determined and influenced by the existence of regional exchange networks? (5) What were the factors responsible for the abandonment of the area during the middle part of the 15th century?

A potential source of research materials dating to this period may lie in the collections made during the early part of this century but never fully reported on. The possibility of locating these collections for restudy, reporting, and reinterpretation should be explored.

Apache and Yavapai Occupations

Although the occupation of the Tonto-Roosevelt area has been documented ethnographically, little is known of the archaeological materials that may relate to these occupations. An archaeological approach to the study of these ethnographically known groups may be guided by several questions: (1) What is the range of material culture remains that may be assigned to Yavapai or Apache groups, and what is the basis for this assignment? (2) To what extent may precontact patterns of Apache and Yavapai subsistence and settlement be studied archaeologically? (3) To what degree may archaeological materials be employed to address the question of the date of Apache arrival in the area? (4) What part, if any, did Apache groups play in the abandonment of the area by 15th century Salado populations? (5) To what extent does the ethnographically documented territory of the Southeastern Yavapai reflect their earlier distribution? (6) What are the nature and extent of modification to archaeological sites in the area through the activities of Yavapai and Apache groups?

The general questions outlined above do not begin to exhaust the set of significant research problems that may be related to the archaeological materials to be found within the Tonto-Roosevelt area. They do provide an organized conception of some of the important problems that remain to be solved and to which future research carried out in the area may be made to speak.

REFERENCES

Abel, Leland J. and Sallie Van Valkenburgh
   1961   The Tonto labyrinth. The Kiva 27: 29-31.

Arizona Bureau of Mines
   1969   Mineral and water resources of Arizona. Arizona Bureau of
          Mines Bulletin 180.

Bandelier, Adolph F.
   1892   Final report of investigations among the Indians of the
          southwestern states, Part II. Papers of the Archaeological
          Institute of America 4. Cambridge.

Basso, Keith H.
   1970   The Cibecue Apache. Case Studies in Cultural Anthropology.
          New York: Holt, Rinehart, and Winston.

Basso, Keith H. and Morris E. Opler, editors
   1971   Apachean culture history and ethnology. University of
          Arizona Anthropological Papers 21. Tucson: University of Arizona Press.

Bolton, Herbert Eugene
   1919   Father Escobar's relation of the Oñate expedition to
          California. Catholic Historical Review 5: 19-41.

Borher, Vorsila L.
   1962   Ethnobotanical materials from Tonto National Monument.
          In Steen and others, pp. 75-114.

Bourke, John Gregory
   1891   On the border with Crook. New York: Scribner.

Brandes, Raymond
   1957a   An archaeological survey within Gila County. MS. Arizona
          State Museum, University of Arizona, Tucson.

   1957b   An early ballcourt near Globe, Arizona. The Kiva 23: 10-11.

Buskirk, Winfred
   1949   Western Apache subsistence economy. Unpublished Ph.D.
          dissertation, Department of Anthropology, University of
          New Mexico, Albuquerque.

Cartledge, Thomas R.
   1976   Prehistory in Vosberg Valley, central Arizona. The Kiva
          42: 95-104.

Dice, L. R.
1943   The biotic provinces of North America.   Ann Arbor:
        University of Michigan Press.

Doyel, David E.
1974   The Miami Wash Project: a preliminary report on excavations
        in Hohokam and Salado sites near Miami, central Arizona.
        Arizona Highway Salvage Preliminary Report 11.

1976a   Hohokam and Salado small sites and small site methodology.
        Contribution to Highway Salvage Archaeology in Arizona 46.

1976b   Revised phase system for the Tonto Basin and Globe-Miami
        areas, central Arizona.   The Kiva 41: 241-266.

1976c   Salado cultural development in the Tonto Basin and Globe-
        Miami areas, central Arizona.   The Kiva 42: 5-16.

1978   The Miami Wash Project: Hohokam and Salado in the Globe-
        Miami area, central Arizona.   Contribution to Highway
        Salvage Archaeology in Arizona 52.

Doyel, David E. and Emil W. Haury, editors
1976   The 1976 Salado Conference.   The Kiva 42 (1).

Duffen, William A.
1962   Addendum: Tonto Ruins stabilization, May 27 to June 30,
        1937.   In Steen and others, pp. 69-73.

Ellison, Glenn R.
1968   Cowboys under the Mogollon Rim.   Tucson: University of
        Arizona Press.

Franklin, Hayward H. and W. Bruce Masse
1976   The San Pedro Salado: a case of prehistoric migration.
        The Kiva 42: 47-55.

Fuller, Steven L., A. E. Rogge, and Linda M. Gregonis
1976   Orme alternatives: the archaeological resources of
        Roosevelt Lake and Horseshoe Reservoir (Vol. 2).   Arizona
        State Museum Archaeological Series 98.

Gifford, E. W.
1932   The southeastern Yavapai.   University of California
        Publications in American Archaeology and Ethnology 29 (3).

1936   Northeastern and western Yavapai.   University of California
        Publications in American Archaeology and Ethnology 34 (4).

Gladwin, Harold S.
1957   History of the ancient Southwest. Portland, Maine: Bond-Wheelright.

Gladwin, Winifred and Harold S. Gladwin
1930   Some southwestern pottery types, series 1. Medallion Papers 8.
        Globe: Gila Pueblo.

1934   A method for the designation of cultures and their variations.
        Medallion Papers 15. Globe: Gila Pueblo.

1935   The eastern range of the Red-on-buff culture. Medallion
        Papers 16. Globe: Gila Pueblo.

Goodwin, Grenville
1942   The social organization of the Western Apache. Chicago:
        University of Chicago Press.

1971   Western Apache raiding and warfare: from the notes of
        Grenville Goodwin, edited by Keith H. Basso. Tucson:
        University of Arizona Press.

Goodyear, Albert C.
1975   A general research design for highway archeology in
        South Carolina. The Institute of Archeology and Anthropology
        Notebook 7 (1). Columbia: University of South Carolina.

Grady, Mark A.
1974   Archaeological sites within the Copper Cities Mine area:
        a preliminary report. Arizona State Museum Archaeological
        Series 55.

Griffin, P. Bion, Mark P. Leone, and Keith H. Basso
1971   Western Apache ecology: from horticulture to agriculture.
        In Basso and Opler, editors, pp. 69-73.

Haas, Jonathan
1971   The Ushklish Ruin: a preliminary report on excavations in
        a Colonial Hohokam Period site in the lower Tonto Basin,
        central Arizona. Arizona Highway Salvage Preliminary Report.

Hammond, George P. and Agapito Rey
1929   Expedition into New Mexico made by Antonio de Espejo
        1582-1583, as revealed in the journal of Diego Perez de
        Luxan, a member of the party. The Quivira
        Society, University of Southern California.

Haury, Emil W.
   1932   Roosevelt 9:6: a Hohokam site of the Colonial Period.
           Medallion Papers 4. Globe: Gila Pueblo.

   1934   Canyon Creek Ruin and the cliff dwellings of the Sierra
           Ancha. Medallion Papers 14. Globe: Gila Pueblo.

   1940   Excavations in the Forestdale Valley, east-central Arizona.
           University of Arizona Social Science Bulletin 12.

   1950   The stratigraphy and archaeology of Ventana Cave, Arizona.
           Tucson: University of Arizona Press.

   1976   The Hohokam: desert farmers and craftsmen. Excavations
           at Snaketown, 1964-1965. Tucson: University of Arizona
           Press.

Hawley, Florence M.
   1928   Pottery and culture relations in the Middle Gila. MS. M.A.
           Thesis, Department of Anthropology, University of Arizona, Tucson.

   1932   The Bead Mountain Pueblos of southern Arizona. Art and
           Archaeology 33(5)226-236.

Hester, James J. and Philip M. Hobler
   1969   Prehistoric settlement patterns in the Libyan Desert.
           University of Utah Anthropological Papers 92, Nubian
           Series 4.   Salt Lake City: University of Utah Press.

Hough, Walter
   1907   Antiquities of the upper Gila and Salt River valleys in
           Arizona and New Mexico. Bureau of American Ethnology
           Bulletin 35. Washington.

Huckell, Bruce B.
   1973   The Hardt Creek Site. The Kiva 39: 171-197.

   1978   The Oxbow Hill Payson Project.
           Contribution to Highway Salvage Archaeology in Arizona 48.

Irwin-Williams, Cynthia
   1967   Picosa: the elementary Southwestern culture. American
           Antiquity 32: 441-457.

Jeter, Marvin D.
   1978   The Reno-Park Creek Project.
           Contribution to Highway Salvage Archaeology in Arizona 49.

Kearney, Thomas H. and Robert H. Peebles
    1960   Arizona flora. Berkeley: University of California Press.

Kent, Kate Peck
    1962   An analysis and interpretation of the cotton textiles from
            Tonto National Monument. In Steen and others, pp. 115-155.

Lange, Charles H. and Carroll L. Riley, editors
    1966   The southwestern journals of Adolph F. Bandelier (Vol. 2:
            1883-84). Albuquerque: University of New Mexico Press.

Lowe, Charles H., editor
    1964   The vertebrates of Arizona. Tucson: University of Arizona
            Press.
Lytle-Webb, Jamie
    1978   Environmental background. In Doyel, pp. 6-16.

Mange, Juan Mateo
    1954   Unknown Arizona and Sonora 1692-1721. From the Francisco
            Fernandez del Castillo version of Luz de Tierra Incognita,
            translated by Harry J. Karns. Tucson: Arizona Silhouettes.

Martin, Paul S. and Fred T. Plog
    1973   The archaeology of Arizona. New York: Doubleday.

McGuire, Randall H.
    1975   The Central Heights Site. MS. Arizona State Museum,
            University of Arizona, Tucson.

    1977   The Copper Canyon-McGuireville Project: archaeological
            investigations in the middle Verde Valley, Arizona.
            Contribution to Highway Salvage Archaeology in Arizona 45.

Minnis, Paul E. and Stephen E. Plog
    1976   A study of the site specific distribution of Agave Parryi
            in east central Arizona. The Kiva 41: 299-308.

Morris, Donald H.
    1970   Walnut Creek Village: a ninth century Hohokam-Anasazi
            settlement in the mountains of central Arizona.
            American Antiquity 35: 49-61.

Peterson, Nels P.
    1962   Geology and ore deposits of the Globe-Miami district,
            Arizona. U.S.G.S. Professional Paper 342. Washington:
            Government Printing Office.

Pierson, Lloyd M.
    1962   Excavations at the Lower Ruin, Tonto National Monument.
            In Steen and others, pp. 33-69.

Plog, Fred T.
    1978   Explaining change in the Hohokam Pre-Classic. Paper
            presented at the 43rd Annual Meeting of the Society for
            American Archaeology, Tucson.

Reagan, Albert B.
    1929   Plants used by the White Mountain Apache Indians of
            Arizona. The Wisconsin Archaeologist 8: 143-161.

    1930   Notes on the Indians of the Fort Apache region.
            Anthropological Papers of the American Museum of Natural
            History 31, Part 5. New York.

Sayles, E. B.
    1945   The San Simon Branch: excavations at Cave Creek and in the
            San Simon Valley. 1: Material culture. Medallion Papers 34.
            Globe: Gila Pueblo.

Sayles, E. B. and Ernst Antevs
    1941   The Cochise Culture. Medallion Papers 29. Globe: Gila Pueblo.

Schmidt, Erich F.
    1926   The Mrs. William Boyce Thompson Expedition. Natural History 26:
            635-644.

    1927   A stratigraphic study in the Gila-Salt region, Arizona.
            Proceedings of the National Academy of Sciences 13 (5).

    1928   Time-relations of prehistoric pottery types in southern
            Arizona. Anthropological Papers of the American Museum of
            Natural History 30, Part 5. New York.

Schroeder, Albert H.
    1963a   Diffusion north out of south-central Arizona. El Palacio 70
            (1-2) 13-24.

    1974   A study of the Apache Indians (Vols. 1, 4). New York: Garland.

Sellers, William D. and Richard H. Hill, editors
    1974   Arizona climate, 1931-1972. Tucson: University of Arizona Press.

Shiner, Joel L.
    1961   A room at Gila Pueblo. The Kiva 27(2) 3-11.

Sparling, John B.
    1978   Analysis of the faunal remains from the Miami Wash Project.
            In Doyel, pp. 283-299.

Steen, Charlie R.
    1962   Excavations at the Upper Ruin, Tonto National Monument.
            In Steen and others, pp. 1-30.

Steen, Charlie R., Lloyd M. Pierson, Vorsila L. Bohrer, and Kate Peck Kent
    1962   Archaeological studies at Tonto National Monument, Arizona,
            edited by Louis R. Caywood. Southwestern Monuments Association
            Technical Series 2.

Struever, Stuart
    1971   Comments on archaeological data requirements and research
            strategy. American Antiquity 36: 9-19.

Van Valkenburgh, Sallie
    1962   Addendum: study of additional Upper Ruin textiles from
            the "Cron Collection", Tonto National Monument. In Steen
            and others, pp. 156-159.

Vickery, Irene
    1939   Besh-ba-go-wah. The Kiva 4: 19-22.

    1945   Inspiration I. The Kiva 10: 22-28.

Vivian, R. Gwinn
    1970   An Apache site on Ranch Creek, southeast Arizona. The Kiva 35:
            125-130.

Weed, Carol S.
    1972   The Beardsley Canal Site. The Kiva 38: 57-94.

Weed, Carol S. and Albert E. Ward
    1970   The Henderson Site: Colonial Hohokam in north central
            Arizona. A preliminary report. The Kiva 36(2) 1-12.

Wells, Wesley
    1971   Prehistoric settlement patterns of lower Cherry Creek.
            MS. Department of Anthropology, Arizona State University,
            Tempe.

Wilson, Eldred D.
    1962   A résumé of the geology of Arizona. Arizona Bureau of
            Mines Bulletin 171.

Windmiller, Ric
    1971a   A partial archaeological survey of the Castle Dome-Pinto
              Creek Project Area, near Miami, Arizona. _Arizona State_
              Museum Archaeological Series 5.

    1971b   Recent archaeological work in Salado settlements. Paper
              presented at the 18th Annual Meeting of the Arizona
              Academy of Science, Flagstaff.

    1972a   An archaeological survey of the Castle Dome-Pinto Creek
              Area, near Miami, Arizona: final report. _Arizona State_
              Museum Archaeological Series 22.

    1972b   The Hagan excavations: pottery. MS. National Park Service,
              Western Archaeological Center, Tucson.

    1972c   Ta-e-wun: a Colonial Period Hohokam campsite in east-
              central Arizona. _The Kiva_ 38: 1-26.

    1974a   Archaeological excavations at Scorpion Ridge Ruin, east-
              central Arizona. _Arizona State Museum Archaeological_
              Series 48.

    1974b   Contributions to Pinto Valley archaeology. _Arizona State_
              Museum Archaeological Series 51.

Winter, Joseph C.
    1973   Cultural modifications of the Gila Pima, A.D. 1697-1846.
            Ethnohistory 20: 65-77.

Wood, Jon Scott
    1978   Settlement and reoccupation along Queen Creek, central
            Arizona. MS. National Park Service, Tonto National Forest.

Wood, Jon Scott and Martin E. McAllister
    1978   Foundation and empire: the colonization of the northeastern
            Hohokam periphery. Paper presented at the 43rd Annual
            Meeting of the Society for American Archaeology, Tucson.

Wood, J. Scott and Martin E. McAllister
    in preparation
            Archaeological studies from the Globe-Miami and Queen
            Creek areas, central Arizona, Tonto National Forest.
            USDA Forest Service, Southwestern Region, Archaeological
            Report. Albuquerque.

Young, Jon N.
    1972   The Hagan Site at Gila Pueblo. MS. National
            Park Service, Western Archaeological Center, Tucson.

CHAPTER 7

THE SOUTHERN DESERT STUDY AREA
by Neal W. Ackerly

Introduction

This section concerns survey and data recovery within the right-
of-way of the southern portion of the APS Cholla-Saguaro transmission line
from Red Rock to Superior (Figure 29). As noted in Chapter 3, this southern
portion was surveyed in two sections. In June, 1974, the section from
Antelope Peak (southwest of Winkelman) to Red Rock was surveyed, and
recommendations were submitted to APS for mitigation of impacts to sites
(Kinkade and Gilman 1974). One historic and five prehistoric sites were
recorded, all of which were subsequently subjected to various data recovery
procedures. The data from these investigations were not analyzed at that
time, and form the basis for the interpretive section of this chapter.

A few important problems must be pointed out that bear on the
analysis and interpretation of the material recovered from the investigated sites. When data recovery in the field was completed, the majority
of field notes and site records were packed into one vehicle for return
to the Arizona State Museum. Unfortunately, the vehicle overturned while
attempting to cross the Gila River, which was in flood at the time. Lives
were spared, but some data were irretrievably lost. Additionally, numerous
personnel and policy changes from 1974 to the present time have resulted
in additional records being lost. Therefore, little contextual information was available. Nevertheless, it was possible to conduct a productive
analysis. Therefore, statistical programs were run on the data to determine
if the archaeological material exhibited significant relationships or
differences that could explain site variability in the Southern Desert
portion of the project corridor.

The second survey of the southern portion of the APS line was conducted in June-July, 1975 (Canouts 1975). This survey concerned the
section from Antelope Peak north to Superior. Eight sites were recorded
in this section, plus two sites originally recorded in the Buttes Reservoir
survey (Debowski and others 1976). In addition, survey of access road
routes located three more sites (one within and two outside the right-of-
way), producing a total of 13 sites in the Antelope Peak-Superior section.
The Arizona State Museum recommended that adjustments be made in engineering to minimize disturbance of the sites whenever possible. Accordingly,
construction adjustments were made by APS, access roads were rerouted, and

268

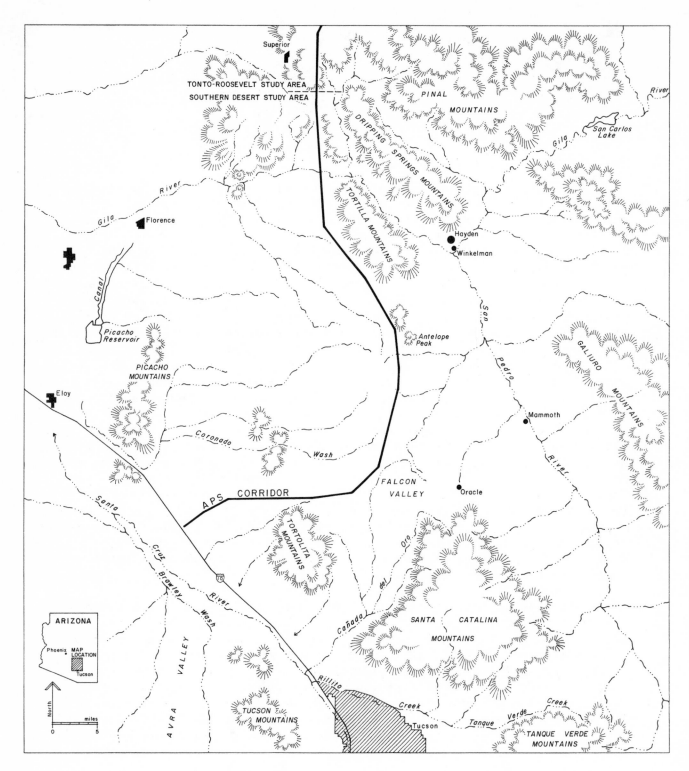

Figure 29.   The Southern Desert study area

archaeologists monitored construction activities in sensitive areas. No data recovery was conducted at any sites in the Antelope Peak-Superior section.

Of the 19 sites (Table 49) recorded for the entire Red Rock-Superior segment, all but two occur south of the Gila River. The transmission line corridor passes through an "interriverine" area bounded by the Gila River on the west and the Santa Catalina Mountains on the south (Figure 28). These boundaries provided a convenient means for examining the cultural resources within the context of a specific set of environmental variables that ultimately could be used to construct prehistoric land use in this region.

Table 49. Archaeological sites in the Southern Desert segment of the Cholla-Saguaro corridor

ASM Number	Field Number	Cultural-temporal Affiliation	Site Type	Approximate Size (m²)	USGS Quad	Elevation (feet)
AZ AA:8:6	CS-16	Historic: Anglo (1881-1892)	Mine	139,000	Tortolita Mtn. 15 min.	3240
AZ BB:1:8	CS-11	Prehistoric: Hohokam	Features with artifact scatter	166,250	Black Mtn. 7.5 min.	3920
AZ BB:1:9	CS-12	Prehistoric: Hohokam Salado	Features with artifact scatter	9000	Black Mtn. 7.5 min.	3960
AZ BB:1:10	CS-13	Prehistoric: Hohokam Salado	Features with artifact scatter	24,300	Black Mtn. 7.5 min.	3960
AZ BB:1:11	CS-19	Prehistoric: Hohokam	Structures with artifact scatter	3750	Black Mtn. 7.5 min.	3920
AZ BB:1:12	CS-23	Prehistoric: Hohokam (A.D. 900-1150)	Artifact scatter	8450	Crozier Peak 7.5 min.	3740
AZ BB:1:13	CS-25	Prehistoric: Hohokam (A.D. 1150)	Features with artifact scatter	1000	Crozier Peak 7.5 min.	3880
AZ BB:1:14	JR-1	Prehistoric (unknown)	Artifact scatter	1750	Crozier Peak 7.5 min.	3840
AZ BB:1:15	JR-2	Prehistoric: Hohokam(?)	Structures with artifact scatter	4900	Crozier Peak 7.5 min.	3860
AZ BB:1:16	JR-3	Prehistoric (unknown)	Structure with artifact scatter	1400	Crozier Peak 7.5 min.	3840

Table 49. Archaeological sites in the Southern Desert segment of the Cholla-Saguaro corridor (continued)

ASM Number	Field Number	Cultural-temporal Affiliation	Site Type	Approximate Size (m²)	USGS Quad	Elevation (feet)
AZ BB:5:21	CS-14	Prehistoric: Hohokam-Salado	Features with artifact scatter	66,500	Oracle 15 min.	3930
AZ BB 5:22	CS-15	Prehistoric: Hohokam-Salado	Features with artifact scatter	6000	Oracle 15 min.	3920
AZ BB:5:23	CS-18	Prehistoric (unknown)	Features with artifact scatter	1600	Oracle 15 min.	3940
AZ BB:5:24	CS-17	Prehistoric (unknown)	Features with artifact scatter	7500	Oracle 15 min.	3940
AZ U:16:27	BR-1-19	Prehistoric: Hohokam Historic: Anglo	Structures with artifact scatter	32,500	Grayback 7.5 min.	1760
AZ U:16:116	CS-37	Prehistoric: Hohokam	Artifact scatter	4900	Grayback 7.5 min.	3180
AZ U:16:128	CS-242 BR-11-88	Prehistoric: Hohokam(?)	Artifact scatter	5200	Grayback 7.5 min.	1780-1860
AZ U:16:181	CS-22	Prehistoric (unknown)	Rock shelter and midden	336	Teapot Mtn. 7.5 min.	2480-2560
AZ U:16:182	CS-24	Prehistoric (unknown)	Lithic quarry	1125	Teapot Mtn. 7.5 min.	3960

Environmental Background

Physiography

The study area lies within the Basin and Range physiographic province. Tectonic and erosional forces have created a landscape characterized by broad, semiarid valleys oriented northwest to southeast and separated by mountain ranges which rise abruptly above the valleys. Within the study area, the province is subdivided into the Sonoran Desert and Mexican Highland sections.

Valley elevations in the Sonoran Desert section range from less than 1000 feet above sea level to 3500 feet on the bajadas of the Upper Santa Cruz Basin. While the mountain ranges are relatively short and narrow and occupy a subordinate share of the Sonoran Desert, they nevertheless stand as bold, rugged landmarks jutting out of the desert. Their summit elevations range from less than 2400 feet above sea level to 4788 feet on Mt. Devine Peak in southern Pinal County (USDA 1977:2.13).

The Red Rock-Antelope Peak segment lies entirely in the Sonoran Desert section. At Red Rock the desert is generally flat and dominated by a creosote-bush--bur-sage community. As the line approaches the Tortolita Mountains, the topography becomes more hilly, and palo-verde--saguaro communities dominate the vegetation. The central portion, from the Tortolitas northeastward to Antelope Peak, contains low rolling hills dissected by numerous shallow arroyos. Vegetation in this section consists of snakeweed, yucca, cholla, prickly-pear, mesquite, and catclaw. Around Antelope Peak, the elevation rises and the predominant land forms are deep, steep-sided washes with high ridges. The vegetation is mainly wild buckwheat with large amounts of cholla, prickly-pear, mesquite, and catclaw acacia; the latter two are especially dense in the washes (Kinkade 1974:2).

The corridor from Antelope Peak to Superior descends northward to a low elevational point at 1710 feet at the Gila River crossing, but then ascends rapidly to elevations exceeding 4000 feet in the mountainous terrain to the north. Within the 2200-foot drop in elevation from Antelope Peak to the Gila River (a distance of 32.2 km or 20 miles), the only substantial change is from a desert grassland biome characteristic of the Mexican Highland section to a Sonoran desertscrub/mixed palo-verde--cacti community 8 km (5 miles) south of the Gila River. The banks of the river itself and the adjacent floodplain support a dense riparian community characterized by mesquite bosques. North from the Gila River, Sonoran desertscrub persists from some 11.3 km (7 miles) with alternating mosaics of jojoba, palo-verde, brittle-bush, and bur-sage. At a point 12 km (7.5 miles) north of the Gila, this Lower Sonoran desert community gives way to scrub oak and manzanita associations, indicating the transition to the Upper Sonoran Life Zone (Spain n.d.).

Geology

Rocks ranging in age from the Precambrian through Quaternary are exposed in the study area and provided sources of raw material for prehistoric lithic tools and building material. Older Precambrian granitic and metamorphic rocks occur as outcrops in the Tortilla, Tortolita, and northern end of the Santa Catalina mountain areas. Younger Precambrian rocks (quartzite, shale, limestone, diabase, and basalt) exist in the Tortilla and Santa Catalina mountains. Paleozoic sedimentary rocks also occur in these mountain regions. Volcanic activity in the Cretaceous System laid down new beds of igneous rock; this activity, which continued into the Quaternary and Tertiary periods, has given the region much of its rugged landscape. During the latter two periods, alluvium accumulated to great thicknesses in the present-day valleys, which currently contain a mixture of a great variety of rock types derived from eroding mountains. These semiconsolidated deposits contain the principal water supplies of the study area (USDA 1977:2.14).

Soils

Those soil types crossed by the southern portion of the line include: (a) the Gilman-Antho-Pimer association, (b) the Mohall-Pinamt association, (c) the White House-Caralampi association, (d) the Chiricahua association, and (e) the granite and schist rock land association (Adams 1972). The Gilman-Antho-Pimer is a mixed, coarse-loamy, alkaline soil found in floodplains east of Red Rock, Arizona, and in the lower Gila River Basin. Adams (1972: Table A) has classified this soil as poor for wild game. The Mohall-Pinamt and White House Caralampi associations are classified as fine silt-loam that is slightly alkaline and nonsaline. These soils are found east of the Gila River. The productivity of wild game on these soils is rated as poor to fair. The Chiricahua association has been characterized as a sandy, loamy, slightly acidic, nonsaline soil typical of foothill locations. This soil is found in the vicinity of Antelope Peak and is rated as fair to poor as a wild game habitat. The granite-schist rock land association, located in the Black Mountain and Cottonwood Hill areas, is typical of steep, mountainous localities and is classified as poor to very poor for wild game. Nonirrigated agriculture is considered almost impossible on any of these soils; while irrigated agriculture is possible only on Gilman-Antho-Pimer soils, the remaining soils are suitable only as range land for cattle production.

Hydrology

The major watercourse in the area is the Gila River, into which flow the Santa Cruz and San Pedro rivers. These provided a permanent water supply and habitat for animals and man, and were the focus of

extensive and long prehistoric occupation. The Santa Cruz is now a dry
bed, flowing only in times of heavy rainfall, and the San Pedro flows
intermittently. At the Gila River crossing of the corridor, water is still
present, but downstream from Roosevelt Dam the Gila rarely holds water.
Survey of the Gila River between the proposed Buttes Dam site and the
town of Kearney has demonstrated that the middle Gila was intensively
occupied by the Hohokam and possibly by earlier prehistoric groups.

No permanent water sources occur in the area transected by the
Red Rock-Antelope Peak segment. Instead, the area is dissected by numerous dry arroyos. Hydrology is considered in more detail in a later section discussing environmental change.

Rainfall

As is the case in most parts of Arizona, rainfall is highly variable
in terms of seasonal and annual yields. Furthermore, cyclical fluctuations
in the amount of rainfall serve to decrease the reliability of agricultural
and cattle production. This is especially true in southern Arizona.

A detailed study of rainfall patterns in Arizona (Steila 1972) has
led to the development of drought indices based on rainfall records from
the period 1931-1971. These indices are indicated in Figure 30 below.
The focus here will be on rainfall data from the east-central and south-
central portions of Arizona (Figure 31). The y-axis in each of the above
figures represents the amount of departure, in inches of rainfall, from
the mean moisture for the entire 40-year period. It may be seen that
there is a high degree of variability from month to month, year to year,
and from one region to another. These data have been summarized within
a single index of annual variation in moisture (Figure 32). These figures
indicate that there is a substantial rainfall deficit from March
to November in the more western portion of the study area and from May
to November in its more eastern portions.

Thus, in upland nonriverine locations typical of the kind of environment crossed by most of the APS Cholla line corridor, soil conditions and
the high degree of seasonal/annual fluctuations in rainfall (associated
with high drought indices) combine to limit the degree to which agriculture
can be practiced. In the case of prehistoric agriculturalists, these limiting factors could have been offset to some degree by the use of water-control
and storage facilities such as check dams, terraces, waffle gardens, and
reservoirs. However, these features are not common in upland environments.
For this reason, it is more likely that agricultural production in upland
zones was marginal, if such production depended solely on seasonally
available rainfall.

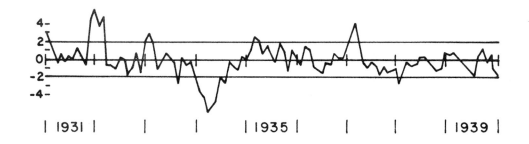

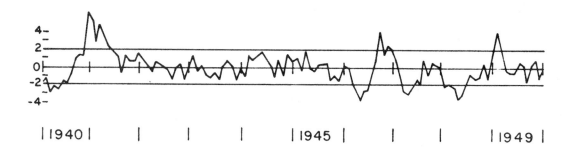

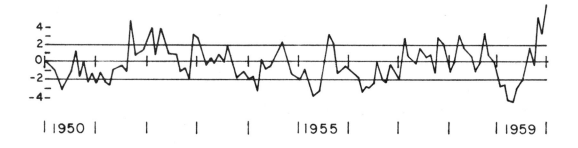

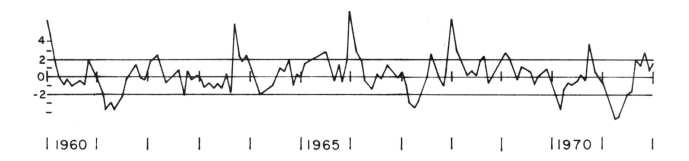

DROUGHT INDICES-EAST CENTRAL CLIMATIC DIVISION

Figure 30

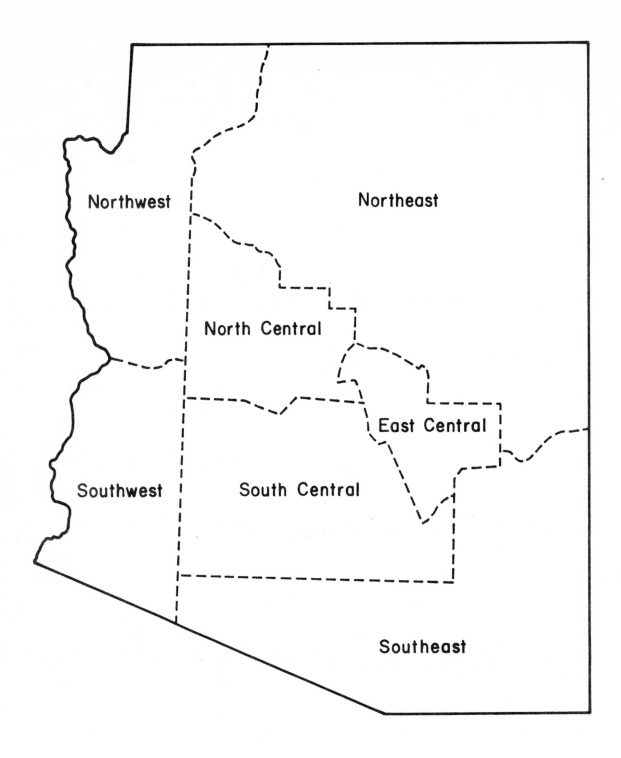

MAP OF
ARIZONA CLIMATIC DIVISIONS

Figure 31

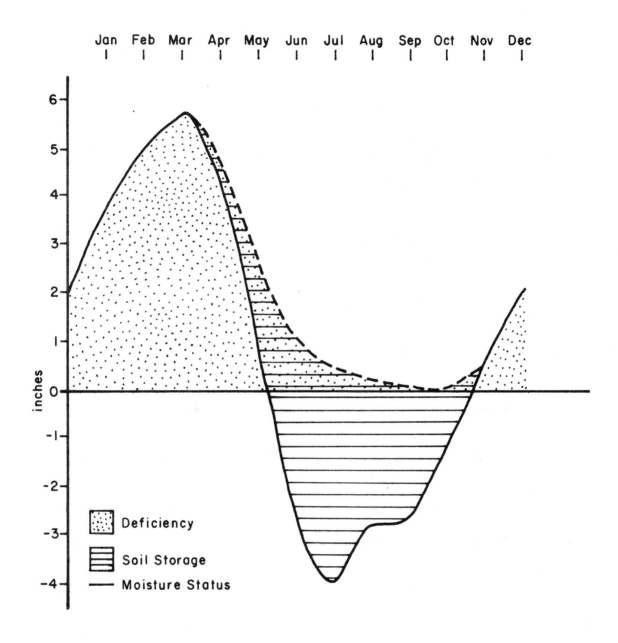

MEAN MOISTURE STATUS: EAST CENTRAL CLIMATIC DIVISION

Figure 32

Biotic Resources

The southern portion of the APS Cholla-Saguaro transmission line corridor from Red Rock to the Gila River is situated primarily in the Lower Sonoran Life Zone. Within this life zone, three biotic communities are present (Lowe 1964).

The Lower Sonoran creosote-bur-sage and palo-verde-saguaro communities are found at lower elevations towards the southern terminus of the transmission line at Red Rock. The creosote-bur-sage community consists mainly of small shrubs typical of areas having low relief and less rocky soils (Lowe 1964:27), while the palo-verde--saguaro community is usually associated with areas having more rocky substrates. Overstory species include the codominant palo-verde and saguaro; subdominant species usually consist of ironwood, crucifixion-thorn, and cholla in varying proportions (Lowe 1964:24-6).

The riparian plant community is localized along perennial streams, floodplains, springs, and seeps. This community is usually characterized by cottonwoods, tamarisk, willow, sycamore, and walnut species. The APS transmission line crosses riparian communities -- moving from south to north-- at Cruz Wash, Big Bertha Wash, Bloodsucker Wash, Palmer Wash, a second Bloodsucker Wash, Putnam Wash, the Gila River, Walnut Canyon, Oak Creek, and Hackberry Creek. Altogether, the southern portion of the line intersects about 11.3 km (7 miles) of riparian environment along its 108.6-km (67.5-mile) length.

Further northward along the line, but still south of the Gila River, the corridor crosses a limited portion of the Upper Sonoran desert grasslands. As Lowe has indicated, the approximate lower limit for this biotic community is at 3500 feet, and its best development is between 4000-5000 feet (1964:40). Those plant species common in this zone include varying proportions of prickly-pear, cholla, agave, yucca, ocotillo, catclaw, mesquite, and, where the soils are more shallow, sotol and bear-grass (Lowe 1964:41-2).

The last environmental zone crossed by the Antelope Peak-Superior segment is the Upper Sonoran interior chaparral ecozone. This zone begins about 1.2 km (0.75 miles) north of the Gila River at elevations between 4000 and 6000 feet in an area of rugged terrain. The more common plants found in this environment include manzanita, sumac, turpentine-brush, and buck-thorn (Lowe 1964:49-50). Overstory vegetation usually consists of mountain-mahogany and a variety of oak species. Localized stands of evergreen woodlands, another biotic community of the Upper Sonoran Life Zone, occur near Superior. These localized stands usually exhibit a higher density of oak trees and an increase in the frequency of juniper.

During the survey of the Antelope Peak-Superior section, detailed data were collected on plants and soils (Spain n.d.) in order to measure environmental variability within the corridor. Of the more than 50 plant species recorded along this 51.5-km (32-mile) stretch, several are known to have been of economic importance to the historic Pima and Papago who once inhabited the general area (Castetter and Bell 1942). While the contribution of wild plant resources to prehistoric subsistence is not quantified as yet, it is probable that the prehistoric inhabitants of this region relied on these resources also (Table 50).

- - - - - - - - - - - - - - - - - -

Table 50. Plant species recorded along the Antelope Peak-Superior section of the APS-CS survey

Genera	Common Name	Genera	Common Name
Acacia	catclaw *	Ferocactus	barrel cactus*
Agave	agave*	Fouquieria	ocotillo*
Aplopappus	turpentine-brush	Franseria	bur-sage
Arctostaphylos	manzanita	Gutierrezia	snake-weed
Artemisia	sagebrush	Hymenoclea	burro-brush
Baccharis	desert-broom	Juniperus	juniper*
Berberis	desert-holly	Krameria	white ratany
Brickellia		Larrea	creosote-bush
Calliandra	false-mesquite	Lycium	wolf-berry
Canotia	false-palo-verde	Menodora	
Carnegiea	saguaro*	Mimosa	mimosa
Ceanothus	buck-brush	Nolina	bear-grass
Celtis	hackberry*	Opuntia	prickly - pear* and cholla*
Cercidium	palo-verde*	Pinus	pinyon pine*
Cereus		Prosopis	mesquite*
Cercocarpus	mountain-mahogany	Psilostrophe	paperflower
Condalia	gray-thorn	Quercus	scrub oak*
Dasylirion	sotol*	Rhamnus	buck-thorn
Echinocereus	hedgehog cactus*	Rhus	skunk-bush
Encelia	brittle-bush	Sambucus	elderberry*
Ephedra	joint-fir	Simmondsia	jojoba
Eriogonum	wild-buckwheat	Yucca	yucca*

* indicates species of economic importance.

Treating the segment as a whole, the mean species diversity is approximately 11 species. The coefficient of variation is just over 30 percent, indicating that there is not a high degree of variation in the number of plant species from one location to another. Furthermore, if the area north of the Gila River is compared with the area south of the Gila, few significant differences in the numbers of plant species can be defined in spite of differences in elevation and drainage in these two areas.

The data used to test the hypothesis that these two areas are different with respect to the variance and mean number of plant species are indicated below (Lentner 1975).

- - - - - - - - - - - - - - -

Table 51. Plant diversity information: north and south of the Gila River

North   South

Number of plant transects   = 16   Number of plant transects   = 18
Mean number of plant species = 12.38 Mean number of plant species = 10.06
Standard deviation   = 4.06   Standard deviation   = 2.31
Sums of squares   = 2698.00   Sums of squares   = 1911.00

$$F_{17, 15} = .6249 \text{ is } > F_{17, 15, \frac{.05}{2}} \text{ of } .367$$

$$\text{is } < F_{17, 15, 1-\frac{.05}{2}} \text{ of } 2.81$$

and Calculated $t_{30} = .5626$, is $< t_{30}$ at .05 of 2.042

The test results show that variances in terms of plant diversity are not significant. A t-test run on the data shows that the mean numbers of species per sample transect in the areas north and south of the Gila River are not significantly different either. In other words, plant diversity within the Antelope Peak-Superior segment is low.

However, there are considerable differences between the areas with regard to the proportional contributions of economically important plants to the overall plant assemblage (see Table 52). Plots of these plant densities revealed a bimodal distribution of 33 percent and 60 percent of the total coverage. For analytical purposes, each plant transect was examined to determine whether the percentage of economically important plants was greater than or less than 33 percent. The results of this examination are shown in the following chi-square test.

Table 52. Relative contributions of economic plants in the areas north and south of the Gila River

	Less than 33 percent	More than 33 percent	
North	5	11	16 transects
South	13	5	18 transects
	18 transects	16 transects	34 transects

$x^2 = 48.1914$; d.f.= 1
$P < .001$; $C = .77$

The above chi-square test indicates that there is a significant (p<.001) difference between the areas north and south of the Gila River with respect to the proportional contributions of economically important plants. Specifically, the area north of the Gila River contains a much larger incidence of economically important plant species than does the area south of the Gila. Since most of the sites recorded along the Red Rock-Superior segment occur in the area south of the Gila, one obvious problem is to determine the possible kinds of plant resources that site inhabitants might have been exploiting. Most of the sites recorded in this segment are situated in what seems to be a marginal zone in terms of economically significant wild plant resources. This factor is important to consider in interpretations regarding the nature of settlement-subsistence strategies in the study area. Long-term environmental change is another important consideration, and will be discussed at length later.

Fauna

There is little substantial information concerning the density and population dynamics of animals in the study area. A recent publication of the U.S. Department of Agriculture (1977) contains a comprehensive listing of present animal species in various habitats in the Santa Cruz and San Pedro river basins; some of these are listed in Table 53. Not all species are listed in this table; only some of those known to be of economic importance to prehistoric and historic aboriginal groups are shown.

Ethnobiological studies on the Pima and Papago (Castetter and Underhill 1935; Russell 1908) demonstrate that mule deer and rabbits formed an important part of Pima and Papago diet. Archaeological sites in the Sonoran Desert also have yielded the remains of specific animals that were hunted and consumed by the Hohokam and early Papago. Escalante Ruin, on the Gila River northwest of the study area (Doyel 1974), and Ventana Cave, in the Papaguería to the west (Haury 1950), are the best examples. Species found at these sites are so indicated in the table. In general, the data show that there was wide variation in animal exploitation by the Hohokam that centered around a few important species, notably mule deer and rabbits (Gasser 1976:36).

Environmental Change

The topic of environmental change in the southern Arizona desert has been addressed by a number of different researchers (Hastings and Turner 1965; Schulman 1956; Humphrey 1958). In a descriptive sense, only the rough outlines of the kinds of changes that have occurred in the study area are known. What follows is a brief review of historic documents and recent paleoenvironmental studies that provide some information on the kinds of changes that have been observed, either directly or indirectly, in the environment of the study area.

Table 53. Common animals of the Southern Desert study area

Species		Habitat		
Common name	Scientific name	Lower Sonoran	Upper Sonoran	Riparian
*+mule deer	Odocoileus hemionus	X	X	X
* white-tailed deer	Odocoileus virginianus	X	X	X
*+cottontail rabbit	Sylvilagus spp.	X	X	X
*+jackrabbit	Lepus sp.	X	X	X
ground squirrel	Citellus spp.	X	X	X
*+pocket gopher	Thomomys spp.	X	X	X
* pocket mouse	Perognathus spp.	X		
*+kangaroo rat	Dipodomys spp.	X		
*+coyote	Canis latrans	X	X	X
* bighorn sheep	Ovis canadensis	X		
* prairie dog	Cynomys gunnisoni		X	
* porcupine	Erethizon dorsatum		X	X
* black bear	Euarctos americanus		X	X
raccoon	Procyon lotor	X	X	X
coati	Nasua narica		X	X
long-tailed weasel	Mustela frenata	X	X	X
badger	Taxidea taxus	X	X	X
beaver	Castor canadensis			X
muskrat	Ondatra zibethicus			X
Mearns' quail	Cyrtonyx montezumae	X	X	X
+Gambel's quail	Lophortyx gambelii	X	X	X
mourning dove	Zenaidura macroura		X	X
+white-winged dove	Zenaida asiatica	X	X	X
other small birds		X	X	X
*+hawks	Buteo spp.		X	X
lizards		X	X	X
snakes		X	X	X

* Remains found at Ventana Cave
+ Remains found at Escalante Ruin

In 1716, Father Velarde described the San Pedro Valley as follows:

...its hills [are covered]with mesquites, bell trees, and other trees and shrubs and there are thickets along the banks of the rivers, composed of poplars, willows, tamarisks, walnuts and gueribos, and in some of the sierras [there are] many and good pines for the building of the churches of the towns....in its rivers there are catfish and other small fish... (quoted in DiPeso 1953:7).

The Santa Cruz River Valley in the vicinity of Tucson was described by Browne in 1869 as

one of the richest and most beautiful grazing and agricultural regions I have ever seen. Occasionally the river sinks [beneath the channel], but even at these points the grass is abundant and luxuriant. We travelled, league after league, through waving fields of grass, from two to four feet high, and this at a season when cattle were dying of starvation all over the middle and southern parts of California (Browne 1869:144).

Prior to 1890, the Santa Cruz was characterized as containing marshes, beavers, and fish (Hastings and Turner 1965:3). It appears that the water table in the Tucson Basin has lowered since the latter portion of the 19th century. In 1697, for example, Bernal described Indian wells that extended 15 to 18 feet below the ground surface to reach the water table (Betancourt 1978a:4).

The Gila River drainage has similarly undergone substantial changes in the vegetation that is known in the area. In 1697, Father Kino indicated that extensive cottonwood groves lined the banks of the Gila (Bolton 1919:171-2), and, in 1699, described Piman groups near the mouth of the Gila as follows: "its inhabitants are fishermen, and have many nets and other tackle with which they fish all the year, sustaining themselves with abundant fish and with their maize, beans, calabashes, etc." (Bolton 1919:195). In 1846, during a traverse of the Gila drainage by a military expedition led by Kearney, the Gila River drainage was described as follows: "[In an area east of the confluence of the San Pedro and Gila rivers] we found, at places, a luxuriant growth of sycamore, ash, cedar, pine...some walnut ...and cottonwood" (Emory 1848:74). In the same location, Johnston (1848:592-3) described the Gila bottom lands as

covered with coarse grass, which abounds in the bottom of [the Gila]; then comes the willows..., which stand thick along the water in many places, but not more than 12 feet high; the cottonwoods are generally a foot or more in diameter, in irregular groves, not more than 100 yards wide along down the river.

On the following day, further west of the Gila-San Pedro confluence, in the vicinity of Mineral Creek, the Gila River bottom lands were described as follows: "Along the very edge of the water of the river the grass and other verdure grew luxuriantly. . . .Signs of the wild hog, and the deer, and the turkey were numerous" (Johnston 1848:593). Emory (1848:77-8) continues this characterization of the bottom lands, noting that they are "principally of deep dust and sand, overgrown with cotton wood, mezquite, chamiza, willow, and black willow."

These and other historical references to certain portions of the study area crossed by the Red Rock-Superior corridor show that the modern environment is considerably different. The crucial question, however, is how much change there has been. In order to adequately address this problem, paleoclimatic and paleoenvironmental research must be considered.

Paleoclimatological research, depending on the completeness of tree-ring series and temperature/rainfall records, does have the potential for allowing the retrodiction of seasonal variations in temperature and rainfall well into the prehistoric period (see Rose 1978). For most of the study area, however, these data are fragmentary. Accordingly, only an approximate notion of environmental change in the study area is possible at present.

The preliminary results of tree-ring studies in the uppper Gila River Basin (situated in New Mexico) and in the Catalina, Rincon, and Chiricahua mountains indicate significant variations in tree-ring growth patterns at various times (Schulman 1945, 1956). While there is a lag between   the time that a given amount of rainfall is received and tree response in the form of ring growth, studies thus far tend to show cyclical periods of decreased rainfall as evidenced in ring widths. Schulman (1956:Figure 32) has found an overall decrease in the amount of annual growth in tree rings in both the upper Gila Basin and for localities in the Catalina, Rincon, and Chiricahua mountains. This tends to signal a gradual decrease in available annual rainfall beginning about 1800 that has culminated, starting about 1930, in perhaps the most severe dessication that the study area has experienced since the early 1200s. Schulman (1956:65) states that "the average annual growth, and, perhaps to a first approximation, rainfall and runoff, during the 85-year drought of 1215-1299 seems to have been about <u>half</u> [of that known] during the drought [of] 1930 in the [upper Gila] basin" [emphasis added].

It seems, therefore, that the natural environment of the study area has undergone a series of significant changes.   The overall decline evident in the amount of tree-ring growth has been interpreted as a "drying out" of the environment, beginning in the early 1800s. While this cannot be expected to have led to the extinction of any particular biotic community, it probably has resulted in a contraction of the more mesic plant species along with the concomitant expansion of the more xeric species. This dessication-induced change in the distribution of plant species has been exacerbated by heavy groundwater pumpage that has lowered the water table over most of the study area (Betancourt 1978a:2-4).

In the Lower Sonoran Life Zone in the Red Rock area, there has been a decline in semiwoody perennials (for example, bur-sage and brittle-bush) and an upslope expansion of the palo-verde-saguaro community into Upper Sonoran desert grassland communities (Hastings and Turner 1965:270).

To briefly summarize the result of this characterization of the territory transected by the Red Rock-Superior segment, it has been shown that the line crosses a wide variety of biotic communities that occur in the Lower and Upper Sonoran life zones as defined by Lowe (1964). The sites in the Red Rock-Antelope Peak section are situated in the Lower Sonoran zone; no sites were recorded in that segment of the line near Superior which crosses the Upper Sonoran Life Zone. An analysis of data from vegetation transects in the areas north and south of the Gila River shows that, while there are no significant differences between these two areas with regard to overall species diversity, the part of the line north of the Gila River exhibits a greater incidence of economically significant plant species than does the line south of the river. Little is known of the density and spatial distribution of faunal resources in the study area, although ethnological and archaeological data show that a wide variety of animals were available, and were hunted by prehistoric and historic aboriginal groups. Soils and rainfall patterns have been shown to exhibit a high degree of variability throughout the study area. Most of the soils are of marginal value for agriculture, unless irrigation is practiced. Rainfall is seasonally and annually variable with the result that drought is quite common throughout the study area. Finally, the question of environmental change has been approached through the use of historic documents as well as recent paleoclimatological research. These sources indicate that contemporary patterns in the distribution of plant resources and, by extension, animal resources are probably not indicative of pre-historic conditions, since the study area is at the end of a long period of dessication originating in the early 1800s. This factor, combined with heavy groundwater usage, has resulted in the expansion of the more xeric plant species and the contraction of the more mesic species.

Culture History and Previous Research

The Southern Desert study area has produced evidence of prehistoric and historic occupations ranging from early Paleo-Indian hunters (around 10,000 B.C.) to recent indigenous Indian and Anglo inhabitants (Figure 33). What follows is a synthesis of information concerning those groups that inhabited the study area outlined above. The focus will be on the chang-ing nature of man-land relationships within this area and, in addition, the presentation of data regarding the changing material culture associated with these temporally distinct adaptations.

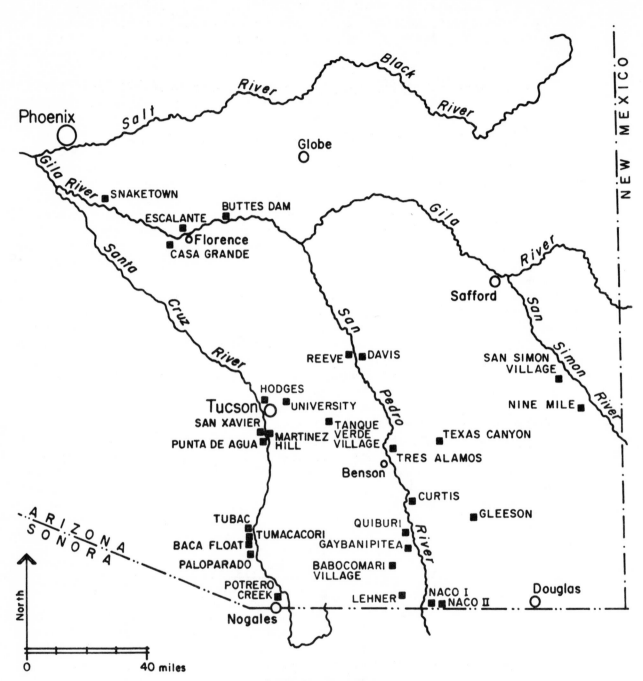

LOCATOR MAP
SHOWING ARCHAEOLOGICAL SITES IN THE REGION

Figure 33

Paleo-Indian

Paleo-Indian occupation is known throughout much of southern Arizona, especially along the U.S.-Mexican border in the southeastern part of the state. The Paleo-Indian period is roughly dated to approximately 12,000-8000 B.C. and has been divided into two traditions--the Clovis and Folsom complexes. Although this distinction is based primarily on morphological differences between projectile point styles, research has indicated that these two styles are temporally and spatially coincident (Agenbroad 1967:133-120). Originally, it was thought that Clovis groups hunted now-extinct mammoth, while Folsom hunters hunted bison. This led to the inference that these traditions had different subsistence strategies, possibly as a result of overhunting of earlier mammoth species (Martin and Wright 1967). However, recent research at the Murray Springs Site (Hemmings 1969) has shown that Clovis projectile points are also associated with bison remains. Thus, it seems likely that these two projectile point traditions may represent similar adaptations to the hunting of the same species of late Pleistocene megafauna (Irwin-Williams 1977:296-8). Clear associations between Paleo-Indian artifacts and faunal remains such as those found at the Naco, Lehner, and Blackwater Draw localities are rare; Paleo-Indian remains are more often found as isolated surface remains. In the study area, isolated Paleo-Indian projectile points have been found in a number of different localities; thus, Clovis points are reported from the Gila River north of Coolidge, Arizona, and from the vicinity of Florence, Arizona (Agenbroad 1967:114-6), while another projectile point exhibiting both Clovis and Folsom attributes has been found in the Tucson Mountains west of Tucson (Agenbroad 1967:118). Based on these findings, it is likely that Paleo-Indian groups traversed this area at one time.

Cochise Culture

Some of the most definite evidence of early prehistoric occupation in southern Arizona has resulted from the recovery of remains associated with the Cochise Culture. First defined by Sayles and Antevs (1941), Cochise remains are thought to represent a group of hunters and gatherers that exploited a wide range of wild plant and animal resources prior to the domestication and production of corn, beans, and squash.

Although the primary area of Cochise occupation is in the Sulphur Spring and upper San Pedro valleys, isolated occurrences of Cochise remains have been reported in the Tucson Basin and Santa Cruz River Basin (Stacy and Hayden 1975; Betancourt 1978b).

The original Cochise Culture chronology was a three-stage sequence based on the correlation of archaeological material with radiocarbon dates and geological events (Sayles and Antevs 1941). Subsequent research has since altered the chronological sequence and included a fourth stage (the Cazador), although there is still some dispute over the segregation of the Cochise Culture stages on the basis of stylistic attributes of their respective artifact assemblages (Whalen 1971; Quinn and Roney 1973). The differing chronologies with respect to author are indicated below.

Table 54. Variant sequences for the Cochise Culture

Stage	Sayles and Antevs (1941)	Whalen (1971)	Sayles and others (n.d.)
San Pedro	3000- 500 B.C.	1500- 200 B.C.	1000 B.C.-A.D.1
Chiricahua	8000-3000 B.C.	3500-1500 B.C.	6000-1500 B.C.
Cazador	N/A	N/A	9000-6000 B.C
Sulphur Spring	? -8000 B.C.	7500-3500 B.C.	10,500-9000 B.C.

Sulphur Spring Stage

The Sulphur Spring Stage is usually characterized as representing a hunting and gathering adaptation to a more mesic environment than that occurring presently in Arizona (Sayles and others n.d.). Assemblages from sites of this time period usually consist of unshaped grinding slabs, hammerstones, lithic flakes indicative of a percussion-flake technology, unifacial scrapers, and utilized flakes (Sayles and others n.d.). While the early investigations disclosed no projectile points at Sulphur Spring Stage sites, subsequent research at sites elsewhere revealed both stemmed and barbed leaf-shaped points associated with this early time period (Willey and Phillips 1958:90-3). Although these artifacts are associated with extinct late Pleistocene fauna, as well as modern fauna, the relative scarcity of projectile points at Cochise sites has led to the inference that gathering of wild plant resources was of greater importance than hunting at this time.

Cazador Stage

The Cazador Stage was identified as a stage transitional between the Sulphur Spring and Chiricahua stages. Geological and climatic evidence shows that the moist Anathermal was ending and the drier Altithermal beginning at this time. Due to climatic change and other factors, the large

Pleistocene mammals had begun to die out. Thus, sites of the Cazador Stage exhibit only the remains of modern fauna (Sayles and others n.d.). The few ground stone tools found are similar to those of the Sulphur Spring Stage, and chipped stone tools are more frequent. Also, projectile point types occurring at Cazador sites were not found at the earlier Sulphur Spring sites. This aspect of site artifact assemblages has long been a bone of contention. Quinn and Roney (1973) and Whalen (1971) suggest that Cazador sites may represent hunting sites of the Sulphur Spring Stage (and that Sulphur Spring sites may actually be the gathering sites of the same stage). However, there are still numerous problems regarding correlation of radiocarbon dates with geological events for this early time period, and the problem of the relationship between these two stages (or two types of sites) still has not been satisfactorily resolved.

Chiricahua Stage

The Chiricahua Stage is known primarily from a sample of sites situated in floodplain, lower bajada, and upper bajada/pediment locales in the San Pedro Basin. Unlike the Sulphur Spring and Cazador stages, a far larger number of sites are known for the Chiricahua Stage; in addition, regional surveys have provided some indications of the settlement-subsistence system of this time. Chiricahua artifact assemblages usually consist of shallow basin and flat slab metates, shaped manos, side-notched and concave-based projectile points, and gravers (Sayles and others n.d.). Scraping implements show considerably greater diversity and density compared with those of the Sulphur Spring Stage. Furthermore, bone tool assemblages first appear in Chiricahua deposits (Sayles and others n.d.). Regional survey and surface sampling in the upper San Pedro Valley have revealed that Chiricahua Stage sites are found in riverine, lower bajada/terrace, and upper bajada/pediment environmental zones (Whalen 1975:207-9) on the eastern slope of the Whetstone Mountains.

One documented example of Chiricahua Stage occupation near the study area is the Gila Dunes Site (AZ U:15:8-ASU) near the Gila River (Fish n.d.). This site contained a Hohokam component overlying an earlier Chiricahua Stage component.

San Pedro Stage

San Pedro Stage remains are somewhat better known than those of the preceding Cochise stages. Research by Windmiller (1973) in the Sulphur Spring Valley and Huckell (1973) in the San Pedro Valley has shown that San Pedro Stage sites exhibit a high degree of functional variability. Limited-activity sites include chipped stone manufacturing sites (Huckell 1973),

possible plant-processing loci (Whalen 1971), and habitation sites
(Windmiller 1973) that may have been seasonally occupied. Habitation
sites differ from other sites in that they evidence a wider range of
inferred activities, have higher artifact densities, and contain possible
storage features. Artifact populations remain similar to those described
from preceding stages. Unifacial and bifacial tools, bone implements,
and a preponderance of basin and slab-shaped metates have been recovered
in varying proportions at these sites.

The San Pedro Stage came to a close around A.D. 1 with the appearance
of a more settled way of life and incipient agriculture. The hunting and
gathering Cochise tradition gave way to the pottery-producing, agriculturally-
based early Mogollon culture, which found expression in southeastern Arizona
as the San Simon Branch (Sayles 1945). Mogollon occupation of the study
area has not as yet been documented, and accordingly will not be discussed
at length here.

Hohokam

Hohokam materials are found throughout the region crossed by the
southern segment of the APS Cholla-Saguaro transmission line. Because of
the great amount of research that has been done at Hohokam sites in various
portions of southern Arizona, more is known of the Hohokam occupations in
the study area than of any other prehistoric group.

The Hohokam continuum is divided into four periods, with differing
local phases for each period. These periods and phases along with the
associated time dimensions are indicated below.

Table 55. Hohokam cultural chronology

Period		Gila River Basin	Papaguería	Local phase designations Santa Cruz Basin	San Pedro Basin
A.D. 1400	Classic	Civano	Sells	Tucson	Reeve
A.D. 1270		Soho		Tanque Verde	Tanque Verde
A.D. 1100	Sedentary	Sacaton	Sacaton	Late Rincon	
				Early Rincon	Tres Alamos
A.D. 900	Colonial	Santa Cruz	Santa Cruz	Rillito	Cascabel
A.D. 700		Gila Butte		Cañada del Oro	
A.D. 500	Pioneer	Snaketown		Snaketown	
A.D. 300		Sweetwater		Sweetwater	
100 B.C.		Estrella			
300 B.C.		Vahki			

Any attempt to synthesize what is known of Hohokam occupation in an area as large as that bounded by the middle Gila, San Pedro, and Santa Cruz drainages must, of necessity, focus on rather general patterns.

From an environmental perspective, human adaptations during this time period were oriented toward at least four main microenvironments. These include riverine, upper and lower mountain bajada, and mountain locales. While it is assumed that each of these environmental zones was of variable importance at different time periods, the fact remains that Hohokam use of riverine environments is best known in the study area. This bias results from a traditional emphasis in archaeology on large stratified sites that, in general, tend to occur more often in riverine locales. Information concerning Hohokam riverine adaptations is available for major drainages such as the Gila, San Pedro, and Santa Cruz basins. From survey research, Hohokam occupation of subsidiary drainages (for example, Aravaipa Canyon in the San Pedro; Donnelly Wash in the Gila; and the Rillito, Cañada del Oro, and Pantano washes in the Santa Cruz) are also known. Knowledge of interriverine adaptations of relevance to this APS study area, however, remains scanty.

Pioneer Period

A number of Pioneer Period occupations are known in the middle Gila River Basin, including the Gila Butte Site (Shipek 1951), the Grewe Site (Hayden 1931), Snaketown (Haury 1976), and AZ U:16:29 and AZ U:15:9 (ASU) (Debowski and others 1976:167; Doelle 1976: Table 3). The Santa Cruz Basin shows evidence of limited Pioneer Hohokam occupation at the Hodges and Hardy sites (Betancourt 1978a:18), while, in the middle reaches of the Santa Cruz, limited late Pioneer occupations have been documented (Greenleaf 1975; Kelly 1938:9-11; Grebinger 1971:28). Pioneer Period sites are not yet documented in the San Pedro drainage, although this probably reflects limited survey coverage rather than a "real" absence of sites. Based on what limited regional data are presently available, however, the incidence of Pioneer Period occupations tends to decrease south of the Gila River.

With the exception of the Grewe, Gila Butte, and Snaketown sites, relatively little is known of Pioneer occupations other than the fact that they do occur in the study area. Excavated information is available only from riverine sites. Although the incidence of hunting-related artifacts (such as projectile points, scrapers, and gravers) is very low at Pioneer Period sites (Haury 1976:296; Shipek 1951:6), the relatively small amount of data from interriverine survey completed so far does not allow a test of the proposition that these inhabitants may have exploited wild plant and animal resources in the interriverine zone. Greene and

Mathews' (1976) analysis of faunal remains from Snaketown indicates an emphasis on various rabbit species and white-tailed and mule deer during the Pioneer Period. An analysis of deer skeletal elements shows a preponderance of vertebrae, scapulae, femurs, and innominate bones, and a scarcity of crania and lower leg bones. While there is some evidence to support the notion of Pioneer Period exploitation of interriverine zones (Doelle 1976:166), the interpretation currently accepted is that irrigation agriculture formed the primary mode of subsistence during this period. This inference is partially substantiated by the discovery of the Pioneer Period canals at Snaketown (Haury 1976:132-7).

Pioneer Period occupation is indicated by the presence of Snaketown Red-on-buff, Sweetwater Red-on-gray, Sweetwater Polychrome, Estrella Red-on-gray, Vahki Red, Vahki Plain, and Gila Plain ceramic types (Haury 1976:214-223). Both jar and bowl forms are present in these types, although there are no data regarding the relative preponderance of one vessel form over another at different periods. Ground stone implements include trough metates and shaped, oblong manos, as well as mortars, pestles, and palettes (Haury 1976:280-9). Residential structures during the Pioneer Period exhibit a high degree of diversity in terms of size. Most structures were rectangular in shape, with floor areas varying between 6.5 and 52 meters square (Haury 1976:65-71). Larger structures also had two entrances, leading Haury (1976:72) to suggest that these structures may have been used by multiple families. Little is known of storage facilities during the period. Haury (1976:119) suggests that surplus agricultural produce may have been parched and then stored in baskets and jars. Haury (1976:77) has further indicated that social organization during this time period was not tightly integrated at the village level. The fact that structures within villages are widely dispersed would seem to support this interpretation.

Colonial Period

Hohokam occupation during the Colonial Period is best known from the Gila River Basin. Continued occupation of Snaketown and the Gila Butte Site during the Colonial Period has been documented (Haury 1976; Shipek 1951), and there is evidence of a late Colonial occupation near Florence, Arizona (Windmiller 1972). Surface reconnaissance in the proposed Buttes Reservoir area (Debowski and others 1976) and on the Gila River Indian Reservation to the west (Wood 1972; Debowski and Fritz 1974) has revealed the presence of a number of sites with evidence of Colonial Period occupations. Excavation data regarding Colonial Period occupations in the San Pedro River Valley are available from only two locales: the Gleeson and Tres Alamos sites (Fulton and Tuthill 1940; Tuthill 1947). Limited surface reconnaissance has provided some information concerning Colonial settlement patterns in the San Pedro Valley (Teague 1974; Gilman and Richards 1975; Ferguson and Beezley 1974). Excavations in the Santa

Cruz Valley south of Tucson (Frick 1954), in the proposed Santa Cruz
Riverpark in Tucson (Betancourt 1978b), and in the Tortolita Mountains
east of Red Rock, Arizona (James Hewitt, personal communication) have
provided a tentative indication of regional settlement patterns during
this time. Generally speaking, however, detailed information is available only from riverine sites containing evidence of Colonial Period
occupations; interriverine areas have yet to be subjected to the same
kind of intensive study.

The Colonial Period in the Gila Basin has been best characterized
by the excavations at Snaketown (Gladwin and others 1937; Haury 1976).
Colonial occupations are indicated by the presence of Santa Cruz and
Gila Butte Red-on-buff jar, bowl, and dish forms (Haury 1976:210-4).
Ground stone assemblages are essentially the same as those found in the
preceding Pioneer Period. Shaped trough metates and oblong-shaped manos
continue to predominate at Snaketown (Haury 1976:280-2). Chipped stone
implements include choppers, scrapers, utilized flakes, and projectile
points. The major difference in projectile points of this period is the
proliferation of multibarb and serrated forms probably produced by pressure
flaking (Haury 1976:296). The rather narrow range of variation among projectile points with regard to raw material, dimensions, and so forth has
led Haury (1976:297) to suggest that specialists in the production of projectile points may have appeared during the Colonial Period. Negative
evidence concerning this interpretation is derived from the lack of definitive knapping loci such as those found at specialized obsidian workshops in
Teotihuacan (Spence n.d.). Furthermore, the fact that these projectile
points are associated with restricted numbers of burials has led to the
suggestion that a social elite may have existed during the Colonial Period
(Haury 1976:296-7). Further evidence of possible social stratification is
found in the rapid expansion of canal systems during the Santa Cruz Phase
(Haury 1976:139), in the construction of a large platform mound (Mound 39)
(Haury 1976:83), and in the construction of Ball Court 1 during the Gila
Butte Phase (Haury 1976:78). These events are taken to indicate that a
higher degree of social integration existed during this period.

While the expansion of canal systems during this period is thought
to indicate a greater emphasis on the cultivation of domesticated crops,
Greene and Mathews' (1976) analysis of faunal remains shows an increased
emphasis on the exploitation of wild animals--especially deer and rabbits--
during the Colonial Period. Similarly, the collection and consumption
of wild plant resources appear to continue during this period (Haury
1976:113-4). It seems, therefore, that while agricultural production
may have been increasing during the Colonial Period, occupants of Snaketown
continued to rely to some extent on wild resources for subsistence.

Structures from the Colonial Period are similar to those of the
preceding Pioneer Period in terms of construction. Floor areas vary from
13 to 48 meters square, with a single entrance (Haury 1976:65). While
there are at least two size modes in terms of floor area (20 meters square

and 33 meters square), houses all tend to be rectangular in shape. The functional or cultural significance of these size differences is unknown. An increase in the relative frequency of Colonial structures may indicate a possible increase in the population of Snaketown. Also increasing in number during the Colonial Period are trash mounds, as opposed to localized trash pits more commonly found in the Pioneer Period. The approximate characteristics of the Colonial Period as described here have been partially confirmed through excavations at the smaller Gila Butte Site (Shipek 1951) and at the Buttes Dam Site (Wasley and Benham 1968). Little information is available on nonriverine site distributions in the greater Gila River Basin.

Excavations at the Gleeson and Tres Alamos sites in the San Pedro drainage (Fulton and Tuthill 1940; Tuthill 1947) have shown that the Cascabel Phase (late Colonial) occupations, while considerably smaller than those at Snaketown, are similar to Snaketown in terms of the artifact assemblages, trash mounds, pit house sizes and shapes, and ball courts that have been described there. As in the Gila River Basin, most survey work has occurred in riverine locales, with the result that little is known of nonriverine Colonial adaptations.

Colonial Period occupation in the Santa Cruz Valley has been best documented through excavations by Grebinger (1971) and Doyel (1977). Their research has shown a scarcity of early Colonial (Cañada del Oro Phase) occupations and a preponderance of late Colonial (Rillito Phase) occupations in much of the upper and lower Santa Cruz Basin. While there are some similarities between Colonial remains in the Gila and Santa Cruz basins (pit houses of similar shape and dimensions, trash mounds, and ceramic and lithic assemblages), the relative scarcity of ball courts and canal systems indicates that the subsistence strategies and social organizational aspects of Colonial occupation were considerably different in the Santa Cruz Basin than those known from the Gila Basin (Doyel 1977:101-3; Grebinger 1971:78-80; Kelly 978). Grebinger (1976:40) has suggested that the increased incidence of Colonial occupations in the Santa Cruz drainage was the result of a population expansion into marginal areas, caused by increased stress on critical resources (for example, land suitable for irrigation farming) in the Gila River area. Grebinger further suggests that during the period of initial expansion, canal irrigation constituted the primary means of agricultural production. This interpretation has been disputed by Doyel (1977:101-2), who, while agreeing with the notion of a population expansion into areas south of the Gila, notes that there is little evidence of canal systems in the Santa Cruz Basin. Thus, he postulates an emphasis on dry farming based on methods similar to those documented ethnohistorically. Such cultivation is usually associated with the presence of check dams, small diversion ditches, and waffle-gardens. Remains of these types have been found throughout the Santa Cruz Valley (Doyel 1977:101; Kinkade and Fritz 1975:29).

To briefly summarize, then, Colonial Period occupation is known mainly from riverine environments in the Gila, San Pedro, and Santa Cruz drainages. Population growth in the Gila Basin is thought to have caused an expansion of Colonial groups into areas that were more marginal in terms of the irrigation system used in the Gila for agricultural production. These environmental differences are reflected in an increased emphasis on dry farming in the Santa Cruz and San Pedro basins, with a continuing use of irrigation systems in the Gila Basin. Settlement and subsistence strategies during this period appear to be reflected in the continuing exploitation of wild flora and faunal resources in non-riverine and mountain zones.

Sedentary Period

Sedentary Period occupations are known from all riverine locales in the Gila, San Pedro, and Santa Cruz drainages. The Sedentary Period is usually indicated by the presence of Sacaton Red-on-buff ceramics, with jars, bowls, plates, and "cauldrons" (Haury 1976:205-8) being common vessel forms. One major difference in the Sedentary Period ceramic assemblage in relation to those of preceding periods is the sheer size of the vessels produced (Haury 1976:205-7). This increase in the size of ceramics is thought to be related to the storage of surplus agricultural produce (Haury 1976:207). While ground stone assemblages (metates and manos) differ little from those of preceding periods, the overall density of these presumed grain-processing implements does not suggest an increase in the amounts of grain being processed (Haury 1976:280-1). Ground stone rings, which are thought to have been used for removing dried corn kernels from the cob, increase in number during the Sacaton Phase at Snaketown (Haury 1976:290-1). Chipped stone implements are essentially the same as those known from the Colonial Period, with the exception that points tend to decrease in frequency. Generally speaking, the density of chipped stone implements and debitage is greatly increased during the Sedentary Period (Haury 1976:294-8), in spite of the proposition that agricultural pursuits constitute the primary mode of subsistence. Interestingly enough, Greene and Mathews' (1976) analysis of faunal remains from the Sacaton Phase indicates an increasing emphasis on the exploitation of mountain sheep, with a decrease in the proportional contribution of deer to the recovered faunal assemblage. Since mountain sheep occur in areas away from Snaketown proper, it appears that Sedentary Period inhabitants may have been going farther afield to collect faunal resources. In any case, while agricultural production may have increased during this period, wild plants and animals continue to constitute a significant portion of the subsistence sources exploited.

The construction of irrigation canals at Snaketown during this period decreases in relation to that observed during the preceding Colonial Period (Haury 1976:139). More fill was added to two platform mounds dating to the Pioneer Period, and a third platform mound (Mound 16) was constructed during the Sacaton Phase (Haury 1976:82-9). Further population growth at Snaketown is evidenced by the fact that most of the trash mounds excavated at the site dated to the Sacaton Phase (Haury 1976:81).

Sedentary Period pit house structures exhibit a great degree of variability in size (floor area) and shape (oval to rectangular with rounded corners). Floor areas generally approximate one of four sizes: 9, 22, 42, or 54 meters square (Haury 1976:53-63). The postulated function of the smallest of these structures is that of menstrual huts or houses for old people (Haury 1976:62). Structures of the two intermediate sizes are suggested to have been family residential units (Haury 1976:57), while structures of the largest size are thought to represent possible "council houses" (Haury 1976:62). The large increase in the number and size of Sedentary Period houses is taken to indicate rapid population growth during this period.

Patterns in artifact assemblages, architectural features, canals, mounds, and so forth, as described here for Snaketown, have been observed at a number of other sites in the Gila Basin (Wasley and Benham 1968; Vivian and Spaulding 1974; Doyel 1974; Wood 1972).

In the San Pedro Valley, materials from the Tres Alamos Site show similar patterns to those described for Snaketown (Tuthill 1947). Remains from the Gleeson Site, however, exhibit more Mogollon characteristics during this time period (Fulton and Tuthill 1940:17-19), even though the remains are considered to be representative of a Hohokam occupation (see DiPeso 1956 for a contrary opinion). Like the Gila River area, regional surveys in the San Pedro are rare, and little information is available concerning settlement patterns during the Sedentary Period (Teague 1974:13). There is some indication of further expansion of Sedentary Hohokam groups into tributary drainages (Gilman and Richards 1975:5).

Considerably more information concerning Sedentary Period occupations is available from the Santa Cruz drainage. While ball courts remain conspicuously absent, artifact assemblages, the presence of trash mounds, and other features associated with the Sedentary Period as defined in the Gila Basin are found in the Santa Cruz (Doyel 1977:9-94; Greenleaf 1975:20-78). Betancourt (1978b:45) found evidence for Sedentary Period occupation at 36 sites within the proposed Santa Cruz Riverpark in Tucson. Excavations at a Sedentary Period occupation in a nonriverine locale (Grebinger 1971:30) have revealed significant differences in the artifact assemblages, floral and faunal remains, and seasonality of occupation in comparison with more thoroughly documented riverine sites. This evidence has been interpreted as indicating movement into zones that are marginal for agricultural production, thus bringing about a greater emphasis on the exploitation of wild plant and animal resources.

Unlike most of the research discussed thus far, regional surveys of limited scale have been completed for many parts of the Santa Cruz Basin. Consequently, a rough notion of Sedentary Period settlement patterns in that area has been obtained. Frick (1954), in a surface survey of the middle Santa Cruz, found Sedentary Period sites mostly on upper and lower terraces of the Santa Cruz. Twelve (30 percent) of the Rincon Phase sites were located in the foothills of the Sierrita Mountains, while another site was situated near the mouth of Madera Canyon in the Santa Rita Mountains. Betancourt (1978b:42-5) found that sites are equally represented in floodplain locations and on higher alluvial fans and terraces flanking the Santa Cruz River.

Classic Period

The transition from the Sedentary to the Classic Period was a time of rapid changes in the material culture and internal structure of Hohokam sites in the Gila and Salt basins. These changes include an increase in the frequency of platform mounds, the appearance of a well-developed canal system that seems to have irrigated substantially larger acreage than what is estimated for preceding periods, an apparent increase in population, the appearance of materials likely to have been brought in via long-distance trade networks, the differential distribution of grave goods (possibly indicative of rank-status distinctions), and a shift from spatially discrete residential structures to multiple dwelling areas enclosed by compound walls (Wilcox and Shenk 1977:190-8). These dramatic changes have been attributed to (1) an invasion of the area by other pre-historic groups (Schroeder 1960), (2) Mesoamerican contact (Haury 1976:93), and (3) the indigenous development of chiefdoms and redistributive economic systems (Wilcox and Shenk 1977:192-7). While it is not yet certain which of these varied causes of these changes is correct, the bulk of present evidence tends to support the last interpretation.

The Classic Period is not well represented at Snaketown, since the population of this time was breaking up and reorganizing into smaller units. Three small sites (AZ U:13:21, 22, and 24) on the western edge of Snaketown represent the only documented Classic Period occupation there. Canals show continued use during the Classic Period, but their degree of use is unknown and subsistence patterns during the period are poorly understood. This problem will be further explored later.

Ceramic types considered to be typical of the Classic Period include Casa Grande Red-on-buff, Gila Polychrome, Gila Red, and Gila Smudged (Haury 1976:202-4). As Haury has noted, bowl forms diminish in frequency, with a concomitant increase in the proportional number of jars within the

total ceramic assemblage at Snaketown; in addition, the overall capacity
of vessels tends to be less than that observed in the preceding Colonial
and Sedentary periods (Haury 1976:203). If we assume that large vessel
capacity is related to storage (Haury 1976:207), the relative decrease
in vessel capacity during the Classic Period may indicate either a shift
in storage technology or an absence of surplus agricultural production
requiring storage.

At Snaketown ground stone implements exhibit few changes in
morphology or density of distribution compared with preceding phases,
while chipped stone implements (especially formal tool classes such as
projectile points and scrapers) show a notable decrease in overall density compared to Sedentary Period deposits.

Another significant change associated with the Classic Period
occupation of the Gila River Basin is the higher frequency of platform
mounds. Precursors of Classic Period platform mounds have been noted
during the Pioneer and Sedentary periods (Haury 1976:82-9), but it is
during the Classic Period that platform mounds become common features
at Hohokam sites. Also, in contrast to mounds known from earlier periods,
platform mounds during the Classic Period often have structures located
on their tops (Haury 1976:93; Doyel 1974:175-7). Some researchers
(Wasley 1966; Haury 1976:93) have suggested that the occurrence of platform mounds is the result of Mesoamerican contact. Large platform mounds
have been recorded at Snaketown, the Escalante Ruin group (Doyel 1974:175-7),
Las Colinas (Hammack 1969), the Gatlin Site (Wasley 1960), and Casa Grande
in the Gila drainage.

Striking changes are also noted in architectural features during
this time period. Settlement patterns of preceding periods have been
characterized as consisting of pit houses dispersed throughout all portions of a site; that is, structures exhibit little spatial clustering.
During the Classic Period, there is a shift from semisubterranean pit
houses to aboveground coursed-masonry structures usually clustered into
a series of compounds or multiple-structure units, although pit houses
do continue to be built. While this change did not occur at Snaketown,
excavations in the Escalante Ruin group have increased our knowledge of
this change (Doyel 1974). Data from AZ U:15:22 and 27 show that aboveground structures were initially built as isolated units that were
incorporated within a compound at some later date (Doyel 1974:49, 64).
Within the compound walls were other rooms, as well as large plaza areas
devoid of structures. Doyel (1974:88) suggested that the plaza served
"a variety of functions associated with household activities such as
food preparation, cooking, storage, and tool manufacture." Evidence
in favor of this interpretation includes the discovery of hearths, caliche-
mixing pits associated with wall construction, and artifactual remains.
The internal arrangement of rooms is similar to that found in pit houses
that have hearths, pits, and postholes as common features. Rooms appear
to have been extensively remodeled at various times (Doyel 1974:65).
Most of this remodeling involved the further subdividing of existing

rooms by constructing internal partitions. Whether or not this reflects
changes in room function (such as storage), occurrence of extended families,
or other socioeconomic factors related to the use of space remains unknown.
One consequence of remodeling activities was that rooms were often stripped
of artifacts, with the result that it is difficult to acquire the kinds
of information necessary to test propositions regarding room functions
(Doyel 1974:64-5).

The social implications of these changes in the archaeological
record during the Classic Hohokam Period are as yet unresolved. As Doyel
(1976:32) has indicated, several theories include an influx of Toltec
(Mexico) missionaries, Mesoamerican merchants bringing in new ideas,
migrations of Sinaguan and/or Saladoan groups from the north, and, lastly,
a change in adaptive strategies in response to a generalized decrease in
available moisture during this period. Given the data base that is
presently available, it is almost impossible to reject any of these
notions as possible explanations for Classic Period changes. Doyel
(1976:34-5) has suggested that the demise of large population centers
such as Snaketown during the early Classic Period resulted in a fragmen-
tation of groups into smaller residential units. The impetus for this
shift is thought to have been the result of rainfall fluctuations leading to substantial variations in annual crop yields. The smaller and
more tightly integrated residential units typical of the late Classic
Period (as characterized by Doyel 1974) may be the result of a readjust-
ment of previous land-use patterns; more specifically, the ratio of population to available agricultural land may have decreased. One concomitant
of this agricultural deintensification is an increased use of wild plant
and animal resources. The few regional surveys that have been completed
indicate an increased incidence of Classic Period gathering loci in nonriverine areas (Goodyear 1975; Doelle 1976; Weaver 1973:82, 85). However,
data from late Classic sites are incomplete, and we know little about
subsistence changes at Classic sites proper.

Classic Period Hohokam remains are not documented in the San Pedro
Valley. It has been suggested that the San Pedro region was reoccupied
by Saladoan groups following the abandonment of the San Pedro at the close
of the Sedentary Hohokam Period (Franklin and Masse 1976:49). This reoccupation, as evidenced by significant differences in the kinds of
cultural remains found during this period, is thought to have occurred
as a result of immigration of Salado peoples originally from the Tonto
Basin near Globe, Arizona (Franklin and Masse 1976:53-5). The Salado
occupation of the project area has been discussed in Chapter 6 and will
not be considered here in detail.

Classic Period Hohokam remains also occur in the Santa Cruz Valley.
As before, most of our knowledge is based on limited excavations from
riverine sites. Thus, there is little information regarding Classic Period
land-use patterns in nonriverine localities. Riverine sites for which
information is available include the Hodges Site (Kelly 1978), Martinez

Hill Ruin (Gabel 1931), the University Indian Ruin (Hayden 1957), and Palo Parado Ruin (DiPeso 1956). Betancourt (1978b:45) found Tanque Verde Phase pottery at 33 locales within the proposed Santa Cruz Riverpark in Tucson. Later Tucson Phase sites were recognized by the presence of Gila Polychrome or other late Classic intrusives. Sites with Gila Polychrome and other northern intrusives were found to cluster in the northernmost and southernmost portions of the riverpark. The southernmost sites may be associated with the large Martinez Hill Ruin (Betancourt 1978b:46).

In summarizing the information available on the Classic Period in the Santa Cruz area, it is readily apparent that there are many similarities to the Classic Period in the Gila River Basin. Ceramic assemblages contain many types known to occur in the Gila, as well as what appear to be local varieties of plainwares, buffwares, and polychromes (Hayden 1957:219-321). A detailed analysis of design elements on these local ceramic types has led Grebinger (1971:150) to conclude that there are subtle "microtraditions" within many of these so-called types. Intra- and intersite variations in the relative frequency of ceramic design elements have produced two alternate models of social interaction in the Tucson Basin during the Classic Period. The first hypothesis is that there was an amalgamation of people from spatially segregated sites into a single site during the late Classic (Tucson Phase). The second hypothesis is that these microtraditions of the late Classic Period may have resulted from the exchange of women (who are assumed to have been the producers of pottery) between different sites, based on the principle of exogamous marriage and patrilocal postmarital residence rules (that is, females must marry out of their villages and reside in the male's village after marriage). The reader is referred to Grebinger (1971:151-2) for a more complete discussion of these models explaining ceramic variability in the Tucson Basin.

The relative incidence of ground stone metates and manos from the University Indian Ruin is considerably higher than that reported from either Snaketown or the Escalante Ruin group in the Gila Basin (Hayden 1957:134-140). Similarly, chipped stone assemblages (especially formal tools such as end-scrapers, gravers, and side-scrapers) are considerably more diverse and frequent at the University Indian Ruin than at sites described in the Gila. These patterns tend to indicate a greater emphasis during the Classic Period in the Tucson area on the collecting and processing of wild plant and animal resources. This inference tends to be confirmed by the recovery of cholla and mesquite remains at Rabid Ruin (Huckell 1976) and deer, elk, and mountain sheep remains at University Indian Ruin (Hayden 1957:100).

As in the Gila drainage, structures and settlement patterns evidence significant changes during the Classic Period in the Santa Cruz. While published information is relatively scarce, data from the University Indian Ruin show the development of caliche-reinforced structures (Hayden 1957:7-37). Initially constructed as isolated units, rooms were incorporated into compounds similar to those described by Doyel (1974) at the

Escalante Ruin group (Hayden 1957:36-8). While canals are poorly known
from the greater Santa Cruz drainage during the Classic Period, Tucson
Phase platform mounds (which were superimposed upon preceding Tanque
Verde Phase pit houses) have been documented in the region. Hayden's
work at the University Indian Ruin shows a sequence of mound-building
episodes in which various structures were constructed on the top of the
mound (Hayden 1957:57-94). As at Escalante, rooms appear to have been
extensively remodeled during their period of use.

Relatively little is known of the regional distribution of Classic
Period sites in the greater Santa Cruz Basin. A survey by Frick (1954)
in the middle Santa Cruz shows that Classic Period sites occur in riverine
locales with less frequency than do preceding Sedentary Period sites.
Foothill and pediment zones also contain few Classic Period sites. Recent
surveys in the Cañada del Oro and Falcon Valley areas northwest of Tucson
reveal fairly large Classic Period habitation sites situated in pediment
areas as well as riverine localities (James Hewitt, personal communication;
Brew 1975; Betancourt 1978b). These distributional patterns tend to confirm Grebinger's (1976:40-1) and Doyel's (1976:34-5) notion that there was
an expansion of Classic Hohokam groups into more marginal zones during
the Tanque Verde (early Classic Period) Phase as a result of increasingly
variable rainfall. Subsequently, populations aggregated into a more
limited number of villages in riverine locales. If this hypothesis is
correct, then we would expect to find late Sedentary - early Classic
Period sites in more marginal hinterland zones, while late Classic sites
would tend to cluster in riverine locales. Furthermore, the relative
frequency of late Sedentary - early Classic sites is expected to be higher
than that of late Classic sites. While these patterns tend to be confirmed
in the middle Santa Cruz Valley, information from the Santa Rosa Valley
immediately west of the Santa Cruz does not conform to this expected pattern. In the Santa Rosa Valley, there is considerably more evidence of
upland exploitation sites than what has been found in the Santa Cruz
(Goodyear 1975). While some sites appear to have experienced a population decline during the Classic Period, ther are little data to suggest
population aggregations into larger villages during the late Classic
Period (Raab 1976). As a result, land—use patterns during the Classic
Period remain unclear at present.

Historic Indian Groups

Relatively little information is available concerning Indian groups
in the study area between the end of the Hohokam occupation and early contact with the Spanish. As previously mentioned, the earliest documented
contacts between Anglos and Indians occurred during Kino's many expeditions
in the Santa Cruz-San Pedro-Gila basins. Because most of the study area
falls within the territory inhabited by the Pima, the following discussion
will be restricted to the nature of Piman occupations in the study area.
The Apache were known to have inhabited the mouth and eastern side of the
San Pedro River, but little is known of their initial occupation in southern Arizona.

Sobaipuri (Pima)

It should be noted that the distinction between the Sobaipuri and the Upper Pima (to be discussed) is, to a great extent, an analytical one. As DiPeso has pointed out, the term "Sobaipuri" originated with early Spanish explorers who maintained a distinction between the Pima of the Santa Cruz and Gila basins and the Pima (Sobaipuri) of the San Pedro Basin (1953:4). While recent research indicates that there may be more similarities than differences between these two groups (Doyel 1977:134-140), this terminological distinction has been maintained in the archaeological literature concerning the study area.

Almost nothing is known about the period between the abandonment of the San Pedro Valley by prehistoric groups and the earliest Spanish contact. The earliest record of Spanish contact with the Sobaipuri is contained in documents relating to the Marcos expedition of 1539 (DiPeso 1953:23). According to Bolton (1936:248-9), the territory inhabited by the Sobaipuri Pima included most of the San Pedro Valley. DiPeso has further suggested that the Sobaipuri may have migrated into the San Pedro from Chihuahua or Sonora during the period 1500-1600 (1951:7). Thus, while the origins of the Sobaipuri are as yet unclear, they were definitely in the upper and middle reaches of the San Pedro Valley by the early 1500s.

Most of our information regarding the Sobaipuri comes from DiPeso's excavations at the village of Quiburi. According to Kino, who visited Quiburi in December of 1696, the village had "more than four hundred souls assembled together, and a fortification, or earthen enclosure, since it is on the frontier of the hostile [Apache]" (quoted in DiPeso 1953:27). A description of the village in 1697 notes that its inhabitants "raised by irrigation large quantities of maize, frijoles, and cotton, the last of which they used for clothing. Quiburi had five hundred souls" (quoted in DiPeso 1953:27). Subject to intense Apache raiding, Quiburi was abandoned in the spring of 1698 (DiPeso 1953:32). It was later reoccupied by the original inhabitants in 1705, but entered a long period of decline both as a center of power and in terms of population. Abandoned by the Sobaipuri for a second time in 1769, the village site was used as a Spanish military garrison (under the name of Santa Cruz de Terrenate) beginning in 1772. This garrison failed to deter Apache raiding in the San Pedro Valley, and Quiburi was again abandoned.

DiPeso's excavations at Quiburi show that, during the two periods in which the site was occupied by the Sobaipuri, defensive structures (compound walls enclosing residential structures) were the main architectural features found at the site (1953:58-60). The 1692-1698 compound wall enclosed an area about 4340 meters square and contained at least 66 residential structures (DiPeso 1953:111). Residential units usually had common entrances, with a number of individual rooms combined into a single structure (DiPeso 1953:111). While Spanish documents indicate interaction between Spaniards and Sobaipuri, the recovery of only limited amounts of metal from Sobaipuri deposits during the 1692-1698 occupation shows that this interaction did not emphasize trade (DiPeso 1953:166-9). Ceramic, lithic, and ground stone assemblages exhibit few differences from those described for late Hohokam occupations in the Gila and Santa Cruz drainages (DiPeso 1953:142-181), with a notable exception in the relative decrease in bone tools and the apparent replacement of stone projectile points and knives by iron substitutes (DiPeso 1953:169, 173).

The Sobaipuri occupation of 1704-1762 at Quiburi differs considerably from that of the earlier period. The compound wall built during the preceding period was reused during the later occupation (DiPeso 1953:95), but fewer residential structures were situated within it--only 25 structures as compared with an earlier count of 66 structures (DiPeso 1953:95) DiPeso (1953:107-8) has interpreted these findings as indicating a decrease in the population due to (a) the failure of many former inhabitants to return when the site was reoccupied, and (b) the effects of smallpox epidemics that were increasingly frequent in the San Pedro during this period. The nature of Spanish-Sobaipuri interaction also changed significantly during this period. Following the Pima Revolt of 1751, Jesuit priests established a mission at Quiburi (DiPeso 1953:88-94). These priests tried to induce the Sobaipuri to repair the compound walls and establish lookout posts in areas surrounding Quiburi. These preparations were evidently made in anticipation of continuing Apache raids into the upper San Pedro Valley. One consequence of this shift is the higher incidence of Spanish trade goods found in later Sobaipuri deposits. It should also be remembered that the Spaniards were trying to establish a buffer between themselves and the Apache, and were using the Sobaipuri as mercenaries toward this end. This is known to have affected inter- and intravillage social organization, in that there now developed hierarchies of villages, according to their military importance to the Spanish, and a hierarchical ordering of individuals, depending on their ability to mobilize their followers against the Apache.

Another major impact of Spanish occupation in the upper San Pedro was the introduction of large numbers of livestock (horses, cattle, sheep, and pigs) (DiPeso 1953:233-6). Although Apache raids had occurred during the preceding 1692-1698 occupation, these became more intense during the early and middle 1700s, probably because of the relative ease in capturing these "slow elk", as well as the Apaches' desire for horses. Among the Sobaipuri, as well as among the Apache raiders, domestic livestock appears, on the basis of relative bone frequencies, to have replaced wild animals as a major source of protein (DiPeso 1953:235-7). Corn agriculture appears to have been a major subsistence activity, and the introduction of European domesticates, notably wheat, barley, and sweet potato, presaged a significant shift in the cultivation strategies of the Sobaipuri and other groups. The impact of these cultigens will be discussed in more detail regarding the Santa Cruz and Gila Piman groups. Apache pressure on Sobaipuri settlements in the San Pedro culminated in the abandonment of the area about 1762.

The most warlike amount all the Pima (tribes?) are those we call
the Sobaipuris, for they are born and reared on the border of the
Apaches; but they have become tired of living in constant warfare,
and have, during the present year of 1762, abandoned their beautiful and fertile valley, retiring some to Santa Maria Soanca, and
some to San Xavier del Bac and to Tucson, thus leaving to the
enemies a free entrance to the high region of the Pimas (quoted in
DiPeso 1953:41).

Upper Pima

Piman groups in the Santa Cruz and Gila drainages have been referred
to as "Upper Pima" (Doyel 1977:134). Spanish contact with the Pima first
occurred in the Santa Cruz Basin in the early 1690s. At this time, Father
Kino traversed the length of the Santa Cruz making contact with a number
of Pima villages (Bolton 1919). During a second expedition in 1697, Kino
traversed the Gila from its confluence with the San Pedro westward to its
confluence with the Santa Cruz (Dobyns 1974:318). Pima villages were not
noted along this stretch of the river until the expedition arrived at
Tucsan, just northwest of the ruins of Casa Grande. Three other villages
(Tusonimoo, San Andres, and Comac) were located farther to the west.
Ezell (1961:16) indicates that the villages of Tucsan and Tusonimoo
were abandoned in 1698 and 1699, respectively. Doelle (1975:6) has
shown that there appears to be a gradual decline in overall population
density during this early period, moving from south to north along the
San Pedro. This decline is evidenced by a decrease in the number of villages, as well as a decrease in the number of inhabitants in each village.

One possible factor relating to these differences in population
and settlemnt is that of different agricultural adaptations in the Santa
Cruz and Gila drainages. Cultivation strategies in the Santa Cruz appear
to have focused on irrigation agriculture (Doelle 1975:7), while flood-
water farming without irrigation appears to have been practiced in the
Gila (Winter 1973:69). Doelle (1975:9-10) has recently suggested that
the use of the latter strategy is confirmed by the fact that Pima villages in the Gila tend to coincide with locations at which the Gila River
(which sometimes flowed underground) rose to the surface.   One
other alternative is that Gila Pima practiced both irrigation and flood-
water farming (Dobyns 1974:325). Irrigation was practiced in areas with
a minimum of surface and subsurface water by enlarging existing springs
and constructing canals to divert sheetwash, while floodwater farming
was practiced in areas that were less marginal in terms of available water.
At present, the best evidence tends to support the notion that both alternatives were practiced under differing environmental conditions.

In addition to agriculture, early explorers also noted that there was a great emphasis on hunting, gathering, and fishing. Piman groups along the Gila were described as "fishermen" (Bolton 1919:195), while Spanish documents indicate that mesquite and mescal were gathered (Doelle 1975:6-7). Present evidence suggests that, unlike Sobaipuri groups in the San Pedro or Piman groups in the Santa Cruz, the Gila Pima practiced a more mixed subsistence strategy focusing on a wider variety of resources.

Upper Piman social organization during the early historic contact period is unclear. Winter (1973:69) has suggested that "there is no evidence for a tribal leader or extra-village structure." Dobyns, on the other hand, has argued that there were two levels of leadership: one on a village level and another directing a multiple number of villages (1974:324). The latter reconstruction is more in accord with what is presently known of Sobaipuri social organization in the San Pedro; however, the question of Piman social organization is not settled.

During the first half of the 1700s, Spanish contacts among the Pima increased dramatically. The effects of this contact are most noticeable on the subsistence base of the Pima. Wheat and livestock were among the important additions to Piman economies. This shift from earlier subsistence strategies that had focused on a wider variety of resources resulted in the increasing sedentism of the Santa Cruz and Gila Pima. The major drawback, however, was that, as with the Sobaipuri, the Pima became targets of Apache raids. During the period 1700-1775, Apache raids caused the Pima to abandon more than two-thirds of the area that they had previously inhabited (Hackenberg 1955:25). This contraction of Pima territory effectively doubled or tripled population density within the area that remained under their control. Hackenberg has indicated that the introduction of European crops greatly increased the relative productive capacity of Piman agricultural systems (1955:27). The most important change engendered by this shift in productive strategies involved an intensification of labor. As the Pima became increasingly dependent on agriculture, they could no longer be certain that flood-water farming would produce sufficient annual agricultural yields. As a consequence, labor intensification in the form of the construction of canals, dikes, diversion ditches, and reservoirs became common (Hackenberg 1955:27). Increased village size, greater dependence on agriculture, and increasing Apache raids are thought to have led to the development of greater social controls in the form of more powerful village and tribal "chiefs" (Hackenberg 1955:26).

Relatively little is known of the Pima between 1750 and 1853. This is due mostly to the fact that, following the Pima Revolt of 1751, there were considerably fewer Spaniards in the area. Following the expulsion of the Jesuits in 1767, most contacts were between the Pima and Spanish military forces in the immediate vicinity of Tucson. American contact with the Pima occurred occasionally during the early part of the

1800s, but increased in frequency following the Mexican War and the
discovery of gold in California in 1849. During the Civil War, when
Union forces withdrew from Arizona, the Pima were supplied with firearms
and acted as an impromptu military force against Apache raiders. They
continued in this role as soldiers and scouts under the command of American
officers until 1873.

The Gadsden Purchase of 1853 led to the inevitable influx of Anglos
into Arizona. By 1859, the Pima were restricted to a 64,000-acre reservation; an additional 81,000 acres was granted in 1869 (Hackenberg 1955:37-8).
However, none of this land encompassed the water resources that were
necessary to ensure continued agricultural productivity. By 1868, American
settlers were diverting so much water from the Gila River upstream from
the reservation that drought conditions prevailed over five continuous
years. This water shortage led to a relocation of villages to areas containing permanent springs or seeps or to places where the Gila rose to
the surface all year round (Hackenberg 1955:46-9). Agricultural productivity began to decline until, by 1895, the federal government had to
provide the Pima with one-quarter million pounds of wheat annually, where
before there had always been surplus production (Hackenberg 1955:53-4).
This trend continued until the late 1920s when the San Carlos Dam was
built to provide water for the reservation. Economic conditions among
the Pima, though still fairly grim, are considerably better than those
that obtained during the late 1800s and early 1900s.

Relatively little is known archaeologically of Upper Pima occupation of the study area. Surveys in the Santa Rita Mountains south of
Tucson show Pima-like early historic occupations (Debowski, in preparation),
while surveys in riverine areas indicate the existence of possible Pima
village sites in the Santa Cruz. Only one Pima site in the Middle Santa
Cruz drainage has been excavated (Doyel 1977:112-135). This site has been
dated to some time in the 17th or 18th centuries. Excavation has shown
the site to consist of a series of oval to elongated structures defined
by cobbles along their perimeters. The size of the structures varies
from 9.25 to more than 18 square meters in area. Prepared floors were
not present, and hearths tended to be located outside the structures
(Doyel 1977:133-7). Ground stone implements show a lack of shaping prior
to use, while chipped stone assemblages emphasize utilized flakes as
opposed to formal tools (Doyel 1977:188-121). The relative incidence
of projectile points is also high (Doyel 1977:121). Ceramics consist
mostly of plainwares; of these, jars tend to predominate over bowls
(Doyel 1977:122).

Doyel (1977:130-4) has interpreted this site as a hunting camp
at which small quantities of plant resources may have been processed.
This inference is based primarily on the low incidence of ground stone
and the high incidence of projectile points. The production of stone
tools may have been a major activity at the site. Intrasite spatial
patterning of structures with allied outdoor hearths has been interpreted
as suggestive of single-family or extended-family residential units, with
the site made up of a number of such units (Doyel 1977:130-4).

Based on the discovery of similar sites in mountain locales, Doyel (1977:132, 134) has suggested that the Pima may have been practicing seasonal transhumance in which they resided part of the year in lowlands and part of the year in the mountains. The major subsistence activities within these two spatially distinct locales consisted of hunting in the lowlands and plant gathering in the more mountainous areas. It should be noted that this conforms in a rough way to Dobyns' (1974:325) suggestion that seasonal transhumance was common among the Gila Pima; the major difference is that Doyel stresses the practice of hunting and gathering while Dobyns focuses on agricultural production.

Spanish and Anglo Occupations in the Study Area

Early Spanish activities in the study area consisted mostly of explorations, followed by the establishment of missions in the Santa Cruz Valley. The information below has been synthesized from the following sources: Debowski and others 1976; Debowski and Fritz 1974; Doelle 1976; and Betancourt 1978a.

The earliest known Spanish incursion into the study area is that of the Diaz expedition. According to Corle (1950:59), Melchior Diaz led an expedition into the San Pedro Valley near the Gila-San Pedro confluence around 1539. The area supposedly explored included an area east and west of the Gila-San Pedro junction. Historical documentation of this expedition is lacking.

In 1694, Father Eusebio Kino traveled down the Santa Cruz River to the Gila to visit the site of Casa Grande. In November, 1697, he again visited Casa Grande with an escort of 20 soldiers. The route taken on this trip was down the San Pedro and then westward along the Gila to Casa Grande. On the 17th of November, they camped on the Gila near South Butte. Their camp location has been tentatively identified by Ives (1973). In 1698 and 1699, Kino made additional trips down the San Pedro to the Gila. Documents from these trips include many descriptions of Indian villages in the Tucson area, and note the approximate distances between villages, the number of structures in some villages, and the number of inhabitants. Kino's last trip was in April of 1700 to lay the foundations for San Xavier del Bac.

During the period 1700-1756, mission activities in the Santa Cruz region accounted for most Spanish occupations in the study area. Documentary evidence indicates that there were troubles with mission Indians and, further, that Spanish influence did not extend much beyond the limits of the mission itself. The Pima Revolt of 1751, followed by the expulsion of the Jesuits in 1767, led to the eventual downfall of the mission system in southern Arizona. With the missions replaced by military garrisons, Spanish activities during the period 1767-1800 consisted mostly of attempting to pacify Western Apache raiders who preyed on the relatively defenseless mission Indians (mostly Piman groups) farming in the Tucson Valley. During this period, the presidio and mission of San Augustín del Tucson was built. The Mexican Revolution of 1810 led to a decline of Spanish influence in the area; in 1821, the presidio was abandoned.

Following the Mexican Revolution in 1810, the primary activity of Spanish in the study area consisted of cattle ranching. In the upper Santa Cruz Basin, the Ortiz brothers maintained two large rancheros; in 1833, they expanded their holdings because their herds were too large to maintain without additional land (Wagoner 1952:24). The Gonzales family controlled most of the San Pedro Basin, with large ranches located at Agua Prieta, Babocomari, Nogales, Elias, and San Juan de las Boquillas. Again, the reason cited in the request for additional land was livestock pressure on existing holdings (Wagoner 1952:25). Most of the land around Tumacacori was owned by Francisco Aguilar and used for herding. During this period, however, Apache raids made ranching in almost any part of southern Arizona rather hazardous. In 1854, approximately 3000 head were lost along trails south of the Gila River, mostly to the Apache (Wagoner 1952:30).

To the north, Anglo expeditions continued after a 100-year hiatus. In 1824, 1826, and 1827, Sylvester and James Pattie undertook a series of fur-trapping expeditions from the headwaters of the Gila River to the San Pedro and west to the Mineral Creek area. Their only long-term occupation in the area was at the mouth of the San Pedro in 1827; this site has not been documented archaeologically. In 1846, Colonel Steven Kearney and Christopher "Kit" Carson passed down the Gila River on the way to California. In 1849, an expedition of gold-rush miners passed through the Upper Gila on their way to California. Archaeological evidence for these various excursions is not presently available.

Following the Mexican Revolution in 1810 and continuing until after the Gadsden Purchase of 1853, Mexican troops maintained a small garrison in Tucson. Farming and limited commercial enterprises were the major activities during this period. In 1856, Mexican troops were replaced by four companies of American dragoons. During this period, Tucson was best known for the Silver Lake milling operations which supplied flour to all of the military garrisons in Arizona. These operations were expanded under the ownership of William S. Grant up until 1862 when, threatened by Confederate troops from Texas, Union forces burned the mills and retreated. Most businessmen in Tucson were Union sympathizers and, consequently, were forced to leave when the Confederates occupied Tucson. Shortly afterward, Tucson was re-captured by the California Volunteers. However, during the period 1862-1864, commercial milling operations ceased under the provisions of martial law. Thus, the Civil War postponed economic and commercial development in the southern Arizona region through the destruction of mills, the abandonment of Tucson and outlying ranches by Union sympa-thizers when Confederate forces invaded the area, and the depredations of Apache raiders who, in the absence of American military control, continued unchecked against those ranchers who tried to maintain herds in the area.

American enterprises in the study area following the Civil War focused mostly on ranching and mining. However, until the Apache were removed to reservations in 1872, most of the cattle in Arizona were brought in from Oregon, California, and Texas (Wagoner 1952:36). Col. H. C. Hooker was the first American to establish a cattle ranch using Texan, rather than Mexican, stock. Prior to this time, smaller Mexican livestock were herded in the area. Hooker's ranch was located in the Baboquivira Valley southwest of Tucson and supplied beef to military installations and Indian reservations for a number of years. While the largest ranches were run by Americans, most of the livestock in the region was owned by Mexican ranchers running considerably smaller herds than their American counterparts (Wagoner 1952:39-40). In 1876, cattle operations began in the San Pedro Basin with the establishment of the Empire and Cienega ranches. The Gila River area did not witness the same magnitude of cattle ranching as did the Santa Cruz or San Pedro; small ranchers running Mexican cattle were more common in this area.

In response to the high demand for beef and the relatively low capital required to begin a ranch, the available range land rapidly became overstocked. By the early 1800s, the range land was becoming severely overgrazed. A drought in 1892-1893, coupled with a severe drop in the market price of beef, ruined small ranchers and forced even large ranchers to pool their stock in order to make up price losses through volume sales (Wagoner 1952:45). By the late 1880s, ranchers had learned that the maximum herd size that could be profitable raised was that which could be maintained during the poorest years (Wagoner 1952:54). However, by the early 1890s, increased rainfall and improved range conditions resulted in a return to the philosophy of maximizing returns rather than minimizing potential losses. Consequently, cattle production over much of Arizona proceeded through a series of "boom and bust" cycles that coincided with periodic droughts and forage shortages. By 1925, ranchers had returned to a more conservative strategy of minimizing their losses (Wagoner 1952:58-9). The only ranch of any importance along the APS line is the Zelleweger Ranch site in the Gila River Basin (Debowski and others 1976).

Mining was the other major activity associated with the arrival of Americans in Arizona. Mining claims were made throughout the 1850s and 1860s, but extraction of gold, silver, and copper ores did not really begin until the later 1870s. Gold ore deposits could not be profitably mined because of poor extraction techniques, and silver mining soon supplanted that of gold as an economic venture. The Silver King Mine in the northern part of the study area, near Superior, was started in the mid-1870s. In 1874, the Mineral Creek Mining Company began operations in the Gila River near its confluence with Mineral Creek (McClintock 1916:419). The now-abandoned town of Riverside on the Gila River served

as a support center for these operations, and, by 1877, Riverside was
a stage stop along the Wells, Fargo, and Company stage line between
Florence and Globe (Gressinger 1963:39). By 1880, a mill and coke ovens
had been established by the Pinal Consolidated Mining Company near the
now-abandoned town of Butte, and, by 1883, the Ray Copper Company began
operations on 17 claims along the Gila River (Debowski and others 1976:117).
Further south, the Jesse Benton Mine conducted silver-mining operations
during the period 1881-1892. Archaeological investigations were made at
this mine, and are discussed in a later section. Following the Panic of
1893, in which the price of silver dropped from $1.29 to $.78 an ounce,
almost all silver mines closed. Copper mining soon became of foremost
importance to the economy of Arizona, and has maintained that position
until the present.

Survey Results and Site Significance

Survey methods and logistics have been described in Chapter 3 and
are briefly summarized here. The results of the survey of the Red Rock-
to-Antelope Peak section were reported by Kinkade and Gilman (1974), and
later, a research design was prepared by Kinkade (1974) for recovery of
information from sites that would be disturbed by proposed construction
activities. The results of the survey of the section from Antelope Peak
to Superior were prepared by Canouts (1975), with recommendations
for engineering adjustments and monitoring of sensitive areas.
No data recovery was undertaken at sites in this section. Survey
of proposed access roads found an additional three sites, and two more
sites near the Gila River had been previously recorded during the Buttes
Reservoir survey (Debowski and others 1976). A total of one historic
and 18 prehistoric sites was recorded for this entire corridor segment;
these sites are discussed below. Individual site descriptions will be
found in the volume accompanying this report.

Not all sites can be easily placed into a site typology, since
surface observations alone can be potentially misleading. Several sherd
and lithic scatters, for example, could represent pit house villages
(habitation sites), but this cannot be determined without subsurface
testing. The sites, then, are ordered in Table 56 according to their
visible characteristics; these descriptions are not absolute functional
determinations.

It must be noted that the majority of sites are high-density
artifact scatters and sites with obvious architectural features. The
criteria for site recognition in use at the time of the survey stipulated that a
site exhibit an artifact density of at least five artifacts per square meter
to warrant its recording on the survey form. Thus, "non-sites" (low-density,
widely dispersed artifact scatters) are not represented in the table.

Table 56. Typology of APS-CS sites located in Southern Desert study area

Site Numbers	Diagnostic Pottery Types	Tentative Dates	Cultural Affiliation
Sites with rock features			
AZ BB:1:9	Plainwares	Late Hohokam-Early Salado?	Hohokam-Salado
AZ BB:1:10	Plainwares, red corrugated	Post-A.D. 1150	Hohokam-Salado
AZ BB:1:11	Red-on-buff, plainwares	?	Hohokam
AZ BB:1:15	Plainwares, redwares	?	Hohokam ?
AZ BB:1:16	None	?	
AZ BB:5:21	Tanque Verde Red-on-brown	Late Rincon-Early Tanque Verde phases; Sedentary-Classic Period transition	Hohokam-Salado
AZ BB:5:22	Tanque Verde Red-on-brown, Gila Plain	Sedentary-Classic Period transition (about A.D. 1100-1270)	Hohokam-Salado
AZ BB:5:23	Plainware, redware, black-on-white	?	?
AZ BB:5:24	Plainwares	?	
AZ U:16:27	Santa Cruz Red-on-buff, Sacaton Red-on-buff	Santa Cruz-Sacaton phases	Hohokam
Sherd and lithic scatter without rock features			
AZ BB:1:8	Santa Cruz Red-on-buff, Sacaton Red-on-buff	Santa Cruz-Sacaton phases	Hohokam
AZ BB:1:12	Sacaton Red-on-buff	A.D. 900-1100	Hohokam
AZ BB:1:13	Sacaton Red-on-buff	A.D. 900-1100	Hohokam
AZ BB:1:14	Plainwares, redware	?	?
AZ U:16:116	Unidentified red-on-buff	?	Hohokam
AZ U:16:128	Plainwares	?	Hohokam?
Lithic scatter site			
AZ U:16:182	None	?	?
Rock shelter			
AZ U:16:181	None	?	Unknown
Historic			
AZ AA:8:6	Jesse Benton Mine		

It is likely, however, that sites of transitory or brief activity do exist in the area transected by the corridor. This point is made to demonstrate why "habitation" sites and high-density artifact scatters are over-represented in the southern corridor segment. A partial reconstruction of occupation of the study area by certain cultural groups is possible, however, because of the occurrence of diagnostic artifact types at several sites. These data are useful for assessing the significance of the sites with respect to regional prehistory.

Sites with rock features (which could be rooms, storage features, or terraces) contain recognizable Hohokam and Salado pottery and artifacts. Table 56 shows that three sites contain Sacaton Phase sherds, two sites exhibit sherds indicative of the Sacaton-Santa Cruz phases, and two sites indicate occupation during the Hohokam Sedentary-Classic Period transition. The remaining sites contain unidentified plainwares. Interestingly, rock features (possible rooms) occur at the later Sedentary-Classic Period sites, while they are absent at the Sacaton Phase sites (which could be pit house sites). Santa Cruz-Sacaton sherds are present at one site with rock features and at one sherd and lithic scatter with no rock features. Despite the biased nature of site types in this segment, the data do demonstrate that certain site characteristics correspond to those of Hohokam sites of known age reported elsewhere in the Santa Cruz, San Pedro, and Middle Gila valleys. There are insufficient data, however, to determine if significant differences exist with respect to site location in a particular area with attendant environmental factors that might have acted upon site formation processes.

In addition to answering questions about cultural and chronological problems, the recorded sites are significant in that they can provide information on prehistoric land use, particularly during the Hohokam occupation of the study area. As noted previously, most Hohokam research has focused on sites situated along the major river valleys; little is known of Hohokam use of the drier interriverine desert areas. Thus, research goals for future investigations were developed to test hypotheses about prehistoric land use in nonriverine areas.

Data Recovery: Field Recovery Methods and the Variables Measured in the Analysis of Artifact Populations

Introduction

Data recovery was recommended for six sites in the corridor between Red Rock and Antelope Peak. Recommendations were made to avoid construction impacts to the sites in the Antelope Peak-Superior section; hence, no further archaeological investigations were necessary for this latter section. Total data recovery (that is, complete excavation and recording of the sites) was not a goal of the proposed investigations, since

in setting up the methodology for this phase of the project, we are assuming that tower relocation and access suggestions made to

A.P.S. will be followed. Therefore, the mitigation proposed here is the minimum required based on this assumption. More intensive testing and excavation, hence a new research plan, will be needed if new roads are built or transmission line towers are not relocated. The information now available is that these sites will remain intact and will be preserved for future investigation (Kinkade 1974:11).

Data recovery at one historic and five prehistoric sites, then, was oriented toward obtaining an artifact sample which, together with collected environmental data, would fulfill proposed research goals.

Research Design for Data Recovery

According to Kinkade (1974), activities at the five prehistoric sites were ultimately directed at procuring, processing, and consuming natural resources. These sites can then be classified according to the type of activity or combination of activities conducted at them, and these data used to obtain some idea of prehistoric subsistence practices. There was no evidence of agriculture at the sites in the Red Rock-Antelope Peak corridor; hence, hypotheses were not developed to test assumptions about this activity. Kinkade (1974:5) proposed that "a quantifiably significant relationship between environmental diversity and the subsistence-related assemblage diversity [would be] found between sites."

In order to test this hypothesis, the research design for data recovery focused on obtaining an artifact sample that would be representative of site activities. It was hoped that assumptions about site function could be validated through detailed analysis of certain classes of artifacts related to food procurement, processing, and consumption. Accordingly, field recovery methods involved the following procedures (Kinkade 1974:11-12):

1) Mapping of the sites, showing all prehistoric features and artifact concentrations.

2) Sampling and collecting of ceramics. Depending on site size and artifact density, sample size varied from 10 to 25 percent; a stratified random sample scheme was used.

3) Sampling and collecting of lithic artifacts. Due to the importance of lithics in testing research hypotheses, a 100 percent collection was proposed, and each artifact mapped.

4) Recording data on features.

5) Recording and collecting vegetation data, using plant transects.

6) Collecting pollen and flotation samples from features.

7) Test excavations within features, time permitting.

8) Localized survey of the area surrounding each site.

Due to lack of time, not all objectives were completely fulfilled. The recovered artifacts were reexamined and the analysis redesigned to obtain as much information as possible from what was available to the author.

Procedures for Data Recovery

Four of the five prehistoric sites that were examined were subjected to controlled surface collections; the fifth site was subjected to "grab" sampling. Because of these differing methods of data collection, the kinds of information that were obtained from the sites are not directly comparable. Those sites subjected to controlled surface collections were sampled using a stratified random sampling technique (Cochran 1977). Subareas of a given site were first defined and treated as separate strata. A simple random sample of collection units was then drawn from each stratum. In most cases, 10 m by 10 m collection units were used. Sampling fractions, or the percentage of a site's surface that was collected, varied from one site to another. While ceramics were always collected by collection units, the lithic population was treated differently. At some sites, lithics were recovered by collection unit but not individually mapped, while at other sites, all of the surface lithics were mapped and collected.

The sampling approach, collection unit sizes, sample fractions, and methods used to collect lithics at each of the investigated sites are indicated in Table 57.

Table 57. Summary of sampling strategies at prehistoric
sites in the southern portion of the APS Cholla-Saguaro corridor

Site	Sampling approach	Sample fraction*	Unit size	Lithic collection
AZ BB:1:8	Grab	Unknown	N/A	Grab
AZ BB:1:9	Stratified random	10 percent	10 m by 10 m	By collection unit
AZ BB:1:10	Stratified random	10 percent	10 m by 10 m	By collection unit
AZ BB:5:21	Stratified random	3.4 percent	10 m by 10 m	100 percent point provenience
AZ BB:5:22	Stratified random	16 percent	10 m by 10 m	100 percent point provenience

*Sample fractions chosen arbitrarily

The Data Base

If various artifact classes are considered as distinct populations, the aggregate of which form an archaeological site, then the objective of the sampling procedures described above is to acquire a representative sample of these various artifact populations. Using data from these samples, it is possible to begin to estimate various relevant parameters of each artifact population.

In the field, samples were collected from a number of subpopulations within the more general populations of sherds, lithic (chipped stone) debris, lithic implements, battered stone tools, and ground stone tools. Data regarding features (for example, terraces and structures) were also collected.

A number of points should be noted concerning these samples of artifacts and features. The samples that were collected are unbiased in the sense that, with two exceptions, the samples were collected randomly. The samples are not representative, since not all of the artifact populations that could have been collected were recovered. For example, the artifact population of "debitage" or waste flakes is underrepresented at most of the sites. Furthermore, many of the samples that were collected are inadequate for the present analysis in terms of their size. This is reflected in the rather large confidence intervals about the mean values of many of the attributes (for example, orifice diameter, lithic edge angles, and others) that were measured. In spite of these problems, the fact that the collection of those artifacts was based on a random design allows the use of various descriptive statistics and statistical tests. As a result, it is possible to statistically assess hypotheses concerning the behavior that led to the deposition of these artifacts, even though some potential hypotheses cannot be tested and some of the tests may be less conclusive than is desirable.

Analytical Procedures

The distinct artifact and feature populations and subpopulations were first examined singly in order to estimate the parameters of each population. These parameters include lengths, widths, counts, weights, and other discrete and continuous sources of variation within each population. Having established intrapopulation variability, the next step in the analysis was to examine the nature of interpopulation covariation at each site. This was done in order to characterize intrasite variability in terms of aggregated artifact populations. Lastly, intersite variability was compared in order to interpret similarities and differences in the kinds of remains and activities that occurred at the sites.

Below is a discussion of the artifact populations and subpopulations that were distinguished for analytical purposes. Variables constituting sources of variation and the behavioral importance of this variation within each analytical group are also indicated. This discussion is presented in an outline format for greater clarity.

Population: Ceramics

Subpopulation: Plainwares - refers to ceramics with little or no surface modification (such as incising, painting, or other modifications) other than polishing.

Variable: Type - typological classification of sherds is used to determine basic cultural chronology.

Variable: Counts/Weights - were used to determine mean sherd density and weight (as well as coefficients of variation per colleciton unit) across various portions of a site. This variable is behaviorally significant, since DeBoer and Lathrap (n.d.:17-19) have demonstrated differences in sherd sizes depending on how much activity occurs in areas where sherds are deposited. They have also shown that the differential spatial distribution of sherds is directly related to certain kinds of discard/disposal behavior. In addition, Alan P. Sullivan has recently suggested to the author that occupational duration is related to variation in the density of artifacts per recovery unit.

Variable: Vessel form - since complete or partially restorable vessels were not recovered from most sites, determinations of vessel form are based on rim sherds. The technique is discussed by Shepard (1956:125-130). Since vessel forms are indicators of the kinds of activities that occurred at a site (Goodyear 1975), the relative frequencies of different vessel forms can allow tentative functional interpretations of a site. Furthermore, ethnoarchaeological research has revealed significant differences in the rates at which different vessel forms are deposited into archaeological contexts (DeBoer and Lathrap n.d.:16; Longacre 1974:7). These findings have obvious implications regarding the duration of site occupation.

Subpopulation: Decorated wares - comprise less than two percent of the ceramic assemblages at the sites. While detailed analyses of decorated ceramics have been done for other sites in the region, too few sherds were collected from APS-CS sites to conduct an intensive analysis. Thus, the variables considered for plainwares were also used to analyze decorated ceramics. David E. Doyel (University of Arizona) assisted in identifying chronologically sensitive pottery types.

To arrive at a functional interpretation of the ceramics, information was needed on vessel form, function, and frequency. Assuming that
narrow orifice vessels are jars and wide orifice vessels are bowls
(Shepard 1956:125-130), the relative proportions of bowls and jars at
a site can be determined by examining rim sherds. This was done for each
site from which sherds were collected (see Figure 34).

A second research objective was to determine what the vessels were
used for. There is considerable ethnographic evidence showing variations
in surface treatment, temper, and porosity of pottery depending on the
intended use of a vessel. For example, Fontana and others (1962:34) have
shown that large water storage jars were more porous than other vessels
made by Papago potters, in order to promote evaporative cooling. Similarily, vessels for storing cactus fruit syrup are also porous (Fontana
and others 1962:37). Russell (1908:127) indicates that Pima water
storage vessels are also quite porous. Fontana and others (1962:37)
have also indicated that some cooking vessels can be of the same shape--
and presumably the same porosity--as large water storage vessels. Assuming
that variations in temper and porosity will, in the long run, reflect
differences in the use of a vessel, we can expect that sherd collections
will exhibit at least two differences in porosity distributed across two
vessel forms. Thus, two hypotheses regarding possible vessel functions
were proposed with corollary test implications:

Hypothesis 1: If jars were used primarily for the storage of
liquids, then expect

Test Implication 1: jars to exhibit a high degree of porosity.
Test Implication 1: on the exteriors of jar sherds, little or
no soot deposits resulting from cooking.
Test Implication 3: fewer broken jars since, with less handling,
the probability of breakage is decreased.

Hypothesis 2: If bowls were used primarily for cooking and serving
activities, then expect

Test Implication 1: soot deposits on the exteriors of large
bowls, since these would be used more often
for cooking.
Test Implication 2: bowl forms to be less porous.
Test Implication 3: more broken bowls in terms of relative
frequencies.

To test these functional propositions, porosity studies of sherds
were undertaken by the original investigators, Kinkade and Gilman.
These researchers selected a sample of body sherds with differing tempers
and subjected them to a porosity test similar to that described by Shepard
(1956:125-130). Dry sherds are first weighed and then boiled for two
hours and reweighed. The relative change in the weight of the sample of

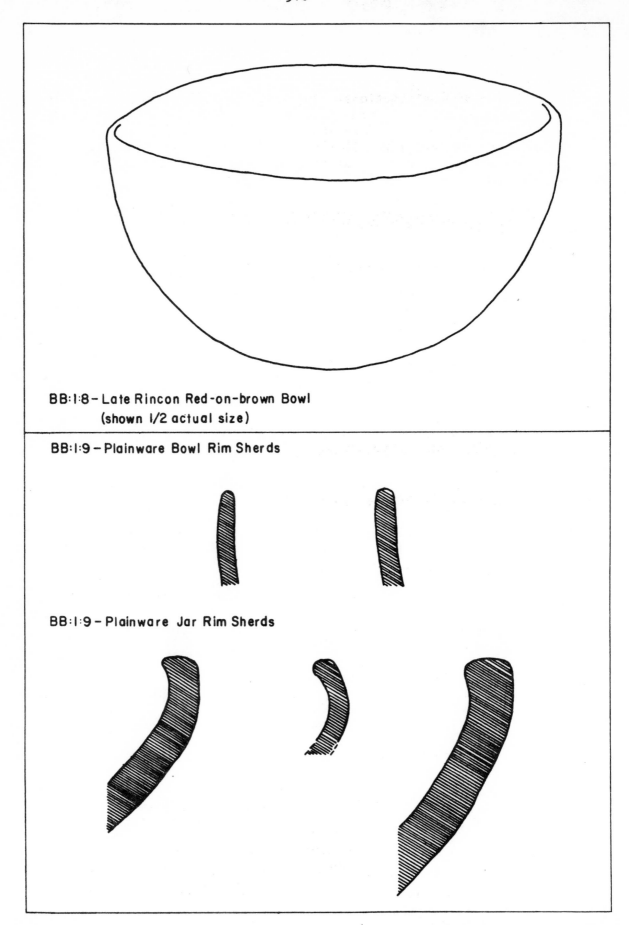

BB:1:8 – Late Rincon Red-on-brown Bowl
(shown 1/2 actual size)

BB:1:9 – Plainware Bowl Rim Sherds

BB:1:9 – Plainware Jar Rim Sherds

Figure 34.   Examples of ceramic vessel and rim forms from AZ BB:1:8 and AZ BB:1:9

sherds when dry and when saturated provides an index of the relative porosity of the sherds. Kinkade and Gilman originally sorted sherds into four categories: quartz-tempered, schist-tempered, interior smudged, and exterior polished. Assuming that porosity estimates for these four kinds of sherds were valid for all sherds of each kind, the present investigator classified jar and bowl rim sherds into one of these four types for each site's sherd collection. The results of statistical tests run on these data were then examined to determine functional attributes.

Population: Lithics

    Subpopulation: Debitage/Flakes (unmodified)

        Sub-subpopulation: Primary decortication flakes - flakes having cortex (weathered surface) on more than 75 percent of their dorsal surfaces. The presence of these flakes is usually indicative of early-stage reduction of lithic raw materials associated with on-site manufacturing or quarrying activities.

        Sub-subpopulation: Secondary decortication flakes - flakes having cortex on 25 to 75 percent of their dorsal surfaces. These flakes are indicative of middle-stage reduction of lithic raw materials.

        Sub-subpopulation: Tertiary decortication flakes - flakes having less than 25 percent cortex on their dorsal surfaces. These flakes are usually indicative of late-stage reduction of lithic raw materials.

        Sub-subpopulation: Thinning flakes or flakes of bifacial retouch - these flakes have no cortex on their dorsal surfaces and are thought to be produced by the thinning or resharpening of bifacial implements. The occurrence of these flakes is associated with tool production and/or tool use.

    The following variables were measured for each of these sub-subpopulations:

        Variable: Counts/Weights - used to determine differences in density, weight, and ratio between one sub-subpopulation and another. This variable is important for establishing the kinds and structure of activities involving the manufacture of chipped stone implements.

        Variable: Length - refers to the maximum dimension perpendicular to the striking platform or proximal end of the flake (see discussion below for importance).

Variable: Width - refers to the maximum dimension perpendicular to the length of the flake as defined above.

Variable: Thickness - refers to maximum thickness at the center of the flake.

Discussion: The metric attributes of length, width, and thickness are important correlates of the size of the raw material from which the flakes were removed. If flakes were being produced for a specific use related to the size of the flake, we would expect to see a relatively low range of variability in the metric attributes associated with any one flake category. If, on the other hand, size was not an important factor, then overall variability would be greater.

Subpopulation: Chunks/Shatter - irregularly shaped (blocky) fragments of stone that are usually by-products of core reduction. Unlike flakes, which exhibit relatively unambiguous dorsal and ventral surfaces, chunks exhibit surfaces that cannot clearly be classified as dorsal or ventral.

Variable: Counts/Weights - used to determine the differential density of these remains across the surface of a site. If chipped stone manufacturing occurred at a site, especially early-stage manufacture, then the incidence of chunks relative to other flake classes should be high.

Subpopulation: Cores - nodules and other relatively large pieces of stone from which flakes are removed (Figure 35).

Variable: Counts/Weights - needed to establish the variation in the frequency and size of different raw materials that are processed at a site, and to establish correlations with the sizes of flakes that would be expected if the cores were reduced at a site.

Variable: Raw material/Geological classification - needed to examine differences within and between sites in the kinds of stone being used. This is directly related to interpreting the procurement behavior involved in the production of chipped stone artifacts.

Variable: Number of flakes removed - the number of flake scars that occur on each core. Variations in the number of flake scars are expected to indicate the intensity of reduction of different kinds of raw materials. This, in turn, allows tentative interpretations concerning the degree to which a given raw material was selected for tool production.

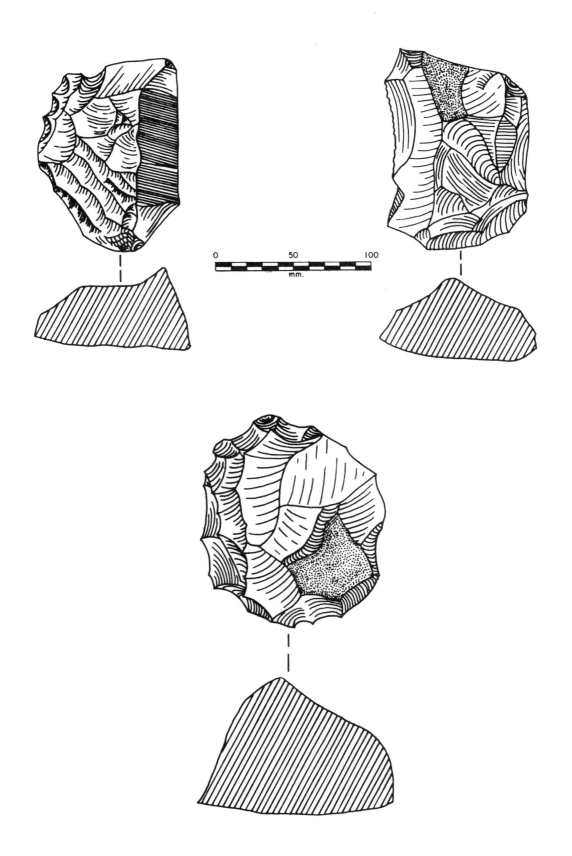

Figure 35. Utilized cores from APS-CS sites in the Southern Desert study area

322

Subpopulation: Modified flakes - primary, secondary, or tertiary
flakes used without any shaping after their removal
from a core. These flakes are usually associated
with rather "extemporaneous" usage (Goodyear 1975)
and are often used and discarded at the same place
where they are produced (Figure 36).

Variables: Length, width, and thickness - measured as described
for unmodified flakes. This information is needed
to determine if there was selection of flakes for
use on the basis of size. If so, then we would expect
that the overall variability among these flakes would
be low when compared with those flakes that are not
utilized.

Variable: Number of used edges - the ratio of used edges to
total edges. This establishes a "use intensity"
coefficient (Schiffer 1976:156) by which differential
use of flakes according to size, raw material, and
so forth can be established.

Variable: Edge length - the length (in centimeters) of an edge
on which use-wear attributes appear. This is measured
for each of the edges that have been used on any one
artifact. From a behavioral standpoint, if there is
great variability among edge lengths, then there is a
greater probability that there was a wider range of
different-sized materials being worked at a site.

Variable: Edge angle - the angle formed between the ventral
surface of a flake and the face of the edge that has
been used (Wilmsen 1968). Ethnoarchaeological and
experimental research has demonstrated that chipped
stone implements with different edge angles are
used for different tasks (Tringham and others 1974;
White and Thomas 1972; Gould, Koster, and Sontz 1971).
Generally speaking, implements with acute edge angles
are used for cutting/slicing, while implements with
more obtuse edge angles are used for scraping.

Variable: Edge shape - is based on a four-way nominally scaled
classification of edge shapes according to the following format: straight, concave, convex, and irregular edges. Significant correlations have been
found between specific edge shapes, edge angles, and
overall flake size. These aid in interpretations
of tool function.

a-c: utilized flakes
d: projectile point
e-f: serrated tools
g: double-spur graver

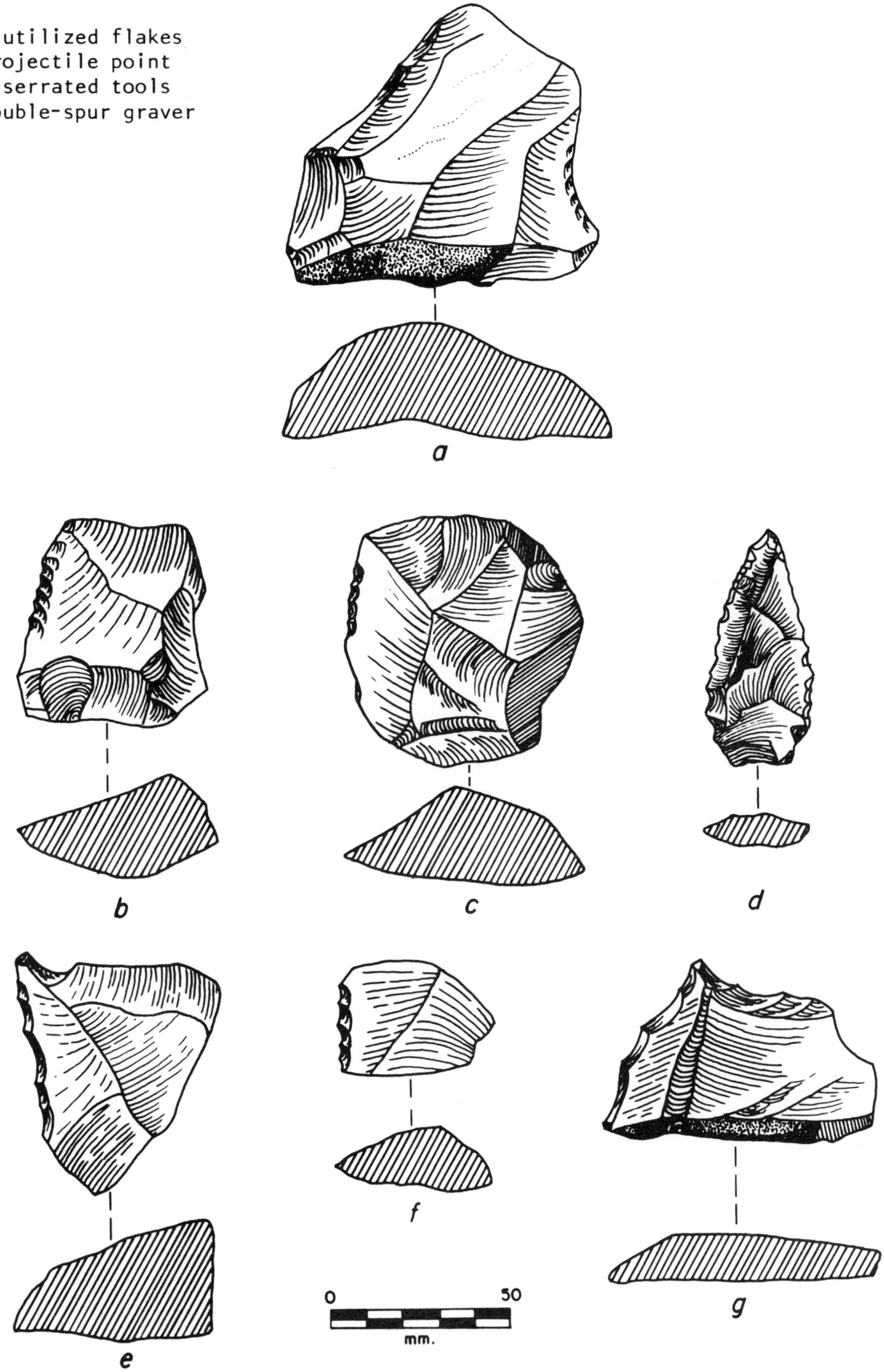

Figure 36.   Flake tools from APS-CS sites in the Southern Desert study area

Subpopulation: Formal Tools - (projectile points, end-scrapers, gravers) are conspicuous by their absence at most of the sites in the APS-CS corridor. The most common classes of formal tools are --in order of frequency--projectile points,denticulates, and serrated tools. Because of the low numbers of these artifacts, detailed discussions will not be presented; only counts will be provided.

Several hypotheses were developed in order to test for variation within the chipped stone assemblage at each site. The first series of hypotheses is related to the procurement of stone and the process of manufacturing stone implements that occurred at the sites. The second series of hypotheses is related to the use of stone tools. These two sets of hypotheses are described below.

Procurement of Stone

Hypothesis 1: If indigenous stone resources were being utilized at the site, then expect

Test Implication 1: cores to consist mostly of stone that occurs in the immediate vicinity of the site (for example, andesite, quartzite, rhyolite, and so forth).

Test Implication 2: do not expect cores of materials such as chert, obsidian, and other nonlocal stone.

Hypothesis 2: If certain kinds of stone were being deliberately selected for by the occupants of the site, expect

Test Implication 1: a highly nonrandom distribution of certain kinds of stone.

Test Implication 2: more intensive utilization of the selected material.

All four of the implications associated with these two hypotheses can be examined using a single statistical test, the Kolmogorov-Smirnov One-Sample Test for Significant Differences. Cores are used in testing these propositions, since it proved easier to identify larger pieces of stone than a large sample of flakes. Thus, this test is based on the assumption that cores and flakes from the sites tend to mirror one another in terms of the kinds and relative frequencies of stone that are present.

A third series of hypotheses concerns the mode of manufacture of stone. The test implications are drawn from the results of testing the previous two hypotheses.

Mode of Manufacture

Hypothesis 1: If core reduction occurred at the site, expect

Test Implication 1: a low core to other flake ratio.
Test Implication 2: a high core to chunk/shatter ratio.
Test Implication 3: a low primary flake to tertiary flake ratio.
Test Implication 4: a moderate secondary flake to tertiary flake ratio.

Hypothesis 2: If the reduction of primary flakes was the major mode of manufacture, expect

Test Implication 1: a high core to primary flake ratio.
Test Implication 2: a high secondary flake to primary flake ratio.
Test Implication 3: a high tertiary flake to primary flake ratio.
Test Implication 4: a low chunk/shatter to core ratio.

Hypothesis 3: If the manufacture of formal tools occurred at the site, expect

Test Implication 1: a relatively high formal tool to other flake ratio.
Test Implication 2: a high tertiary flake to other flake ratio.
Test Implication 3: a high flake with bifacial retouch to other flake ratio.

Several hypotheses to determine the function of the chipped stone tools were also developed.

Use of Unmodified Flakes

Hypothesis 1: If the use of stone implements focused on relatively unmodified flakes, expect

Test Implication 1: a high ratio of utilized flakes to formal tools.
Test Implication 2: a low ratio of retouched flakes to other flakes.

Hypothesis 2: If flakes were used for similar tasks and exhibit little functional variation, expect

Test Implication 1: little variability in the intensity of use as evidenced by the relative proportion of edges used on each implement.

326

Test Implication 2: little variability in edge angles.
Test Implication 3: little variability in the length of used edges.
Test Implication 4: little variability in the overall dimensions of implements.

Population: Ground stone implements (Figure 37).

Subpopulation: Manos

Subpopulation: Metates

Variable: Length, width, and thickness - because most of the ground stone implements from these sites are fragmentary, dimension measurements are not useful.

Variable: Grain size - a nominally scaled variable referring to the relative coarseness of the material out of which manos or metates were made. Grain size may be related to the kinds of materials that are processed with these implements. This variable was recorded according to one of three classifications (fine, medium, and coarse), using a reference set of ground stone implements selected from the sites.

Variable: Surface configuration of grinding facets--a nominally scaled variable. Manos were classified into those with flat or convex surfaces, while metates were classified into basin, slab, and trough-shaped varieties.

Functional interpretations of ground stone can be found in the archaeological literature. It has been suggested that fine-grained stone is more suitable for the processing of small seeds, while more coarsely grained stone is better suited for processing large seeds or kernels such as corn (Sayles and others n.d.). It has been further suggested that there is a shift from slab and basin metates to trough-shaped metates following the introduction of corn into prehistoric subsistence economies (Sayles and others n.d.). Given these presumed functional differences between ground stone tool forms, the first hypothesis relating to ground stone used at a site may be stated as follows:

Hypothesis 1: If small items such as grass and cacti seeds were being processed at the site, expect

Test Implication 1: a preponderance of medium to fine-grained manos and metates at the site.
Test Implication 2: a preponderance of slab and/or basin-shaped metates.

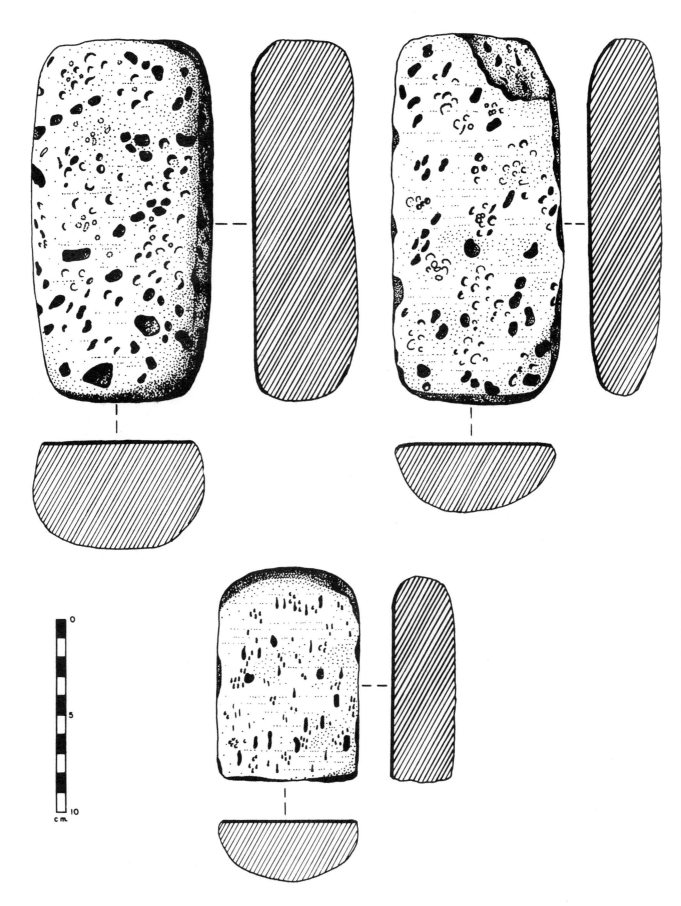

Figure 37. Ground stone artifacts from APS-CS sites in the Southern Desert study area

Population: Features

    Subpopulation: Structures

    Subpopulation: Rock piles

    Subpopulation: Unknown other

        Variable: Area - measures of length and width were made to assess variability in the size of features, in that size might be related to function.

        Variable: Presence of upright slabs - often associated with ramada-like structures throughout much of the southwestern Arizona desert (Doyel 1977; Goodyear and Dittert 1973). This variable is recorded as present or absent.

        Variable: Wall fall - the absence of wall fall is also associated with ramada-like structures. As with upright slabs, wall fall is recorded as present or absent.

Since none of the features at the investigated sites was excavated (although one was tested), data are lacking regarding the subsurface nature of these features. Some could be shallow, ramada-like structures. Doyel (1977:113), in discussing a probable protohistoric Pima site in the upper Santa Cruz Basin, described a series of ramada-like structures in the following manner:

> They were oval in plan...and were outlined by cobbles. ...In most structures, many of the wall stones were placed vertically into either individual holes or in trenches....so that they [occasionally] abutted one another to form a line...other stones appear to have been simply placed along the wall on the ground surface.... The floors...[evidenced] no prepared surfaces.

Doyel further indicates that wall fall is seldom associated with these structures. Goodyear and Dittert (1973:26) have indicated that recent historic Papago ramadas tend to have few artifacts within the confines of the ramada, while Doelle (1976) has implied that a large number of activity areas occur peripheral to contemporary Papago ramadas.

These descriptions lead to the following hypothesis regarding the possible function of the structural features recorded at the sites:

    Hypothesis 1: If the features at a site are ramada-like structures, then expect

    Test Implication 1: cobble alignments to predominate with an absence of wall fall/coursed walls.

Test Implication 2:   a high incidence of upright stone slabs
around the perimeter of the structure.

Test Implication 3:   floors with no prepared surfaces.

Intrasite Activity Structure

Interpretations of activities performed at a particular site are
possible depending on the kinds of associations exhibited among various
artifact classes at that site. Such interpretations are predicated,
however, upon an understanding of the relationship between the depositional context in which the archaeologist finds artifacts and the dynamics of the prehistoric cultural system that led to the deposition of those artifacts
(Schiffer 1976). It is no longer possible to assume a one-to-one relationship between these two sets of phenomena. Accordingly, it becomes necessary
for archaeologists to attempt to model site formation processes in order to
delineate the relationship between archaeological depositional contexts
and past behavioral contexts.

One of the primary difficulties facing archaeologists is that of
determining whether archaeological remains are deposited at their loci
of use or, alternatively, whether remains were gathered together and
deposited at some place other than where they were used. The former
situation produces what has been termed primary refuse, while the latter
produces secondary refuse (Schiffer 1976:30). The important distinction
is that the spatial relations between two or more artifacts that may have
been used in the performance of a given activity have a greater likelihood
of being preserved in primary refuse. The formation of secondary refuse
through the process   of removing artifacts from their use loci effectively
destroys these spatial relationships and as a result is not as useful for
reconstructing activity structure at a site. Below is a series of tests
of hypotheses regarding the kinds of depositional processes that occurred
at the sites during and subsequent to the period of their occupation.

Hypothesis 1: If the remains at a site consist of primary refuse,
expect

Test Implication 1:   clusters of refuse corresponding to use
areas.

Test Implication 2:   a high degree of redundancy in terms of
the kinds of artifacts found in each use
area.

Test Implication 3:   on the basis of ethnographic analogy
(DeBoer and Lathrap n.d.), sherds to
be of relatively small size due to
repeated trampling.

Test Implication 4:   assuming that trampling occurs at equal
                      intensities in each use area, a low
                      amount of variability in sherd size
                      (by weight).

The first implication requires that clusters of artifacts correspond to use areas at a site. The complicating factor, however, is that clusters can also occur as a result of the localized dumping of trash into secondary refuse deposits. As a result, the occurrence of clusters by itself does not necessarily provide a good discriminating variable between the presence of primary or secondary refuse. Examination of the coefficients of variation among collection units with respect to certain artifact classes aids in determining the degree of clustering. For example, a high coefficient of variation would indicate a high degree of clustering.

The second implication calls for a high degree of redundancy among collection units in terms of the kinds, not density, of artifacts that are found. Assuming that the site contains multiple overlapping primary refuse areas, it is expected that there will be few differences among collection units in terms of the kinds of artifacts that are found. The measure of redundancy can be expressed as follows:

$$\text{Redundancy} = \frac{\text{Sum of the number of units x number of artifact classes in each unit}}{\text{Total number of units x total number of classes}}$$

If it is assumed that the deposits at a site consist of multiple overlapping primary refuse areas, and that all of the activities which occurred in these areas are the same, the expected result would be complete redundancy. If, on the other hand, a site consists of a series of discrete trash areas, it is expected that the redundancy ratio will vary depending on the number of trash areas encountered relative to the total number of collection units that are taken from the site. It is reasonable to expect that as refuse disposal becomes more localized (that is, as secondary refuse begins to predominate), the relative probability of a single collection unit intersecting that trash area will decrease and the probability of intersecting nontrash areas will increase. This follows the statistical notion that there is a direct relationship between the frequency of occurrence of a given item and the probability of encountering that item. Once a trash area was encountered or intersected by a collection unit, the probability of encountering additional trash areas would decrease. Consequently, it is expected that, while trash units may be exptected to contain all of the kinds of artifact populations that occur at a site, the frequency of such trash areas in a sample from a site would be relatively low. Furthermore, there would be a concomitantly greater incidence of collection units containing only a few artifact populations. Thus, in a general sense, the redundancy ratio would be lower. The remaining alternative is that of a situation in which a site consists of multiple nonoverlapping primary refuse areas in which none of the activities are the same.

The third implication is that, if archaeological deposits consist of primary refuse and these deposits have been subject to repeated trampling,there should be relatively small sherd sizes. This inference is based on ethnographic analogy from a study by DeBoer and Lathrap (n.d.) of Shipibo ceramic manufacture, use, and discard behavior. Summarizing their results, they found that those areas in which sherds were deposited as primary refuse were subjected to repeated trampling. This continued trampling tended, over the long run, to result in the reduction of sherds in main activity areas to small sizes.

The last implication is that, if sherds are deposited at their loci of use, and if each of these loci are subject to the same degree of trampling, there should be a low coefficient of variation in sherd size (DeBoer and Lathrap n.d.). Again, these investigators found that those sherds that were removed from their loci of use and redeposited in another area as secondary refuse were subject to less trampling and thus tended to be of larger size. It follows logically that if trampling is differentially distributed in primary and secondary refuse deposits, there should be a greater degree of variation in sherd size over the site as a whole, and mean sherd sizes should be somewhat greater than what would be found in equally trampled primary refuse deposits. These observations cannot, however, be applied without reservation to material in archaeological contexts, particularly those associated with long-term postoccupational exposure on the surface.

Site Descriptions and Results of Analysis

AZ BB:1:8

Very little information is available for this site. AZ BB:1:8 was recorded by the original 1974 survey as consisting of a sparse plain-ware sherd scatter and two vesicular basalt cobble concentrations. One concentration is a small circular arrangement of cobbles with a depressed center. The second is a larger (4 m-diameter) concentration from which several rocks had been removed to stabilize an APS survey marker.

Heavy ground cover and lack of time prevented mapping and surface sampling of the site. A "grab" sample of sherds and lithics was collected, but no information can be found for this collection. One of the cobble concentrations was tested by excavating a 1 m by 6 m north-south trench inside the feature and parallel to its east wall. At a depth 10 to 10.5 cm below the surface, several whole and partial vessels were encountered, representing four jars, three bowls, and one ceramic scoop. The feature floor was defined at a depth of 20 to 25 cm. The feature appears to be a single ramada-like structure with a cobble perimeter and a shallow unprepared floor. The several vessels found within the trench may be <u>de facto</u> refuse, which has been described by Schiffer (1976:33) as "the tools, facilities, and other cultural materials that, although still usable, are abandoned with an activity area."

The ceramics from this test trench indicate an occupation during the Santa Cruz-Sacaton phases of the Hohokam late Colonial-early Sedentary periods (around A.D. 900-1100).

In November 1976, the site was revisited during an access road survey, and additional features were discovered on the ridge immediately southeast of the site, outside the transmission line corridor. These features consist of 16 cobble alignments and cobble concentrations in a dispersed east-west pattern across the ridge top. A jeep trail runs east-west through the long axis of the site but does not appear to have disturbed any of the remains. The sketch map indicates that many of the features are rectilinear and U-shaped cobble alignments suggestive of architectural structures; some may represent terraces. At any rate, little can be said about the function of these features and about site activities at AZ BB:1:8.

AZ BB:1:9

Surface indications at AZ BB:1:9 consist of a scatter of sherd, lithic, and ground stone items associated with terraces, contiguous room blocks, and isolated cobble alignments possibly indicative of other structures. APS Tower 616 is on the site, which is bisected by an east-west access road. Data recovery at this site consisted of surface collection and mapping of artifacts and features. No sub-surface testing was undertaken.

The site measures approximately 11,200 square meters in area. A 10-percent simple random sample of the total site area resulted in the collection of eleven 10 m by 10 m units. All sherds and lithics within each of these units were collected but not mapped individually. The resultant sample of artifact populations from this site is small, due in part to the low sample fraction that was collected and in part to the low overall surface density of artifacts. The mean surface density for both sherds and lithics--the most common artifact popula-tions--is 1.09 items per square meter. All of the artifacts collected were analyzed.

Most of the sherds are of a sand-tempered, brown plainware, and could not be assigned to recognized ceramic types, although they appear to fall somewhere between late Hohokam and early Salado varieties as defined in the Gila and San Pedro basins. No decorated Hohokam sherds were recovered and the lack of corrugated wares tends to indicate that the occupation does not contain a Salado component. Thus, the cultural affiliation of the occupation of AZ BB:1:9 is ambiguous. The site characteristics and entire artifact collection suggest a date between A.D. 1150-1350.

Ceramic Population: Characteristics and Functional Interpretations

The ceramic assemblage from AZ BB:1:9 consists primarily of plainwares. Sherds were relatively scarce over most of the site, averaging one sherd per square meter, with a 103-percent coefficient of variation in sherd density (by count) among collection units. This high degree of variation among collection units indicates spatial clustering in ceramic distributions over portions of the site. Similarly, the average weight of sherds is about 3.6 grams, with a coefficient of variation of 23 percent. This indicates that, in general, sherds tend toward a consistent size in terms of weight. These two factors, small sherd size and low density, made it difficult to estimate the relative proportions of different vessel forms at AZ BB:1:9. Assuming that narrow-orifice vessels are jars and wide-orifice vessels are bowls (Shepard 1956:125-130), rim sherds were analyzed to determine the relative proportions of these two generalized vessel forms. Of the 30 rim sherds recovered from the site, 14 were from jars and 16 from bowls. Measurement of orifice diameters was possible on only 14 of the 30 rim sherds. Variations in orifice diameters between jars and bowls are shown in Table 58.

Table 58. Metric attributes of jar and bowl orifice diameters from AZ BB:1:9

Item	N	Mean	Standard deviation	Sample range	CV*	95% CI**
Jars	7	18.85 cm	3.80 cm	15.05-22.65 cm	20.2%	±5.05 cm
Bowls	7	22.43 cm	6.32 cm	16.11-28.75 cm	28.2%	±2.39 cm

* Coefficient of variation
** CI - Confidence interval of the population mean

These data indicate that while the sample means for orifice diameters of jars and bowls do not appear to be significantly different, the relatively large 95-percent confidence intervals about the means of jar and bowl orifices show that there may be differences in orifices that cannot be detected based on the sample of rim sherds obtained at AZ BB:1:9.

As regards the frequencies of various orifice sizes in jars and bowls, jars exhibit a unimodal frequency distribution, with more than half of the jar rims falling within the range of 15 to 20 cm in diameter. Bowls, on the other hand, exhibit a bimodal frequency distribution, with more than half of the bowls falling equally within the ranges of 15 to 20 cm and 26 to 30 cm in diameter.

The functional analysis of the plainware pottery was conducted in accordance with the hypotheses and test implications presented earlier. The jar and bowl rim sherds were classified into four groups on the basis of temper and surface treatment attributes, as shown in Table 59.

Table 59. Cross-classification of jar and bowl rim sherds from AZ BB:1:9 by temper and surface treatment

	Jars	Bowls	Mean gram weight increase
Quartz-tempered	10	3	1.24 grams
Schist-tempered	1	4	1.29 grams
Interior smudged	1	7	.51 grams
Exterior polished	2	1	.74 grams
Total	14	Total 15 with 1 indeterminate	

The first test implication is that jars tend, on the whole, to be more porous than bowls. The use of the Fischer's exact test to examine this implication is dictated by the small sample size. The results of this comparison are indicated below.

Table 60. Fischer's exact test of rim sherds from AZ BB:1:9

	Jars	Bowls	Totals
More porous (quartz, schist)	11	7	18
Less porous (smudged, polished)	3	8	11
Total	14	15	29

This assessment of the first implication indicates that there are less than seven chances in one hundred that the jar and bowl samples were drawn from the same population with regard to porosity. While this result does not fall within generally accepted levels of significant differences, it nonetheless suggests a strong trend toward more porous jars and less porous bowls at AZ BB:1:9. This trend might be statistically demonstrated as significant if a larger sample were available. Consequently, the first implication will be considered partially confirmed for this study.

The second implication is that if jars were used for storage and bowls were used more often for cooking (all other things being equal), bowls should exhibit a greater frequency of soot deposition on their exteriors. This implication could not be tested due to the fact that natural erosion had altered sherd surfaces.

The third implication is that if bowls are used more for cooking and serving, they are handled more than storage jars and may be expected to have a higher rate of breakage and discard. One alternative to the third implication is that both storage and cooking/serving vessels were subject to varying degrees of handling and movement, although the breakage rate for cooking/serving vessels would still be greater than that for storage vessels. If the storage vessels at AZ BB:1:9 were for all purposes nonportable, then their breakage rate would be very low, in which case, the expected jar:bowl ratio would be very low. If, on the other hand, storage vessels were relatively portable, then their breakage rate would be somewhat higher and the expected jar:bowl ratio would be higher. Since the jar:bowl ratio at AZ BB:1:9 is 14:16, or 0.88, the latter alternative seems more plausible.

To briefly summarize, two confirmed implications, those regarding porosity and breakage/discard rates, indicate that jars were probably used for liquid storage and were less portable than bowls. Furthermore, jars were more portable than so-called "permanent" storage vessels. Bowls, on the other hand, appear to have been less suitable for liquid storage and exhibit breakage patterns indicating somewhat higher "portability".

Lithic Population: Characteristics and Functional Interpretations

Procurement of Raw Materials. The lithic data from AZ BB:1:9 were examined to determine the significance of observed variables. The first major hypothesis concerned raw material procurement (Table 61).

Table 61. Number of cores of various raw materials at AZ BB:1:9

Raw material	Number of Cores
Quartz	4
Quartzite	4
Basalt	1
Andesite	1
Diorite	1
Total	11

All of the cores from AZ BB:1:9 are of stones that are immediately available in the site vicinity; artifacts made from nonlocal stones such as chert and obsidian are absent. Consequently the first hypothesis regarding raw material procurement, that raw material procurement focused on indigenous raw materials, is confirmed. The second hypothesis, that there is a non-random distribution of kinds of stone that reflects deliberate selection of certain stone types, cannot be statistically tested using the cores from the site, given the small size of the available sample. However, if one includes quartz and quartzite cores within one category and cores of other igneous stones within a second, the data suggest a certain emphasis on quartz and quartzite for lithic manufacture at AZ BB:1:9.

The second index of the intensity of core reduction with respect to a particular raw material is the ratio of the number of flakes removed from a core to core size. The table below reflects an attempt to measure intensity of core reduction by means of a ratio of the average number of flake scars per core to average core size. Admittedly, the number of flake scars visible on a discarded core does not necessarily accurately represent the total number of flakes removed. Therefore, this is not a particularly strong basis for inferences regarding intensity of core reduction. Nevertheless, the calculations below may at least suggest some trends within these data. According to these calculations, the ratio of average number of flake scars per core to average core weight seems to suggest a high degree of variablility at AZ BB:1:9.

Table 62. Relationships between core size and number of flake scars per core from AZ BB:1:9

Raw material	N	Mean core size	Standard deviation	Mean number of flake scars per core	Standard deviation	Ratio
Quartzite	4	98.5125 cc	41.384	8.25	.96	.0837
Quartz	4	407.575 cc	250.489	7.25	1.89	.0178
Basalt	1	N/A	---	---	---	.0281
Diorite	1	N/A	---	---	---	.0092
Andesite	1	N/A	---	---	---	.0110

These data indicate that quartzite cores are more highly reduced, thus confirming the second implication that raw material procurement for lithic manufacture was selective.

Mode of Manufacture. The second major hypothesis to be tested concerns the mode of lithic manufacture at AZ BB:1:9. Table 63 below shows the comparative ratio of artifact classes that were used in relation to the implications described earlier.

Table 63. Ratios of lithic artifact classes from AZ BB:1:9

	Ratio	Test results
Primary flake reduction		
Cores: Primary flakes	11:4 (2.75)	Confirmed
Secondary flakes: Primary flakes	20:4 (5.00)	Confirmed
Tertiary flakes: Primary flakes	15:4 (3.75)	Confirmed
Chunks/shatter: Cores	3:11 (0.273)	Not confirmed
Tool manufacture		
Formal tools: Other flakes	1:39 (0.026)	Not confirmed
Tertiary flakes: Other flakes	15:24 (0.625)	Not confirmed

Given the rather small size of the lithic sample, the test results nonetheless seem to confirm the hypothesis that the reduction of primary flakes was the primary mode of manufacture at AZ BB:1:9. This leads to the conclusion that there is a very high probability that flake reduction occurred at the site. The ratios of formal tools and tertiary flakes to other flakes is low; thus, the hypothesis that formal tools weremanufactured at the site must be rejected.

Summarizing the foregoing tests and observations, the lithic data from AZ BB:1:9 seem to indicate a relatively strong emphasis on the procurement of locally available quartzite and quartz. The primary mode of manufacture appears to have been flake (as opposed to core) reduction. Furthermore, flake production seems to have been directed toward the manufacture of flakes suitable for use with only a limited amount of modification.

Use of Unmodified Flakes. The third major hypothesis concerns the use of unmodified flakes to perform tasks. It has already been demonstrated that the intensive production of formal tools at AZ BB:1:9 is highly unlikely. Since the ratio of utilized flakes to formal tools is 9:1, and the ratio of flakes with bifacial retouch to other flakes is 0:39 (0), it seems likely that the inhabitants of AZ BB:1:9 predominantly used implements with relatively little formal shaping.

Utilized flakes at the site consist almost entirely of secondary and tertiary flakes. It was originally expected that secondary and tertiary flakes might have been used for two different purposes, and the analysis proceeded by segregating utilized flakes into these two categories. Data relevant to the first implication, that there is little variability in the intensity of flake use, were not statistically tested due to the small size of the available sample. However, the examination and comparison of these flakes revealed no apparent differences between secondary and tertiary utilized flakes with regard to the intensity with which their edges were used; thus, the first implication is here considered confirmed.

Data relevant to the second implication, that there would be few differences in the variability of edge angles associated with utilized flakes, likewise were too few to warrant statistical testing. Figure 38 indicates the frequency distribution of edge angles on secondary and tertiary flakes; given the small size of the sample, this figure nonetheless suggests a significant difference between the edge angles of secondary and tertiary flakes. Thus, the second implication is considered here as rejected.

Although the small sample size did not warrant the use of statistical tests in evaluating the third implication (that the amount of edge used on secondary and tertiary flakes is not significantly different), an examination of Figure 39, which illustrates the frequency distribution of utilized flake edge lengths from AZ BB:1:9, indicates that there seems to be no such difference. Accordingly, this implication can be considered confirmed.

Data relevant to the fourth implication, that the overall dimensions of utilized flakes are basically the same, are illustrated in Figure 40, which plots mean flake widths and lengths plus and minus one standard deviation to illustrate overlaps in the dimensions of secondary and tertiary utilized flakes. Given the small size of the sample, this figure indicates that secondary and tertiary flakes exhibit the same basic variability with regard to lengths and widths. These artifacts also seem to exhibit no significant differences among themselves in terms of thicknesses. Thus, on the basis of the available data, the fourth implication would seem to be at least tentatively confirmed.

The last implication is that, assuming there are no significant differences among utilized flakes with respect to intensity of use, edge angles, edge lengths, or overall dimensions, there should also be no differences with regard to edge shape. The data relevant to this implication are shown in Table 64.

Table 64. Summary of edge configurations of secondary and tertiary utilized flakes from AZ BB:1:9

	Secondary	Tertiary
Straight	2	2
Concave	1	0
Convex	1	4
Concavo-convex	2	1
Totals	6	7

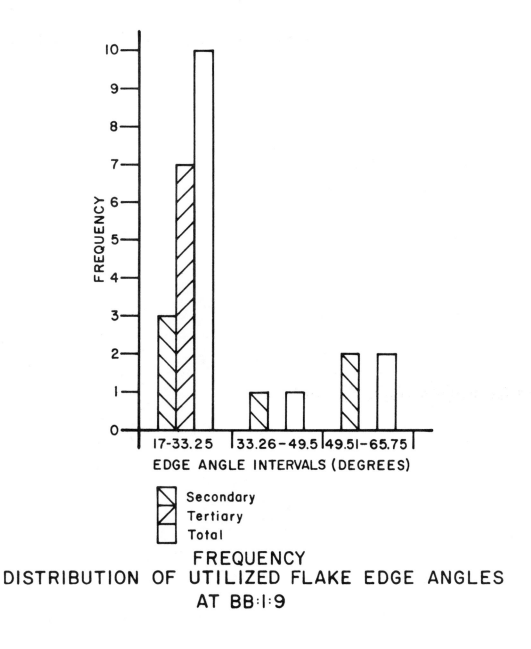

FREQUENCY
DISTRIBUTION OF UTILIZED FLAKE EDGE ANGLES
AT BB:1:9

Figure 38

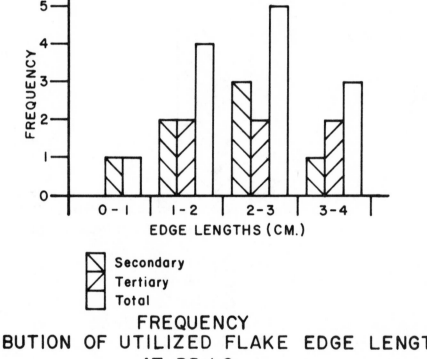

FREQUENCY
DISTRIBUTION OF UTILIZED FLAKE EDGE LENGTHS
AT BB:1:9

Figure 39

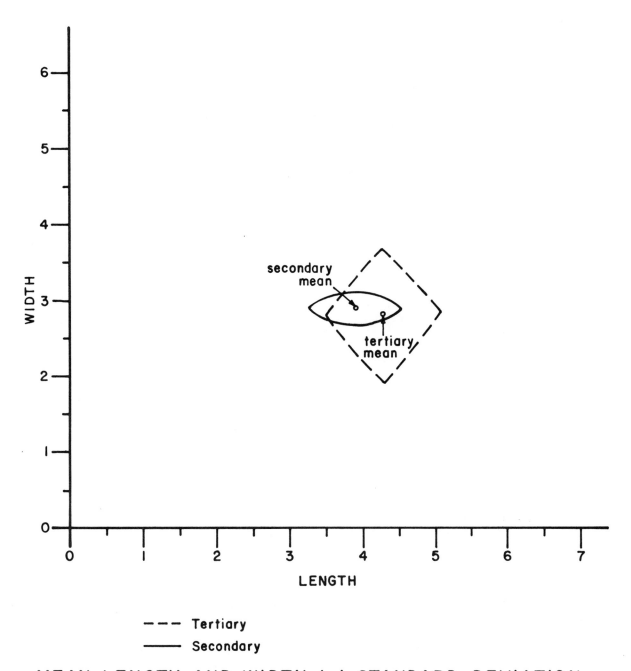

WIDTH

secondary
mean

tertiary
mean

LENGTH

- - - Tertiary
——— Secondary

MEAN LENGTH AND WIDTH ± I STANDARD DEVIATION
OF UTILIZED FLAKES
AT BB·I·9

Figure 40

While it is impossible to assess statistically the probabilities associated with this distribution, it is evident that there is a slight tendency for tertiary utilized flakes to exhibit convex edges. However, this distribution is not considerably different from what would be expected under purely random conditions. Provisionally, then, the implication that there is little variability in edge shape among all utilized flakes will be accepted.

To briefly summarize the results of tests regarding the use of unmodified flakes as implements, it has been demonstrated that formal tools such as projectile points, end scrapers, gravers, and so forth were probably not produced at AZ BB:1:9. Instead, the bulk of the lithic tool assemblage at the site consists of relatively unmodified flakes. These utilized secondary and tertiary flakes exhibit few significant differences in intensity of use, edge angles, overall dimensions, amount of edge modified by use, and, lastly, in the edge configurations associated with these implements. The relatively acute edge angles observed on these tools have been interpreted by some researchers as indicative of a "cutting-slicing" action (Tringham and others 1974). The last remaining test concerns the materials that might have been processed with these rather generalized implements. In the absence of any data informing on the procurement, processing, consumption, and discard of artifact and bone material related to hunting activities at AZ BB:1:9, the most plausible inference is that these utilized flakes were involved in processing the fleshy portions of plants or small game animals. The edge damage observed on these implements tends toward what has been called "nibbling" (Goodyear 1975) and has been experimentally produced by processing rabbits (Wyant and Bayham 1976). Scalar and step fractures usually associated with the processing of tougher, more resistant materials such as wood and bone are not evident in the sample of utilized flakes from the site.

Ground Stone Population: Characteristics and Functional Interpretations

The few ground stone artifacts recovered from AZ BB:1:9 include one rhyolite slab metate and one biconvex basalt mano. Subsequent investigations revealed that a few additional ground stone fragments were present at the site; these, however, were not collected. The two artifacts noted above do not warrant extended consideration here.

Feature Population: Characteristics and Functional Interpretations

The features at AZ BB:1:9 are difficult to interpret since none of them were tested or excavated to determine their true function. Most of them are best described as single-course rock alignments. Five consist of L-shaped cobble alignments, and two of three walls forming an open-ended U-shape; one is rectilinear. These eight features could represent habitation or storage rooms. None of them contained upright slabs, but rather were constructed of rows of cobbles and angular fragments. Two features are single lines of rocks forming a total of five alignments. They are situated in cleared areas on the east side of the ridge on which the site is located. From surface observations, it might be inferred that these cleared areas were agricultural or horticultural plots. The "terraces" are situated on ridge slopes, and some cleared areas are bordered by bedrock outcrops. These features would have allowed soil and water retention either for small farm plots or to enhance moisture requirements for natural vegetation.

In order to test hypotheses concerning the function of these features (as outlined earlier), the frequency of measurable structures by size is shown below.

Table 65. Frequency of structural features at AZ BB:1:9 by size

Size Intervals	Frequency
Less than 5 m^2	3
6 - 10 m^2	1
11 - 20 m^2	1
Greater than 21 m^2	1

The frequency of structures by size does not appear to deviate significantly from what would be expected under chance conditions. Consequently, there does not appear to be an emphasis on structures of a specific size at AZ BB:1:9. While the larger structures probably represent residential units, the function of the smaller structures is as yet uncertain.

Intrasite Activity Structure at AZ BB:1:9

In order to derive a functional interpretation of this site, the data were examined in accordance with the test hypotheses outlined earlier to determine if the cultural deposits reflect primary refuse.

The first implication requires that clusters of artifacts correspond to use areas at a site. The coefficients of variation among the relative densities of artifacts from collection units at AZ BB:1:9 are: ceramics, 98.3 percent; debitage, 111.8 percent; utilized flakes, 70.7 percent; and ground stone, 300.0 percent. These values tend to indicate a high degree of clustering, thus confirming the first implication.

The second implication calls for a high degree of redundancy among collection units in terms of the kinds of artifacts recovered from them. Applying the formula for redundancy described earlier, at AZ BB:1:9 there is one unit with one artifact class, five units with two artifact classes, and five units with three artifact classes. The ratio is therefore

$$\text{Redundancy} = \frac{(1 \times 1)+(5 \times 2)+(5 \times 3)}{(11+3)} = \frac{26}{33} = .7879$$

indicating high redundancy. Thus, the second implication is confirmed.

The third implication calls for relatively small sherd sizes. Since the mean sherd size (by weight) at the site is 3.6 grams, this implication tends to be confirmed.

The last implication is that if sherds are deposited at their loci of use and are subject to the same degree of trampling, there should be a low coefficient of variation in sherd size. Since the coefficient of variation in sherd size among collection units is 23 percent, it appears that sherds were trampled to the same degree; thus, the probability of primary refuse deposition is greater.

Because all of the four test implications associated with the proposition that primary refuse deposits occur at AZ BB:1:9 have been confirmed, it will be argued that the bulk of deposits at the site consists of primary refuse and, consequently, that behaviorally significant spatial relationships among various artifact populations have been preserved.

The reconstruction of activity areas on the basis of the spatial association of different artifact populations is still a somewhat novel undertaking in archaeology. As other researchers have indicated, the different methods currently available, including nearest-neighbor analysis and dimensional analysis of variance (Whallon 1973, 1974), are not without their problems. For example, nearest-neighbor analysis requires that the location of all artifacts be recorded in two-dimensional space. Similarly, dimensional analysis of variance requires that large contiguous areas of a site be collected. Because the artifacts were recorded by collection unit and the site not collected in contiguous blocks, these two approaches are not applicable at AZ BB:1:9. The only alternative available, then, is to assume that each artifact population has an equal chance of occurring in each collection unit on the surface of a site, and to assess the magnitude of deviations from this theoretical random distribution.

Hypothesis: If jars and bowls were jointly used in the performance of a given activity, and if these two vessel forms were deposited at their loci of use, then expect a high spatial correlation between the occurrences of jars and bowls.

Of the seven collection units that contained identifiable jar and bowl rims at AZ BB:1:9, six contained both jars and bowls. Thus, the hypothesis that jars and bowls were jointly used is confirmed. Furthermore, the occurrences of jars and bowls are not spatially correlated with the occurrence of utilized flakes (Fischer's p = .4762 and .381, respectively), nor are jars and bowls spatially coincident with cores (Fischer's p = .833 and .429, respectively). Thus, it seems possible to define a spatially distinct ceramic "tool kit" involving the joint usage of jars and bowls at AZ BB:1:9.

AZ BB:1:10

Surface indications at AZ BB:1:10 consist of a scatter of sherds, lithics, and ground stone artifacts associated with a series of non-contiguous rooms. The site is located immediately south of APS Tower 616 on the same ridge system as AZ BB:1:9. The site is not directly impacted by APS tower pad construction, although the access road to the tower crosses the western margin of the site. Data recovery at the site consisted of surface collections; no subsurface excavations were undertaken.

The total site area incorporates about 30,800 square meters. A 10-percent stratified random sample of the area resulted in the collection of thirty 10 m by 10 m units. All of the sherds, lithics, and ground stone within these units were collected but not mapped. As at the adjacent site, AZ BB:1:9, the surface density of archaeological remains at AZ BB:1:10 is low. All of the artifacts collected from the site were analyzed.

The plainware sherds from AZ BB:1:10 exhibit a higher degree of variability in temper and surface treatment than do the sherds from AZ BB:1:9. There is noticeably more mica, phyllite, and quartz temper (in varying proportions), with a higher frequency of mica-tempered varieties. The plainwares resemble those which occur during the Hohokam Classic Period occupation at Escalante Ruin (Doyel 1974:55, 74, 140), although most of the sherds from AZ BB:1:10 could not be identified with traditional ceramic types. The presence of a red corrugated variety at the site indicates a post-A.D. 1150 occupation that may have extended to about A.D. 1250. Masse's research at the Alder Wash Ruin in the San Pedro Basin indicates that corrugated ceramics occur in significant numbers during the period A.D. 1150-1250 (personal communication).

Ceramic Population: Characteristics and Functional Interpretations

The ceramic assemblage from AZ BB:1:10, like that from AZ BB:1:9, consists mostly of plainwares. There is an average of 0.49 sherds per square meter with a coefficient of variation among collection units of 97.1 percent (using count data). This interunit variability estimate indicates a high degree of differential density across the surface of the site, which is usually associated with the presence of spatially distinct clusters. The mean sherd weight is approximately 2.96 grams with a coefficient of variation of 32.9 percent. This shows that sherd

sizes (measured by weight) are relatively small, but that there is a
fair degree of variation in sherd size among   collection units.

Although AZ BB:1:10 was sampled at an intensity comparable to
AZ BB:1:9, the combination of low surface artifact density and small
sherd size allows only minimal analysis of vessel form and orifice characteristics. Rim sherds from AZ BB:1:10 were sorted into bowl and jar
types (Table 66). Of the total of 22 rim sherds collected, only ten were
measurable. More than half of the jars fall into the 18-22 cm range of
orifice diameters, while more than half the bowls fall into a range of
22-26 cm.

Table 66. Metric attributes of jar and bowl orifice diameters
from AZ BB:1:10

Item	N	Mean	Standard deviation	Sample range	CV	95% CI
Jars	5	22.8 cm	3.63	19.17 - 26.43 cm	15.9%	±4.14 cm
Bowls	5	25.6 cm	3.58	22.02 - 29.18 cm	14.0%	±4.01 cm

These data indicate that while the sample means for orifice diameters
of jars and bowls do not appear to be significantly different, the extremely
low sample sizes of each vessel form result in relatively large confidence
intervals about the mean. Consequently, there may be significant differences
between the orifice diameters of these two vessel forms that cannot be
detected using the sample obtained from AZ BB:1:10.

The same series of hypotheses concerning vessel function that was
examined for AZ BB:1:9 was examined for AZ BB:1:10. Again on the basis
of data from sherd porosity studies conducted by Kinkade and Gilman, it
was assumed that rim sherds having the same kinds of temper as the body
sherds used in the porosity analysis would have the same basic porosity
indices. Rim sherds were accordingly classified into four categories. The
resulting distribution is shown in Table 67.

Table 67. Cross-classification of jar and bowl rim sherds from
AZ BB:1:10 by temper and surface treatment

	Jars	Bowls	Mean gram weight increase
Quartz-tempered	8	2	.39 grams
Schist-tempered	2	0	.74 grams
Interior smudged	1	2	.42 grams
Exterior polished	2	5	.76 grams

The first implication is that jars tend, on the whole, to be more porous than bowls. The Fischer's exact test is used to examine this implication.

Table 68. Fischer's exact test for significant differences in the porosity of jars and bowls from AZ BB:1:10

	Jars	Bowls	Totals
More porous (schist, polished)	4	6	10
Less porous (quartz, smudged)	9	3	12
Totals	13	9	22

p = .0929

The results indicate that there are nine chances in one hundred that the jars and bowls from AZ BB:1:10 do not come from the same population with regard to vessel porosity. This represents a relatively strong trend toward more porous bowls and less porous jars that might well be confirmed if the sample sizes were larger. Since this pattern is the exact opposite of what the implication requires, it is evident that the first implication is not confirmed.

The second implication requires that there be differential soot deposition on jar and bowl sherds and that bowls exhibit more soot deposition. Since these sherds are from a surface context in which organic remains have not been preserved, this implication cannot be examined using the data from AZ BB:1:10.

The third implication is that bowls are subject to more handling if they are used for cooking and serving, and that they accordingly have a greater probability of breakage than do less handled "storage" jars. If, on the other hand, jars were used for purposes other than relatively permanent storage, they might be expected to have higher breakage rates. Since the jar to bowl ratio at this site is approximately 13:9 (1.44), the latter alternative seems plausible. It seems likely, therefore, that even though bowls may have been used for cooking and serving activities, the relative breakage and discard rate of jars is significantly higher than what would be expected if jars were being used only for storage; some other use is indicated.

To briefly summarize, the test results show that jars and bowls do not have porosity values indicative of liquid storage, given the hypothesis that has been presented. In contrast to AZ BB:1:9, at AZ BB:1:10 jars are less porous than bowls. The jar to bowl sherd ratio indicates that both jars and bowls were deposited in equal proportions. Thus, the presumed function of jars as essentially nonportable storage vessels is not confirmed.

Lithic Population: Characteristics and Functional Interpretations

Procurement of Raw Materials. The same series of test hypotheses regarding the lithic artifacts at AZ BB:1:9 was used to test assumptions about the lithic assemblage at AZ BB:1:10. The range of lithic raw materials present among cores is shown in Table 69.

Table 69. Frequency distribution of cores by raw material type at AZ BB:1:10 (Kolmogorov-Smirnov test for significant differences)

| Raw material | Number of Cores Observed | | Number of Cores Expected | | Differences (K_D) |
	Frequency	Cumulative percentage	Frequency	Cumulative percentage	
Quartz	5	.1282	7.8	.2000	.0718
Quartzite	25	.7692	15.6	.4000	.3692
Basalt	5	.8974	23.4	.6000	.2974
Diorite	3	.9744	31.2	.8000	.1744
Rhyolite	1	1.0000	39.0	1.0000	.0000

Minimum K_D at .05 = .2177

Observed K_D = .3692 (significant differences)

These results indicate that all of the lithic raw materials utilized at AZ BB:1:10 consist of locally available stones; nonlocal cherts and obsidians are not represented at the site. Consequently, the first hypothesis is confirmed. The hypothesis of nonrandom selection of stone for manufacture is also confirmed insofar as the first implication is concerned. There is clearly a strong emphasis on the use of quartzite at AZ BB:1:10.

The second implication of the second hypothesis is that, if raw material procurement was nonrandom, there should also be evidence of more intensive utilization of the emphasized stone. It has already been demonstrated that the focus of raw material procurement at AZ BB:1:10 was on quartzite. Thus, we would also expect quartzite cores to show a greater intensity of reduction. The figures below (Table 70) were calculated by the same process described in the similar discussion for AZ BB:1:9.

Table 70. Relationships between core size and the number of flake scars per core from AZ BB:1:10

Item	N	Mean Size	Standard deviation	Mean number of flake scars per core	Standard deviation	Ratio
Quartzite	25	111.314 cc	78.8412	8.04	3.6226	.0722
Quartz	5	130.116 cc	61.3450	5.60	1.3416	.0430
Basalt	5	143.091 cc	45.6162	5.40	1.1402	.0377
Diorite	4	659.045 cc	449.8737	5.75	2.8723	.0087
Rhyolite	1	N/A	N/A	N/A	N/A	.0102

It is evident that quartzite shows a much greater intensity of use as measured by the number of flake scars per core against the average size of a core. Consequently, the second implication of the second hypothesis is confirmed.

Mode of Manufacture. The same series of hypotheses concerning the manufacture of stone items that was tested for AZ BB:1:9 was also tested for AZ BB:1:10. The different ratios of lithic artifact classes were examined to determine if core reduction, primary flake reduction, or formal tool manufacture was the primary mode of manufacture at the site. These data are presented in Table 71 below.

Core reduction, in which the final implement is formed out of the core, does not appear to have been the primary mode of manufacture at AZ BB:1:10; instead, the reduction of primary decortication flakes into implements appears to have been practiced. Reduction activities at the site do not appear to have been oriented towards the production of formal tools. Only one projectile point and one end scraper were recovered from surface contexts at the site. The production of large flakes suitable for use without any further modification appears to have predominated at AZ BB:1:10.

Table 71. Ratios of lithic artifact classes from AZ BB:1:10

	Ratio	Test Results
Core Reduction		
Cores:Other flakes	43:172 (0.25)	Not confirmed
Cores:Chunks/shatter	43: 33 (1.30)	Not confirmed
Primary flakes:Tertiary flakes	26: 59 (0.44)	Not confirmed
Secondary flakes:Tertiary flakes	87: 59 (1.47)	Not confirmed
Primary Flake Reduction		
Cores:Primary flakes	43: 26 (1.65)	Confirmed
Secondary flakes:Primary flakes	87: 26 (3.34)	Confirmed
Tertiary flakes:Primary flakes	59: 26 (2.27)	Confirmed
Chunks/shatter:Cores	33: 43 (0.77)	Confirmed
Cores:Other flakes	43:172 (0.25)	Confirmed
Tool Manufacture		
Formal tools:Other flakes	2:172 (0.012)	Not confirmed
Tertiary flakes:Other flakes	59:113 (0.52)	Not confirmed
Thinning flakes:Other flakes	0:172 (0)	Not confirmed

Use of Unmodified Flakes. The same hypotheses regarding use-modified flake functions that were examined for AZ BB:1:9 were examined for AZ BB:1:10. Utilized flakes recovered from AZ BB:1:10 consist predominantly of secondary flakes, with a secondary emphasis on tertiary flakes. As at AZ BB:1:9, utilized flakes were sorted into primary, secondary, and tertiary categories since it was thought that some functional differentiations might be discernible among these three categories. An examination of the implication that there are no significant differences in the intensity of flake use is shown below (Table 72).

These results indicate that while there is moderate variability among primary, secondary, and tertiary flakes with regard to the intensity with which they were used, the utilized flakes come from the same population with regard to intensity of use. Thus, the first test implication is confirmed.

The second implication, that there is little variability among the edge angles of all utilized flakes, whether primary, secondary, or tertiary, is examined below (Table 73).

Table 72. F-test for significant differences in the intensity
of edge utilization of utilized flakes from AZ BB:1:10

	Primary	Secondary	Tertiary
Number of cases	5	30	13
Mean edge use	.31	.26	.34
Sums of squares	.0558	.6374	.3868
Coefficient of variation	39.7%	57.7%	55.9%

Primary: Secondary calculated $F_{4,29,.95}$ = .8463 > $F_{4,29,.025}$ of .118

$< F_{4,29,.975}$ of 3.25

Secondary: Tertiary calculated $F_{29,12,.95}$ = .682 > $F_{29,4,.025}$ of .415

$< F_{29,4,.975}$ of 2.96

Primary: Tertiary calculated $F_{4,12,.95}$ = .4328 > $F_{4,12,.025}$ of .114

$< F_{4,12,.975}$ of 4.12

Table 73. F-test for significant differences in the variability
of edge angles among utilized flakes from AZ BB:1:10

	Primary	Secondary	Tertiary
Number of cases	6	37	18
Mean edge angle	47.0°	46.7°	39.4°
Sums of squares	1158.00	14,006.13	3106.28
Coefficient of variation	32.4%	41.6%	34.3%

Primary: Secondary calculated $F_{5,36,.95}$ = .5953 > $F_{5,36,.025}$ of .162

$< F_{5,36,.975}$ of 2.90

Secondary: Tertiary calculated $F_{36,17,.95}$ = 2.129 > $F_{36,17,.025}$ of .47

$< F_{36,17,.975}$ of 2.44

Primary: Tertiary calculated $F_{5,17,.95}$ = 1.268 > $F_{5,17,.025}$ of .157

$< F_{5,17.975}$ of 3.44

These results indicate that, while there is a moderate degree of variability among utilized flakes with regard to edge angles, the utilized flakes from AZ BB:1:10 come from the same population of edge angles. Thus, variability among edge angles is the same for primary, secondary, and tertiary utilized flakes, and the second implication is confirmed. The frequency distribution of edge angles on utilized flakes is illustrated in Figure 41.

The third implication, that there are no significant differences in the length of the used edges among primary, secondary, and tertiary flakes, is examined in the following table.

- - - - - - - - - - - - - - -

Table 74. F-test for significant differences in the variability of edge lengths among utilized flakes from AZ BB:1:10

	Primary	Secondary	Tertiary
Number of cases	6	36	16
Mean edge length	2.52 cm	2.34 cm	2.11 cm
Sums of squares	6.4835	18.6686	14.7531
Coefficient of variation	45.2%	31.1%	42.6%

Primary: Secondary calculated $F_{5,35,.95} = 2.431 > F_{5,35,.025}$ of .162

$< F_{5,35,.975}$ of 2.90

Secondary: Tertiary calculated $F_{35,15,.95} = .5423 > F_{35,15,.025}$ of .464

$< F_{35,15,.975}$ of 2.51

Primary: Tertiary calculated $F_{5,15,.95} = 1.318 > F_{5,15,.025}$ of .156

$< F_{5,15,.975}$ of 3.58

These results show, again, that the utilized flakes come from the same population with regard to edge lengths. Consequently, the third implication is confirmed. The distribution of edge lengths on utilized flakes is shown in Figure 42.

The last implication is that there are few differences among the overall morphologies of utilized flakes. The data used to show the overlap of these flakes in terms of length and width are shown in Figure 43.

Assuming that there are no differences among utilized flakes with respect to intensity of use, edge angles, length of use edges, and overall morphology, there should be no significant differences in the relative proportions of edge shapes. The data to examine this last implication are presented in Table 75.

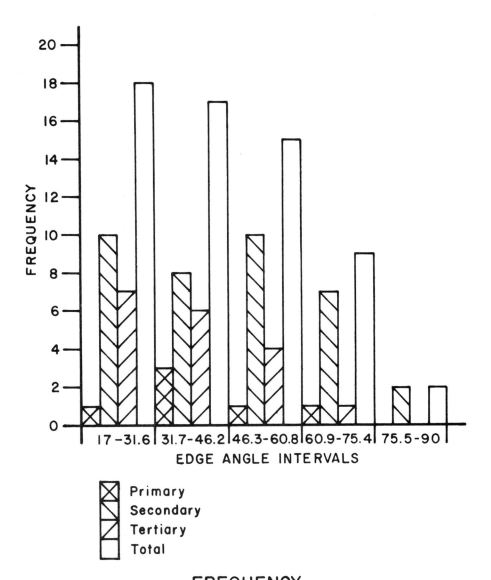

FREQUENCY
DISTRIBUTION OF UTILIZED FLAKE EDGE ANGLES
AT BB:I:IO

Figure 41

354

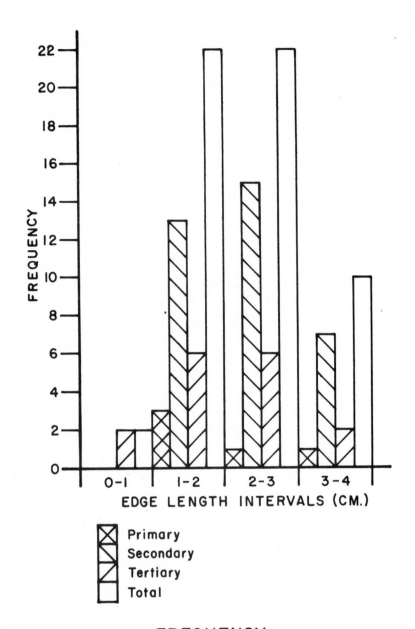

FREQUENCY
DISTRIBUTION OF UTILIZED FLAKE EDGE LENGTHS
AT BB:1:10

Figure 42

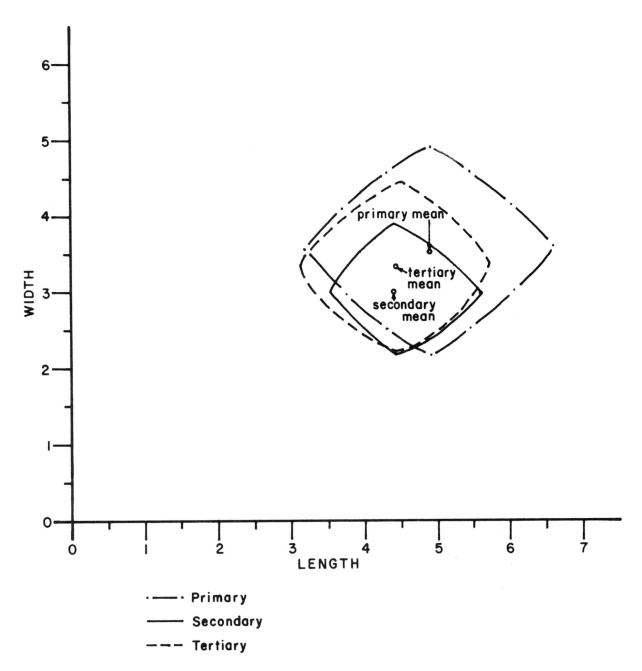

MEAN LENGTH AND WIDTH ± I STANDARD DEVIATION
OF UTILIZED FLAKES
AT BB:1:10

Figure 43

Table 75. Summary of edge configurations of primary, secondary, and tertiary utilized flakes from AZ BB:1:10

	Primary	Secondary	Tertiary
Straight	4	16	7
Concave	0	5	4
Convex	1	4	4
Concavo-convex	1	10	3

Since more than 20 percent of the cells in Table 75 have observed values of less than 5, and since the table is not symmetrical, it is impossible to assess frequency distributions using either a chi-square test or a Fischer's exact test. However, within each utilized flake class, primary and tertiary utilized flakes do not show a distribution significantly different from what would be expected under random conditions. Secondary flakes, however, show a significantly nonrandom distribution (X^2 = 10.372, d.f. =3, .01<.02<p).

Assuming that variations in edge shape may indicate differences in function, then the variability among secondary utilized flakes from AZ BB:1:10 should be examined to see if there are correlations between edge shape and other functionally significant variables. The cross-classification of secondary utilized flakes by edge shape and edge angle is shown in Table 76.

Table 76. Cross-classification of secondary utilized flakes from AZ BB:1:10 by edge shape and edge angle

Edge angle (degrees)	Edge shape			
	Straight	Concave	Convex	Concavo-convex
17-35.25	6	3	2	3
35.26-53.5	5	0	2	3
53.51-71.75	5	2	0	2
71.76-90.0	2	0	0	2

Again, cell sizes do not permit the calculation of valid chi-square values for this classification. However, there appear to be no significant correlations between edge configuration and edge angle that might enable the identification of functionally distinct classes of artifacts. Consequently, it must be concluded that there is no functional significance to the nonrandom distribution of edge shapes among secondary flakes.

Summarizing the tests of hypotheses concerning utilized flakes, it has been shown that there is little variability among utilized flakes from AZ BB:1:10. No significant differences can be seen among primary, secondary, and tertiary utilized flakes with respect to use intensity, amount of edge used, edge angles, or gross morphology. These factors, in conjunction with the relative scarcity of formal tools, suggest that lithic manufacture at the site focused on easy-to-acquire raw materials and easy-to-produce implements (utilized flakes). Relatively low use-intensity indices indicate that flakes were used for a short time and then discarded. Assuming that acute edges are used more for cutting/slicing activities, and that obtuse edges are more suitable for scraping activities (Wilmsen 1968), it is apparent that utilized flakes were used for both kinds of activities at AZ BB:1:10. It is interesting to note, however, that the utilized flakes from AZ BB:1:9 predominantly exhibit acute edges, while most of the utilized flakes from AZ BB:1:10 bear obtuse edges. This may indicate that scraping activities were more common at AZ BB:1:10 than at AZ BB:1:9.

Ground Stone Population: Characteristics and Functional Interpretations

Manos and metates are relatively infrequent at AZ BB:1:10, although they appear more often than at AZ BB:1:9. The mean density of manos per unit area is approximately .02 per square meter, while metates show a surface density of .03 per square meter. The coefficients of variation of manos and metates per collection unit are 226.3 percent and 59.1 percent, respectively. These values show that manos are more dispersed about the site than metates. All of the manos and metates recovered from AZ BB:1:10 are fragmentary, and few pieces were reconstructible. Assuming that each fragment represents a single implement, the mano to metate ratio at AZ BB:1:10 is 11:20 (0.55). Since the sample of ground stone from this site is unbiased, it can then be assumed that the frequency of metates was higher than that of manos. Whether this indicates the use of many metates or the possibility that they were moved more (and were thus more likely to break) is not known. Present evidence concerning the use of metates, as measured by the amount of surface wear in relation to the amount of remaining surface area, shows that the useful life of these implements had not been exhausted. Consequently, there is a greater probability that they were broken as a result of being moved.

In accordance with the test hypotheses outlined previously regarding ground stone function, the data were examined to determine if significant associations existed within the assemblage. All of the manos and metates at AZ BB:1:10 were rank-ordered into fine, medium, and coarse-grained

varieties of stone on the basis of a reference set of stones from the
site. Manos were further classified into those having flat as opposed
to convex working surfaces; flat surfaces indicate use on a slab metate,
while convex working surfaces indicate use in a trough metate. Metate
fragments were classified into slab and trough varieties. This information is presented in Table 77.

Table 77. Cross-classification of manos and metates
from AZ BB:1:10 by grain size and shape of working surfaces

Grain size	Manos		Metates	
	Flat	Convex	Slab	Trough
Fine	4	2	3	0
Medium	2	1	7	3
Coarse	1	1	3	4
Total	7	4	13	7

The small sizes of these cell values do not allow the use of the chi-square
test. However, within the class of manos, there seems to be an emphasis
on flat working surfaces and on fine-grained stone for both flat and convex working surfaces. There is a strong emphasis on slab metates over
trough metates, and slab metates do exhibit a trend toward medium-grained
stone types. Consequently, at least one of the two implications listed
above can be confirmed, and the hypothesis that small items were processed
at AZ BB:1:10 is provisionally accepted.

Feature Population: Characteristics and Functional Interpretations

A total of six features was recorded at AZ BB:1:10, five of which
were contiguous rectilinear cobble alignments; the sixth was a rock pile
(Figure 44). Four of these features each extended over an area less than
10 meters square; two were of 10-20 square meters in area. Thus, there
is approximately the same frequency of structures in each size range that
was noted at AZ BB:1:9. The larger structures probably represent residential units. The function of the smaller structures is as yet unclear,
but will be examined in the conclusions to this chapter.

Intrasite Activity Structure at AZ BB:1:10

The earlier discussion of intrasite activity structure presented
a tentative means of discriminating between primary and secondary refuse
at archaeological sites. This problem is important since the spatial

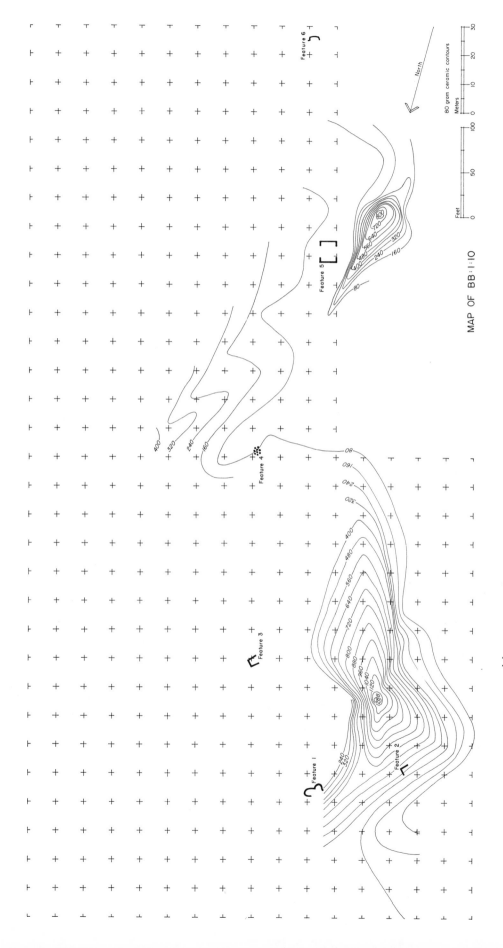

Figure 44. Map of AZ BB:1:10, showing location of features and ceramic density contours

relationship of two or more artifacts used in the performance of a given activity tends to be preserved in contexts of primary refuse. Such spatial relationships allow further interpretations regarding activity structure that cannot be defined through a technological analysis of discrete artifact populations. What follows is an attempt, using the same methods applied at AZ BB:1:9, to determine the probability that primary refuse occurs at AZ BB:1:10.

The first implication is that clusters of refuse correspond to use areas. Coefficients of variation among collection units at AZ BB:1:10 reveal a high degree of clustering in the surface distribution of ceramics, debitage, ground stone, utilized flakes, and cores. Ceramics show a coefficient of variation of 103.32 percent and debitage a coefficient of 98.7 percent. The coefficient of variation for ground stone is 177.62 percent and 129.18 percent for utilized flakes. Lastly, cores have a coefficient of variation of 125.66 percent. These data tend to confirm the first implication.

The second implication calls for a high degree of redundancy among collection units with regard to the diversity of the artifact populations recovered from each unit. Using the five artifact populations noted above, there are five units with all five populations, eleven units with four populations, nine units with three populations, four units with two populations, and one unit with one population. Redundancy is then expressed as follows:

$$\text{Redundancy} = \frac{(5\times5) + (11\times4) + (9\times3) + (4\times2) + (1\times1)}{(5\times30)} = \frac{105}{150} = .70$$

This shows that there is a relatively high degree of redundancy among collection units at AZ BB:1:10 in terms of the kinds of artifact populations that have been recovered; the second implication is therefore confirmed.

The third and fourth implications call for relatively small sherd sizes and a low coefficient of variation for sherd sizes among collection units. The mean sherd size (measured by weight) is 2.65 grams, and the coefficient of variation for sherd weight among collection units is 32.9 percent. These data tend to confirm the third and fourth implications.

On the basis of the above analysis, it is suggested that there is a high probability that most of the surface remains at AZ BB:1:10 consist of primary refuse, although the somewhat greater coefficient of variation for sherd weights (as compared with 23 percent at AZ BB:1:9) may indicate the presence of some secondary refuse at the site. For present purposes, however, surface remains at AZ BB:1:10 will be treated as if the bulk of the remains is primary refuse.

As with AZ BB:1:9, the spatial co-occurrence of artifacts can only be approached on a collection-unit basis. Assuming that each artifact population has an equal chance of occurring in each collection unit, deviations from random values will be used to measure spatial associations.

Hypothesis 1: If jars and bowls were used together in the performance of a given activity and were deposited at their loci of use (that is, are primary refuse), expect a strong spatial correlation between the incidences of jars and bowls.

Jar and bowl rims could be identified in only 15 of the units collected at AZ BB:1:10. Of these units, eleven contained either jars or bowls, while only four units contained both jars and bowls. A chi-square one-sample test tentatively disconfirms the above hypothesis ($X^2 = 3.267$, d.f. = 1, $.05 < p < .10$); jars and bowls do not tend to occur in the same collection units. This value, as it is not within accepted limits of significance, does not by itself warrant rejecting the hypothesis; nonetheless, it does indicate a strong trend towards spatially distinct activity areas where jars and bowls were used.

Hypothesis 2: If ground stone implements were used with either jars or bowls and were deposited at their loci of use, expect a high spatial correlation between ground stone implements and jars and/or bowls.

In a sample of 16 units in which either jar rims or ground stone or both could be identified, ten contained either jars or ground stone implements, while, six units contained both jars and ground stone ($X^2 = 1.00$, d.f. = 1, $.3 < p < .5$). On the other hand, of the 12 units containing identifiable bowl rims, ground stone, or both, nine contained either bowls or ground stone, while three contained both ($X^2 = 3.00$, d.f. = 1, $.05 < p < .10$). These data show that ground stone implements occur either with or without jars, but that there is a strong trend for such implements not to occur with bowls in the same collection units.

Hypothesis 3: If utilized flakes were used with either jars or bowls and were deposited at their loci of use, expect a high spatial correlation between utilized flakes and jars and/or bowls.

Of 21 collection units, 13 contained either utilized flakes or jars, while eight contained both ($X^2 = 1.1905$, d.f. = 1, $.2 < p < .3$). This relationship is essentially the same for bowls ($X^2 = .80$, d.f. = 1, $.3 < p < .5$). Thus, there is no strong association between utilized flakes and bowls and jars with respect to collection units.

Hypothesis 4:   If primary flake reduction constituted the major
mode of manufacture at AZ BB:1:10, and if utilized
flakes were produced and used at flake reduction loci,
expect a high spatial correlation between debitage
and utilized flakes.

Of the 26 collection units that contained debitage and/or utilized
flakes, seven units contained either debitage or utilized flakes, while
19 units contained both (X^2 = 5.5385, d.f.= 1, .01<p<.02). This distribution indicates a highly nonrandom spatial association between debitage
and utilized flakes.

Thus, at least four spatial associations indicative of activity
areas are present at AZ BB:1:10. These include areas in which jars were
used, areas in which bowls were used, areas in which ground stone implements were used, and areas in which utilized flakes were produced and
used. There is, of course, a certain amount of spatial overlap between
some of these activity areas, although this overlap does not appear to
be very important.

AZ BB:5:21

Surface indications at AZ BB:5:21 consist of a scatter of sherds,
lithics, and ground stone artifacts associated with cobble alignments
indicative of structures. APS Tower 632 is located on the site, which
is bisected east to west by a jeep trail. Tower construction at the site
had minimal impact on archaeological remains with the result that data
recovery consisted solely of surface collections.

The total area encompassed by AZ BB:5:21 is about 100,000 square
meters, within which are situated numerous discrete loci. A 3.4-percent
stratified random sample of this site resulted in the collection of 34
10 m by 10 m units at the site; these collection units were used to
acquire samples of ceramics. The proveniences of all surface lithics
on the site were mapped prior to the collection. Consequently, while
there is a 3.4-percent sample of ceramics from the site, there is a
100-percent sample of lithics from the site's surface. The resulting
sample of artifacts from the site is small due to the low sherd sample
fractions that were collected as well as the low surface density of remains from the site. The mean surface density for both sherds and lithics
is approximately 0.49 artifacts per square meter. All of the artifacts
collected were analyzed.

The sherds from AZ BB:5:21 are more chronologically sensitive
than those from AZ BB:1:9 and AZ BB:1:10. The presence of Tanque Verde
Red-on-brown, smudged corrugated wares, unidentified whitewares, mug strap-
handles, and high-necked jars indicates occupation during the late Rincon-
early Tanque Verde phases (around A.D. 1100-1270) during the Sedentary

to Classic Period Hohokam transition. Because the sherds were compared
to those found at sites in the Santa Cruz Basin, and because in the Santa
Cruz and San Pedro drainages different dates are associated with similar
ceramic types, these dates should be considered tentative, since AZ BB:5:21
is located in the San Pedro drainage. Nevertheless, the temporal placement of this site is considerably better than what was possible for
AZ BB:1:9 and AZ BB:1:10. The sherds are generally quite thin and exhibit
a mica-schist temper, with a fairly high amount of quartz sand temper
included in the sherd matrix. Many of the sherds show exterior polish.

Ceramic Population: Characteristics and Functional Interpretations

The sherds from AZ BB:5:21 consist mostly of plainwares, although
smudged corrugated varieties are noticeably more common than at the other
sites investigated. As at most of the sites, sherds are sparsely distributed; the mean density by count is approximately 0.51 sherds per square
meter, with a coefficient of variation among collection units of 94.5
percent. The mean weight of sherds from the site is 2.43 grams, with a
coefficient of variation of 32.7 percent. These data indicate that while
there is considerable differential distribution of ceramics across the
site, the size of sherds generally tends to be fairly constant in all
parts of the site.

Because the sherds were so small, a detailed analysis of vessel
form could not be performed. Of the 67 rim sherds recovered from the
site, only 33 could be reliably measured in order to determine variations
in orifice diameter (Table 78).

Table 78. Metric attributes of jar and bowl orifice diameters
from AZ BB:5:21

Item	N	Mean	Standard deviation	Sample range	CV	95% CI
Jars	20	24.20 cm	4.0988	20.1 - 28.3 cm	16.9%	±1.796 cm
Bowls	13	23.54 cm	7.2642	16.3 - 30.8 cm	30.9%	±3.949 cm

These data show that while there do not appear to be any differences
between mean orifice diameters of jars and bowls as determined from
sample estimates, the true population means of jars and bowls, given the
relatively wide confidence intervals around the mean bowl values, may be
significantly different. It should be noted that 69 percent of the bowl
orifice diameters are greater than the mean, while only 55 percent of the
jar orifice diameters are greater than the mean. Consequently, jar
orifice diameters tend to be normally distributed about the mean, while
bowl orifice diameters are positively skewed towards sizes larger than
the mean.

Using the results of Kinkade and Gilman's porosity study of sherds from AZ BB:5:21, each jar or bowl rim sherd was sorted into one of five categories discussed earlier to determine whether there were significant porosity differences (Table 79).

Table 79. Cross-classification of jar and bowl rim sherds from AZ BB:5:21 by temper and surface treatment

	Jars	Bowls	Mean gram weight increase
Quartz-tempered	7	8	.8750 grams
Schist-tempered	5	2	1.0000 grams
Interior smudged	4	11	.5606 grams
Exterior polished	23	5	.1539 grams
Mica-tempered	2	0	.4429 grams

The first implication is that jars tend to be more porous than bowls. A chi-square test is used to examine this implication.

Table 80. Chi-square test for significant differences in the porosity of jars and bowls from AZ BB:5:21

	Jars	Bowls	Total
Low porosity (polished)	23	5	28
Medium porosity (mica, smudged)	6	11	17
High porosity (quartz, schist)	12	10	22
Total	41	26	67

$$x^2 = 10.3863$$
$$d.f. = 2$$

$$.001 < p < .01$$

This test indicates that while there are significant differences between jars and bowls with respect to porosity, the correlation of specific levels of porosity with any one vessel type is not very strong. If Table 80 is examined in more detail, it becomes evident that jars have a bimodal distribution with respect to porosity while bowls exhibit a unimodal distribution. Generally speaking, jars are less

porous than bowls. This finding is the exact opposite of what is required
by the hypotheses;   consequently, these hypotheses are not confirmed.

As before, the recovery of these sherds from surface contexts in
which organic remains (soot deposits, for example) are not preserved does
not allow an examination of the second implication, which concerns vessel
use for cooking.

The third implication is that bowls are subject to higher probabilities of breakage if they are used for cooking and serving activities, while
jars, if they are used for relatively permanent storage functions, will have
a lower probability of breakage. Alternatively, if jars were used for
some activity other than permanent storage, they would be expected to have
higher breakage probabilities and hence greater discard rates. Because
the jar to bowl ratio at AZ BB:5:21 is 41:26 (1.58), the latter alternative
seems more plausible. Although bowls may have been used for cooking and
serving activities, the breakage rates of jars seem to indicate that they
were used for some activity other than permanent liquid storage.

To summarize the results of the ceramic analysis, there is some
indication that two functionally distinct subclasses may occur within
the more general class of jars, with one subclass evidencing low porosity
and the other having considerably greater porosity indices. Thus, while
some of the jars may have been used for the storage of liquids, other jars
have porosity indices that do not indicate liquid storage. Bowls, on the other
hand, exhibit consistently higher porosity indices. As a result, the
hypothesis as it is stated cannot be decisively confirmed or rejected.
Breakage rates, as indicated by jar to bowl ratios, tend to indicate
that jars were used for some purpose other than nonportable storage.

Lithic Population: Characteristics and Functional Interpretations

The same series of hypotheses regarding the procurement, processing, use, and discard of chipped stone that were examined for AZ BB:1:9
and AZ BB:1:10 will be considered for AZ BB:5:21.

Procurement of Raw Materials.   It has already been demonstrated that lithic raw material procurement at AZ BB:1:9 and AZ BB:1:10
focused on local resources such as quartzite, quartz, and basalt. The
kinds of stone recovered from AZ BB:5:21 are similar to those recovered
from the other sites investigated. Raw data concerning the frequencies
with which various kinds of stone appear among the sample of cores from
the site is presented in Table 81. This statistical assessment indicates
that there is a significantly nonrandom distribution of cores according
to stone type and, further, that all of the stone types recovered from
the site consist of locally available varieties. Cherts, obsidians, and
other "exotic" stones are notable by their absence. These data confirm
both implications of the first hypothesis and confirm the first implication of the second (that stone use is nonrandom).

Table 81. Frequency distribution of cores by raw material type at AZ BB:5:21
(Kolmogorov-Smirnov test for significant differences)

Item	Observed		Expected		Differences (K_D)
	Frequency	Cumulative percentage	Frequency	Cumulative percentage	
Quartz	7	.1429	9.8	.2000	.0571
Quartzite	24	.6327	19.6	.4000	.2327
Rhyolite	9	.8163	29.4	.6000	.2163
Basalt	6	.9388	39.2	.8000	.1388
Andesite	3	1.0000	49.0	1.0000	.0000

Minimum K_D at .05 = .1943

Observed K_D = .2327 (significant differences)

There is a high degree of variability in the relationship between stone type and the intensity of reduction of certain stone types. By standardizing core size and the number of flake scars per core as an index of the intensity of reduction of a stone type, the following frequency distribution is obtained.

Table 82. Relationship between core size and the number of flake scars per core at AZ BB:5:21

Item	N	Mean size	Standard deviation	Mean number of flake scars per core	Standard deviation	Ratio
Quartzite	24	289.0234 cc	379.299	7.375	3.4239	.0255
Quartz	7	418.1721 cc	127.169	6.857	1.8645	.0164
Rhyolite	9	743.1478 cc	757.334	7.333	3.0000	.0099
Basalt	6	287.6206 cc	167.335	8.167	2.8577	.0284
Andesite	3	318.4302 cc	266.647	6.667	1.5275	.0209

These data indicate that quartzites, while by far the predominant stone type used at AZ BB:5:21, were not used as intensively as was basalt. Consequently, the implication that stone utilization is nonrandom in terms of intensity is only partially confirmed. It is interesting to note that the intensity of basalt reduction is higher at AZ BB:5:21 than at AZ BB:1:9, although it is not higher than at AZ BB:1:10. Whether this signals a technofunctional shift in lithic tool production is as yet unclear.

To briefly summarize, it has been demonstrated that raw material procurement at AZ BB:5:21 focused on locally available stone varieties such as quartzites, quartz, basalt, and rhyolite. While quartzites appear to have been used with greater frequency than other stone types, use-intensity indices show that basalt was more intensively reduced than quartzite.

Mode of Manufacture. The same series of hypotheses relating to mode of manufacture that was tested for AZ BB:1:9 and AZ BB:1:10 also was tested for AZ BB:5:21. The following ratios were examined to determine whether core reduction or formal tool manufacture was the primary mode of manufacture.

Table 83. Ratios of lithic artifact classes from AZ BB:5:21

	Ratio		Test Results
Core Reduction			
Core:Other flake	50:305	(0.164)	Confirmed
Primary flake:Tertiary flake	43:141	(0.305)	Confirmed
Secondary flake: Tertiary flake	121:141	(0.858)	Confirmed
Core:Chunk/shatter	50:18	(2.778)	Not confirmed
Formal Tool Manufacture			
Formal tool:Other flake	7:305	(0.023)	Not confirmed
Tertiary flake:Other flake	141:164	(0.859)	Not confirmed
Thinning flake:Other flake	0:305	(0)	Not confirmed

Regarding core reduction, three of the four implications are confirmed using sample data from AZ BB:5:21. One implication is not confirmed due to the low core to chunk/shatter ratio. Since chunk/shatter is relatively difficult to recognize in the field, it is possible that the failure to confirm this implication results from observational difficulties. Since three of the four implications have been confirmed, this hypothesis will be considered partially confirmed.

The data from the site do not confirm any of the implications regarding formal tool manufacture.

One last hypothesis concerns what types of lithic implements were being manufactured at AZ BB:5:21. It has already been demonstrated that core reduction constituted the primary mode of manufacture at the site. Furthermore, manufacturing activities at the site do not appear to have been oriented toward the production of formal tools. Instead, reduction appears directed toward production of flakes for expedient use. Consequently, a new hypothesis can be forwarded:

If utilized flakes were the main implement type produced at the site, and if core reduction was the major mode of manufacture, then expect (a) a high ratio of utilized flakes to other flakes, and (b) most of the utilized flakes to consist of late-stage core reduction flakes such as secondary and tertiary flakes.

The ratio of utilized flakes to other flakes at AZ BB:5:21 is 198:305 (.649). As this ratio is extremely high,   the first implication is confirmed. The implication that most utilized flakes should consist of late-stage core reduction flakes is examined below.

Table 84. Chi-square one-sample test for significant differences in the proportion of late-stage utilized flakes at AZ BB:5:21

	Observed	Expected	
Primary utilized flakes	33	66	$\chi^2 = 25.1212$
Secondary utilized flakes	79	66	d.f. = 2
Tertiary utilized flakes	86	66	p<.001

These results show that there is a significantly nonrandom distribution of utilized flakes. There is a unimodal distribution of utilized flakes positively skewed toward late-stage flakes such as secondary and tertiary flakes. Thus, the second implication is confirmed. This leads to the conclusion that utilized flakes appear to have been the major implement type produced at AZ BB:5:21.

Use of Unmodified Flakes. The previous discussion has shown that use-modified flakes constituted the major class of implements produced, used, and discarded at AZ BB:5:21. What follows is a series of tests of hypotheses   concerning the possible function of these flakes. These are the same hypotheses that were examined for AZ BB:1:9 and AZ BB:1:10.

Utilized flakes were sorted into primary, secondary, and tertiary flake categories since it was thought that there might be some functional differentiation among these classes of flakes. The implication that there are differences in the intensity with which these three flake types were used is examined in Table 85. These data indicate that there are no significant differences (p<.05) between (a) primary and secondary utilized flakes and (b) secondary and tertiary utilized flakes with regard to variability in the intensity of use. However, there is a low probability that primary and tertiary flakes do not come from the same population with respect to variability in intensity of use. Specifically, tertiary flakes appear to be slightly more variable than primary flakes. Since about 85 percent of the utilized flakes are classed as secondary or primary flakes, this implication will be considered strongly confirmed in spite of the differences outlined below.

Table 85. F-test for significant differences in the
intensity of edge utilization on utilized flakes from AZ BB:5:21

	Primary	Secondary	Tertiary
Number of cases	29	66	63
Mean edge use	.24	.24	.29
Sums of squares	.1691	.5639	.7432
Coefficient of variation	33.3%	37.5%	41.4%

Primary:Secondary calculated $F_{28,65,.95}$ = .6961 > $F_{30,60,.025}$ of .515
$< F_{30,60,.975}$ of 1.82

Secondary:Tertiary calculated $F_{65,62,.95}$ = .7237 > $F_{60,60,.025}$ of .600
$< F_{60,60,.975}$ of 1.67

Primary:Tertiary calculated $F_{28,62,.95}$ = .5038 > $F_{30,60,.025}$ of .515
$< F_{30,60,.975}$ of 1.82

The second implication is that there is little variability among
edge angles on primary, secondary, and tertiary utilized flakes at
AZ BB:5:21. The frequency distribution of utilized flake edge angles
is shown in Figure 45.

The implication that there are no significant differences in the
variability of edge angles among primary, secondary, and tertiary utilized
flakes is examined in Table 86.

Table 86. F-test for significant differences in the variability of
edge angles among utilized flakes from AZ BB:5:21

	Primary	Secondary	Tertiary
Number of cases	33	79	86
Mean edge angle	47.8°	45.9°	46.5°
Sums of squares	9147.52	25,167.59	29,880.50
Coefficient of variation	35.4%	39.1%	38.7%

Primary:Secondary calculated $F_{32,78,.95}$ = .886 > $F_{30,60,.025}$ of .515

$< F_{30,60,.975}$ of 1.82

Secondary:Tertiary calculated $F_{78,85,.95}$ = .918 > $F_{120,120,.025}$ of .698
$< F_{120,120,.975}$ of 1.43

Primary:Tertiary calculated $F_{32,85,.95}$ = .813 > $F_{30,60,.025}$ of .515
$< F_{30,60,.975}$ of 1.82

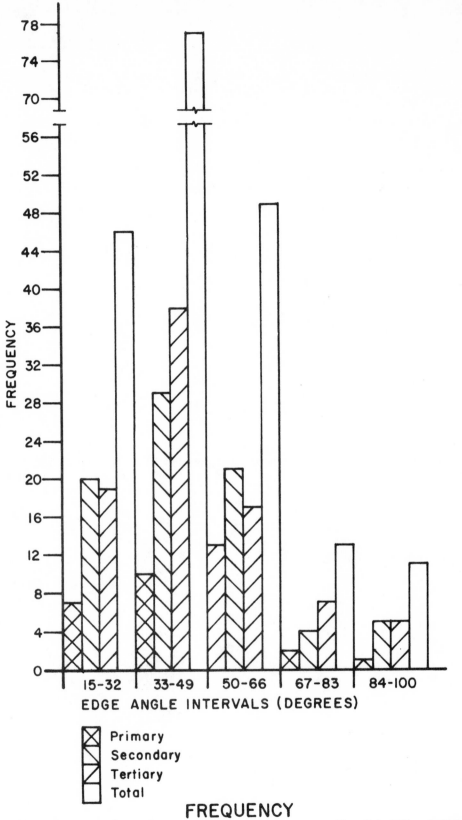

FREQUENCY
DISTRIBUTION OF UTILIZED FLAKE EDGE ANGLES
AT BB:5:21

Figure 45

These data indicate that variability in edge angles does not differ significantly (p<.05) among primary, secondary, and tertiary utilized flakes, and that the mean edge angles associated with these implements are essentially the same. Consequently, the second implication is confirmed.

The third implication is that there are few differences in the amount of edge length used on each of these three classes of implements. The frequency distribution of utilized flake edge lengths is shown in Figure 46. The data required to examine this implication are presented in Table 87.

Table 87. F-test for significant differences in the variability of edge lengths among utilized flakes from AZ BB:5:21

	Primary	Secondary	Tertiary
Number of cases	33	79	86
Mean edge length	2.72 cm	2.46 cm	2.15 cm
Sums of quares	43.0928	74.7122	89.3089
Coefficient of variation	47.9%	40.2%	42.7%

Primary:Secondary calculated $F_{32,78,.95} = 1.4059 > F_{30,60,.025}$ of .515

$< F_{30,60,.975}$ of 1.82

Secondary:Tertiary calculated $F_{78,85,.95} = .9116 > F_{60,60,.025}$ of .60

$< F_{60,60,.975}$ of 1.67

Primary:Tertiary calculated $F_{32,85,.95} = 1.2817 > F_{30,60,.025}$ of .515

$< F_{30,60,.975}$ of 1.82

These data indicate that there are no significant differences among primary, secondary, and tertiary utilized flakes with respect to variability in edge length. As a result, the third implication is confirmed.

The last implication, that there should be no significant differences in the relative proportions of edge shapes associated with primary, secondary, and tertiary utilized flakes, is examined with data presented in Table 88. These data indicate that the observed distribution of edge configurations among primary, secondary, and tertiary utilized flakes strongly tends not to conform with the distribution expected.

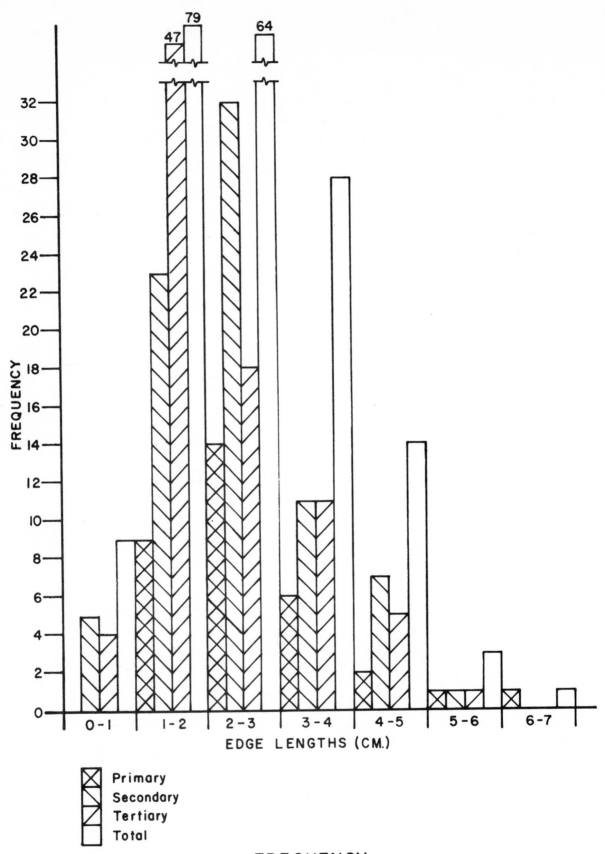

FREQUENCY
DISTRIBUTION OF UTILIZED FLAKE EDGE LENGTHS
AT BB:5:21

Figure 46

Table 88. Summary of edge configurations of primary, secondary, and tertiary utilized flakes from AZ BB:5:21

	Primary	Secondary	Tertiary	
Straight	14	28	30	72
Concave	2	6	14	22
Convex	14	23	21	58
Concavo-convex	3	22	21	46
	33	79	86	198

$$X^2 = 10.3836$$
$$d.f. = 6$$
$$.05 < p < .10$$

In an attempt to determine if variations in edge shape can be correlated with other functionally significant variables, utilized flakes were then cross-classified according to edge shape and edge angle. The resulting distribution is shown below.

Table 89. Cross-classification of utilized flakes from AZ BB:5:21 by edge shape and edge angle

Edge angle (degrees)	Edge Shape											
	Straight			Concave			Convex			Concavo-convex		
	P	S	T	P	S	T	P	S	T	P	S	T
15-32	3	6	7	1	0	1	3	6	8	0	8	3
33-49	5	11	12	0	6	6	4	6	10	1	6	10
50-66	5	8	6	1	0	6	5	9	1	2	4	4
67-83	1	1	2	0	0	0	1	1	1	0	2	4
84-100	0	2	3	0	0	1	1	1	1	0	2	0

It can be seen that there is a bimodal distribution of primary utilized flakes according to edge configuration, with the majority of the flakes exhibiting straight and convex edges. However, within these two edge-shape categories, primary flakes exhibit a unimodal edge angle distribution of 33-66 degrees. Secondary utilized flakes, on the other hand, are equally distributed among the edge configuration categories--straight, convex, and concavo-convex. To determine whether there were any significant differences between the observed and expected distributions of these edge shapes with different edge angles, secondary utilized flakes in each of the three edge shape classes were correlated with the most common edge angle modes. The results of this test are shown below.

Table 90. Chi-square test for significant differences in the distribution of edge shapes and edge angles among secondary utilized flakes from AZ BB:5:21

Edge Angles (degrees)	Straight	Convex	Concavo-convex
15-32	6	6	8
33-49	11	6	6
50-66	8	9	4

$$X^2 = 3.5409$$
$$d.f. = 4$$
$$.3 < p < .5$$

These results show that there is a 30 to 50 percent chance that these edge shapes come from the same population with regard to edge angles. Consequently, there does not appear to be any functionally significant clustering of secondary utilized flakes according to edge shape or edge angle. Tertiary utilized flakes appear to be randomly distributed across straight, convex, and concavo-convex edges within edge angle intervals of 15-66 degrees ($X^2 = 1.0164$, d.f. = 4, .90 < p < .95). A test of the proposition that these edge shapes are correlated with specified edge angle intervals is presented below.

Table 91. Chi-square test for significant differences in the distribution of edge shapes and edge angles among tertiary utilized flakes from AZ BB:5:21

Edge Angles (degrees)	Straight	Convex	Concavo-convex
15-33	7	8	3
33-49	12	10	10
50-66	6	1	4

It is impossible to compute a chi-square value for this distribution, since more than 20 percent of the cells have an expected value of less than five (Siegel 1956:178). However, there does not appear to be a high degree of clustering of any one edge shape with any one edge angle interval. For this reason, it will be tentatively concluded that there is little functional variation within the class of tertiary utilized flakes.

In summarizing this discussion of functional variability among utilized flakes at AZ BB:5:21, it has been demonstrated that there are few differences among primary, secondary, and tertiary utilized flakes with regard to intensity of use, edge angles, and edge lengths. Furthermore, there do not appear to be significant correlations between edge angles and edge shapes such that functionally distinct classes of implements can be defined. Generally speaking, the utilized flakes from this site seem to have enjoyed short-term use, with little or no emphasis placed on retouch/resharpening to increase the use-life of the implement. The wide range of edge angles and edge shapes that occurs within the various flake classes tends to indicate generalized cutting and scraping activities. It should be noted that the modal edge angle is higher than that observed at AZ BB:1:9 (although not at AZ BB:1:10), and may indicate a greater emphasis on scraping activities.

Ground Stone Population: Characteristics and Functional Interpretations

Manos and metates are rare at AZ BB:5:21. The mean surface density of manos is .002 per square meter, while metates exhibit a surface density of .005 per square meter. These surface densities are higher than those observed at AZ BB:1:9, but lower than those at AZ BB:1:10. Almost all of the manos and metates recovered at the site are fragmentary, and few matching fragments could be found. Assuming again that each fragment represents a single implement, the mano to metate ratio at AZ BB:5:21 is 8:18 (.444). These data indicate that the flow rate of metates into the archaeological record is higher than that of manos. Furthermore, since most of the metates exhibit no evidence of heavy surface grinding, it appears that they were broken and discarded prior to being exhausted.

The same functional relationship examined for AZ BB:1:10 will be examined for the ground stone assemblage from AZ BB:5:21. Specifically, it has been suggested that fine-grained slab metates are associated with seed grinding. Consequently, if seed-grinding activities occurred at AZ BB:5:21, we would expect a high incidence of flat-surfaced manos and slab metates exhibiting a medium to fine-grained texture. To test this proposition, manos and metates were classified into rank-ordered grain-size categories varying from fine to medium to coarse-grained stone. Manos were subdivided into those with flat and convex working surfaces. Metates were classified as slab or trough varieties. The resulting distribution is presented in Table 92.

Table 92. Cross-classification of manos and metates from
AZ BB:5:21 by grain size and shape of working surfaces

Grain Size	Manos		Metates	
	Flat	Convex	Slab	Trough
Fine	1	1	2	0
Medium	2	1	8	2
Coarse	0	3	2	4

It is readily apparent that cell values in Table 92 are too small to cal-
culate a chi-square test of deviations from a random distribution. If,
however, medium and fine-grained classes are lumped within a single
category and the coarse-grained category is retained, it is possible to
examine the two implications discussed earlier using a Fischer's exact
test. This test reveals that there is a .1786 probability that manos
with flat and convex surfaces come from the same population with regard
to grain size. On the other hand, there is only a .0533 probability
that metates come from the same population with regard to grain size.
The first implication is not confirmed, since there does not appear to
be a nonrandom distribution of manos toward medium and fine-grained varieties with flat surfaces. The second implication is confirmed, since
there does appear to be a significantly nonrandom distribution of metates
toward medium and fine-grained slab varieties.

It is evident that the sample sizes of ground stone implements
from AZ BB:5:21 are far too small to resolve this difficulty. Manos do
not conform to the expected distribution, given the hypothesis of seed-
grinding activities at the site; metates - of which there is a larger
sample - do tend to conform to the expected distribution, given the above
hypothesis. While it seems that the grinding of both small (seeds) and
large items occurred at AZ BB:5:21, the findings obtained from the sample
of metates are weighted more heavily in favor of accepting the hypothesis
that primarily small items were being processed at AZ BB:5:21.

Feature Population: Characteristics and Functional Interpretations

In contract to the other sites investigated, the number of permanent
features at AZ BB:5:21 is very large, totaling 30 features. Of this
total, 14 consist of L-shaped cobble alignments, four consist of roughly
U-shaped cobble alignments, four are rectilinear cobble alignments, seven
are single rows of cobbles, and one is a bedrock mortar. The features
are dispersed across the site area; no clustering is apparent and there are no
contiguous rooms (Figure 47). In an attempt to distinguish possible functional
differences among them, features on the site were analyzed for total areal

variations. The resulting distribution of structural features by size at AZ BB:5:21 is described in Table 93 below. Single-row alignments and features of dubious form are exluded from this test.

Table 93. Frequency distribution of structural
features by size at AZ BB:5:21
(Kolmogorov-Smirnov test for significant differences)

Size intervals	Observed		Expected	
	Frequency	Cumulative percentage	Frequency	Cumulative percentage
Less than 5 m^2	8	(.4)	4	(.2)
6-10 m^2	2	(.5)	4	(.4)
11-15 m^2	4	(.7)	4	(.6)
16-20 m^2	3	(.85)	4	(.8)
More than 21 m^2	3	(1.0)	4	(1.0)

Minimum K_D at .05 = .3041; Observed K_D = .200   (not significant)

These data indicate that the distribution of structural features by size is not significantly different from what would be expected under random conditions. There is an approximately equal distribution of large and small structures across the surface of AZ BB:5:21.

The actual function of these features is uncertain, since there are no data on their subsurface nature. Because they could represent ramada-like structures, the test hypothesis outlined earlier was applied to data relevant to these features. The first implication requires that cobble alignments predominate, and that wall fall and coursed masonry be absent. The second test implication requires a high incidence of upright stone slabs around the perimeters of these structures.

The structural data from the site reveal a predominance of single-course cobble alignments over structures exhibiting multiple coursing (N = 21, 19 without multiple coursing, X^2 = 13.8, d.f. = 1, p<.001). There does not appear to be an emphasis on upright stone slabs/cobbles at AZ BB:5:21 (N = 21, 11 with upright slabs, X^2 = .0476, d.f. = 1, .8<p<.9). Interestingly enough, however, considerable differences appear when the sizes of structures are compared with the incidence of upright slabs/cobbles. These data are indicated in Table 94.

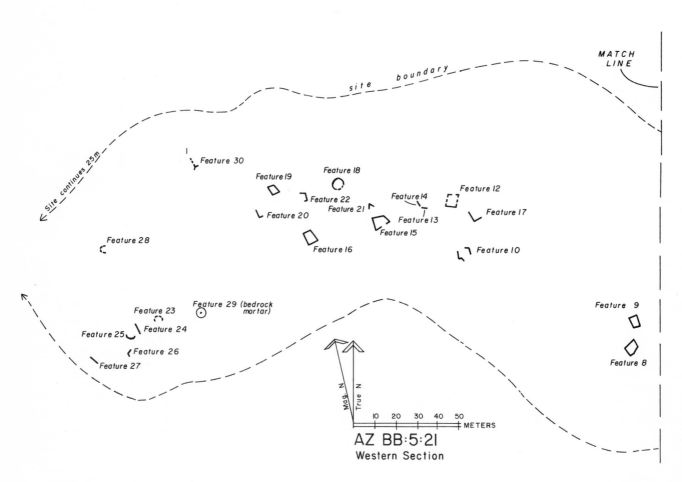

Figure 47a. Map of AZ BB:5:21, showing location of features: western half

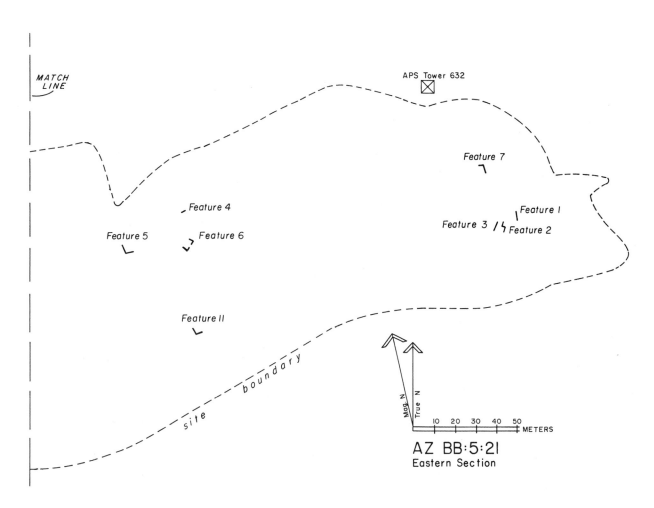

Figure 47b. Map of AZ BB:5:21, showing location of features: eastern half

Table 94. Frequency distribution of upright slabs
by the size of structures at AZ BB:5:21

Size of Structures	Upright Slabs	
	Present	Absent
Less than 10 m^2	2	8
10 - 20 m^2	5	2
Greater than 20 m^2	2	1

If structures in the larger size modes (that is, those greater than 10 m^2) are combined within one category, the resulting distribution can be examined using a Fischer's exact test.

Table 95. Fischer's exact test for significant differences in the distribution of upright slabs by structure size at AZ BB:5:21

Structure Size	Upright Slabs		
	Present	Absent	
Less than 10 m^2	2	8	p = .0322
More than 10 m^2	7	3	

These data show rather conclusively that the occurrence of upright slabs is strongly associated with larger structures, while small structures do not evidence upright slabs. Consequently, there is some indication that upright slabs occur primarily with large structures at AZ BB:5:21, and that these could be ramada-like structures. However, it should be noted that distinctions between single-course and multiple-course cobble alignments were made without benefit of excavation. Multiple coursing could, in fact, only be detected in those features which had suffered some pot hunting.

Intrasite Activity Structure at AZ BB:5:21

In order to examine the test implications related to depositional processes, data from AZ BB:5:21 were examined to determine the relative probability that the artifact distribution at the site reflects the presence of primary refuse.

The first implication requires a clustering of artifacts that corresponds to use areas at the site. The coefficients of variation in the density of various artifact classes per collection unit are as follows: ceramics, 94.5 percent; debitage, 178.1 percent; utilized flakes, 278.0 percent; and cores 210.8 percent. All of these values indicate a high degree of clustering, thereby confirming the first implication.

The second implication calls for a high degree of redundancy among collection units in terms of the kinds of artifacts recovered from them. At AZ BB:5:21 there are 19 units exhibiting one artifact class, eleven units with two artifact classes, two units with three artifact classes, and two units with four artifact classes. The ratio is therefore:

$$\text{Redundancy} = \frac{(19 \times 1) + (11 \times 2) + (2 \times 3) + (2 \times 4)}{(34 \times 4)} = \frac{55}{136} = .4044$$

This is the lowest redundancy index found among the sites considered here. As a result, the second implication is not confirmed.

The third and fourth implications call for small sherd sizes and little variation in sherd sizes among collection units. The mean sherd size (by weight) at AZ BB:5:21 is 2.43 grams, with a coefficient of variation of 32.7 percent. Thus, the third and fourth implications tend to be confirmed. While there is some possibility that secondary refuse occurs at the site, the bulk of the remains seems to be primary refuse.

Hypothesis 1: If jars and bowls were jointly used in task performance, expect a high spatial correlation between jars and bowls.

Of the 13 collection units in which jar and/or bowl rims could be identified, nine units contained either jar rims or bowl rims; only four units contained both. The resulting distribution does not differ from what would be expected under random conditions (X^2 = 1.9231, d.f. = 1, .75<p<.90).

Hypothesis 2: If ground stone implements were used in conjunction with jars and/or bowls, expect a high spatial association between jars and/or bowls and ground stone.

Of the eight units containing jars or ground stone or both, none contained both jars and ground stone This was also true of those units containing bowls. As a result, this hypothesis is not confirmed.

> Hypothesis 3: If utilized flakes were used with either jars or bowls, expect a high spatial correlation between utilized flakes and jars and/or bowls.

Of eight collection units containing jars and/or utilized flakes, five have either jars or bowls, while only three units contain both. Of 12 units containing bowls and/or utilized flakes, ten contain either bowls or utilized flakes; only two units contain both. The resulting distribution suggests a significant negative spatial correlation between bowls and utilized flakes ($X^2 = 5.333$, d.f. = 1, $.1<p<.2$). Thus, the above hypothesis does not appear to be confirmed.

These data show that there are at least three kinds of spatially discrete activity areas at AZ BB:5:21. These include areas where jars and/or bowls were used, areas where utilized flakes were used, and areas where ground stone implements were used. Together with the low redundancy index, the patterns indicate that the majority of the remains at AZ BB:5:21 consist of multiple nonoverlapping refuse deposits. The fact that some units exhibit spatial overlap of different artifact classes may indicate the presence of some secondary refuse.

AZ BB:5:22

Surface indications at AZ BB:5:22 resemble those at the other sites situated in the Red Rock-Antelope Peak section of the APS-CS corridor. The site consists of a scatter of sherd, lithic, and ground stone artifacts associated with a number of noncontiguous structures. The site is situated 200 meters north of AZ BB:5:21 in the vicinity of

APS Tower 632. A jeep trail intersects the northern margin of the site but does not appear to have directly impacted much of the site. Data recovery at AZ BB:5:22 consisted of surface collections; excavations were not conducted.

The total site area encompasses approximately 15,000 square meters. A 16-percent stratified random sample of the site resulted in the collection of 22 10 m by 10 m units; as with AZ BB:5:21, only ceramics were collected in these units. One hundred percent of the lithics on the surface of the site were mapped and then collected. The average surface density of sherds and lithics at AZ BB:5:22 is about .51 items per square meter, which is comparable to the surface density of artifacts at AZ BB:5:21. The combination of low surface artifact density and small sample fractions produced small sample sizes for analysis of various artifact populations from the site. All of the artifacts collected were analyzed.

The occupation of AZ BB:5:22 appears to have been contemporaneous with that of AZ BB:5:21. An examination of the sherds shows that the ceramics are more homogeneous with respect to such variables as temper, paste, and surface treatment than those observed at the other investigated sites. Most of the sherds exhibit a micaceous schist temper with variable amounts of quartz sand included in the sherd matrix. Most of the sherds appear to represent a variant of Gila Plain, with a light color and mica temper. The sherds are generally much thinner than those observed at AZ BB:1:9 and AZ BB:1:10. The presence of Tanque Verde or Rincon Phase Red-on-brown varieties (as well as a slipped redware similar to Gila Red) and the limited occurrence of strap-handles on sherds at the site suggest that AZ BB:5:22 was occupied during the period A.D. 1150-1350, which coincides with the transition from the Sedentary to Classic Period in the Hohokam sequence.

Ceramic Population: Characteristics and Functional Interpretations

The majority of the ceramic assemblage from AZ BB:5:22 consists of plainwares. The mean surface density of sherds is approximately .50 per square meter, with a coefficient of variation of 95.0 percent among collection units. The average weight of sherds is 2.65 grams, with a coefficient of variation of 40.4 percent among collection units. These data tend to indicate that the surface distribution of sherds at AZ BB:5:22 is highly clustered and that there is a moderate degree of variation in the size of sherds - as measured by weight - among collection units. The sherds were too small and dispersed to enable vessel reconstruction. A total of 18 rim sherds was recovered from the sample of ceramics taken from the site, although only eleven could be reliably sorted into jar and bowl categories. The resulting jar to bowl ratio at the site is 4:7 (0.57). The metric attributes of the vessel orifice diameters are presented in Table 96.

Table 96. Metric attributes of jar and bowl orifice diameters
from AZ BB:5:22

Item	N	Mean	Standard deviation	Sample range	CV	95% CI
Jars	4	22.0 cm	7.30	14.7 - 29.3 cm	33.2	±7.15 cm
Bowls	7	23.4 cm	3.60	19.8 - 27.0 cm	15.4	±2.67 cm

These data show that while there do not appear to be significant differences, using mean values, between the orifice diameters of jars and bowls, the large confidence intervals about the means - especially in the case of jars - emphasize the possibility that the low sample sizes from the site may be obscuring functionally significant differences between these diameters. Most (71 percent) of the bowls from the site fall within the 24 to 30 cm orifice diameter range, while jars are evenly distributed through all orifice diameter ranges.

The same series of hypotheses regarding vessel function that has been tested with data from the other investigated sites was tested with data from AZ BB:5:22. Sherd porosity studies made by Kinkade and Gilman of ceramics from the site provided the basis for this analysis. Assuming that rim sherds have the same basic porosity as the body sherds used in the porosity study, rim sherds were sorted into various temper and surface treatment categories, and the porosity indices associated with these categories recorded. The resulting distribution is presented in Table 97.

Table 97. Cross-classification of jar and bowl rim sherds
from AZ BB:5:22 by temper and surface treatment

	Jars	Bowls	Mean gram weight increase
Quartz-tempered	2	0	.6923
Interior smudged	0	5	.4688
Exterior polished	2	2	.3750

The first implication, that jars tend generally to be more porous than bowls, is examined with data presented in Table 98.

Table 98. Fischer's exact test for significant differences
in the porosity of jars and bowls from AZ BB:5:22

	Jars	Bowls	Total
More porous (quartz-tempered)	2	0	2
Less porous (smudged, polished)	2	7	0
Totals	4	7	11

These results indicate that there are eleven chances in one hundred that
jars and bowls from AZ BB:5:22 do not come from the same population with
regard to porosity. This represents a relatively strong trend toward
more porous jars and less porous bowls that might be confirmed if larger
sample sizes were available. Consequently, the first implication will be
considered partially confirmed.

The second implication is that jars are subject to less handling
and moving if used for relatively permanent storage, while bowls, because
they are handled in cooking and serving activities, have higher probabilities
of breakage; this leads to the expectation that more bowls will be broken
than jars. Since the jar to bowl ratio at AZ BB:5:22 is 4:7 (.57), this
implication tends not to be confirmed (x^2 = .8182, d.f. = 1, .5<p).

These data indicate that there are no statistically significant
differences between jars and bowls with respect to porosity or apparent
breakage rates such that functionally distinct classes can be identified.
However, they do suggest at least a strong trend toward porosity differences
between these two vessel categories. These interpretive difficulties are
probably the result of the small sample sizes from the site.

Lithic Population: Characteristics and Functional Interpretations

What follows is a series of tests of hypotheses regarding the procurement, manufacture, use, and discard of chipped stone implements at
AZ BB:5:22. These are the same series of hypotheses that have been examined
for the other sites discussed previously, with some modifications. It
should be indicated that the discussion of the procurement and manufacture
of stone tools will not be very detailed due to the very small sample of
debitage from the site. While 12 cores were recovered from the surface
collections, only 14 pieces of debitage were obtained.

Procurement of Raw Materials.   An examination of the data
from AZ BB:5:21 indicates that raw material procurement focused on locally
available resources. Since AZ BB:5:22 is temporally and spatially associated with AZ BB:5:21, it is expected that the pattern of stone procurement
may be similar.

As with other sites, tests on the data from AZ BB:5:22 indicate a strong emphasis on the use of quartzites. Of the 12 cores recovered from the site, eleven were quartzite and one was basalt. This pattern confirms the first hypothesis (that indigenous stone was procured), as well as the first implication of the second hypothesis, in which a highly nonrandom pattern of procurement is expected. The intensity with which these quartzite cores were reduced, as measured by the average number of flake scars per core in relation to the overall size of the cores, is comparable to those ratios obtained for AZ BB:5:21. The mean quartzite core size is 403.6 cc, and the mean number of flakes per core is 8.27, thus producing a ratio of .0205 of flakes to core size. Since cores of other kinds of raw material (except basalt) are not present at the site, it is impossible to assess this ratio in relation to other raw material types in terms of the intensity of core reduction. However, the hypothesis of nonrandom selection for a given stone type - in this case, quartzites - will be provisionally accepted.

Mode of Manufacture. The following series of hypotheses deals with the mode of manufacture of lithic implements at AZ BB:5:22.

Hypothesis 1: If flake reduction occurred at the site, expect
(a) a high core to other flake ratio,
(b) a high core to chunk/shatter ratio,
(c) a high primary flake to tertiary flake ratio, and
(d) a moderate secondary flake to tertiary flake ratio.

Only two of these implications are confirmed using the sample data. The core to other flake ratio is 12:14 (.9231), and the core to chunk/shatter ratio is 12:3 (4.00). The ratio of primary flakes to tertiary flakes is a low 1:4 (0.25), while the ratio of secondary flakes to tertiary flakes is a high 9:4 (2.25); these ratios do not confirm the related implications. These data tend to indicate that core reduction was not a major activity at the site, although it is unclear whether primary flake reduction occurred at the site either.

Hypothesis 2: If the manufacture, use, and discard of formal tools occurred at AZ BB:5:22, expect
(a) a high formal tool to other flake ratio,
(b) a high tertiary flake to other flake ratio,
(c) a high thinning flake to other flake ratio, and
(d) a high formal tool to utilized flake ratio.

Again, data from the site do not tend to confirm these implications. The formal tool to other flake ratio is 4:14 (.2857), while the tertiary flake to other flake ratio is 4:10 (.4). At the same time, the thinning flake to other flake ratio is 0:14 (0), and the ratio of formal tools to utilized flakes is 4:17 (.2325). These data indicate that while there is an increased incidence of formal tools at AZ BB:5:22 in comparison with other sites in the corridor, these implements were not produced at this site, even though they appear to have been used and discarded there.

Hypothesis 3:   If utilized flakes constitute the major item produced at the site, and if flake reduction constitutes
the dominant mode of manufacture, then expect
(a) a high ratio of utilized flakes to other flakes, and
(b) most of the utilized flakes to consist of later-
stage flakes such as secondary and tertiary flakes.

As at AZ BB:5:21, this hypothesis is confirmed. The ratio of utilized
flakes to other flakes at AZ BB:5:22 is 17:14 (1.2143), a value considerably
higher than that found at AZ BB:5:21. The implication that most of the
utilized flakes should consist of later-stage flakes cannot be closely
examined with the meager data available. The lithic sample collected
includes one primary flake, eight secondary utilized flakes, and eight
tertiary utilized flakes. Thus, there does appear to be a strong trend
toward later-stage utilized flakes, which at least provisionally confirms
the last implication.

Use of Unmodified Flakes. It has been demonstrated that there is
a high probability that lithic manufacturing activities at AZ BB:5:22
revolved around the production of flakes that were subsequently used
for short periods and then discarded. There are, however, a number of
questions regarding the uses to which these flakes were put.

Maintaining the distinction between secondary and tertiary utilized
flakes that has been used throughout this report, utilized flakes from
AZ BB:5:22 were first analyzed to determine the relative proportions of
edges that were used on each implement. The results are shown in Table 99.

Table 99. F-test for significant differences in the intensity
of edge utilization among utilized flakes from AZ BB:5:22

	Secondary	Tertiary
Number of cases	8	5
Mean edge use	.2308	.458
Sums of squares	.0181	.0658
Coefficient of variation	21.9%	28.0%

Calculated $F_{7,4,.95} = 4.1572 > F_{7,4,.025}$ of .181
$< F_{7,4,.975}$ of 9.07

These data indicate that there are less than five chances in one hundred
that these different classes of utilized flakes do not come from the
same population with regard to the intensity of flake utilization. Thus,
the implication that there are few differences in the intensity of use
is confirmed.

The second implication is that there are no significant differences in the variation of edge angles between secondary and tertiary utilized flakes. The frequency distribution of utilized flake edge angles is shown in Figure 48. The data required to examine this proposition are presented below.

Table 100. F- test for significant differences in variability of edge angles among utilized flakes from AZ BB:5:22

	Secondary	Tertiary
Number of cases	8	9
Mean edge angle	48.875°	51.0°
Sums of squares	1598.8748	4094.000
Coefficient of variation	30.9%	44.4%

Calculated $F_{7,8,.95}$ = .4463 > $F_{7,8,.025}$ of .204

< $F_{7,8,.975}$ of 4.53

These data confirm the second implication, since there are less than five chances in one hundred that these implements do not come from the same population with regard to variability in edge angles.

The third implication calls for a similar degree of variability among utilized flakes with respect to the amount of edge used. The frequency distribution of utilized flake edge lengths is shown in Figure 49. The information concerning variability in used edge lengths is presented in Table 101.

Table 101. F-test for significant differences in the variability of edge lengths among utilized flakes from AZ BB:5:22

	Secondary	Tertiary
Number of cases	8	9
Mean edge length	2.35	1.87
Sums of squares	6.5328	1.6670
Coefficient of variation	41.2%	24.5%

Calculated $F_{7,8,.95}$ = 4.452 > $F_{7,8,.025}$ of .204

< $F_{7,8,.975}$ of 4.53

It should be indicated that while there is a strong trend toward significant differences between secondary and tertiary utilized flake with regard to the amount of edge used, more than one half of the sums of squares values for secondary flakes result from a single "wild" measure. If

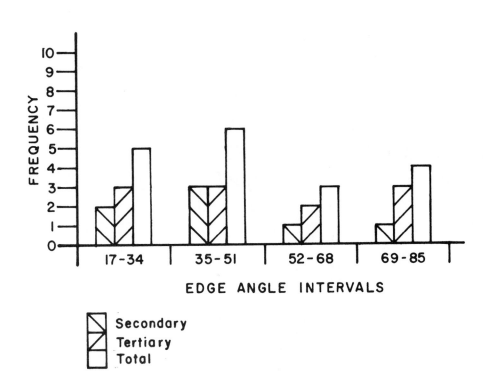

FREQUENCY
DISTRIBUTION OF UTILIZED FLAKE EDGE ANGLES
AT BB:5:22

Figure 48

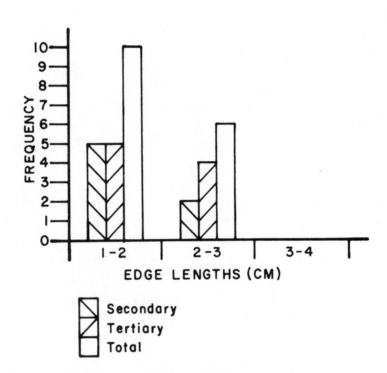

FREQUENCY
DISTRIBUTION OF UTILIZED FLAKE EDGE LENGTHS
AT BB:5:22

Figure 49

this one secondary utilized flake is removed, this trend disappears. As a result, the third implication is confirmed.

The last remaining implication is that there is no significant correlation between edge angles and edge shapes between secondary and tertiary utilized flakes. This implication is examined using a plot of mean flake lengths and widths to illustrate overlaps in the dimensions of secondary and tertiary utilized flakes (Figure 50). The following table is a cross-classification of secondary and tertiary utilized flakes by edge angle and edge shape.

Table 102. Summary of edge angles and configurations of secondary and tertiary utilized flakes from AZ BB:5:22

Degree intervals	Straight S	Straight T	Concave S	Concave T	Convex S	Convex T	Concavo-convex S	Concavo-convex T
17 - 34 (low)	0	1	1	0	0	1	1	0
35 - 51 (medium)	2	3	1	0	0	1	0	0
52 - 68 (medium)	0	0	0	0	0	0	0	1
69 - 85 (high)	0	0	0	3	1	0	0	0

Extremely low cell values preclude an assessment of this distribution in its present form.

To briefly summarize, these tests demonstrate nonrandom selection of quartzite as the raw material for lithic tool manufacture at AZ BB:5:22. Modes of manufacture - whether core or flake reduction - are unclear. The ambiguous test results are probably a function of small sample sizes. While formal tools (especially projectile points) were found at AZ BB:5:22, debitage analyses do not indicate that these implements were produced at the site.

Ground Stone Population: Characteristics and Functional Interpretations

The relative incidence of ground stone implements from AZ BB:5:22 is low. Only two mano fragments and two metate fragments were recovered from the site. The manos have convex working surfaces, while all of the metates are of a trough variety; all of these implements tend to be medium to coarse-grained. Consequently, given the hypothesis regarding the function of these implements depending on shape and grain size, it is unlikely that they were involved in processing seeds or other small items.

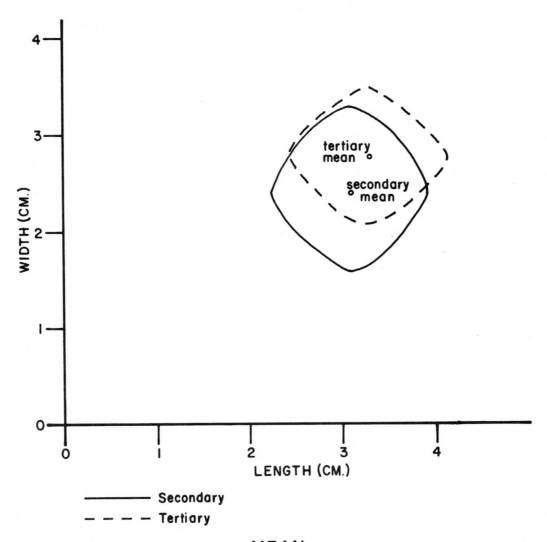

MEAN
LENGTH AND WIDTH ± I STANDARD DEVIATION OF UTILIZED FLAKES
AT BB:5:22

Figure 50

Feature Population: Characteristics and Functional Interpretations

Nine features were recorded at AZ BB:5:22 (Figure 51). Three of these are rectilinear cobble alignments, one is an L-shaped cobble alignment, one is a semicircular cobble alignment, two are circular rock piles, and two are bedrock mortars. Of those features whose areas could be measured, two encompass areas less than 5 meters square, two areas   of 10 to 20 square meters, and two others areas   of more than 20 square meters. Features in the smallest size mode are circular in shape, while features in the larger size modes are rectilinear. Furthermore, the original investigators, Kinkade and Gilman, indicate that the small features may be rock piles and not residential units. Assuming that the small features do not represent residential units, the question of the function of the larger structures remains to be answered.   Drawing upon ethnographic and archaeological findings, the same hypotheses tested for AZ BB:5:21 regarding the presence of ramada-like structures were also tested for AZ BB:5:22.

Of the four structures in the larger size modes (that is, greater than 10 square meters in area), none exhibits enough wall fall to indicate the presence of coursed, aboveground walls. Three of the four structures are indicated by single courses of cobbles and the presence of upright stone slabs. Since excavations were not undertaken in these features, there is no information regarding the preparation (or lack) of floors. Thus, these test results do not prove conclusively that the larger features at AZ BB:5:22 represent ramada-like structures or rooms.

Intrasite Activity Structure at AZ BB:5:22

As has been indicated in previous discussions of intrasite activity structure, it is necessary to determine whether archaeological remains have been deposited as primary or secondary refuse before the question of spatial patterning within a site can be addressed. A tentative method of determining whether remains have been deposited as primary or secondary refuse has been outlined in the earlier section on site-activity hypotheses.

The first test implication is that there are clusters of refuse corresponding to use areas. Coefficients of variation at AZ BB:5:22 indicate that ceramic and chipped stone remains are highly clustered. The ceramic coefficient of variation (according to sherd counts) among collection units is 90.5 percent; those for debitage and utilized flakes are 203 percent and 167 percent, respectively. The coefficient of variation among collection units with respect to the occurrence of cores is 217.2 percent. Thus, the first implication is confirmed.

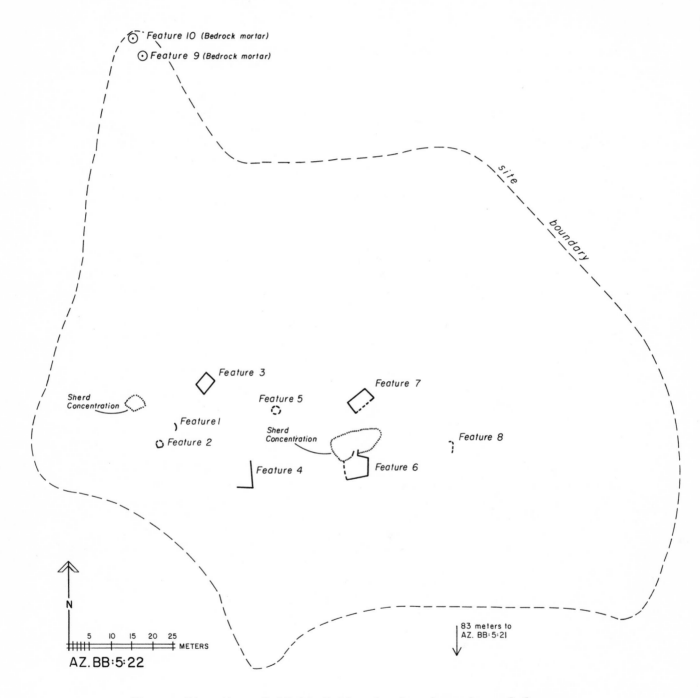

Figure 51.   Map of AZ BB:5:22, showing location of features

The second test implication is that a high degree of redundancy will be found among collection units with regard to the kinds of artifacts found therein. The degree of redundancy at AZ BB:5:22 is not very high. There are eleven units with only one of the four artifact populations. The resulting redundancy index is:

$$\text{Redundancy} = \frac{(11 \times 1) + (6 \times 2) + (3 \times 3) + (1 \times 4)}{(21 \times 4)} = .4286$$

This is one of the lowest redundancy indices found among the sites, and indicates that collection units at AZ BB:5:21 tend to be dissimilar in terms of the diversity of artifacts found in each unit. Thus, the second implication is not confirmed.

The third and fourth implications call for small sherd sizes and little variation among collection units in sherd sizes, assuming that all activity areas are subject to equal trampling. The mean sherd size at AZ BB:5:22 is 2.65 grams, and the coefficient of variation in sherd size among collection units is 40.4 percent. These data indicate that, while sherd sizes tend to be small across the site as a whole, there is a moderate degree of variation among units that may indicate the presence of some secondary refuse.

The combination of low redundancy and an increased probability of secondary refuse deposits at AZ BB:5:22, in conjunction with extremely small sample sizes, warrants caution in discussing intrasite activity structure there. The low redundancy index would lead to the expectation that there will be few spatial associations between artifact populations in terms of collection units. This is, in fact, verified by the data. Jars and bowls tend to occur in spatially discrete areas, while chipped stone populations (including debitage, utilized flakes, and cores) do not appear to be spatially correlated. This leads to the inference that, rather than representing a series of multiple overlapping primary refuse deposits, the bulk of the remains at AZ BB:5:22 consists of multiple non-overlapping refuse deposits. Some of these materials were probably secondarily deposited, while others were deposited at their loci of use, as primary refuse.

AZ AA:8:6--the Jesse Benton Mine

The Jesse Benton Mine represents the only historic Anglo occupation that was examined during the 1974 survey of the southern portion of the APS Cholla-Saguaro transmission line corridor. The mine is located in the northern portion of the Tortolita Mountains, west of Oracle Junction.

In 1882, a newspaper story described the structure of the mine and the milling operation associated with it:

> We entered an enclined shaft,--which had been driven down on the porphyry foot wall near the west end of the claim,--we proceeded to a depth of fifty feet, noting as we descended an eight-inch streak of free milling chloride ore lying on the foot wall. Fifty feet from the surface we entered a level driven west on the foot wall to a distance of forty feet showing all the way the pay streak we had observed in coming down the shaft. At some points in this drift the pay streak widens out to ten and twelve inches. Retracing our steps to the face of the level, we entered another one directly opposite and extending east sixty feet. Here we found the same pay streak showing the entire length of the drift, except at one point where the dike had forced it out. Returning to the face of the drift we descended the shaft to the bottom,--a distance of 75 feet from the surface,--and found a continuation of the pay ore. The hanging wall is granite and the width of the vein matter is several feet. Returning from this point to the surface we examined the dump and found about forty tons of ore, the mill average of which is over three hundred dollars per ton. Just east of this shaft is an open cut extending along the ledge. It is 20 feet long, six feet wide and 12 feet deep, and has yielded about thirty tons of ore, as good in grade and the same in character as that on the dump at the shaft. Just west of the shaft is an open cut on the ledge, 95 feet long, 12 feet deep and about four feet wide. From this a large quantity of rich chloride ore has been extracted. Near the center of the claim is an enclined shaft running down on the foot wall to a depth of about seventy feet and cross-cut at a depth of about sixty feet. It shows a greater breadth of vein matter than the west shaft and the ore occurs in bunches scattered through the vein. Some of the ore from the shaft has been shipped but a considerable amount of high grade rock remains on the dump. On the east end of the claim another enclined shaft goes down on the foot wall to a depth of eighty feet, but we did not explore it owing to a lack of time. It shows some fine ore on the dump, but most of the metal taken out at this point has been shipped and sold for something over $300 per ton....
> The Jessie Benton mill stands in a canyon at the base of the Tortillitas and about three and a half miles west of the Jessie Benton mine. A splendid hard road of gradual descent leads from the latter to the mill. The mill site could not have been better addapted to the purpose had it been designed especially for that use. It is located on a solid rock bluff which has been blasted down in the form of terraces and the machinery so arranged that the ore works down from the rock crusher to the settler without being handled more than once. The machinery consists of five 700-pound stamps, two five foot pans, one eight foot settler, one three foot clean up pan, a rock crusher, a thirty horse power engine, a large steam pump with boiler capacity to furnish more steam than will be needed. The machinery was all

made at Becket & McDowell's, New York, and is handsomely finished. The mill will be completed by the 15th of next month and ready for business....(Arizona Weekly Enterprise, July 29, 1882).

A retrospective account provides some indication of the magnitude of the operations at the Jesse Benton Mine.

The Jesse Benton silver property was being worked night and day with a large crew of miners, and it is reported that between 1,000,000 and 1,500,000 ounces of silver was taken out of the mine. The ore was freighted some five miles further down the gulch to the west where it was put through a five-stamp mill and the silver milled. Then there was a village of some 300 souls at the mine and it was truly a lively mining camp...(Arizona Blade Tribune, May 5, 1923).

The development and decline of the Jesse Benton Mine can be directly linked to technological and economic innovations that occurred during the 1870s. The major technological innovation that affected the operation of mines such as the Jesse Benton was the advent of air-drilling systems and high explosives. These allowed suitable profit margins when exploiting low-grade or multiveined deposits, since fewer men could extract a much greater amount of ore (Young 1967:87).

The economic stimulus for the extraction of silver ore was provided by the Bland-Allison Act of 1878, which provided that the price of silver be increased to $1.29 per ounce. During the 1880s, the question of whether to use silver or gold as the standard of currency was debated throughout the United States. The decision to use gold as a standard contributed directly to a major financial panic in 1893 in which the price of silver dropped from $1.29 per ounce to $0.78 per ounce. Almost all of the silver mining operations in Arizona, including the Jesse Benton Mine, ceased operations in anticipation of, or immediately following, the decision to shift to the gold standard.

Archaeological research at AZ AA:8:6 was extremely limited. The 17 surface features, most of which consist of residential structures, were mapped. Collections from the site consisted of "grab" samples of temporally diagnostic artifacts from some of the features. The major classes of artifacts recovered consisted of cans, nails, cartridges, glass, and ceramics. Because the collections were not comprehensive, the underlying proportions of these artifact classes cannot be estimated. What follows is a brief discussion of temporal and functional variability within and between these artifact classes.

Cans

Almost all of the cans that were recovered from the site were of the "hole-in-the-top" variety. Hole-in-the-top cans consisted of separate

pieces of metal that were soldered together. Sterilization of the contents of the cans involved a heating process that required that a small
hole remain in the top of the can. After heating, the hole was soldered
over and the can allowed to cool. The result was an early form of vacuum-
packing (Fontana and Greenleaf 1962). Starting in 1897, this canning
process was gradually replaced by other forms of cans. By 1902, hole-
in-the-top cans were becoming relatively scarce in the United States.

Nails

Most of the nails found at AZ AA:8:6 were of the square-cut variety.
Most of these square-cut nails began to be replaced by wire nails in the
late 1880s (Fontana and Greenleaf 1962:49). The presence of square-cut
nails, then, corresponds well with the period during which the site is
known to have been occupied.

Cartridges

A number of different rifle and pistol cartridges were recovered
from AZ AA:8:6. Rifle cartridges included the .40-60 and .45-70
Winchester calibers; also found were .44-caliber pistol cartridges.
Variations in the head stamps of these cartridges provide a tentative
indication of the time periods during which these cartridges may have
been deposited at the site. The .40-60 and .45-70 cartridges both have
a "WRA Co." head stamp. The "WRA Co." was replaced by the "WRA" head
stamp in the 1930s. Winchester began production of the .40-60 cartridge
in about 1884 (Williamson 1952:456) and halted production in the 1930s.
The .45-70 cartridge was introduced by Winchester in the 1870s and has
been produced until the present. The .44-caliber pistol cartridges
exhibit the "WRA Co." and "UMC" head stamps of the Winchester Repeating
Arms Company and the Union Metallic Cartridge Company, respectively.
The "WRA Co." head stamp indicates production prior to 1930, while the
"UMC" head stamp indicates production prior to 1912, when the Union
Metallic Cartridge Company merged with Remington Arms. According to
Logan (1959), UMC produced the .44-caliber cartridge from 1867 to 1902.
These dates again bracket the period during which the Jesse Benton Mine
was occupied.

Glass

As glass remains from the site were extremely fragmentary, only
two types of bottles could be distinguished: medicine bottles and liquor
bottles. None of the bottle bases exhibit pontil marks, which indicates

that they were produced after 1860 (Kendrick 1967:20-3). The neck fragments recovered do not exhibit seams, lack of which is normally associated with production prior to 1903 (Scoville 1948:329).

Ceramics

Few ceramic fragments were collected from the site. Most of them are stoneware or earthenware (see Fontana and Greenleaf 1962). Maker's marks, though present on some of these pieces, are incomplete and of little use in either dating the site or determining how these items may have been shipped to the mine. The only reasonably complete maker's mark comes from a plate base which is marked "Premium Stone China - Homer Laughlin".

Summary

Because collections from the Jesse Benton Mine (AZ AA:8:6) were not comprehensive, relatively little can be said regarding the significance of the artifacts recovered therefrom. The range of artifacts from the site tends to conform to expected residential refuse and is mirrored, on a smaller scale, at other mining camps in central Arizona (McGuire 1977:95-102). Unlike many small mining camps, however, residential structures at the Jesse Benton Mine are built of masonry; smaller camps tend to consist of tents. This is important since it appears that the labor investment in the construction of these permanent facilities was considerable, and that the operation of the mine was expected to continue long enough to justify this investment.

The bulk of the refuse collected from the site is utilitarian in nature; luxury items appear infrequently. The absence of children's toys and any items that might possibly be associated with the presence of women may indicate that most of the occupants of the site were male. This conclusion is tentative, however, in light of the fact that the collections made were unsystematic.

There is also some evidence that machinery was removed from the site prior to its abandonment. One building exhibited a series of iron bolts set into the foundation of the structure. The original investigators surmised that these bolts may have been used to stabilize some kind of machinery.

In brief, the Jesse Benton Mine Site appears to represent a residential and processing-activity site associated with the operation of an 1880s silver mine. Most of the refuse from the site appears to be associated with exclusively male households and reflects the range of items that might be expected in day-to-day cooking activities. The number of structures and amount of refuse found do not indicate a population of the size described in newspaper accounts from the period during which the site was occupied. This suggests that, if the newspaper accounts are correct, evidence of a large number of more ephemeral structures (for example, tent pads) may be present at the site.

Interpretations and Conclusions

Although numerous tests of various hypotheses concerning human behavior at the prehistoric sites within the Southern Desert study area have been completed, it is not easy to determine what these various occupations at these sites represent. It is, in fact, much easier to show what they do not represent. For example, the probability that these sites are ceremonial centers is extremely low, as is the probability that they represent long-term habitations.

All of the information that has been presented in the preceding section tends to indicate that these sites probably represent seasonal occupations. The artifact assemblages exhibit a high degree of redundancy both within and among sites, indicating that the same kinds of activities occurred at each of these sites, with some minor variations. The bulk of the data suggests that plant procurement and processing, as well as some limited hunting, constituted the primary activities at these sites. Because of gaps in the data base, however, it is difficult to specify in greater detail the nature of prehistoric human occupation at these sites.

Nevertheless, an attempt will be made to more explicitly define what these remains may indicate in terms of prehistoric subsistence-settlement strategies. Specifically, an argument will be presented whereby AZ BB:1:8, AZ BB:1:9, AZ BB:1:10, AZ BB:5:21, and AZ BB:5:22 may be seen to represent similar kinds of cactus extraction and processing loci even though they are separated in time. It has already been demonstrated that these five sites are situated in an area where 33 percent or less of the ground cover consists of economically significant plant species. Based on this contemporary plant distribution, the majority of the plants that are economically important are cacti, essentially including various species of Opuntia, primarily prickly-pear and cholla. Prehistoric cactus exploitation strategies and the kinds of archaeological manifestations of associated activities have been treated in great detail by Goodyear (1975). Goodyear's work is crucial to understanding cactus exploitation in Lower Sonoran environments, and his methodological approach to delineating various components of cactus extraction activities has been adopted for this study.

The main hypothesis is that these sites represent seasonally-occupied loci at which yucca, mescal, prickly-pear, or cholla were procured and processed. There are many ethnographic descriptions concerning the exploitation of these species by Papago and Apache groups (Castetter and Underhill 1935; Castetter and Opler 1936; Buskirk 1949). In describing the use of cholla and prickly-pear by the Papago, Castetter and Underhill have stated:

> The buds and joints of the five species of Opuntia...constitute
> a staple crop....The branches of the chollas are composed of easily
> detachable joints; the flower buds...are gathered as they come out in
> May. Whole cholla joints, as well as the buds, are pit-baked and
> dried....When the picking is ended, a pit is dug, stones placed in it
> and heated with a mesquite fire (1935:15).

Castetter and Underhill further state that, with respect to prickly-pear, "the usual method of utilizing the fruit is to eat it fresh in large quantities while the supply lasts, unused fruit being dried or made into syrup"(1935:23).

Yucca was also an important staple crop that was gathered and preserved. Castetter and Underhill (1935:23) state that the fruit was eaten fresh whenever possible and the seeds were "removed by hand and the pulp ground on the metate."

Mescal (agave), aloe, and sotol are rare in areas near the investigated sites, although they do occur in the area north of Antelope Peak. There are numerous examples of the preparation of these plants and their products in the ethnographic literature. Yucca hearts were prepared by the Mescalero and Chiricahua Apache in a manner similar to that described for mescal:

> The crowns of the mescal plants are dug out with three-foot sticks cut from oak branches ...and flattened at the end....A broad stone knife is used to chop off the leaves....Pits in which the crowns are baked are about ten to twelve feet in diameter and three or four feet deep , lined with large flat rocks....Rocks are piled on the flat stones....Upon this, oak...and juniper wood...are placed. Before the sun comes up this is set on fire and by noon the fire has died down....After the mescal has been covered with the long leaves of bear grass and the whole with earth to a depth sufficient to prevent steam from escaping, the crowns are allowed to bake the rest of the day and all night. Early in the morning the pit is opened and a crown examined and eaten. The pit is again closed.... The following morning all the mescal is removed....The pulpy centers of the black, roasted crowns are...pounded vigorously into thin sheets on a rock (Castetter and Opler 1936:35-37).

Buskirk, who also worked with Apache groups, indicates that winter was the main period during which mescal was gathered (1949:297). According to Apache informants, the best mescal came from south of the Salt River and from the Bylas and Graham mountains (1949:297). Mescal gathering was described as follows:

> The winter camps were temporary habitations. If rain threatened, a ramada could be erected by a man and wife in about two hours....A roasting place was selected in an area where there was a good stand of agave. From this the women of the party fanned out in groups of two or more, frequently searching a radius of a mile or more from the roasting pit to find suitable plants....After the plant had been cut or pried loose [with a chisel like implement made of wood], the leaves were trimmed with the mescal knife....the men dug an earth oven or cleaned an old one, the dimensions varying from three to twelve feet in diameter and from two to four feet in depth. After digging or clearing the pit, they filled it with wood laid in a criss-cross pattern.... Over the wood was placed a layer of stones (1949:289, 299-300).

After the mescal was cooked, the pulp could be treated in one of two ways. "The cooked mescal was pounded flat with stones into sheets an inch or two thick and two or three feet in diameter [and then dried]" (Buskirk 1949:304).

Alternatively, "the cooked mescal crowns were left in a heated pit until they began to ferment. Then they were ground and boiled or boiled first and then ground, and the liquor poured off and allowed to stand until fermented" (Buskirk 1949:305). It should be noted that, unlike Castetter and Bell and Castetter and Opler, Buskirk indicates that cholla and yucca were not used by the Apache. Lastly, Russell described Pima mescal-gathering activities as follows: "Then the men gathered mescal heads by prying them out with the sticks, and trimmed off the leaves with a knife.... Pits were dug, and after the fire built in them had died down small stones were placed on the coals. The mescal was then placed on the stones and the whole covered with earth" (1908:70). Russell also indicates that juice was extracted from the pulp and then boiled for syrup (1908:70); the same pattern of processing was used for various cholla species (1908:71).

These descriptions show a consistent patterning in the behavior and implements associated with the procurement and processing of Opuntia, mescal, and yucca. At the same time, it is evident that, due to these similarities, it is almost impossible to precisely determine which cactus species were being processed at any one locus; the archaeological indicators would all be the same. For this reason, rather than try to identify the species being processed, the behavior associated with the procurement and processing of all of these cacti will be treated as a unit. The patterns thus described lead to the following testable proposition:

Hypothesis 1: If prehistoric methods of procurement and processing of yucca, Opuntia, and mescal were similar to those described for ethnohistoric groups, then one would expect to find

Test Implication 1: evidence of temporary shelters, such as ramadas;

Test Implication 2: a preponderance of stone implements with acute edge angles for cutting and slicing the pads, stalks, and crowns of cacti;

Test Implication 3: a high incidence of implements for pounding and/or grinding cactus pulp after it was roasted;

Test Implication 4: both jars and bowls at these sites. If cactus products were being boiled for syrup, expect jars to predominate;

Test Implication 5: subsurface pits of variable size containing carbonized wood and stones;

Test Implication 6: within these pits, pollen from the above cacti.

Some of these implications can be examined using data from the investigated sites; the last two implications cannot be examined, since no subsurface testing was done at the sites.

Test Implication 1: expect evidence of temporary shelters such as ramadas.

        Seasonally occupied structures have been defined at AZ BB:1:8, AZ BB:1:9, and AZ BB:1:10, although it is by no means certain that they represent ramadas. However, the presence of single-course cobble outlines, coupled with an absence of wall fall and - at AZ BB:1:8 - the absence of prepared floors, does tend to indicate only a small labor investment in these structures. At AZ BB:5:21 and AZ BB:5:22, the interpretation of large features as ramada-like structures is somewhat more justifiable. Of the four attributes associated with ramadas (single-course cobble outlines, upright slabs, an absence of wall fall, and un- prepared floors), the large structures at these two sites exhibit a nonrandom association of at least the first three. Given these patterns, the probability that these structures represent ramada-like structures is increased, and the first implication will be considered tentatively confirmed.

Test Implication 2: expect a high frequency of acute-angled implements for
                     cutting and slicing the pads, stalks, and crowns of cacti.

        The predominance of acute-angled utilized flakes at all of these sites has been conclusively demonstrated.

Test Implication 3: expect implements for pounding and/or grinding cactus pulp
                     after it was roasted.

        This implication does not appear to be confirmed at either AZ BB:1:9 or AZ BB:5:22. The ground stone and battered stone frequencies are such that "a high incidence" cannot be postulated. The ratios of ground/battered stone to all other artifact populations at these two sites are .0017 and .006, respectively. This implication does appear to be confirmed at AZ BB:1:10 and AZ BB:5:21, where the ratios of ground/battered stone to all other artifact populations are .024 and .028, respectively. However, few ethnographic data are available regarding the relative proportions of grinding implements at mescal camps.

Test Implication 4: expect both jars and bowls to occur at these sites.
                     If cactus fruit was being boiled for syrup, expect
                     jar forms to predominate within the sherd assemblages.

        Data from these four sites indicate that both jars and bowls occur in varying proportions within the ceramic assemblages. The strong trend toward a significant preponderance of jars at AZ BB:5:21 could indicate syrup production, although this is not certain.

Test Implication 5:   expect subsurface pits of variable size containing
                       carbonized wood and stones.

Test Implication 6:   expect these pits to contain pollen from mescal, sotol,
                       yucca, or cholla.

        In the absence of any subsurface excavations, it is impossible to test
these implications at present. It has been demonstrated that the smaller cobble
concentrations at the sites are not ramada-like features. For present purposes,
it is proposed that these smaller rock concentrations are, in fact, roasting pits
for the preparation of yucca, cholla, or prickly-pear products. Since these
test implications are crucial to confirming or rejecting the hypothesized function of these features, future research should focus on testing these features.
If they are not roasting pits, then the hypotheses regarding cactus processing
will have to be reexamined.

        In addition to cactus processing, two sites exhibit evidence of legumi-
nous plant processing. Sites AZ BB:5:21 and 22 both contain bedrock mortars,
the presence of which suggests that activities related to the processing of
leguminous plants (mesquite and acacia) were also conducted at these two sites.
Bedrock mortars, boulder mortars, and wooden mortars are known to have been
important in the processing of mesquite pods by the Papago (Castetter and
Underhill 1935; Doelle 1976). Russell (1908:74) reports that, for the Pima,
mesquite beans constituted nearly the most important food resource.

        Goodyear (1975:161) notes that the seeds and beans of mesquite are ex-
tremely rich in proteins and carbohydrates. While acacia has not been analyzed
for nutritional properties, he notes that it should be possible generally to
extend to acacia the chemical properties of mesquite, since the fruit morphologies
are so similar (1975:66).

        With respect to leguminous seed processing, Castetter and Underhill
report the following:

    The technique with all these except the sticky mesquite was to parch,
    sun-dry, and store in sealed jars. The parching was done at the time
    of gathering and was really part of the storing technique to prevent
    mildew, although the seeds were not ground into flour until just before
    they were used. The mesquite beans, too sticky for a metate, were
    pounded in a mortar made either of stone or wood (a mesquite log hollowed
    with a stone axe) (1935:45).

        Doelle's (1976) study involved the demonstration of mesquite-pod processing by
a Papago woman. In this study, the bedrock mortars were located about one-half
mile from the woman's house. Dried mesquite pods were piled into a mortar,
pulverized with a pestle into a fine flour, sifted, then made into cake by
adding a small amount of water. The cake could then be stored away for later
use.

AZ BB:5:21 and 22 are situated on ridge tops where mesquite is rare. However, in the steep drainages flanking the ridges and in the major wash channels, acacia and dense bosques of mesquite are common. While the relative abundance of mesquite and acacia in prehistoric times is unknown, and long-term climatic change has doubtlessly altered the density and distribution of these plants somewhat, this probably did not cause a major change in the availability of these plants at the time the sites were occupied. Thus, it is reasonable to suggest that mesquite-pod gathering and processing constituted one set of activities at these sites.

In summary, the study of five prehistoric sites in the Red Rock-Antelope Peak segment of the APS Cholla-Saguaro transmission line corridor has focused on defining subsistence-related activities in the Southern Desert. Not all study goals could be fulfilled, but the data have helped to augment our knowledge of the use of nonriverine areas by Hohokam and Salado groups.

The ceramic data indicate occupation of the area during several different time periods by groups exhibiting characteristics of the Hohokam and Salado material cultures. AZ BB:1:8 appears to be the earliest of the five sites. The sherds date to the Santa Cruz and Sacaton phases of the late Colonial and early Sedentary periods of the Gila Basin Hohokam. Plainwares, the only sherds recovered from AZ BB:1:9, are not chronologically sensitive. However, site architecture and characteristics of the artifact assemblage suggest a post-A.D. 1150 occupation by late Hohokam or early Salado groups. Similarily, the high frequency of mica-tempered plainware sherds and red corrugated sherds at AZ BB:1:10 also indicates a post-A.D. 1150 date.

AZ BB:5:21 and 22 are not only better dated, but also reveal some mode of occupation by Hohokam groups exhibiting a material culture characteristic of the Tucson Basin and San Pedro Valley. Specifically, the presence of Tanque Verde Red-on-brown, smudged corrugated wares, and intrusive whitewares indicates occupation during the Rincon and Tanque Verde phases of the Hohokam Sedentary-Classic Period transition. The data at hand do not, however, provide any new information that would elucidate the previously discussed problems of settlement and subsistence during the Hohokam Sedentary and Classic periods. We can only say that sites of these periods do exist in nonriverine areas; more data from AZ BB:5:21 and 22 are needed if these sites are to be adequately compared to others in assessing prehistoric land use during the Hohokam Sedentary and Classic periods.

The data from the sites as a whole do indicate that site activities with respect to subsistence pursuits are not markedly different despite their different times of occupation. Procurement and processing of cactus products seem to have been undertaken at all the sites; furthermore, on the basis of the presence of bedrock mortars, leguminous plant processing seems to have been performed at AZ BB:5:21 and 22. This could mean that mesquite and acacia acquired greater importance in later times; however, this cannot be proved since wooden mortars or mortars situated at a distance from AZ BB:1:8, 9, and 10 could have been used. Another consideration is that AZ BB:5:21 and 22 may be representative of the San Pedro Hohokam as opposed to the Gila Basin Hohokam represented at AZ BB:1:8, 9, and 10. Seen from this perspective, the presence of bedrock mortars at AZ BB:5:21 and 22 could reflect a culturally determined emphasis on different types of plant foods, if not an adaptive response to a changing resource base.

The information gained from this study has shown that, regardless of time period, the sites investigated reflect Hohokam (and later Salado) subsistence activities geared toward the procurement and processing of available wild resources. The presence of semipermanent structures indicates that the sites were visited on an occasional basis, although future excavation may well produce evidence of occupation of longer duration. Most importantly, the data show that as early as the late Colonial Period, and well into the Classic Period, the Hohokam were exploiting desert resources well away from riverine areas. More complete data from the sites are needed, however, to understand their role in the overall prehistoric subsistence-settlement system of the Southern Desert.

REFERENCES

Adams, E. D.
   1972   General Soil Map, Pinal County, Arizona. U.S. Department of
           Agriculture Soil Conservation Service, Washington.

Agenbroad, Larry D.
   1967   The distribution of fluted points in Arizona. The Kiva 32:
           113-120.

Anthony, Robert G. and Norman S. Smith
   1977   Ecological relationships between mule deer and whitetail
           deer in southeastern Arizona. Ecological Monographs 47: 255-277.

Arizona Blade Tribune
   1923   "Rich gold strike made in Owl Heads - $2000 ton."
           May 5, 1923. Florence, Arizona.

Arizona Weekly Enterprise
   1882   Jesse Benton consolidated. July 29, 1882. Florence, Arizona.

Ayres, James E.
   1967   A prehistoric farm site near Cave Creek, Arizona. The Kiva 32:
           106-111.

Betancourt, Julio L.
   1978a   An archaeological synthesis of the Tucson Basin: focus on
           the Santa Cruz and its river park. Arizona State Museum
           Archaeological Series 116.

   1978b   Cultural resources within the proposed Santa Cruz Riverpark
           Archaeological District. Arizona State Museum Archaeological
           Series 125.

Bolton, Herbert E.
   1919   Kino's historical memoir of Pimeria Alta (Vol. 2).
           Cleveland: Arthur H. Clark.

   1936   Rim of Christendom. New York: MacMillan.

Brew, Susan A.
   1975   Archaeological assessment of Cañada del Oro. Arizona
           State Museum Archaeological Series 87.

Browne, J. Ross
   1869   Adventures in Apache country: a tour through Arizona and
           Sonora, with notes on the silver regions of Nevada.
           New York: Harper and Brothers.

Buskirk, Winfred
    1949   Western Apache subsistence economy. Unpublished Ph.D.
           dissertation, Department of Anthropology, University of
           Arizona, Tucson.

Canouts, Veletta, editor
    1975   An archaeological survey of the Arizona Public Service
           Cholla to Saguaro 500 kV transmission line proposed route.
           Interim report: Antelope Peak, Arizona to Superior,
           Arizona. Arizona State Museum Archaeological Series 81.

Castetter, E. F. and W. H. Bell
    1942   Pima and Papago Indian agriculture. Inter-Americana
           Studies I. Albuquerque: University of New Mexico Press.

    1951   Yuman Indian agriculture. Albuquerque: University of
           New Mexico Press.

Castetter, E. F. and M. E. Opler
    1936   Ethnobiological studies in the American Southwest: the
           ethnobiology of the Chiricahua and Mescalero Apache.
           University of New Mexico Bulletin 297.

Castetter, E. F. and R. M. Underhill
    1935   Ethnobiological studies in the American Southwest: the
           ethnobiology of the Papago Indians. University of New
           Mexico Bulletin 275.

Cochran, W. G.
    1977   Sampling techniques. Third edition. New York: John Wiley
           and Sons.

Corle, Edwin
    1950   The Gila: river of the Southwest. New York: Rinehart and
           Company.

DeBoer, W. R. and D. W. Lathrap
    n.d.   The making and breaking of Shipibo-Conibo ceramics.
           To be published in Ethnoarchaeology: implications of
           ethnography for archaeology, edited by Carol Kramer.
           New York: Columbia University Press.

Debowski, Sharon S., assembler
    in preparation
           The Anamax-Rosemont Project: an archaeological evaluation
           in the Santa Rita Mountains. Arizona State Museum
           Archaeological Series.

Debowski, Sharon S. and G. Fritz
    1974   The archaeological resources of the Middle Gila Planning
           Unit of the Bureau of Land Management. Arizona State
           Museum Archaeological Series 46.

Debowski, Sharon, Anique George, Richard Goddard, and Deborah Mullon
    1976   An archaeological survey of the Buttes Reservoir.
            Arizona State Museum Archaeological Series 93.

DiPeso, Charles C.
    1951   The Babocomari Village Site on the Babocomari River,
            southeastern Arizona. The Amerind Foundation, Inc.,
            No. 5. Dragoon, Arizona.

    1953   The Sobaipuri Indians of the upper San Pedro River Valley,
            southeastern Arizona. The Amerind Foundation, Inc., No. 6.
            Dragoon, Arizona.

    1956   The Upper Pima of San Cayetano del Tumacacori: an
            archaeological reconstruction of the Ootam of Pimeria
            Alta. The Amerind Foundation, Inc., No. 7. Dragoon,
            Arizona.

Dobyns, Henry F.
    1974   The Kohatk: oasis and ak chin horticulturists. Ethnohistory
            21: 317-328.

Doelle, William H.
    1975   The Gila Pima at first contact. MS. Arizona State Museum
            Library, Tucson.

    1976   Desert resources and Hohokam subsistence: the Conoco
            Florence Project. Arizona State Museum Archaeological
            Series 103.

Doyel, David E.
    1974   Excavations in the Escalante Ruin Group, southern Arizona.
            Arizona State Museum Archaeological Series 37 (revised 1975).

    1976   Classic Period Hohokam in the Gila River Basin, Arizona.
            The Kiva 42: 27-38.

    1977   Excavations in the middle Santa Cruz River Valley,
            southeastern Arizona. Contribution to Highway Salvage
            Archaeology in Arizona 44.

Emory, W. H., Lieut. Col.
    1848   Notes of a military reconnoissance, from Fort Leavenworth,
            in Missouri, to San Diego, in California, including part
            of the Arkansas, Del Norte, and Gila rivers. Thirtieth
            Congress, First Session, Ex. Doc. No. 41. Washington:
            Wendell and Van Benthuysen.

Ezell, Paul H.
    1961   The Hispanic acculturation of the Gila River Pimas.
            Memoirs of the American Anthropological Association 90.
            Menasha, Wisconsin.

Ferguson, T. J. and John Beezley
    1974   A records inventory of the archaeological resources in the
            San Manuel - Red Rock A.P.S. transmission line study area.
            Arizona State Museum Archaeological Series 42.

Fish, Paul R.
    n.d.   Gila Dunes: a Chiricahua Stage site near Florence,
            Arizona. MS. Arizona State Museum Library, Tucson.

Fontana, Bernard and J. Cameron Greenleaf
    1962   Johnny Ward's Ranch: a study in historic archaeology.
            The Kiva 28 (1-2).

Fontana, Bernard, W. J. Robinson, C. W. Cormack, and E. E. Leavitt, Jr.
    1962   Papago Indian pottery. Seattle: University of Washington
            Press.

Franklin, Hayward H. and W. Bruce Masse
    1976   The San Pedro Salado: a case of prehistoric migration.
            The Kiva 42: 47-56.

Frick, Paul S.
    1954   An archaeological survey in the central Santa Cruz Valley,
            southern Arizona. MS. M.A. thesis, Department of Anthropology,
            University of Arizona, Tucson.

Fulton, William S. and Carr Tuthill
    1940   An archaeological site near Gleeson, Arizona. The
            Amerind Foundation, Inc., No. 1. Dragoon, Arizona.

Gabel, N. E.
    1931   Martinez Hill Ruins. MS. M.A. thesis, Department of Anthropology,
            University of Arizona, Tucson.

Gasser, Robert E.
    1976   Hohokam subsistence: a 2000 year continuum in the
            indigenous exploitation of the lower Sonoran Desert.
            USDA Forest Service, Southwestern Region, Report No. 11.
            Albuquerque.

Gilman, Patricia and Barry Richards
    1975   An archaeological survey in Aravaipa Canyon Primitive Area.
            Arizona State Museum Archaeological Series 77.

Gladwin, Harold S., Emil W. Haury, E. B. Sayles, and Nora Gladwin
    1937   Excavations at Snaketown: material culture. Medallion
            Papers 25. Globe: Gila Pueblo.

411

Goodyear, Albert C.
    1975   Hecla II and III: an interpretive study of archaeological remains from the Lakeshore Project, Papago Reservation, south central Arizona. <u>Arizona State University Anthropological Research Paper</u> 9.

Goodyear, Albert C. and A. E. Dittert
    1973   Hecla I: a preliminary report on archaeological investigations at the Lakeshore Project, Papago Reservation, south central Arizona. <u>Arizona State University Anthropological Research Paper</u> 4.

Gould, R. A., D. A. Koster, and A. H. Sontz
    1971   The lithic assemblage of the western desert aborigines of Australia. <u>American Antiquity</u> 36: 149-169.

Grebinger, Paul F.
    1971   Hohokam cultural development in the middle Santa Cruz Valley, Arizona. Ph.D. dissertation, University of Arizona. Ann Arbor: University Microfilms.

    1976   Salado - perspectives from the middle Santa Cruz Valley. <u>The Kiva</u> 42:39-46.

Greene, Jerry L. and Thomas W. Mathews
    1976   Faunal study of unworked mammalian bones. In Haury, pp. 367-373.

Greenleaf, J. Cameron
    1975   <u>Excavations at Punta de Agua.</u> Tucson: University of Arizona Press.

Gressinger, A. W.
    1963   The story of a desert town. <u>Pinal Ways</u> 4: 37-46.

Hackenberg, Robert A.
    1955   Economic and political change among the Gila River Pima Indians. MS. Arizona State Museum Library, Tucson.

Hammack, Laurens C.
    1969   A preliminary report of the excavations at Las Colinas. <u>The Kiva</u> 35: 11-27.

Hastings, James R. and Raymond M. Turner
    1965   <u>The changing mile: an ecological study of vegetation change with time in the lower mile of an arid and semiarid region.</u> Tucson: University of Arizona Press.

Haury, Emil W.
    1950   <u>The stratigraphy and archaeology of Ventana Cave, Arizona.</u> Tucson: University of Arizona Press.

Haury, Emil W.
   1976   The Hohokam: desert farmers and craftsmen. Excavations at
           Snaketown, 1964-1965. Tucson: University of Arizona Press.

Hayden, Irwin
   1931   Field report on major antiquities: Grewe Site, Coolidge,
           Arizona. MS. Arizona State Museum Library, Tucson.

Hayden, Julian D.
   1957   Excavations, 1940, at University Indian Ruin, Tucson, Arizona.
           Southwestern Monuments Association Technical Series 5.
           Globe: Gila Pueblo.

Hemmings, E. Thomas
   1969   Analysis of a Clovis bison kill site and processing area.
           Paper presented at the 34th Annual Meeting of the Society
           for American Archaeology, Milwaukee.

Huckell, Bruce B.
   1973   The Gold Gulch Site: a specialized Cochise site near
           Bowie, Arizona. The Kiva 39: 105-130.

Huckell, Lisa W.
   1976   Analysis of the carbonized plant remains from the Rabid
           Ruin, Arizona, AA:12:46. MS. Arizona State Museum Library,
           Tucson.

Humphrey, Robert R.
   1958   The desert grassland: a history of vegetational change and
           an analysis of causes. University of Arizona Agricultural
           Experiment Station Bulletin 299 (reprinted from The Botanical
           Review 24(4), April 1958).

Irwin-Williams, Cynthia
   1977   Black boxes and multiple working hypotheses: reconstructing
           the economy of early Southwest hunters. The Kiva 42: 285-300.

Ives, Ronald L.
   1973   Father Kino's 1697 entrada to the Casa Grande Ruin in
           Arizona: a reconstruction. Arizona and the West 15: 345-370.

Johnston, A. R., Captain
   1848   Journal of Captain A. R. Johnston, First Dragoons. In
           Emory, pp. 565-614.

Kelly, Isabel T.
   1938   The Hodges Site, Vol. 1 (as revised by James E. Officer).
           MS. Arizona State Museum Library, Tucson.

Kelly, Isabel T., James E. Officer, and Emil W. Haury
   1978   The Hodges Ruin: a Hohokam community in the Tucson Basin,
           edited by Gayle Harrison Hartmann. Tucson: University of
           Arizona Press.

Kendrick, Grace
    1967   Bottle fragments betray age of historical sites.
            El Palacio 74 (2) 19-24.

Kinkade, Gay M. and Patricia Gilman
    1974   An archaeological survey of the Arizona Public Service
            Cholla to Saguaro 500 kV transmission line proposed route.
            Interim report: Winkelman, Arizona to Red Rock, Arizona:
            Saguaro plant. Arizona State Museum Archaeological Series 54.

Kinkade, Gay M. and Gordon L. Fritz
    1975   The Tucson Sewage Project: studies at two archaeological
            sites. Arizona State Museum Archaeological Series 64.

Lentner, Marvin
    1975   Introduction to applied statistics. Boston: Prindle,
            Weber, & Schmidt.

Logan, H. C.
    1959   Cartridges: a pictorial digest of small arms ammunition.
            New York: Bonanza Books.

Longacre, W. A.
    1974   Kalinga pottery making: the evolution of an archaeological
            research design. MS. Arizona State Museum Library, Tucson.

Martin, Paul Schultz and H. E. Wright, editors
    1967   Pleistocene extinctions: the search for a cause. Vol. 6
            of the Proceedings of the VII Congress of the International
            Association for Quaternary Research. New Haven: Yale
            University Press.

McClintock, James H.
    1916 Arizona. Chicago: S. J. Clarke.

McGuire, Randall
    1977   The Copper Canyon - McGuireville Project: archaeological
            investigations in the middle Verde Valley, Arizona.
            Contribution to Highway Salvage Archaeology in Arizona 45.

Quinn, Kathleen and John Roney
    1973   Archaeological resources of the San Simon and Vulture units
            of the Bureau of Land Management. Arizona State Museum
            Archaeological Series 34.

Raab, L. Mark
    1976   The structure of prehistoric community organization at
            Santa Rosa Wash, southern Arizona. Unpublished Ph. D.
            dissertation, Arizona State University. Ann Arbor:
            Microfilms Press.

Rose, Martin R.
    1978   The extension and quantitative retrodiction of intra-annual
            paleoclimatic variability on the Colorado Plateau: a test
            case. Paper presented at the 43rd Annual Meeting of the
            Society for American Archaeology, Tucson.

Russell, Frank
    1908   The Pima Indians. Twenty-sixth Annual Report of the Bureau
            of American Ethnology, 1904-1905, pp. 3-390. Washington:
            Government Printing Office.

Sayles, E. B.
    1945   The San Simon Branch: excavations at Cave Creek and in the
            San Simon Valley. 1: Material culture. Medallion Papers 34.
            Globe: Gila Pueblo.

Sayles, E. B., and E. Antevs
    1941   The Cochise Culture. Medallion Papers 29. Globe: Gila Pueblo.

Sayles, E. B., E. Antevs, T. L. Smiley, W. W. Wasley, and R. H. Thompson
    n.d.   The Cochise Gathering Culture of southeastern Arizona.
            MS. Arizona State Museum, Tucson.

Schiffer, Michael B.
    1976   Behavioral Arch eology. New York: Academic Press.

Schroeder, Albert H.
    1960   The Hohokam, Sinagua and the Hakataya. Archives of Archaeo-
            logy 5. Madison: Society for American Archaeology and
            the University of Wisconsin Press.

Schulman, Edmund
    1945   Tree-ring hydrology of the Colorado River Basin. University
            of Arizona Bulletin 16 (4), Laboratory of Tree-ring
            Research Bulletin 2.

    1956   Dendroclimatic changes in semiarid America. Tucson:
            University of Arizona Press.

Scoville, W. C.
    1948   Revolution in glassmaking. Cambridge: Harvard Press.

Shepard, Anna O.
    1956   Ceramics for the archaeologist. Carnegie Institution of
            Washington Publication 609. Washington.

Shipek, Florence
    1951   Gila Butte Site. MS. Arizona State Museum Library, Tucson.

Siegel, Sidney
   1956   Nonparametric statistics for the behavioral sciences.
           New York: McGraw-Hill.

Spain, Nicholas
   n.d.   Plant density along the APS Cholla - Saguaro transmission
           line corridor: raw data. MS. Arizona State Museum, Tucson.

Spence, Michael W.
   n.d.   The development of the Teotihuacan obsidian production
           system. MS. Arizona State Museum Library, Tucson.

Stacy, V. K. Pheriba and Julian D. Hayden
   1975   Saguaro National Monument: an archaeological overview.
           Arizona Archaeological Center, National Park Service, Tucson.

Steila, Donald
   1972   Drought in Arizona: a drought identification methodology
           and analysis. Division of Economic and Business Research,
           University of Arizona, Tucson.

Teague, Lynn S.
   1974   The archaeological resources of the Winkelman and Black
           Hills Unit of the Bureau of Land Management. Arizona State
           Museum Archaeological Series 47.

Tringham, Ruth, G. Cooper, G. Odell, B. Voytek, and A. Whitman
   1974   Experimentation in the formation of edge damage: a new
           approach to lithic analysis. Journal of Field Archaeology 1:
           171-196.

Tuthill, Carr
   1947   The Tres Alamos Site on the San Pedro River, southeastern
           Arizona. The Amerind Foundation, Inc., No. 4. Dragoon,
           Arizona.

U.S. Department of Agriculture
   1977   Santa Cruz - San Pedro River Basin, Arizona: resource
           inventory.

Vivian, R. Gwinn, Peggy Spaulding, and Walter H. Birkby
   1974   Test excavations at Arizona U:13:27: the Sacaton-Turnkey
           Project. Arizona State Museum Archaeological Series 44.

Wagoner, J. J.
   1952   History of the cattle industry in southern Arizona, 1540-
           1940. University of Arizona Social Science Bulletin 20.

Wasley, William W.
   1960   A Hohokam platform mound at the Gatlin Site, Gila Bend,
           Arizona. American Antiquity 26: 244-262.

Wasley, William W.
    1966   Classic Period Hohokam. Paper presented at the 31st Annual
            Meeting of the Society for American Archaeology, Reno.

Wasley, William W. and Blake Benham
    1968   Salvage excavation in the Buttes Dam Site, southern Arizona.
            The Kiva 33: 244-279.

Weaver, Donald E., Jr.
    1973   Excavations at Pueblo del Monte and the Classic Period
            Hohokam problem. The Kiva 39: 75-88.

Whalen, Norman M.
    1971   Cochise Culture sites in the central San Pedro drainage,
            Arizona. Ph.D. dissertation, University of Arizona.
            Ann Arbor: University Microfilms.

    1975   Cochise site distribution in the San Pedro Valley.
            The Kiva 40: 203-211.

Whallon, Robert Jr.
    1973   Spatial analysis of occupation floors I: the application
            of dimensional analysis of variance. American Antiquity 38:
            266-278.

    1974   Spatial analysis of occupation floors II: the application
            of nearest neighbor analysis. American Antiquity 39: 16-34.

White, J. P. and D. H. Thomas
    1972   What mean these stones?: ethno-taxonomic models and archaeo-
            logical interpretations in the New Guinea highlands. In
            Models in Archaeology, edited by D. L. Clarke, pp. 275-308.
            London: Methuen.

Wilcox, David R. and Lynette O. Shenk
    1977   The architecture of the Casa Grande and its interpretation.
            Arizona State Museum Archaeological Series 115.

Willey, Gordon and Philip Phillips
    1958   Method and theory in American archaeology. Chicago:
            University of Chicago Press.

Williamson, H. F.
    1952   Winchester: the gun that won the West. New York: A. S.
            Barnes.

Wilmsen, Edwin
    1968   Functional analysis of flaked stone artifacts. American
            Antiquity 33: 156-161.

Windmiller, Ric
    1972   Archaeological salvage excavations at two drilling sites
            within Conoco's project area near Florence, Arizona.
            Arizona State Museum Archaeological Series 8.

    1973   The late Cochise Culture in the Sulphur Spring Valley,
            southeastern Arizona: archaeology of the Fairchild Site.
            The Kiva 39: 131-169   (Contribution to Highway Salvage
            Archaeology in Arizona 37).

Winter, Joseph C.
    1973   Cultural modifications of the Gila Pima, A.D. 1697-1846.
            Ethnohistory 20 (1) 65-76.

Wood, Donald D.
    1972   Archaeological reconnaissance of the Gila River Indian
            Reservation: second action year (Phase III). Arizona
            State Museum Archaeological Series 16.

Wyant, Jeffrey R. and Frank E. Bayham
    1976   An experimental study of lithic use wear. In Doelle,
            pp. 231-243.

Young, O. E.
    1967   How they dug gold. Tucson: Arizona Pioneers Historical
            Society.

CHAPTER 8

CONCLUSIONS

by Lynn S. Teague

It is customary to conclude resource management reports with
recommendations for the protection and preservation of significant
qualities of the resources potentially subject to impact. The history
of the Cholla-Saguaro survey has made this superfluous here.

Data recovery along the southern portion of the Cholla-Saguaro
line (Chapter 7 of this report) represents the earliest effort to mitigate the potential adverse effects of transmission line construction
on archaeological sites within the corridor. No further data recovery
was undertaken until 1977. During the intervening period, the Arizona
State Museum worked with Arizona Public Service and U.S. Forest Service
personnel to devise strategies for the avoidance and preservation of
sites. In February, 1977, the Museum submitted a report on sites for
which no feasible avoidance plan had been developed. In March, 1977,
a research proposal for data recovery was submitted. Eventually, 41
sites were investigated within the framework of this proposal, 23
through systematic surface collection and mapping alone and 18 through
collection and additional strategies including excavation. In addition,
limited additional survey outside the corridor was undertaken as a part
of the mitigation effort. Reports now in preparation will describe
this work.
In this report the individual study areas have been dealt with
as discrete units. Later reports will provide evaluations of the
archaeology along the Cholla line in terms of large-scale regional
variability. The absence of regional interpretation in the present
report is a reflection of the cumulative nature of the project; this
report represents only the earlier stages of Cholla-Saguaro research.
To some extent the approaches represented in this report are also a
product of the individual history of this project.

The Cholla-Saguaro survey took place during a period of change
in cultural resource management and in archaeology. It was also faced
with technical problems arising from the nature of transmission line
planning and construction. Because many of the solutions adopted in
the course of the project were necessarily stopgaps, there is still a
need for long-term solutions that would prevent rather than correct
difficulties of the sort that occurred on the Cholla-Saguaro Project.
A review of the problems and an assessment of approaches and methods
likely to prevent these problems will be presented here so that future
projects may benefit from the experiences of this one.

The Design of a Transmission Line Survey

When this survey was begun, it was recognized that the first step must be the development of a research design that would structure the recovery of information and would define the archaeological goals of the project. A basic design was written for the study and was followed by a series of individual designs for corridor segments as they were surveyed. All of these designs shared an assumption that there were two basic study objectives: the inventory and evaluation required for management needs, and a research effort expected to make an identifiable contribution to archaeological knowledge independent of survey management goals. Inadequate integration of these goals can be identified as a basic problem for this survey. The somewhat over-ambitious research goals of the survey could not be achieved, and information that was later needed for design of the mitigation program was not provided.

When the Cholla-Saguaro survey was begun, cultural resource management was, like archaeology as a whole, involved in an effort to produce better directed and more meaningful research. Since widespread major mitigation efforts were still a thing of the future, much of this effort was concentrated in attempts to realize the potential of survey data, previously somewhat neglected in comparison to data from excavation. Out of an effort to correct this long-standing neglect, there occasionally was a tendency to expect too much of limited bodies of information. It should be unnecessary to review here in detail the inherent limits of survey data. However, inferences about site function, the nature and distribution of subsurface features and artifacts, and even the chronological and cultural associations of a site are often inaccurate when based on survey data alone. Attempts to correlate behaviorally significant site types with environmental variables without excavation data are, therefore, often more ambitious than productive. The accuracy and detail that may be achieved are dependent on many variables; the availability of contextual information, the nature of the survey, and the feasibility of test excavations are among the most important of these. In the case of this project, difficulties varied from area to area, but in general the initial research effort was severely impaired by failure to identify and develop a more realistic strategy.

Problems in fulfilling the original survey design arose from attempts to correlate very detailed aspects of site environment (soil chemistry, for example) with site classes based on inferred function. Emphasis was placed on correlation of habitation sites with the potential productivity of arable land. Specific difficulties included insufficient data on present areal environment (since survey and acquisition of detailed data were confined to the corridor) and lack of areal studies in reconstruction of past environments. Furthermore, it was often impossible to determine prior to test excavations whether sites were permanent habitations and, if so, the intensity and duration of occupation. The design was in general more appropriate to an areal study than to a linear one and, in any case, would have required extensive test excavations in order to achieve adequate reliability. A more general focus on availability of arable land, rather than more detailed assessments of relative productivity, would have served better. The identification of site types would still have been heavily dependent on comparison with nearby excavated sites, since testing of sites for which no impact was anticipated would have exceeded the managerial limitations of the project but would have been essential for fulfillment of the design. As the preceding chapters indicate, these necessary comparative data were not always available.

Focus on the research approach chosen for the Cholla-Saguaro survey also limited attention to data classes needed in mitigation planning. The design did not require, for example, any quantification of artifact density within lithic scatters. Many of the sites subsequently investigated during the mitigation phase were lithic scatters, and it was found that relative assessments ("light scatters", "high density") were virtually meaningless for development of efficient recording strategies and estimation of time and cost figures.

The role of the initial survey and evaluation of archaeological resources in the overall research and management project must be clearly defined in order to develop strategies appropriate to the circumstances. The survey report (which, if possible, should be available prior to major decision-making and mitigation) should provide the archaeological context available for the interpretation and evaluation of the resources, an accurate description of site characteristics to the extent that these can be determined, and an assessment of the archaeological significance and potential of the sites based on these information sources.

Transmission Line Survey Scheduling and Field Work

Large transmission line surveys are managerially and logistically among the most complex studies undertaken for purposes of management-related archaeological inventory and evaluation. Unlike reservoirs and land exchanges, a transmission line provides no continuous and fixed areas of direct impact within which consistent presumptions of effect can be made. Many hundreds of towers, access roads, pulling stations, and other facilities are involved. Each is a discrete unit that throughout the planning and construction phases may be relocated entirely, restricted, or modified to meet engineering needs or the management requirements of landholding agencies.

In this often frustrating complexity lies the great advantage of archaeological work associated with transmission lines. Unlike reservoirs and land exchanges, along transmission lines the selective preservation of areas in which significant resources are found is very often feasible. Relatively few of the sites located during survey of this corridor were ultimately subject to disturbance. The intent of federal preservation legislation, which emphasizes in-place protection of significant sites, can be fulfilled much more often in the case of transmission lines than in many other sorts of large-scale construction and land modification projects.

In order to take advantage of this potential for resource protection, it is important that information be available to engineers before facilities are designed. Because the Cholla-Saguaro survey was undertaken after design of most tower locations, the survey was accompanied by a continuing effort to modify facility locations long after much of the potential flexibility had been lost. In a 12-mile corridor segment in the Chevelon region, the failure of the original survey to identify many of the sites within the corridor resulted in impacts to these sites before their discovery. The economic cost of late site identification is high; the cost in resource loss may also be high and is ultimately much more significant since the destruction of resources represents an irreparable loss.

Survey should be initiated after a corridor is identified (early reconnaisance surveys may identify desirable alternate routes and possibly prohibitive problems) and before tower locations are selected. It is also essential that this be done after the corridor is adequately defined on maps and on the ground. The early stages of the Cholla-Saguaro survey suffered in cost-efficiency and to some extent in accuracy through uncertainties about the corridor's location. When the 1975 summer survey was begun, little of the line had been flagged. Maps and low-quality aerial photographs were available, but were inadequate. The Brunton compass, the most common tool of archaeological surveyors for determining location, is subject to an error of several degrees even under the best of conditions. The accuracy needed to follow a narrow corridor hundreds of miles in length is not possible without the more sophisticated instrument-survey methods employed by company professionals. On the Cholla-Saguaro Project, the solution reached was for archaeological survey crews to follow immediately behind or very often accompany engineering surveyors. This was not always an ideal approach. Eight persons (two crews) were employed in order to meet a company request for rapid completion of the survey, but were often unproductively engaged in waiting. Sometimes errors were made by surveyors and because of very short lead time were not detected before archaeological survey. Thus, short segments were archaeologically surveyed twice.

Several generalizations can be made regarding the problem of on-the-ground corridor identification for archaeological survey. Having the archaeological survey crew accompanied by a company engineering surveyor is one method, but is less than ideal if it is intended not as a supplementary aid but as a substitute for engineering survey prior to archaeological survey. As was noted earlier, delays result when problems occur during the engineering survey, and a second archaeological survey may be necessary if lead time is insufficient to identify errors before archaeological crews have proceeded. This approach is, however, effective if an engineering survey has been completed but if flagging is too widely spaced for accurate use by archaeologists.

A better approach involves adequate initial flagging by engineering surveyors. "Adequate" is difficult to quantify in this context because terrain and vegetation significantly affect the difficulty of following the line; ideally, flagging should be visible from any point along the line. If this is not possible, distances between markers should be minimized so that navigation by Brunton compass is feasible. This requires distances of no greater than 500 feet between flags when problems of terrain and vegetation are moderate.

It may be worthwhile to comment here on a misunderstanding that often leads to insufficient on-ground corridor marking and identification. Archaeological survey is virtually unique in requiring accurate on-ground identification of all points along a corridor. For many engineering and construction purposes, it is sufficient simply to be able to find the next marked point from the one preceding it. For example, it may be acceptable if personnel can find their way to the correct ridge top and subsequently identify--perhaps several hundred feet away--the actual center line. For the archaeological surveyor, this lack of precise accuracy would require rewalking the entire segment. The potential cost of repeated situations of this kind is high, and both survey schedules and accuracy may become compromised.

The Cholla-Saguaro survey delays discussed earlier also led to other problems. Personnel engaged on the basis of the original schedule had made other commitments, thus requiring the assembling and organizing of a new crew. Furthermore, survey was geographically discontinuous, causing problems in field logistics. This problem of insufficient continuity could have been largely eliminated through proper scheduling to avoid extended delays in the field.

Other problems include those associated with the recording and marking of sites. Once a site is located, its boundaries must be recorded both on the ground and on maps. High-quality aerial photographs are a very important asset to recording. On the ground, flagging with tape is the customary method of marking site boundaries; this, however, poses yet another scheduling problem, since tape is sometimes worn away and is almost invariably eaten by cattle and wildlife. If the revisiting of a site is delayed by more than a few months after flagging, the need for reflagging can be confidently predicted. Similarly, if archaeologists follow months behind engineering surveyors marking the line, insufficient corridor flagging can be expected.

These considerations suggest a need for careful planning and tight scheduling. Site recording, always the most time-consuming element of archaeological survey, may be a problem; if the engineering of towers, roads, and other facilities is delayed pending completion of the survey, it is unacceptable to have this initial survey proceed slowly. An alternative procedure might be location and partial recording of sites during an initial survey, with subsequent full recording of site data after the pressure of engineering schedules has been reduced. It should be stressed, however, that this is an acceptable rather than an archaeologically ideal sequence of events. Assessments of site significance will be more accurate if full recording and, if needed, testing have been completed. Since the initial survey and assessment serve to guide decision-making regarding avoidance, this sequence presents a serious risk of error. Both the company and the contractor should be prepared at this early stage to evaluate in greater detail any sites that present problems in significance assessment. The possible delay and inconvenience associated with early testing would be repaid in the overall planning process. The need for a very extensive testing program at this stage could be avoided through consultation with engineers to identify sites very unlikely to be affected and those for which the potential for impact is high. Even prior to actual tower engineering, this could be done on the basis of topography (towers are more likely to be located on ridges than in canyons, for example), site size (small sites are easier to avoid than large ones), and other variables.

An acceptable sequence of events for an efficient archaeological survey of a transmission line might include the following steps:

1) records check and reconnaissance survey to provide data for evaluation of alternative corridors;

2) acquisition of good-quality aerial photographs of the corridor and on-the-ground flagging of the corridor by engineering surveyors;

3) no more than two months after engineering survey, initial archaeological survey to identify sites, flag and map boundaries, and record basic data needed for a preliminary evaluation of site significance;

4) more detailed recording and testing of sites for which significance cannot be assessed with sufficient accuracy and for which impact is probable;

5) engineering of tower, road, and other facility locations;

6) full archaeological recording of all sites and checks of project designs in potentially sensitive areas.

This sequence of events could then be followed by test excavations, when needed, to prepare mitigation plans.

Throughout this process, good communication between archaeologists and company personnel, both field and in-house, is needed. During the Cholla-Saguaro Project, it was determined that a field contact was essential to efficient operation. This becomes increasingly critical as schedules become tighter, but is strongly recommended at all project stages. The Museum was fortunate during this project to have had excellent cooperation from project liaisons; it is improbable that the survey and mitigation could have been completed to anyone's satisfaction without this. The functions of a liaison should include assistance in coordinating initial archaeological survey with corridor instrument survey and in resolving field problems related to corridor location. When tower, access road, and other facility locations are later determined, a liaison is indispensable in coordinating field checks of areas that are potentially archaeologically sensitive and in conveying to archaeologists field scheduling priorities. A liaison is particularly important in working with archaeologists and engineers to develop efficient strategies for avoidance and protection of sites.

It is essential that one person be designated to serve this function at any one time. Particularly when projects are large and multiple company crews are working in a variety of areas at all times, the confusion that could develop without a single coordinating individual familiar with all aspects of the project and capable of setting priorities on a daily basis would greatly reduce efficiency of the archaeological work.

The Administration of a Transmission Line Survey

Many of the problems that may occur on transmission line surveys can be avoided through adequate coordination of company, agency, and archaeological contractor efforts. This coordination can most effectively be viewed from the perspective of the three participating organizations since each organization experiences different demands in internal administration of projects. This discussion will focus on aspects of project administration that were most critical during the Cholla-Saguaro Project, and is thus not comprehensive; however, the issues addressed can be expected to be crucial in any large project of this kind.

The Company

The role of the company field liaison has already been discussed. Beyond this level of basic procedural coordination in the field, it is also important that the company's priorities, long-term schedules, and expectations be conveyed to archaeological contractors so that archaeological activities can be efficiently integrated within the overall

planning process. It has been noted previously that detailed field
recording of archaeological sites can be postponed if time allotted
between corridor identification and tower location selection is short.
Efficiently adapting to such constraints requires that the archaeological contractor be informed of schedules before survey is begun. The
customary procedure involves full recording of sites as they are
encountered; particularly when substantial distances are involved in
travel between project areas, it is more time- and cost-efficient
overall to complete work at each site before proceeding. Weighing
this against other scheduling problems can only be done with full and
accurate information regarding company plans.

The Agency

When the Cholla-Saguaro survey was begun, the national forests
having jurisdiction over much of the corridor employed no staff archaeologists. There was virtually no communication of Forest Service
requirements to archaeological contractors or to the company beyond the
general understanding that a full inventory complying with general
federal standards was expected. In 1976, an archaeological staff position was established for the Tonto National Forest, and authority for
Cholla-Saguaro cultural resource coordination in both Tonto and Apache-
Sitgreaves national forests was delegated to the Tonto archaeologist.
The placement of a permanent archaeological staff member at Tonto was
quickly followed by discussions to develop survey and reporting specifi-
cations. This process was accelerated by the discovery shortly thereafter
of problems in the Chevelon survey. Procedures were instituted regarding
what was to be surveyed (for example, acceptable buffer zones on access
roads); frequency, content, and format of interim reports; and verification of survey adequacy.

The development and communication of agency requirements of
these sorts for all projects are essential if management needs are to
be met. Since archaeological situations vary greatly, as do agency
policies and procedures, it cannot be assumed that a single set of
requirements can be universally adopted. The development of archaeological expertise within land-managing agencies has been a major contribution to greater efficiency and effectiveness, making planning and
communication of this sort realistic goals.

The Archaeological Contractor

The role of contract supervisors and administrators is crucial
to achieving project objectives efficiently, both in initially planning
work and in ensuring that all of the work is performed according to
acceptable standards. Many of the aspects of project planning, most
importantly research design and scheduling, have already been reviewed.

The role of the contract project administrative staff in reviewing field work in progress deserves some additional attention.

In planning an archaeological project, the supervisory staff attempts to ensure that the resources needed for the successful completion of that project are available. These include sufficient time and money and adequately trained personnel. The supervisory staff, both field and in-house, can also be expected to design the research in such a way that adequate field data will be gathered efficiently. Inevitably, however, unforeseen problems arise that may compromise the quality of the work. These may develop within any aspect of the field work: personnel may become rushed, environmental conditions may reduce site visibility, or the survey area and individual sites may be incorrectly located on maps and on the ground. Good project planning may minimize these difficulties, but only continuing supervision and survey verification can ensure that no problems have significantly compromised the adequacy of the work in progress. Because conditions change, this must be a continuing process. It is crucial that the project supervisors and administrators determine through direct observation the extent to which project changes (personnel, terrain, vegetation) may have affected the work. Ideally, this should include both observation of the field crew at work and systematic verification of inventory adequacy in areas where survey has been recently completed. The methods appropriate for this vary; in some cases, informal inspections may be sufficient, while in others, probability sampling is called for. In any case, it is the responsibility of the contractor to ensure that archaeological survey is complete and accurate. To do so requires a continuing assessment of field methodologies and techniques and of factors external to the archaeology itself that may adversely affect inventory quality.

Summary

This chapter has reviewed some of the problems that occurred in the course of this project and has discussed potential solutions. Although categorized here as project design, field work, and administration, it should be apparent that these concerns are closely interrelated. Conditions in any of these areas may affect those in the others; all three aspects ultimately affect the quality of the protection provided to the resources.

On the Cholla-Saguaro Project, it was possible to avoid and protect many of the sites within the corridor. Others could not be avoided feasibly and were investigated during the mitigation phase. This survey report presents the information acquired during the course of the survey, but, given the nature of this project and its history, is neither a management document in the usual sense, nor does it represent a completed research study.

APPENDIX A

SUPPLEMENTARY SPECIAL FORMS

USED IN APS-CS SURVEY

Site Filed No._____

ARIZONA STATE MUSEUM
A.P.S. Cholla-Saguaro Project
Field Lithic Analysis

Field No._____   Artifact Type:_____

Provenience:_____   Material:_____

Length:_____   Complete or

Width:_____   Fragment:_____

Thickness:_____   Original Form:

Flaking: Flake

    Unifacial   Core

    Bifacial   Other:_____

Edge angle:_____   Cross section:

Utilization:

    Slight

    Moderate

    Great

    None

Plan view:

AGRICULTURAL POTENTIAL FIELD RECORDING FORM

Station No._____ Site No._____ Sample No._____

Quadrangle_____ Location: T___ R____ Sec. _____ ¼ ¼

Collection Loci:_____ Elevation:_____ Date:_____

I. Topography:*

____ Plains: (use only if sub-category was not determined)

____   (a) Flat plains

____   (b) Irregular plains; slight relief

____   (c) Irregular plains; moderate relief

____ Plains with Hills and Mountains: (use only if sub-category was not determined)

____   (a) Plains with hills

____   (b) Plains with high hills

____   (c) Plains with low mountains

____   (d) Plains with high mountains

____ Open Hills and Mountains: (use only if sub-category was not determined)

____   (a) Open low hills

____   (b) Open high hills

____   (c) Open low mountains

____   (d) Open high mountains

____ Hills and Mountains: (use only if sub-category was not determined)

____   (a) Hills

____   (b) High hills

____   (c) Low mountains

____   (d) High mountains

____ Tablelands - Plateau/Valley; dissected: (use only if sub-category was not determined)

____   (a) Tablelands with moderate relief

____   (b) Tablelands with considerable relief

____   (c) Tablelands with high relief

_____

Slope gradient:*_____%

Gradient variation (100 m):_____%

Gradient variation (1 km): _____%   *Field Observations

Topography (continued)

____ Alluvial Fan		____ Floodplain
____ Arroyo		____ Hill
____ Bajada		____ Hill Slope
____ Barranca		____ Meadow
____ Beach Line		____ Mesa
____ Bluff		____ Plain
____ Canyon		____ Playa
____ Canyon Floor		____ Ridge
____ Canyon Side		____ Rock Shelter
____ Cliff		____ Talus Slope
____ Delta		____ Terrace
____ Dry Lake		____ Valley
____ Dunes		____ Other _____

II. Vegetation:*

Plant Community:_____

Dominant Species:

(1)_____

(2)_____

(3)_____

(4)_____

(5)_____

(6)_____

(7)_____

_____

III.Water Resources:*

(1) Distance to nearest water source (meters): _____; Elev.:_____

(2) Permanance of nearest water source:

      a. impermanent: _____

      b. semi-permanent: _____

      c. permanent: _____

(3) Type of nearest water source:

      a. stream/river: _____

      b. spring: _____

      c. seep: _____

      d. lake/pond   _____

      e. reservoir (extent):   _____

      f. ditch/canal (extent: _____

      g. other:

(4) Distance to nearest stream (if other than VI-1; meters):____; Elev.:_____

(5) Permanence of nearest stream (if other than VI-2):

      a. impermanent: _____

      b. semi-permanent: _____

      c. permanent: _____

Comments:_____

_____

_____

_____

IV. Agricultural/Water Control Features:*

    ____ check dam

    ____ linear terrace

    ____ contour terrace

    ____ channeling border

    ____ diversion dam

    ____ grid border (waffle gardens)

    ____ ditch

    ____ canal   extinct

    ____ reservoir

    ____ other

Comments:

General Remarks:

*Field Observations